Rollyson, Carl E.
(Carl Edmund)

American Isis.

DATE			

2-13

AMERICAN ISIS

ALSO BY CARL ROLLYSON

Marilyn Monroe: A Life of the Actress

Lillian Hellman: Her Legend and Her Legacy

Nothing Ever Happens to the Brave: The Story of Martha Gellhorn

The Lives of Norman Mailer: A Biography

Rebecca West: A Life

Susan Sontag: The Making of an Icon

Beautiful Exile: The Life of Martha Gellhorn

To Be a Woman: The Life of Jill Craigie

Hollywood Enigma: Dana Andrews

AMERICAN ISIS

THE LIFE AND ART OF
SYLVIA PLATH

Carl Rollyson

ST. MARTIN'S PRESS ✹ NEW YORK

www.stmartins.com

Design by Anna Gorovoy

Library of Congress Cataloging-in-Publication Data

Rollyson, Carl E. (Carl Edmund)
    American Isis : the life and art of Sylvia Plath / Carl Rollyson. — 1st U.S. ed.
        p. cm.
    Includes bibliographical references and index.
    ISBN 978-0-312-64024-8 (hardcover)
    ISBN 978-1-250-02315-5 (e-book)
  1. Plath, Sylvia.   2. Poets, American—20th century—Biography.   3. Plath,
Sylvia—Psychology.   4. Plath, Sylvia—Criticism and interpretation.
5. Women and literature—United States—History—20th century.   I. Title.
II. Title: Life and art of Sylvia Plath.
    PS3566.L27Z849 2013
    811'.54—dc23
    [B]

                                                                    2012037393

First Edition: January 2013

10   9   8   7   6   5   4   3   2   1

To Lisa

CONTENTS

Acknowledgments ix

Author's Note xiii

Introduction 1

1. Primordial Child of Time (1932–50) 8

2. Mistress of All the Elements (1950–53) 26

3. Queen of the Dead (1953–55) 60

4. I Am Nature (1955–57) 94

5. Queen of the Ocean (1957–59) 138

6. The Universal Mother (1960–62) 170

7. Queen Also of the Immortals (1962–63) 194

8. In The Temple of Isis: Among the Hierophants (1963–) 232

Appendix A: Sylvia Plath and Carl Jung 269

Appendix B: Sylvia's Plath's Library   273

Appendix C: David Wevill   277

Appendix D: Elizabeth Compton Sigmund   279

Sources   285

Bibliography   297

Index   301

ACKNOWLEDGMENTS

Without the strong support of my agent, Christina Ward, this biography would not have been written. Without Lindsay Sagnette's enthusiastic recommendation to her colleagues at St. Martin's Press, this biography would not have been accepted for publication. Without the enthusiastic backing of my editor, Michael Flamini, this book would not have had such careful encouragement and advice. Without the astute advice of my wife, Lisa Paddock, this book would have lacked a certain polish. Early on, I grew to rely on the expertise, encouragement, and generosity of Peter K. Steinberg, an extraordinary Plath scholar, who pointed me to many important primary sources. He also gave me permission to reproduce his photographs documenting the world of Sylvia Plath. Peter saved me from making several errors. I am very grateful to Susan Plath Winston (Warren Plath's daughter) for giving me permission to reproduce several photographs and for answering my queries. I am very grateful to Ellis B. Levine of Cowan, Debaets, Abrahams & Sheppard, LLP, for his wise counsel.

Karen V. Kukil, a renowned Plath scholar and archivist, went out of her way to address the needs of my biography. The work she has done at the Smith College archive is stupendous. Owing to its openness and accessibility, the archive's policies ought to be a model for the world. It is a detriment to scholarship that other repositories of Plath's papers have surrendered to her estate's restrictive and censorious protocols. Nevertheless, I appreciate the prompt and generous help I received from Kathleen Shoemaker at Emory University, Helen Melody at the British Library collections of the Ted Hughes and Olwyn Hughes papers, and Beth Alvarez and Ann L. Hudak at the University of Maryland. Less helpful, but still indispensable, of course, is the Plath Collection in the Lilly Library at Indiana University. For expert retrieval of various secondary sources, I am indebted to my wonderful Macaulay Honors College student assistant, Tara Gildea. Her diligent and first-rate work represents what is best about the City University of New York.

David Wevill cordially answered my email queries, but he did not wish to be interviewed. He did agree, however, to my request to reproduce his email reply to one of my queries (see Appendix C). My letters to Marcia Brown and Richard Sassoon went unanswered, but I had the benefit of Constance Blackwell's memories of her friendship with Sassoon during Sylvia's time at Smith. What Eddie Cohen had to say seemed bound up in his letters, and that was the story I wanted to tell. W. S. Merwin would vouchsafe almost nothing even to Olwyn Hughes, to whom he replied on 13 October 1987 with the observation that writing about Sylvia "seems to me bad medicine altogether." I couldn't see why he would have talked to me, and so I decided not to hazard his rebuff. But I did get an insight into the friendship between Merwin and Hughes in the course of an unexpected, spontaneous conversation with Grace Schulman, my colleague at Baruch College.

Even to this day, most of Olwyn's friends observe a code of silence. I'm grateful that Marvin Cohen, through the good offices of Charles DeFanti, made an exception for me. For more insight into Olwyn and Ted Hughes, and their treatment of Sylvia Plath, I turned to A. Alvarez, a remarkably generous and welcoming man who patiently went over ground he has eloquently explored in his own writings. I am indebted to him, as well, for discussing his correspondence with Olwyn, now in his papers at the British Library. His wife, Anne, took time during a busy day to discuss with me Olwyn Hughes and Assia Wevill. Similarly, the testimony of Elizabeth Sigmund, married to David Compton when Plath and Hughes resided at Court Green, has been invaluable. Spending nearly two whole days with her, observing her careful recounting of those days in Devon while examining her extensive files, I came away with a greater understanding of why Aurelia Plath believed Elizabeth was essential to Sylvia's well-being. Rather than just cut up Elizabeth's memories into the bits and pieces that can be found in previous Plath biographies, I thought it fitting to let her speak in her own voice (see Appendix D) as a means of conjuring a bygone era. To Elizabeth's husband, William Sigmund, who occasionally joined our conversations and provided delicious lunches and teas— not to mention transportation—I want to express my gratitude and affection.

I have been especially fortunate in speaking and corresponding with several Smith College alumnae who knew Sylvia Plath, and with some who encountered Ted Hughes. Thank you Jody Simon, Constance Blackwell, Kathleen Knight, Judy Denison, Marilyn Martin, Ellen Ouelette, Barbara Russell Kornfield, Anne Mohegan Smith, CB Follett, Barbara Schulz Larson, Daryl Hafter, Clare Goldfarb, Helen Lane, Nanci A. Young, and Ravelle Silberman Brickman. These women provided a fresh perspective, new material, and—in one case—an unpublished photograph of my subject, always a splendid dividend. They all made it a joy to talk about Sylvia Plath, and they inspired my effort to do justice to her protean personality and work. I'm grateful to Aubrey Menard for putting me in touch with Richard Larschan, a friend of Aurelia Plath. Larschan described someone who was very much her own woman, and not just Sylvia's mother, a view corroborated by Aurelia's annotations to Judith Kroll's scholarly study, a copy of which is in the Mortimer Rare Book Room at Smith College. I am also indebted to Professor Larschan for providing a copy of Trevor Thomas's privately printed memoir.

AUTHOR'S NOTE

I wrote this biography, in part, because I felt there were aspects of Sylvia Plath other biographers have overlooked or misunderstood. I confess, however, that as I wrote the book I reread my predecessors—usually after writing a section of my book. I checked to see how others had handled the same material. I think my practice in doing so is worth mentioning because I have dispensed with a good deal of the boilerplate most biographers feel compelled to supply. I say little, for example, about the backgrounds of Plath's parents. I don't describe much of Smith College or its history. I do very little scene setting. Previous biographers do all this and more, and what strikes me about their work is how distracting all that background is for someone wishing to have a vision of Sylvia Plath, of what she was like and what she stood for. To put it another way, since earlier biographers have done so much to contextualize Plath, I have not wanted to repeat that exercise, as valuable as it can be for the Plath novice. Instead, I have tried to concentrate on the intensity of the person who was Sylvia Plath, restricting my discussion of her writing to crucial pieces that advance my narrative. As a result, certain important poems and stories do not appear in my narrative, and others do so only briefly. I cut even paraphrases of poems and stories to an absolute minimum, assuming that the knowledgeable Plath reader will not need them. At the same time, I have tried to write a narrative so focused—without timeouts for exposition of her work—that a reader new to Plath biography may feel some of the exhilaration and despair that marked the poet's life. The timelines at the top of each chapter tell you where we are headed, so that I can get on with the story.

The advantage of my approach, I believe, is that it allows me to do justice to Plath's correspondents, whose letters I read carefully in various archives so as to gauge the impact of their voices on Plath. It is striking, for example, how banal Dick Norton's letters are compared to Eddie Cohen's, and how precious and effete Richard Sassoon's seem in relation to Cohen's robust prose. To read Gordon Lameyer's long letters to Sylvia—especially those written during her treatment in the summer of 1953 after her suicide attempt—is to appreciate how terrifically important she was in guiding his own sense of vocation. Through reading these letters, I came to see how hard Plath tried to live many different sorts of lives, and to be many different things to her correspondents. Of course she did not live by these letters alone, but securing a more prominent place for her correspondents seems to me a way of enforcing the point of this biography: Sylvia Plath was a great poet, yes, but she was also great in other ways that no earlier book has evoked.

AMERICAN ISIS

INTRODUCTION

> I am nature, the universal Mother, mistress of all the elements, primordial child of time, sovereign of all things spiritual, queen of the dead, queen of the ocean, queen also of the immortals, the single manifestation of all gods and goddesses that are, my nod governs the shining heights of Heavens, the wholesome sea breezes. Though I am worshipped in many aspects, known by countless names . . . some know me as Juno, some as Bellona . . . the Egyptians who excel in ancient learning and worship call me by my true name . . . Queen Isis.
>
> **—Apuleius,** *The Golden Ass*

Sylvia Plath is the Marilyn Monroe of modern literature. Plath occupies a place no other writer can supplant. Sister poet Anne Sexton recognized as much when she called Plath's suicide a "good career move." That crass comment reveals a stratospheric ambition Plath and Sexton shared. They wanted to be more than great writers; they wanted nothing less than to become central to the mythology of modern consciousness. Plath has superseded Sexton because—as Marilyn Monroe said, speaking of herself—Plath was dreaming the hardest. At the age of eight Plath was already working herself into the public eye, later winning prizes and exhibiting herself as the epitome of the modern woman who wanted it all. And, in having it all, she would make herself and what she wrote both threatening and alluring, deadly and life affirming. Biographers have puzzled over what Ted Hughes meant when he claimed, rather dramatically, "It was either her or me." This much is clear: He did not want to play Osiris to her Isis. Although he began their marriage thinking she needed him to complete herself, he gradually realized his role was to act as a consort in her mythology.

Biographers have misconstrued Plath, becoming fixated on her psychological problems, on what Ted Hughes did to her—and on one another, with Janet Malcolm heading up the forensic team of those who suppose that it is somehow unseemly to rake up the life of a "silent woman" who cannot speak for herself. In truth, Plath wanted to be wholly known. Hughes was astonished to learn that his wife had entrusted his love letters to her mother. But Aurelia Plath was not surprised, having raised nothing less than a primordial child of time, a woman who wrote for the ages and was unconcerned about her husband's petty notions of privacy.

Plath needs a new biography, one that recognizes her overwhelming desire to be a cynosure, a guiding force and focal point for modern women and men. The pressures on a woman who sees herself in such megalomaniacal terms were enormous, and understanding such pressures and her responses to them yields a fresh and startling perspective that makes Plath's writing, her marriage, and her suicide finally understandable in terms of the way we live now.

Unlike other writers of her generation, Plath realized that the worlds of high art and popular culture were converging. As a young child, she listened to *Superman* and *The Shadow* on the radio. She devoted a letter to a parody of *Dragnet*. She was as attracted to bestselling novels as she was to high art. Before she graduated from high school she had read *Gone with the Wind* three times. Before entering college she published a story in *Seventeen* magazine, and she soon became a protégé of Olive Higgins Prouty, author of tearjerkers such as *Now, Voyager* and *Stella Dallas*, which ran as a radio serial from 1937 to 1955.

During her Fulbright term in England, Plath posed for a photo layout in *Varsity*, Cambridge University's newspaper, to accompany her article, "Sylvia Plath Tours the Stores and Forecasts May Week Fashions." In addition to pictures of her in a ball gown and a white cocktail dress, the piece features a shot of her wearing a typical 1950s cheesecake swimsuit ensemble. One picture shows off the 5' 9" model's long legs, recalling America's iconic World War II pinup. "With love from Betty Grable," Plath amusingly styled herself on clippings she sent to her mother. Plath was certainly not the first American woman poet to glamorize herself—Edna St. Vincent Millay and Elinor Wylie come to mind—but none of her predecessors pursued public renown in quite this determined and strategic way. Plath was a relentless applicant for writing prizes, not only because of their monetary value, but also because they kept her in the public eye. She was no Emily Dickinson, who wrote primarily for herself and let posterity take care of itself. For Plath, an audience had to witness the spectacle of what it meant to be Sylvia Plath.

Ted Hughes was baffled by Plath's desire to write popular prose. Like most "serious" writers of his generation, he drew a line separating vulgar from fine art. He dismissed her efforts to write conventional fiction as "a persistent refusal of her genius." Plath knew better. In college, she tried writing a story for *True Confessions,* only to shrewdly observe in her journal that doing so took "a good tight plot and a slick ease that are not picked up over night like a cheap whore." She knew there was an art to the creation of potboilers, and she wanted to master the form. It was all part of what it meant to be Sylvia Plath. Hughes understood up to a point. After all, in his introduction to *Johnny Panic and the Bible of Dreams,* a collection of her stories, he perceptively argued, "It seems probable that her real creation was her own image, so that all her writing appears like notes and jottings directing attention toward the central problem—herself." But he could not live with the consequences of her all-consuming quest, forestalling biographical inquiry and behaving as though protecting Plath was his business.

Ted's friends, who cared only about poetry, did not like Sylvia— indeed they saw her as an American vulgarian—but she persisted in her multitasking approach to literature. Although much emphasis has been placed on her last brief but brilliant period as a poet, in fact during this time she was also planning and writing two new novels and contemplating a career beyond poetry. "Poetry is an evasion from the real job of writing prose," she wrote.

Susan Sontag, born just a year after Plath, is often treated as a master of melding highbrow and pop in the 1960s, but in fact

Sontag abhorred mass entertainment and retreated to Parnassus as soon as she saw the consequences of mingling mainstream and minority (elitist) audiences. Indeed, in an interview, Sontag explicitly rejected Plath's need for popular approval. Sontag could not conceive of an artist who performed on all levels of culture at once. Plath—much bolder than Sontag and a much greater artist—took on *everything* her society had on offer.

Witness, for example, Plath's riveting journal entry for 4 October 1959:

> Marilyn Monroe appeared to me last night in a dream as a kind of fairy godmother. An occasion of "chatting" with audience much as the occasion with Eliot will turn out, I suppose. I spoke, almost in tears, of how much she and Arthur Miller meant to us, although they could, of course, not know us at all. She gave me an expert manicure. I had not washed my hair, and asked her about hairdressers, saying no matter where I went, they always imposed a horrid cut on me. She invited me to visit during the Christmas holidays, promising a new, flowering life.

No passage in Plath's writings better displays her unique sensibility. And yet her biographers have ignored or misconceived this crucial evidence. In *Rough Magic: A Biography of Sylvia Plath,* Paul Alexander calls the dream "strange." In *The Death and Life of Sylvia Plath,* Ronald Hayman calls the imagined audience with Monroe one of Plath's "less disturbing" dreams. These characterizations typify the misdirected narratives that plague Plath's legacy.

Plath imagines Marilyn Monroe as a healer and source of inspiration at a time when most women and men regarded the actress as little more than a sex symbol, the embodiment of a male fantasy. "What a doll!" the apartment superintendent keeps declaring in *The Seven Year Itch.* And yet, in the same film Monroe functions as a soothing and supportive figure for the clumsy Tom Ewell, telling him he is "just elegant." And she does so in exactly the kind of maternal, fairy godmother way that makes Plath's dream not strange but familiar. Marilyn Monroe "chats" with Sylvia Plath. The sex

goddess girl-talks Sylvia. This concatenation of high and low segues into a reference to T. S. Eliot, whom Plath and Hughes were
going to meet shortly. Plath was anticipating an encounter with
a great poet who might also be someone she could chat up. The
"audience" becomes, in Plath's dream, a very American talk.

Who in 1959 thought of the marriage of Marilyn Monroe and
Arthur Miller as a model to emulate? Only Sylvia Plath. Evidence
discovered by Plath scholar Peter K. Steinberg shows that Plath had
Monroe on her mind for quite some time. In the spring of 1959, *The
New Yorker* rejected a poem, "A Winter's Tale," but the editor suggested that Plath resubmit her work after changing a line in the
third stanza, "hair blonde as Marilyn's," referencing angels' haloes
in a Christmas scene. This fusing of the sacred and profane, so to
speak, was replaced by the more sedate "Haloes lustrous as Sirius,"
the brightest star in the sky, and the poem was published on 9 October, shortly after Sylvia had her Monroe dream.

Plath, like Monroe, was starstruck. Plath regarded Hughes as her
hero, in the same way that Monroe looked up to Miller. The Plath-
Hughes and Monroe-Miller marriages both occurred in June of
1956. Like Miller, Hughes wanted his work to be critically praised
and also broadly accepted. Both men glommed onto wives who
would extend their ranges by expanding their audiences. And just
as Miller wrote for Monroe's movies, Hughes dreamed of selling his
children's fables to Walt Disney. He saw his wife Sylvia as a symbol
of America and a conduit to success—even though he understood
next to nothing about her native land or her motivations. Their
marriage broke down, in part, because Hughes, like Miller, failed to
comprehend his wife's ambition. Indeed, both men shrank from
their wives' devouring aspirations.

That Monroe could give Plath an "expert manicure" seems
strange only to someone who does not understand that Monroe's
gift was to appear available and anodyne. Plath, always meticulous
about personal hygiene, conceived of a domesticated Monroe, now
ensconced in a happy union with a great writer—the same fate
Plath imagined for herself, avoiding the "horrid cut" her culture
imposed even on women of achievement. Marilyn Monroe was all
promise for Sylvia Plath. In an early story, Plath asserts her own

sense of superiority by portraying a young woman telling an eligible man, "So you don't know how to treat Ava Gardner when she also has the brains of Marie Curie. So I am here to tell you I am your fairy godmother in person, complete with chocolate cake." Ted Hughes could be of no help to Sylvia Plath, whose promise included chocolate cake and brains. His desire for a private world went against the very grain of the persona Plath was in the process of building. He let her down in ways far more disturbing than his infidelity.

In *Her Husband,* Diane Middlebrook has written persuasively about how Hughes perceived Plath as an incarnation of Robert Graves's white goddess. But Plath saw herself quite differently. She resembles, it seems to me, an American Isis. She wanted to be an ideal mother and wife—but with her power, her magic, intact. Isis, especially in her earliest Egyptian incarnation (before the imposition of the Osiris myth), seems a perfect metaphor for Plath, since the mythology includes the goddess's association with all levels of society, rich and poor. Because Plath went to the best colleges and was dressed well, Hughes mistakenly thought her wealthy when he first met her. In fact, these privileges were hard won by Plath and her mother, who worked long hours to ensure her daughter's place in society. Hughes was a naïf compared to Plath, who worked a hard eight hours per day as a field hand the summer before she entered Smith so that she would have enough money for the clothes and books her scholarship did not afford.

Small wonder Plath has become such a revered figure. This was a domestic goddess who loved to cook and clean. She appreciated the joys of everyday life. Ted Hughes did not know how to balance a checkbook; Sylvia Plath did. He never washed his clothes; Sylvia Plath did. He did not know how to compete in a quickly changing literary world; Sylvia Plath did. He drew back from her satire of friends and family in *The Bell Jar,* completely misconceiving her work, which deliberately transgressed the separation of art and autobiography. The marriage may have lasted as long as it did because he liked to cook and thought highly of her poetry. But Sylvia shot down his notion that they shared "one mind," as he told interviewer Peter Orr. She told Orr she was "more practical."

Plath is a genre breaker and a cross-cultural heroine. She bridges cultures like the Isis who eventually became a beloved object of worship throughout the Greco-Roman world. Plath has become the object of a cult-like following, her grave a pilgrimage site like the sanctuaries erected in honor of Isis. The repeated defacing of Plath's grave marker—so that "Sylvia Plath Hughes" reads "Sylvia Plath"—is more than simply retribution against Ted Hughes. The erasure is an assertion that his very name is an affront to the mythology of Sylvia Plath.

The Isis-like Plath encompasses characteristics that would seem to be at odds. Plath's suicide—and her poems that flirt with death—have become part of the Eros and Thanatos of her biography. And it is precisely this sort of tension between conflicting elements that transforms Plath into a modern icon, one that will continue to enchant and bedevil biographers. "Another biography of Sylvia Plath?" a reader will ask. Yes, the time to define the Plath myth for a new cohort of readers and writers is now.

CHAPTER I

PRIMORDIAL CHILD OF TIME

(1932–50)

27 October 1932: Sylvia Plath born in Boston while her family lives in Winthrop, Massachusetts; **1934:** Otto Plath publishes *Bumblebees and Their Ways,* a landmark study in entomology; **27 April 1935:** Warren is born; **21 September 1938:** The great New England hurricane; **5 November 1940:** Otto Plath dies of an embolism after an amputation; **10 August 1941:** Sylvia's first poem is published in the *Boston Herald;* **7 December,** The United States enters World War II; **1942:** Aurelia Plath moves her family to Wellesley and begins teaching at Boston University; **1944:** Sylvia begins keeping a journal and writes for her junior high school literary magazine, the *Philippian;* **20 January 1945:** Sylvia and her mother attend a performance of *The Tempest* in Boston; **6, 9 August:** Atomic bombs dropped on Japan; **1947:** Sylvia coedits the school newspaper, the *Bradford,* during her last year of high school; **1950:** Sylvia is accepted as a scholarship student at Smith College, Northampton, Massachusetts, and lives on campus in Haven House. She publishes a story in *Seventeen* and a poem in *The Christian Science Monitor.*

Some writers are born to be perpetual exiles and think of themselves as sea creatures. Sylvia Plath liked to tell the story of her mother setting her infant Sivvy on the beach to see what she would do. The baby scrabbled seaward like an old salt, saved from being submerged in an oncoming wave by a vigilant mother who held onto her daughter's heels. Held on or held back? Sylvia was always of two minds about her mother. Aurelia would later write scholar Judith Kroll that in fact it was Warren who had crawled into the waves—but such facts did not matter to a poet creating her own mythology.

As the poet wrote in an essay broadcast on the BBC near the end of her life, she spent her childhood where the land ended. She described the swells of the Atlantic as "running hills." Peering at the kaleidoscopic interior of a blue mussel shell, she imagined the intake of air the earth's first creatures experienced. Living in a house by the sea, she was rocked by the sounds of the tides. Never again would life feel so buoyant.

Sylvia had eight years of this coastal cradlehood. Then her father died, and the family moved upcountry, sealing Sivvy off from the enchantments of childhood like—to use her expression—"a ship in a bottle." That vision of a seaworld vanished as abruptly as her father, and both seemed to her a "white flying myth," fleeting and pure and unreachable and moribund for a child growing up in a world elsewhere. As angry as Coriolanus, a bereft Sylvia Plath went into exile. She would accomplish many great things, but never with the assurance of someone who has arrived. She was always looking back, full of regret and uncertain of the future, even though she met so many moments of her life with high expectations. Her life—beginning with her adoration of Superman—became a crusade.

Siv was six years old when war came to Europe, old enough for a precocious child with a foreign father to realize the world was full of villains. "Who knows what evil lurks in the hearts of men," the insinuating radio voice of The Shadow asked every Sunday evening, answering, "The Shadow knows." Siv heard Hitler's speeches, which Americans tuned into with the same kind of hearty compulsion they displayed when listening to the harangues of their own home-grown fascist, Father Coughlin. Later, images of the Führer and the Holocaust haunted Plath's poetry, amalgamated in her vision of a hellion husband.

Syl was not alone. She went to school with the children of

immigrants who watched their parents—exhausted after a hard day's work—subside beside the radio, awaiting word about the home country. At school, she stood pledging allegiance not with hyphenated Americans, but with kids still called Irish Catholics, German Jews, Swedes, Negroes, Italians, and what the writer later described as "that rare, pure Mayflower dropping, somebody *English."* Hands over their hearts, these children faced an American flag draped like an "aerial altar cloth over teacher's desk." Not such a different article, really, from Superman's cape, part of a sartorial ensemble that protected "truth, justice, and the American way."

They sang "America the Beautiful," and Syl was weeping by the time they arrived at "from sea to shining sea," a line that made a lot more sense to an elementary school student than "above the fruited plain." Moist sea winds permeated the playground with positive ions, the proverbial breath of fresh air that exuded hope and made them exult—when they were not shooting marbles, jumping rope, or playing dodgeball—"Up in the sky, look! It's a bird, it's a plane, it's Superman!"

The comic book version of Superman had become a staple of Action Comics in the late 1930s, but Sylvia seems to have found the radio serial version especially entertaining. The program premiered on 12 February 1940, opening with an announcer addressing boys and girls, telling them about the Superman clubs being formed around the country. Superman was not only an action hero, he was also the newspaperman Clark Kent, who first got a job on the *Daily Planet* by promising to return to his editor with a good story. Kent got the stories, even as, in the guise of Superman, he rescued young women and others in distress, foiling crimes involving both corruption in American business and threats to national security. A strange dream during summer camp left Sylvia thinking it would not be surprising to hear Superman knocking at her door. By the time she was ten years old, the idea of a powerful man swooping in to save the day had become a constituent of Sylvia Plath's imagination. But so had the idea of the independent woman, embodied by Lois Lane, who treated Clark Kent with considerable suspicion and contempt, even as she idolized Superman. Getting the story, getting the man, in a world in which both individual and country were on the verge of destruction would remain crucial to Sylvia's idea of world order.

For a short while, Sylvia had her own Superman at home: her father Otto Plath. An erudite and imperious entomologist, Professor Plath was old school. He was German, and what he said was law. To his daughter, he was Prospero, a diviner of nature's secrets. He showed her how to catch bumblebees—nobody else's father could do that! But he was aloof and irascible. He did not know how to play with children. It was not easy to placate Otto the Choleric. His wife, Aurelia, Otto's former student, tried soothing words, but her emollients eventually evaporated, and he would erupt with thunderous exclamations, waking Sylvia's younger brother, Warren. The enraged sounds coming from another room in the Plath home would not have been so different from the sound of Hitler's rants.

Otto exhorted excellence, and he enjoyed endowing his daughter with high standards. She loved to watch him correct student assignments; it was like putting the world right. But she had to be quiet if she was to have the privilege of witnessing his improvements. Red pencil marks slashed through papers with improper wording. Otto's sadistic streak showed when he told his daughter that in class the next day there would be "a weeping and wailing and a gnashing of teeth." To Sylvia, this assertion only proved the power of a father who lectured to hundreds about the way the world was put together. He seemed to the young girl a monarch, looking down from the lecture platform, calling his subjects to account. They approached to receive the awful judgment of his corrections. Quite aside from the image Sylvia constructed, one of Otto's colleagues, George Fulton, recalled for biographer Edward Butscher that Professor Plath was friendly and talkative, with a lusty appetite for huge roast pork sandwiches. Elizabeth Hinchliffe, another biographer, spoke with Otto's Harvard classmates, and they remembered his gift for languages and preference for literature over science. Aside from his interest in nature and his special subject, bees, he did not seem like a scientist at all. Indeed, Sylvia delighted her father with her early interest in poetry, and she quickly learned that she could earn his admiration by writing poems for him. Later, her most famous poem, "Daddy," would be addressed to him.

Sylvia loved to watch her father propel himself through the waves like a seagod. He would carry her on his back with apparently no strain, leaving a wake behind him. Her fear of the murky depths vanished in the rocking motion of his body. While asthmatic Warren remained at home, father and daughter romped on the beach. The fair Sylvia never burned, instead turning a beautiful brown. This was all a fairy tale, and Sylvia knew it. Otto, suffering the effects of diabetes, could not have performed the physical feats ascribed to him. As *Letters Home* reveals, the seagod father was actually "Grampy," Aurelia's vigorous middle-aged father. But Sylvia was concerned with re-creating the power of her father's presence, and the prowess she accords him is her way of dramatizing the hold he had on her imagination. As Richard Larschan explains in his myth-busting article, Plath also mythologized some of her early schooling, exaggerating the multicultural aspects of her upbringing to suit the temper of the times.

There was a war on, and Otto the German was under suspicion. Such mistrust was not fair, since he had nothing to do with Hitler or Nazism. But on radio, in comic books, and in movies, the voice of villainy was, in effect, Otto's voice. He was part of a mythology that his daughter could not quite separate from her own experience of the man. For a child, Otto's cruel rule could not be easily severed from a world of concentration camps, of newsreels that depicted the horror of Japanese prisoner of war camps. Like Susan Sontag, another child of the war, Sylvia Plath saw evil documented in graphic images that became embedded in her preteen psyche.

The searing nature of evil, and the way her own family could be contaminated with it, struck hard at a suburban girl living in Winthrop, Massachusetts, six miles from Boston. Disaster could strike at any moment—as it did with the great hurricane of 21 September 1938, when land and sea converged in a toss-up that pitched a shark into grandmother's garden. Sylvia saw the sea rear up with "evil violets in its eyes." All day she heard her mother make frantic phone calls, anticipating the worst from an all-devouring storm that could annihilate the only existence Sylvia knew. It seemed like Armageddon, a toppled world with upended telephone poles and ruined cottages bobbing in roiling waters.

Sylvia felt the elation of terror, the next day finding the wreckage satisfying and somehow commensurate with her imagination of disaster. She was born to a biblical life, calling the torrential rain a "Noah douche." She began writing poetry and stories almost as soon as she learned her letters, and the perfect storm that remade her universe became associated with her own creative cosmos, which could similarly reshape reality into her own realm. That tautological process of inventive perception, in which the world was bent back into the word wrap of phrase making, was the very stuff of life for her. When she succumbed to her first creative dry spell in the summer of 1953, she saw it as a living death and attempted to end her existence. A second, famously successful suicide would come later when she was an exhausted, worded-out poet who could no longer generate the energy that had peaked in her thirtieth year.

Sylvia Plath, however, was no solipsist. More than most children her age, she was a world citizen, enthusiastically learning geography in elementary school lessons and reports that she put together with A+ accuracy. She could not have had a more encouraging mother, one who wrote her daughter notes full of praise and pride. Aurelia Plath, herself a top student, well-read and self-sacrificing, seemed the perfect parent, and Sylvia would often tell her so in notes written during summers spent away from home at camp. Unlike Otto, who made demands on his children, Aurelia offered suggestions, alternatives, and an array of esteem-building exercises— which her daughter would come to loathe. What was wrong with mother? In one sense, nothing. In another, what was wrong with mother was that she was not Otto Plath. He had the mystique and the majesty of higher learning his daughter revered. Aurelia did not expect any less from Sylvia than Otto did, but Aurelia had also been her husband's servant. How could she function as her daughter's master?

Otto's death on 5 November 1940 remained a suppurating wound in Sylvia Plath's life. How could such a powerful man die, especially before his time? He was only fifty-five. But he had refused to see

doctors until it was too late. Even after his diabetes was diagnosed, he continued to consume a diet heavy in fats and sugars
that hastened his demise. Aurelia nursed him through his dying
days, restricting contact with the children to spare them the sight
of their father's agony. She also decided not to have Sylvia and
Warren attend the funeral. But to her daughter, Aurelia's actions
meant that Sylvia was deprived of her father's affection and approval. This reaction made his death seem even more mysterious
and arbitrary, a tyrannical disruption of her childhood that made
him blameworthy, too. How could a father so dominate her world
and then just disappear? It was monstrous. A child who, after her
father dies, says she will stop speaking to God (speaking to, mind
you—not praying to) is one who brooks no equals, let alone superi-
ors, in her cosmos. She may for a moment—even a year—feel over-
powered by another, but all of her writing speaks to a need to
dominate the world's attention.

It was Aurelia who introduced Sylvia Plath to poetry, reading
poems that she thought suited her child's love of rhythm and ca-
dence. Matthew Arnold's "The Forsaken Merman" struck Sylvia as
being addressed to her—or at least to children like her:

> Come, dear children, let us away:
> Down and away below!
> Now my brothers call from the bay,
> Now the great winds shoreward blow,
> Now the salt tides seaward flow . . .

For a child who often visited her grandparents on a strip of Winthrop land called Point Shirley that had views of both ocean and
bay, the merman's call to watery depths would echo in the image
of riding on Otto Plath's back, gradually losing her fear of the dark
and deep sea beneath their bodies as he swam his rhythmical
strokes.

Arnold's poetry was her world "through the surf and the swell . . .
where the sea-beasts ranged all round." Poetry proved to be a me-
dian point between her and the world, a conjoining like that of
land and sea. The merman, forsaken by his beloved Margaret,

yearns for her return. But she remains on land in church, "her eyes . . . sealed to the holy book!" The merman's voice is the poet's and expresses the enchantment of words that Margaret has also forsaken, but that Sylvia, a "sea-girl" like her mother, swooned over, saying they made her want to cry but also made her very happy. Poetry had that power over her. She would live and die by it.

Plath published her first verse, simply titled "Poem," in the *Boston Herald* on 10 August 1941. This brief nature poem featuring the sounds of crickets and the sights of fireflies appeared in the children's section, "The Good Sport Page." Paul Alexander calls this first publication the most important day of that summer. But the occasion was more than that: Sylvia became aware that the world was watching. Publication is a form of judgment that another kind of sensibility—say, Emily Dickinson's—shrinks from, but Sylvia already had a habit of putting herself forward. She measured herself by having others take the measure of her.

Aurelia understood this aspect of her daughter. When in the fall of 1942 Aurelia sold the family house in Winthrop and moved her family to Wellesley, she was thinking of more than situating Sylvia in a college town. Sylvia Plath needed a bigger canvas on which to practice her art. She was already drawing quite well, one year after publishing "Poem" winning a prize for a picture of a woman wearing a hat. Like some other extraordinary writers— Rebecca West, Norman Mailer, and Susan Sontag, for example— Sylvia from an early age regarded writing as a form of serious play.

Jane Eyre and *Gone with the Wind* were favorite novels, but Syl also liked to listen to *The Lone Ranger* and *The Jack Benny Show*. If Aurelia fussed over her child's devotion to radio the way parents today worry over how much television their children watch, such concern left no traces. Sylvia loved paper dolls and was overjoyed to get Rita Hayworth and Hedy Lamarr paper doll books. She also treasured her Bette Davis autograph. Syl may have seemed "brainy" to other kids, but her outgoing nature and wide-ranging interests and activities—swimming, sunbathing, and playing with boys— reveal nothing like the nerdy, introverted behavior often attributed to exceptionally brilliant students. Helen Lawson, Sylvia's ninth grade English teacher, told Edward Butscher that Sylvia, a perfectionist, "seemed to have the complete respect of her fellow pupils—not that of the 'grind.'"

By the age of twelve, Sylvia had scored in the 160 range on an IQ test, well into genius territory, according to Dorothy L. Humphrey, who reported the results to Edward Butscher. Humphrey notes that Sylvia was not only unusually knowledgeable for her age, she took a remarkable interest in the test itself, seeming to enjoy the "whole lengthy procedure," which she prolonged because she kept providing correct answers.

The next year Sylvia attended a performance in Boston of *The Tempest*. Aurelia dated the program 21 January 1945 and preserved it in the Smith archive, noting that her daughter had been "completely transported to the magic island of Prospero," talking about the play on the train home. It was a brilliantly sunny day. To Aurelia, the play's "stuff that dreams are made on" seemed reflected in the shining piles of snow. Sylvia was reading Shakespeare, entranced by a poet who once again brought the sea of her experience home to her.

> Full fathom five thy father lies;
> Of his bones are coral made;
> Those are pearls that were his eyes:
> Nothing of him that doth fade
> But doth suffer a sea-change
> Into something rich and strange.
> Sea-nymphs hourly ring his knell:
> Ding-dong.
> Hark! now I hear them—ding-dong, bell.

The sounds of this poem and the effect of the bell sounding a death knell create a magical resonance that could well captivate a child entranced not merely by poetry, but by all the wonderful sound effects on the radio—portentous music like the "William Tell Overture," heralding the Lone Ranger's appearance. Sylvia loved to create radio melodramas in the schoolyard, and she was already writing short stories and plotting novels, even as she tried to get the fingering right during her piano lessons at camp.

And yet she still had time for fellow campers, taking on a new name, "Sherry," and comforting a homesick girl. She assured Aurelia that her wonderful letters helped her daughter adjust to being away from home. Sylvia was "overwhelmingly happy" and eating well. If her accounts were accurate, she was stuffing herself. Why eat one bowl of tomato soup if she could down three? The same went for coffee cake and watermelon: She ate four slices of each. She reported her achievements, such as swimming sidestroke for a hundred yards and bravely diving into the cold water when everyone else malingered. Making new friends was a competitive activity. Joan Beales, for example, could play piano and violin and tap dance—and, most impressively, she sang on the radio. Ah, but she could not draw, Sylvia told Aurelia.

One feature of camp life that separates Sylvia's world from ours was the minstrel show. She dressed as a "pickaninny" and deemed her performance a "great success." Sylvia had no Negro friends, to use the argot of those times. She would not have seen many African Americans in her neighborhood. As human beings, they were virtually invisible—not just to her, but to millions of Americans, as Ralph Ellison eloquently explained in *Invisible Man*. The most familiar Negro figure in Sylvia's life would have been Rochester, Jack Benny's sly factotum, who was always scheming to get a day off from serving his parsimonious employer. Benny's half-hour Sunday night comedy program delighted millions, who took in stride an anodyne version of house slave humor. Audiences laughed at jokes about Rochester's skin color—for example, his plea that Benny stop scraping the blackened toast in his servant's hands because "Boss, you're getting down to me." The only other Negro role model was Mammy, Scarlett O'Hara's house slave, who insists that her rebellious teenage charge behave with a propriety befitting a woman of her class and race.

Caught up in what the movies purveyed as desirable daughterly behavior, Sylvia sought to please Aurelia and play the dutiful daughter to a mother as saintly as Scarlett O'Hara's mother, Ellen, who was always a lady. Aurelia resembled the kind parent who enforced a strict moral regime not through punishment, but through martyrdom to principles. Sylvia's postcards and letters from camp sound the continual theme of mother love. It was what saved her, Sylvia said, from her own "petty jealousies." Sylvia ran to Aurelia for comfort just as Scarlett sought out Ellen's embraces. But Scarlett O'Hara could never be as nice as her mother, and Sylvia realized early on the same would be true of her.

Sometimes Sylvia relegated Aurelia to the role of an offstage mother like Stella Dallas. Aurelia would eventually watch her beloved daughter depart for England and a life just as separate and unreachable to her as Stella Dallas's daughter's life is to the protagonist of Olive Higgins Prouty's novel. Stella can only stand in the street and gaze yearningly up at the window into her wealthy daughter's grand new world. And yet, as Sylvia's letters show, Aurelia—again like Stella Dallas—had a certain power. On the radio, Stella, like Superman, often got people out of jams. She was a tower of strength for her daughter. It is telling that when Sylvia married Ted Hughes, she wanted only her mother by her side.

Throughout her secondary school years, Sylvia won awards for her writing and her art. Other than her mentor, high school teacher Wilbury Crockett, who ran his literature classes like college seminars, her teachers by and large did not see her as a genius, although Anna C. Craig, a guidance counselor at Wellesley High School, recalled for Edward Butscher that Sylvia "devoured" Shakespeare and was an avid reader and creative writer, a standout who was also a "loner." One of Plath's classmates, Louise Lind, told Butscher that she and Sylvia "laughed and giggled together over school projects." Many years later, when Aurelia was still pondering the reasons for her daughter's suicide, Wilbury Crockett told her:

> As I have said to you several times, those who had asked me about Sylvia seem to disbelieve my recollections. But she was in my presence always affirmative, filled with exuberance, in love with life—with an unquenchable relish for the human adventure. Amusingly she seemed quite out of breath with it all. I loved having her come to the house . . . much hilarity—and, of course, much serious conversation. As you must realize, I came to know her well after three years of having her

in class. And I do look back upon our relationship with great fondness.

If I were to single out a word to describe her, it would be *radiant.*

Sylvia was perhaps too dutiful, too eager to please, to stand out in stereotypical fashion as an aloof, mercurial intellectual destined for greatness. She looked wholesome and, as she frequently said, tanned well. She liked to bike and play tennis, a game a neighbor boy, Phil McCurdy, taught her. Unlike other males, he did not seem especially daunted by a girl who scored 160 on an IQ test and could be formidable in conversation. By her junior year of high school, Sylvia was going out on dates and would not, for very long, be without the attentions of a boy like Perry Norton, who lived close by. There were many others throughout her years in school.

Looks mattered to Sylvia. So did what she wore. So did matters like good manners and diction. She complained that a couple of girls at camp used words like "ain't" and "youse" that hurt her ears. They were "*not* well brought up." A middle-class sense of propriety remained a very strong feature of this poet even when she lived among the loucher types of the literary world. Her acerbic comments about people were a form of scrubbing away the squalor that surrounded some writers and other denizens of arty conclaves. Her favorite radio heroes—the Lone Ranger, The Shadow, and Superman—were part of a sort of cleanup detail, making the world morally immaculate. Sylvia had a visceral dislike of messes—moral and otherwise—that accounts for her extreme reactions later in life to her husband's appalling physical and moral hygiene.

Aurelia, and later Ted Hughes, never felt comfortable with Sylvia's astringent observations about themselves and others. They never seemed to realize that what seemed hurtful to others *entertained* Sylvia, who was by nature a satirist, as Diane Middlebrook clearly shows. This satirical bent explains why Jack Benny was so appealing to Sylvia during her teenage years. Benny's radio program relentlessly mocked his shortcomings, making fun of his violin playing, his toupee, his stinginess, and even his effeminate way of walking. The program ran a nationwide contest with $10,000 in prizes, asking listeners to complete the phrase, "Why I hate Jack Benny." Sad to say, there is no way of knowing if Sylvia submitted an entry. A running gag in the show featured movie star Ronald Colman and his wife, forever trying to avoid meetings with Benny, their bumptious neighbor. And Jack gave as good as he got, making fun of his obese announcer, Don Wilson (who was so fat he got stuck in armchairs), mocking the shiftless Rochester, and ridiculing Phil Harris, the program's band leader, who could not read music—or anything else, for that matter. Sylvia had a habit of mind that naturally reveled in this kind of put down, which audiences encouraged by laughing uproariously at Jack, whether he was the butt of a joke or its author. Benny's kind of joking—the puncturing of pretentions, including his own—had an aggressive edge. His program regulars tried to outdo one another with comic insults, which built to a crescendo of audience laughter in the best shows. The high energy of these Sunday night programs had obvious appeal for Sylvia and millions of others readying themselves for another workweek. Indeed, anything that could make the competitive nature of society a pleasing diversion had enormous appeal for a young mind as serious as Sylvia's.

Wilbury Crockett's classes brought out Sylvia's competitive nature. After Crockett described a lengthy reading list and extensive writing assignments, one third of the first day's class did not return for another lesson, instead transferring to a less demanding section. He developed a cadre of twenty superior students called "Crocketeers." Otto Plath would have approved of Crockett's intellectual esprit de corps. This notion of an elect—an elite literary strike force that was also political in nature, keeping abreast of the latest developments in Europe and elsewhere—spurred Sylvia to write about subjects such as the Korean War and the atomic bomb, faithfully following her father's pacifist politics.

In the spring of 1947, Sylvia began writing to a pen pal, a German teenager named Hans-Joachim Neupert. They would exchange letters over the next five years, revealing, on Sylvia's side, a keen desire to discover what the war had been like for a young boy living in a devastatingly bombed landscape. She was acutely aware of her own safe suburban upbringing, mentioning that the life of an American teenager must seem frivolous to Hans. Didn't he think that, in the end, war was futile? She told him she was considering careers as a foreign correspondent, a newspaper reporter, an author, or an artist. In later letters, she spoke of her writing and the rejections she had received from various publications. These last never seemed to discourage her. She already had the attitude of a professional who realizes that for every acceptance there are scores of dismissals.

In subsequent letters she drew a map of Massachusetts, stretching from Salem to Winthrop to Boston, Cambridge, Wellesley, and Boston Bay, where a sea serpent is shown popping out of the water with a balloon message: "Hello Hans!" The serpent's tongue and perky back flipper are visible above the calm water. But below the water line lurks a dragon-like figure with a long serpentine tongue.

Hans was evidently a good correspondent (his letters have not survived). Sylvia complimented him on his writing, revealing a good deal about her own temperament, which was so much like the sea, changing from "one mood to another—from high waves on dark, stormy days, to tranquil ripples on sunny days." She found it disturbing that so much history was happening while her own surroundings were complacent and placid compared to the horrors Hans had witnessed.

These letters explain a good deal about the poet who wrote "Daddy" and her desire to integrate her own family story with the Holocaust. Even at this young age, she felt touched by history that had not yet touched her. Here was a sensibility that felt implicated in what had been done to Hans and his people. She wanted to "plunge into the vital world," acknowledging ruefully that war could not be as real to her as it had been to Hans. It bothered her that this should be so. Expressions of yearning to go abroad to remedy the insufficiency of her own comfortable upbringing are startling to read in the prose of a tenth grader. Only two years later she would confide to her journal that she felt the "weight of centuries" suffocating her.

Sylvia spoke of her connection to Europe through her Austrian grandparents. Indeed, Aurelia had spoken German growing up in her family, the Schobers, and Sylvia heard stories about the anti-German sentiment abroad in America during World War I, when Aurelia was growing up in a primarily Irish neighborhood. Rather than rejecting her ethnic background, Sylvia said she took "patriotic pride" in it. She made a point of giving an oral report about Thomas Mann, a world famous author and anti-Fascist who had become a celebrated figure in America. She told Hans that in class she had read aloud part of his letter describing Mann's recent visit to Germany.

Sylvia sometimes stayed with her grandparents when her mother was working full time in order to afford extras like camp for both her children. In Sylvia's journal, she mentions Grampy's admiration for everything she does and Grammy's rich recipes, which appealed to a child with an enormous appetite. Sylvia was also fond of her Uncle Frank, who came to her in dreams dressed as Superman. This extended family, with ties to the "old country," made Sylvia acutely conscious of what it meant to be an American, while also giving her, at a very young age, a remarkably cosmopolitan perspective that helped her shy away from any form of jingoism.

In her letter of 30 May 1950, Sylvia announced that she had been accepted to Smith College in Northampton, Massachusetts, about ninety miles from Wellesley. With her high scholastic average and extracurricular record (working on the school newspaper, playing basketball, participating in student government), she could have been admitted to Wellesley on a town scholarship and saved money by living at home. But like many ambitious students, she wanted to test herself by going away to college and, of course, away from her mother. But not too far away. Aurelia was Sylvia's lifeline no matter how much she resented her mother—or at least her overwhelming need to confide in Aurelia. Aurelia bore the weight of what Sylvia expected of herself and seems not to have objected to her daughter's desire to attend Smith. Indeed, Aurelia later told scholar Judith Kroll that she welcomed all signs of her daughter's growing independence.

It obviously pleased Sylvia, as well, that even though she re-

ceived some scholarship aid, she was going to have to work in order to afford her first year at Smith. As she wrote Hans, she would
be laboring on a farm that summer, biking back and forth to work
in fields and in a greenhouse, "rain or shine." Her only previous
experience of this kind had been a day at camp picking blueberries
for ten cents a quart. She anticipated sore muscles but also seemed
to enjoy the prospect of breaking herself in—and yes, getting a
tan. Sylvia would stick it out through a long, tiring summer, making friends with farmworkers and experiencing for a brief period
the hard manual labor of working-class life.

Sylvia told Hans about the Estonian and the Pole who picked
fruits and vegetables beside her. She enjoyed their funny stories—
about the only entertainment she had, since by the time she got
home she was exhausted and was in bed by nine. It felt good to
be working the earth. But it was more than that. The daily rhythms
of hard labor soothed her. Lying in her bed at night thinking of
the strawberry runners she would set the next day, she suddenly
understood how for some people this kind of life was enough.
Why demand more? she asked in her journal.

Sylvia did not tell Hans that Ilo, the Estonian boy, had lured her
to his room—ostensibly to see his artwork—and had bestowed on
her a passionate French kiss, her first. She left abruptly, realizing
she would be teased about falling for Ilo. But she did not really
shrink from the experience. She welcomed the idea of a fulfilling
sex life, but she feared the consequences and wished to put off that
kind of intense physical involvement until she found a mate she
was surer of. In her journal, she called herself "the American virgin, dressed to seduce." With Emile, another boyfriend from that
summer, she necked and petted, feeling his erection as she pressed
her breasts closer to his body. In 1950, casual sexual intercourse for
a girl of her age and background was just too risky.

Talk of the Korean War made her angry. She saw no purpose to
the fighting, except as a manifestation of rabid anticommunism.
You can't kill an idea, she argued. Even if Hans told her she was simply a "silly girl" who did not understand how boys felt about fighting, she would say war was absurd. She had been reading Thomas
Hardy's sad, wistful war poems, such as "The Man He Killed," which

she quoted to Hans. Hardy's lines dramatized not only the humanity of the men firing at one another, but also the oddity and irony of their behavior:

> Yes; quaint and curious war is!
> You shoot a fellow down
> You'd treat, if met where any bar is,
> Or help to half a crown.

What hurt Sylvia was the way war destroyed simple acts of kindness and generosity and the desire to exchange confidences, as she did with Hans. She called the dropping of the atomic bomb "a sin."

She used her summer farm experience to compose a fine poem, "Bitter Strawberries," published on 11 August 1950 in *The Christian Science Monitor*. The work reads a little like Thomas Hardy's war poems, or Siegfried Sassoon's, while also sounding a little like William Carlos Williams's vignettes of American scenes using direct speech. In the fields the talk is about the Russians, culminating in the "head woman" saying, "Bomb them off the map." This was often said in the early 1950s, when certain Americans echoed what General Patton had declared immediately after World War II: Annihilate the Russians before they have the power to retaliate. The call for another atomic bomb drop took on urgency because of the new draft law alluded to in Sylvia's poem. A blue-eyed girl reacts in terror at the harsh words, and she is told sharply not to worry. This little drama ends with everyone returning to their picking, kneeling over the rows and cupping the berries protectively before their stems are snapped off "between thumb and forefinger." The ironic poem's description of a crew organized by a leader dealing in delicate lethality is both a contrast to and evocation of the nuclear age Plath detested—an era of mutually assured destruction that would, she wrote in her journal, deprive her brother Warren of the opportunity to lead a full, productive life.

Sylvia would never forsake her early pacifism, perhaps also influenced by the devastating scenes of destruction depicted in *Gone with the Wind.* For her, pacifism meant not only rejection of war, but also a sense of solidarity with other places, other people. Writing to Hans helped wrest her from Wellesley, as did farm work, so that she could show up at Smith, as she did every summer at camp, with another shot at making something new of herself.

CHAPTER 2

MISTRESS OF ALL THE ELEMENTS

(1950—53)

August 1950: Sylvia publishes "And Summer Will Not Come Again" in *Seventeen;* 1950–53: Korean War; 1950–51: A scholarship student at Smith College, Plath begins dating but does not find her Mr. Big; 1951–52: She works at a hotel and then as a mother's helper to earn spending money; 1952: Sylvia's short story "Sunday at the Mintons" wins a prize and is published in *Mademoiselle;* 1953: First issue of *Playboy,* with Marilyn Monroe on the cover.

On 3 August 1950, Sylvia Plath received her first fan letter. Twenty-one-year-old Eddie Cohen had read her short story "And Summer Will Not Come Again," her first appearance in *Seventeen* after the magazine had rejected more than forty earlier submissions. In this story of a doomed romance between a young girl and her tennis instructor, Cohen detected a temperament that transcended the crude sentiment of popular magazine fiction. The story's title was taken from a Sara Teasdale poem, "An End":

I have no heart for any other joy,
The drenched September day turns to depart,
And I have said goodbye to what I love;
With my own will I vanquished my own heart.

On the long wind I hear the winter coming,
The window panes are cold and blind with rain;
With my own will I turned the summer from me
And summer will not come to me again.

"What I wouldn't give to be able to write like this," fourteen-year-old Sylvia had written in her journal. "Like this" meant not only commanding the simplicity and grace that were Teasdale's signature traits, but also the ability to exquisitely evoke her own sensibility, to describe why the poet wrote out of a melancholy sense of self-injury. Such concerns constitute a leitmotif in Plath's journals.

Critic Steven Gould Axelrod has shown how much of Teasdale's sensibility suffused Sylvia Plath's work. Teasdale developed what he calls the "rhetoric of anguish." Celia, the heroine of "And Summer Will Not Come Again," quotes a part of "An End" that evokes a powerful sense of loss, of getting caught in a self-defeating dynamic. Eddie Cohen, still wondering what to do with his life, identified with Sylvia's heroine when he perused his sister's copy of *Seventeen*. He thought he might have talent as a writer, and like Sylvia, he was checking out the market. He was expecting, however, just to pick up a few pointers. He was taken aback when the story actually moved him. His first letter to Sylvia is rather condescending—in effect a message from an older boy telling a younger girl that maybe she has something there. He wanted to find out.

Over the course of their correspondence Eddie would prove, again and again, that he knew how to read Sylvia, the person and the writer. He detected tensions in her that no one—not even Aurelia—identified. Cohen found in Plath a "trapped voice," to use Axelrod's term for Teasdale's "bereaved speakers." And like Teasdale, Plath wrote poems and stories with inconsolable narrators. Indeed, Plath's affinity for Teasdale, as well as the similarities of their suicides—both triggered by the departure of a powerful man—brought them together, early and late, in Plath's career.

Despair is an underlying theme in much of what these two poets wrote, as both struggled to balance their vocations as writers and their lives as women. Recurring metaphors of nature, especially of the sea, function as calming influences on the exquisitely fragile sensibilities of poets who sought to anchor their work in classical forms, even as they embraced modernity. Somehow Eddie Cohen divined that more was at stake in "And Summer Will Not Come Again" than in the formulaic fiction *Seventeen* ordinarily published.

On 6 August, Sylvia replied to Eddie, telling him she had his number. If he would drop the superior tone and level with her, she would enjoy corresponding with a critic. She had no illusions about her story, saying it resembled the usual *Seventeen* "drivel." So why the "subtle flattery"? she wondered. Did he have a wager with Hemingway about "would-be female writers"? The question shows she already resented the segregation of women in the literary canon. Eddie had aroused her competitive instincts, and she wanted him to know that she was as tough as any male, not some "sweet and trusting" *Seventeen* hopeful he could manipulate.

Two days later, Eddie did open up, calling himself a "cynical idealist," a good handle for a sensibility as earnest as Sylvia's but chastened by a few more years of failed expectations. Sylvia admitted that her own brand of sarcasm masked her fear of getting hurt. Like Eddie, she liked to remain a little aloof and even caustic in her judgments. When Sylvia admitted that she tried not to let her "vulnerable core" show, Eddie eagerly replied that his roommates remembered him saying exactly the same thing about himself.

When Aurelia objected many years later to Sylvia's cruel characterizations of her and others in *The Bell Jar* and in letters, journals, and stories, she did not fully take in her daughter's need to put people in their places, lest she lose her own sense of singularity, the exceptional identity her father had fostered and exemplified. Sylvia shared the power to pinpoint flaws with Virginia Woolf, who shaped her diaries as both literary and identity-strengthening exercises. And like Sara Teasdale, Plath maintained her fragile equilibrium by encasing it in the equipoise of the poetic line.

By the end of September, Sylvia had begun her freshman year at Smith, sending her mother upbeat reports in daily postcards and in letters that provided copious details. It was almost as if Sivvy, the loving and anxious child, were taking her own temperature for her apprehensive and adoring parent, whom she called "my favorite person." Sylvia's room in Haven House was "homey," everyone was friendly, and the food was "fabulous." She had already met Ann Davidow, who would become a lifelong friend. Ann had Jewish parents, as Sylvia told her mother, but was "a free thinker," and loved to discuss God and religion and men. Nearly as tall as Sylvia, Ann sparkled. Sylvia was already being advised that she should enjoy herself, which meant socializing and becoming an "all around" person.

Eddie seemed amused at Sylvia's first gushing letters from Smith, calling them "breathless." He was also pleased that she asked him to keep writing. Not to worry, he assured her; Sylvia had gotten "under my skin." She had found his weak spots. She flattered him "nicely." What male could resist that? But she did not hesitate to contradict him, and he found her independence attractive.

Sylvia never displayed her devastating irony in letters home. They expressed her generosity and genuine desire to include Aurelia in her enthusiasms. Aurelia was a ready-made audience. She understood that for Sylvia decorating her room was as important as meeting a boy who turned out to be a poet. Sylvia blazoned her new identity in capital letters, the equivalent of billboarding herself: "I'M A SMITH GIRL NOW." Her letters did not, however, reflect pressures that were building internally as she sought to equalize her commitments to herself, to her writing, and to the world, now centered on college. Writing in a letter dated 26 September (which Aurelia did not include in *Letters Home),* Sylvia confessed that she loved journalism because it made her less self-conscious and eager to understand others.

Of course, Sylvia could not forget herself for long, especially after a physical exam, a requirement for all freshman instituted in 1924 that ended only in 1969. Daryl Hafter, who graduated a year after Sylvia, remembered, with a shiver in her voice, walking naked into a very large gym to be looked at by a phys ed teacher. Posture photographs were taken to identify conditions such as scoliosis that might result in orthopedic problems. Good posture was considered essential to good health, not just at Smith but also at colleges and schools throughout the country. Only much later were such exams viewed as intruding on student rights and enforcing a standard of conduct deemed coercive.

Sylvia reported to her mother she was now 5' 9", 137 pounds, and so terribly conscious of maintaining a good posture that in aligning her ears and heels she neglected to "tilt up straight." This last comment prompted the teacher's comment, "You have good alignment, but you are in constant danger of falling on your face." Even as Plath worried about her deportment, a copy of Mabel Elsworth Todd's *The Thinking Body* lay on Marilyn Monroe's bedside table. In this era, women—whether in finishing schools, Ivy League colleges, or businesses—did not slouch.

Eddie Cohen, industriously "digging between the lines," as he put it, detected Sylvia's unease in a bewildering new world that was "indifferent" to her and that eluded her full understanding. He had dropped out of the high-powered University of Chicago and only recently begun attending classes at Roosevelt University. Eddie detected "something close to terror" in Sylvia's account of one of her dates. She was so impressed with Eddie's analysis that, surprisingly, she let her mother in on it. Writing on 8 October in another important letter Aurelia did not include in *Letters Home,* Sylvia admitted that she had been frantically seeking refuge, and that Eddie, with his customary perceptiveness, "hit the nail on the head."

Sylvia was already beginning to experience colds, sinus infections, and related ailments that sometimes put her in the infirmary. She worried about grades, telling her mother she did not expect to get a single A, and that she feared failing history, a subject notoriously difficult even for sophomores and juniors. Reading forty pages of history every night persuaded Sylvia she had "no background." It was like beating your head "against the knowledge of centuries," she confided to her journal. For someone Sylvia's age, her understanding of the past and of contemporary affairs was impressive. But now she realized the difference between the scholar and the merely well informed. Too often her worries over her studies have been portrayed merely as a psychological problem, as though she were too hard on herself. And in a sense, she was. But what made Sylvia Plath great—not just as a poet, but as an imaginative mind—was her profound humility, her submission to history as a subject that had to be mastered. Surrendering to the authority of a discipline is part of what ultimately made her a writer of genius. Before she could be bold enough to exert the mastery exhibited in her mature poetry, she had to be mastered by what she studied.

The strange new world that Eddie Cohen described included this daunting desire for mastery. Other than Wilbury Crockett, before college Plath had not had a teacher who could have challenged and unsettled her the way reading history at Smith did. Eddie Cohen, who had had his problems with the demanding University of Chicago curriculum, knew exactly what Plath confronted: an intellectual anxiety that goes far beyond clichés about adjustment to freshman year.

Other aspects of collegiate existence also rattled Sylvia. She wanted to enjoy the social life, but she did not see how she could spend all night playing bridge the way other freshmen did. After three blind dates, she wrote in her journal of feeling undesirable, an astounding admission that left her wondering at herself. She had been so popular before leaving for Smith, full of confidence in her ability to attract males. Now she complained about the dating system, about wandering with boys from one fraternity to another, or visiting them at nearby colleges and then returning with reports on who one saw and what one did. This hardly seemed the way to find a congenial male.

Downhearted, Sylvia leaned heavily on Eddie, telling him he was her "dream," although she hoped never to meet him because as matters stood, their relationship played into "my writing, my desire to be many lives." She was beginning to shrug off his desire to meet her. For all his perspicacity—or perhaps because of it—she dreaded the idea of his coming so close. After all, it was her writing, not herself per se, that first attracted him to her. Eddie, though, thought of himself as more than her alter ego and served notice that he saw no reason why they should not meet. He was looking for the one "Golden Woman" capable of sharing "all facets" of his existence. Sylvia was seeking essentially the same thing: a tall, handsome, sensuous, but also intellectually serious young man—in essence, Ashley Wilkes. She had already told Eddie that, judging by the photograph he sent, he was good looking, and he was starting to hope that maybe he and Sylvia were suitable—although he recognized that they shared only a "paper world," one that she had called "unreal," much to Eddie's dismay. He admitted that he was pleased when her dates did not work out and jealous when they did.

Sylvia's mood swings at Smith are apparent in a postcard dated 28 October that Aurelia chose not to include in *Letters Home*. At the library a professor sat next to her, and she discovered he knew her name. Smith suddenly seemed much less impersonal: "*Are* there any colleges other than Smith?" she asked. Like her contemporary, Susan Sontag, then attending the University of Chicago, Plath was an enthusiast. But while the inevitable disappointments made Sontag bitter, wary, and cynical, Plath felt hurt and betrayed any time a person or place she built up proved unworthy. The letdown would be devastating, and it could occur at a moment's notice. Sontag was more broody and introverted. Not learning to play bridge would never bother her. She saw no value in conforming, but not playing the game troubled Plath, who wanted to fit in. She was as self-absorbed as Sontag, but Sylvia was also incredibly alive to her culture, allowing it to impinge on her in ways that Sontag, with her strongly defended sense of self, could reject at will. Both women were insecure and could hide their vulnerability in haughtiness, but only Sontag made that haughtiness into the armature of her identity. The walls of Plath's fortress would be breached again and again, so that she felt overrun. In an 11 November letter to her mother, she casually mentions suicide, saying she advised her close friend Ann Davidow against it because "something unexpected always happens."

In the midst of her hectic fall, Sylvia was thrilled to learn she had received a scholarship from Olive Higgins Prouty, the author of the novel *Stella Dallas,* a tearjerker made into a radio soap opera, as well as two films. Prouty wanted Sylvia to write about her future plans. The scholarship bolstered Sylvia. To Aurelia, she declared that Smith was stretching her, pulling her to "heights and depths of thought I never dreamed possible." She believed she was storing up experiences—and even pain—that would produce art.

In her 1 December thank you letter to Prouty, a rattled Sylvia wrote about watching the faces of six hundred freshmen on the steps of Scott Gym, and feeling that she was "drowning in a sea of

personalities, each one as eager to be a whole individual as I was."
What makes Sylvia such a significant figure—a cynosure, in fact—is
her refusal to simply play the alienated artist or disaffected individual, even though she believed her true calling as an artist was
elsewhere. Beginning with her first year at Smith, she was trying,
in earnest, to live through her contradictions.

When a twenty-five-year-old soldier, a Korean War veteran who
had spent two years in a hospital convalescing from a lung wound,
attacked her during a late night walk on campus, Sylvia was shocked
by how little she knew about the world. He desisted when she cried
out, but she was amazed at how offended *he* was, since he pre-
sumed their night out would culminate in a rape—although neither
he nor Sylvia would have used the word then. A chagrined Sylvia
realized how naïve she had been and actually comforted the ag-
grieved man, who put his head in her lap. She understood something was wrong with this picture. Shouldn't he be apologizing to
her? Yet the times were such that neither of them could see past
what were then conventional cultural markers of their encounter. It
perplexed Sylvia that she should have made such an elementary
blunder, and she vowed never again to put herself in such a vulnerable position. Back at Haven House, a shaken Sylvia talked over the
episode with friends and discovered they had had similar experiences.

On 8 December, Eddie Cohen set her straight:

Although you have an unusual understanding of the world
in terms of ideas and groups of people, you as yet do not understand the individual in conflict with himself or society,
or the impact of emotion upon an individual to the extent
that it overcomes his rational aspects. This results from two
things: never having had the experience of facing a demanding personal situation on your own; and never having had a
really compelling, overwhelming love affair. In these shortcomings, time will bring you through—your attitude is almost exactly my own two years ago, and I have since learned
those things which only experience can bring. Logic isn't
everything.

No one talked to Sylvia Plath this way. She fell silent, as Eddie noted in two follow-up letters.

Because she was depressed, Sylvia did not write. She admitted as much to her mother, saying she had given up carving a block of wood that now represented her own blankness. To counteract her "black despair," she had attended a life class and felt her spirits lift as she made sketches of a posing Smith girl. But Sylvia still wondered how she would make it to Christmas. She also told Aurelia that Ann Davidow was dropping out of Smith because she did not feel smart enough to do the work. Ann, in fact, was suicidal, Sylvia said. In *Letters Home,* Aurelia would add a note suggesting her daughter was exaggerating and that Ann's mood was, in fact, a projection of Sylvia's own.

On 24 December 1950, Sylvia wrote to her pen pal Hans, describing Smith in very positive terms, though she admitted she felt "a little lost." She still believed the world was likely to come to a grim end: America was like the Roman Empire, "new and bright," and yet falling apart. *On the Beach,* Nevil Shute's novel about the aftermath of nuclear holocaust, would not be published for another seven years, and yet Sylvia was already imagining not only the extinction of her hopes, but of the world's. She made it through the Christmas season but returned to Smith in a glum mood. She missed Ann Davidow. Sylvia wrote to Ann, addressing her as "Davy," to say she was lost without her confidant. Sylvia was not unhappy for long, though. She made friends with Marcia Brown, a cheerful companion who loved debating ideas on long walks. Sylvia went home with Marcia to New Hampshire in early February for a brief visit.

Eddie Cohen suddenly appeared at Smith in early April, exhausted from his cross-country drive from Chicago and ill-prepared for Sylvia's frigid reception. He drove her home in near silence. Their awkward meeting shook his confidence. He wondered if perhaps he had misled her and was not the good-looking guy in the photograph he had sent her. At any rate, he took the blame for their misadventure and told her he was going to therapy. He suspected that somewhere in him a piece was missing, and he was "rather anxious to find what and where it is."

Eddie had been replaced by Dick Norton, a med student at Yale, tall and handsome, and the older brother of Perry Norton, whom Sylvia had dated in high school. The older neighbor boy noticed she had grown up, and he invited her for a weekend at his school— always a special kind of invitation, requiring arrangements for travel by train and a place to stay, insuring all was in order for a Smith girl intent on preserving her chastity. Dick was a master of the routine, and at first he impressed Sylvia. He was friendly but not too familiar, writing correct letters that inquired about her studies, discussed their families, and expressed interest in what she was writing. He also described events on his campus, including the visit of Reinhold Neibuhr, a theologian then popular owing to his talent for addressing a broad range of readers concerned about America's place in history. Like Plath, Niebuhr feared the country was going the way of the Roman Empire.

If Dick was promising, he also needed work, Sylvia confided to Ann. He acted like an "indulgent older cousin," memorizing poetry and reciting it to her, even though he had discounted "emotional expression" unless it had a scientific basis "or something," Sylvia trailed off. Whereas go-for-broke Eddie saw a glorious future for Sylvia as a writer, the practical Dick observed, "You won't be badly off, Syl, if she [Aurelia] can teach you shorthand and if I can impart some enthusiasm for natural science. One or both may come in time." Sylvia had to set aside such small-minded advice in hopes that there was more to Dick. Right then, it was Dick—or more of those dreadful blind dates.

Their first weekend was a great success. Dick made headway, it seems, because he was gentlemanly and sure of himself, traits Sylvia admired. Unlike her blind dates, he was not cowed by her intelligence; indeed, he found it lacking in some respects. The very idea that *she* might have shortcomings sent Sylvia to the moon over Dick, as she revealed in a 5 March letter to Ann: "I never felt so shallow in my life." And he knew how to show a girl a good time, attending an exciting swim meet, biking, and dining at a Chinese restaurant. Reporting to her mother about the weekend with Dick, Sylvia summed it up this way: "He knows everything."

In her journal, Sylvia gave Dick a portentous fanfare. She might as well have written a Harlequin romance, for the scene is set at night, with the wind whipping up a froth of expectation, as she strides forward on "silver feet," holding hands with her beloved under the starkly shining street lights, "Two of us, strong and together." Overhead she observes a cathedral of constellations, and Dick says it is like "being in church." They kiss, again and again. Sylvia salivated over that "glorious specimen of Dick-hood," who addressed one letter to her, "Dear Incomparable One" and signed another "Your willing slave."

To her mother, Sylvia spoke in conventional terms of catching a man. In her journal she chided herself, "so proud and disdainful of custom," for thinking of marriage as a viable option, one that required her to subordinate herself to a husband and to channel her creativity through his career. Even so, Sylvia hoped her man would tolerate her freelancing writer's life. The idea of a career—the very word—bothered her. She had not entirely abandoned the idea of earning an advanced degree, but like Susan Sontag, born just a year after Plath, she regarded the routines of academic institutions and the paraphernalia of the scholar's life with ambivalence. How could a creative person function in so much harness? Marriage itself, Sylvia confided to her journal, might drain her of creativity, although she conceded that having children might do just the opposite, making her a more fulfilled artist.

Marcia Brown, so logical and sensible according to Sylvia, offered solace and companionship, and Sylvia was heartened in May when they both secured summer babysitting jobs in Swampscott, Massachusetts. By this time, after a month or so of rhapsodizing about Dick, Sylvia was beginning to have her doubts. What was behind his jocular tone? She suspected, for all his casual confidence, that he was uneasy about something. On 14 May, she told her mother that she had ripped off part of his irritating "jovial mask."

Sylvia took the typical Smith safety route, finding summer employment babysitting the Mayo family's children, aged six, four, and two. She called them three "adorable" kids, but they seemed far less lovable after a long day of helping with breakfast, making beds, doing the laundry, ironing, and bathing the baby at night. In her journal she lamented the tragedy of womanhood. She wanted to be out in the world, hitting the road and consorting with soldiers and sailors, hanging out at bars—doing the scene like Jack Kerouac. But her mere presence would be taken as an invitation to have sex.

Sylvia felt awkward in the kitchen, since she knew little about cooking. She now realized how her capable mother had spoiled her by not ever requiring her to learn the rudiments of meal making. It was a lot of work, and she was having murderous thoughts about her "darlings." By July, she was fed up with the peripatetic schedule that had her going "in spurts" from 7 a.m. to 9 p.m. She was well treated and did take some pleasure in caring for her charges, but inevitably she suffered in the role of supernumerary, which brilliant women before her—Marie Curie and the Brontë sisters, among others—had endured in their demeaning apprenticeship years. She had to grit her teeth, as they did, and deal every day with unruly children. In her journal and letters she actually sounds rather like Anne Brontë's Agnes Grey. What is most unbearable about such situations is that no one notices the beautiful genius in their midst. No one complimented Sylvia on how well she looked. She admitted to Ann Davidow that she felt diminished. The recognition of others was always important to Sylvia, who did not care for the role of solitary genius. She longed to hear from Eddie, but he had fallen silent after she failed to answer his last two letters. To Aurelia, she confessed to feeling "cut off from humankind." She could do no work of her own, since her main task was always to superintend the children. She had lost her tan and looked hollow-eyed. So no trysts with Dick, she decided, although she eventually did see him when he could get away from waiting tables at the Latham Inn. Marcia had taken a job similar to Sylvia's with the Blodgett family and saw Sylvia frequently. Even so, in her journal Sylvia reprimanded herself for allowing fear and insecurity to dominate her.

Sylvia's forlorn letters after a month of babysitting reflect how much her grandiose sense of herself had been affronted by her employment. Her 7 July letter to Aurelia suggests how keenly she felt the discrepancy between the fan letters forwarded to her from *Seventeen* and her own uncertainty about herself. Reading fan mail provoked an ironic comment in the third person: "Sylvia Plath sure has something—but who is she anyhow?" She quoted a line from William Ernest Henley's famous poem, "Invictus": "My head is bloody, but unbowed," to which she added her own line, "May children's bones bedeck my shroud." Those children would be the death of her, she implied in her gruesome poetic joke, which was such a counterpoint to Henley's own concluding lines: "I am the master of my fate: / I am the captain of my soul." Sylvia had a few inconsequential dates that summer, and in late August she enjoyed a few days with Dick. But mostly she was learning, as she wrote to Aurelia on 4 August, the "limitations of the woman's sphere."

As so often, though, what Sylvia said on one page would be contradicted on another. Her shifting moods made it impossible for her to settle down. Thus a journal passage written after her return to Smith for a second year pays tribute to blind dates and the thirty-odd boys who had made her more conversant and confident. She was making her entrances downstairs in Haven House with a "practiced casualness," no longer worrying whether her slip was showing or her hair uncurling. Now Sylvia could see herself as an attractive creation. It was show time at Smith College. What had bothered her so much about her babysitting stint in Swampscott was, as she put it in her journal, living in the "shadow of the lives of others." The very expression of this sentiment in the passive voice suggests how much Sylvia missed the spotlight.

Resuming correspondence with Eddie Cohen was one sure sign that Sylvia had recovered from her summer in shadow. She had also come to realize how awful she had been to Eddie after his long ride to see her. She told him about Dick's tentative courtship, which Eddie diagnosed as her suitor's uncertainty about himself and Sylvia. Eddie did not need to read her journal to sum up her problem: the huge discrepancy between the way she was living and her ambitious plans, a discrepancy that marriage would complicate. But he did not know that Sylvia was also keeping score, estimating that a woman had only about eight years before the wrinkles began to show and she was no longer physically attractive.

Then Sylvia had one of those Jane Eyre/Thornfield Hall episodes. Everyone in Haven House was invited to Maureen Buckley's coming-out party at her family's mansion in Sharon, Connecticut. Maureen was the sister of William F. Buckley Jr., then a senior at Yale and later the founder of the *National Review* and one of the guiding lights of American conservatism. Bill had brought along his Yale class to meet all the Smith girls. Sylvia, sought after by several dance partners, gloried, perhaps for the first time, in her womanhood, feeling like a princess escorted by the scions of wealthy families, including Plato Skouras, son of Spyros Skouras, head of 20th Century Fox. One of her courtiers actually addressed her as "Milady." Another said she looked like the Botticelli Madonna hanging over the Buckleys' fireplace. That night, as she drifted off to sleep and into "exquisite dreams" in what might as well have been Thornfield Hall, she could hear the wind "wuthering outside the stone walls."

This idyll—coming so soon after a summer of baby-minding and Sylvia's provisional romance with Dick—she transformed into lines that placed her in the pastoral world of Renaissance poetry, picturing the sculpture of a bronze boy "kneedeep in centuries," bedecked with leaves heralding the passage of time. From longing to frequent barrooms to frolicking on landed estates, Sylvia Plath could hardly contain herself. Returning to the Smith campus, however, she confessed to Aurelia that the course work frightened her, and she could not keep up. She saw her future as only work and more work.

Eddie was talking of coming east again, and this time Sylvia wanted to show him a better time, alerting her mother that she would like to invite him to their home. He remained a kind of reality check on Sylvia's tendency to romanticize events. When she described Constantine, one of the Buckley party cavaliers who had invited her for a Princeton weekend, Eddie (sounding like Nelson Algren) observed: "He reminds me, in a vague way, of someone I know. I dunno some romantic type critter I run into now & again who discusses love & literature & atomic power with equal glibness & appears and disappears with the suddenness of Mephistopheles." Sylvia quoted Eddie's verdict to Aurelia, concluding succinctly, "Not bad for a thumbnail sketch!"

Sylvia, for all her worries, survived the fall semester of 1951 and, as usual, did well in her studies. In January 1952, she spent a weekend at Yale with Dick, who took her on his rounds as a medical student. She witnessed a birth, which she seemed to take in stride. She was not prepared, though, for the shocking revelation that Dick, who had led her to think otherwise, was not a virgin. She was angry about his deception and sudden confession. She was generally mad at men, who could play around in ways that women could not. Her reference to him now as a "blond god" was surely sarcastic. Sylvia was no prude, but Dick was different. She had built him up into a pristine idol. Now he seemed just like other men, some of whom she might have bedded if she had loved them or was not so worried about emotional involvements and pregnancy. She was still holding out for a taller, more romantic figure than Dick, so that she could wear heels and do the romantically impractical thing. Even at her most passionate, sooner or later Sylvia took the measure of her men. She yearned for the recklessness of romance, but she also read the newspapers and worried about world events, still pouring out her anxieties about nuclear war in letters she had resumed writing to Hans.

Only Eddie, though, saw what really troubled Sylvia about Dick. Did it ever occur to her, Eddie asked, that she was not so much a woman deceived as "an engineer whose latest airplane design didn't quite come up to specifications in performance?" Eddie had no interest in defending Dick, but he thought the larger issue was Sylvia's fear of what sex would do to her in a committed relationship. Her quest for a "Golden God" seemed a symptom of her desire to force some kind of resolution of her anxieties. He noticed that in her latest letter she had used the word "rape" at least five times. "Keerful, gal, your dynamics might be slipping," he cautioned her. Had she noticed that every sinus attack, as well as other illnesses, had come just after a breakup or some other contretemps with a male? Eddie was no expert on psychosomatic sickness, but he was beginning to wonder.

Dick, on the other hand, continued to sound in his letters very much like Samuel Richardson's unreal gentleman, Sir Charles Grandison. "I am aware of the joy, the honor of being near you and under your spell," Dick wrote on 28 January 1952. That kind of banality could be briefly soothing, but his formulaic letters explain why Sylvia said she sought someone "more intuitive." Dick wrote in phrases that could have been copied out of a conduct primer. Sylvia wanted the praise, of course, but it had to be delivered with panache. If Eddie had been able to confect a style that brought Sylvia both to the drawing room and the barroom, he might have succeeded in winning her.

Eddie Cohen never lost sight of Sylvia the writer. But Dick did, as he mused about the life of a doctor's wife, making Sylvia doubt he had any idea of the space and time required to write. Her work was not a sideline, and she believed she would lose respect for herself if she simply became absorbed in her husband's career—especially since Dick had become more assertive on their well-planned dates. Was this the result of a "mother complex"? Like Aurelia, Dick's mother was a "sweet, subtle matriarch," but she was also the manipulative mom that Sylvia had been reading about in Philip Wylie's influential *Generation of Vipers.* Momism, Wylie argued, was emasculating men and pacifying women into a conformism that would become one of the dominant themes in books about the American family in the 1950s. Mrs. Norton handled the family's finances and ruled the home, reducing her husband, at times, to a supplicant, the weak father that was also a feature of 1950s situation comedies. Perhaps Dick's seduction of the Vassar girl he told Sylvia about was his own version of rebelling against Momism, Sylvia speculated. And would he now seek to impose a submissive pattern of behavior on Sylvia, so as to forestall her domination of him? A medical career might well represent the best way to fend off a demanding wife and mother. His not entirely successful bid to achieve supremacy over Sylvia perhaps accounted for their contradictory denial and acceptance of one another. In sum, she believed they were both scared of what they might do to one another—as she would later reveal in her story, "The Fifty-Ninth Bear."

Sylvia confessed in her journal that she was not capable of love—at least not then—because she was so entirely dedicated to her art. She wanted the freedom to try on other lives the way she tried on dresses. Nagging at her, though, was the middle-class yearning for security, for settling into the comfortable. Forsaking Dick could mean a lost opportunity. Or, as she put it while summing up her sophomore year, she was now more aware of her limitations. She believed she had a more sober sense of her ambitions to publish and to go abroad as a Fulbrighter, which would entail not merely hard work but campaigning for herself. She would need to get elected to honor board and become involved in Smith's journalism program, as well as work on the *Smith Review*. In effect, she acknowledged the politics of excellence, which the more introverted Sylvia of her freshman year had not been prepared to pursue.

Eddie thought Sylvia was overcomplicating her love life. He bluntly stated that her troubles with Dick and other males had more to do with her superiority than anything else. Usually Eddie found her rather haughty words about her dates off-putting. (Both the number of unworthy suitors and Sylvia's superior tone are reminiscent of Scarlett O'Hara.) He could see that Sylvia had already destroyed whatever love she had for Dick, and if their relationship continued, that only meant she was not yet ready to relinquish the dependability Dick offered. Of course, Eddie was not a disinterested party. By the spring of 1952, he was openly declaring his love for Sylvia. He admitted his jealousy and his desire for her, especially after Sylvia said that she still felt a strong physical attraction to Dick.

Throughout Sylvia's sophomore year she continued to work on her fiction, staying up late at night in the Haven House kitchen typing away. Much of her work met with rejection slips that hardly seemed to dent her determination, which was rewarded in early June when she won *Mademoiselle*'s $500 fiction prize for "Sunday at the Mintons." Plath put her hostile feelings about Dick into the story, transforming him into Elizabeth Minton's fussy brother, Henry, who chides his sister for daydreaming and for an impractical nature that has left her directionless—barely able, in his view, to perform her duties as a town librarian. She is an aging spinster who has come to live with her brother in his retirement. This, of course, is the fate that Sylvia was determined to avoid: getting stuck with a male companion whose intellectual arteries would harden and in turn ossify her own existence.

She wondered in a letter to her mother if Dick would recognize himself in the story. It only becomes clear in the conclusion that Elizabeth has daydreamed Henry's drowning during a gallant effort to retrieve their mother's brooch, which Elizabeth has dropped on a rock about to be washed by the waves of an approaching storm. In a neat reversal that made the story palatable for a juvenile audience, Elizabeth's revenge fantasy actually stimulates her sympathy for her brother, who would no longer have anyone to look after him in the slimy, murky depths of the sea. But the story's saving grace is surely its ironic commentary on the expired, smug male reflected in Elizabeth's question to herself: "Who would listen to him talk about the way the moon controlled the tides or about the density of atmospheric pressure?"

Sylvia was working a summer job scrubbing tables at the Belmont Hotel when she received the good news about the *Mademoiselle* prize in a telegram from Aurelia. Sylvia screamed with delight and hugged the startled head waitress. Plath had just begun her job, but she was already disgruntled, again discovering she was ill prepared to deal with the menial side of life. Even more disappointing, she had been assigned to the side hall because of her inexperience. That assignment meant she would not be getting big tips in the main dining room. More than money was at stake, though, since Sylvia always wanted to be seen and admired. Even waitressing, to her, had rankings, and she realized she did not rate.

The day before learning of her prize, Sylvia wrote in a note not included in *Letters Home* that carrying trays one-handed terrified her. She knew nothing about her job, she confessed. She consoled herself by saying she would be harvesting a good deal of the summer for her writing. Indeed, in her journal, she catalogued no fewer than twenty-two characters, each labeled with an appropriate epithet: "Oscar, the birdlike, picayune, humorous band leader . . . stoic-faced Harvard law student and straight-backed busboy Clark Williams . . . Mrs. Johnson, the tall, sharp Irish chef's wife with the acid brogue and the fiery temper," and so on.

Even so, it was difficult for Sylvia to overcome the Belmont Hotel experience by turning it into fiction. She felt humiliated by her physical clumsiness and envious of waitresses expertly handling special dishes. She had believed she could somehow fit in. Intelligence and imagination seemed to count for little in occupations and organizations that depended on fast footwork and excellent coordination. Not being a quick study in a summer job is humbling indeed for a writer with a superiority complex. Sylvia Plath wanted not just the praise of the elites, but also the respect of the rank and file. Otherwise, Sylvia could not have written, less than a week after Aurelia's telegram, that her life seemed awful and the prize "unreal." The work terrified and unnerved her, although she refused to slink back home to mother—always a temptation when she felt overwhelmed.

Another troubling concern absent from *Letters Home* is Sylvia's disappointment that the other girls did not take to her. Why is not hard to understand. Sylvia assured her mother that she was self-contained and independent enough not to need the girls' affection. And yet that was probably just the problem: They did not warm to Sylvia because she seemed so self-involved. The other irritation was Dick. He had retreated from his know-it-all stance. Had he read "Summer at the Mintons"? At any rate, Sylvia wished he would "stop being *nice* and leave me alone."

On the one hand, Plath was receiving letters from New York editors expressing interest in her future work and wanting to know what books she planned. On the other hand, she slept through restless dreams that had her waitressing all the time. Ideas for stories continued to occur to her, and she decided to stick it out at for another month—until early August—so she would have a full month to work on her fiction before returning to Smith. But a sinus infection so depleted her that after three weeks at the Belmont she had to quit. A doctor advised her to return home to recuperate.

When the hotel called to say she could have her job back, Sylvia asked her mother to say it was not certain when her daughter could return. Reflecting on her three weeks at the Belmont, Sylvia realized that she had been caught up in a sort of squirrel cage that she detested. And yet she felt compelled to perform there. Looking at those days now she compared her view of them to lifting a bell jar off a "clockwork functioning community." Routine ruled, and no matter how trying the repetitive nature of the work, that rigid structure gave purpose to the lives of those within that world. In an 8 July letter to Marcia Brown, Sylvia was already casting a retrospective glow on the Belmont episode, referring to the "blissful routine" of working hard for six hours, the weekends she managed to see Dick, and the girls who she had begun to enjoy and who were sending her nice notes. Now Sylvia had to regenerate her own sense of purpose. She apparently could not remain at home and write. Home, in fact, would never again be a refuge, one that she had forsaken as soon as she entered Smith. She could sense her own depressions reverberating in Aurelia. In effect, Sylvia confided to Marcia, Aurelia empathized too much and prolonged her daughter's down periods. Returning to the Cape brought her back to the beach and closer to where Dick was working that summer.

It seemed imperative now to have "a Job," she confided to her journal. Searching the want ads, she considered the possibilities: painting parchment lampshades, filing, typing, or assisting a real estate agent. She actually spent a day with a realtor, fascinated by the woman's manipulative methods, but concluding that serving as her Girl Friday was not likely to pay very well. Even waitressing remained an option, but then Sylvia saw an ad for a housekeeper/babysitting position with well-to-do Christian Scientists, the Cantors. In spite of her vow of "NEVER AGAIN" when it came to such jobs, Sylvia liked the sound of Mrs. Cantor's voice over the phone and enjoyed her interview, she wrote Marcia Brown. This time Sylvia would be in charge of two small children, but would also have the company of the Cantor's teenage daughter. Sylvia could not resist the comfortable surroundings of this charming family in Chatham, Massachusetts, near the sea—always a draw for her— and a two-hour drive southeast from Wellesley.

Sylvia was treated well, more like a member of the family than in her previous home care experience. She had long conversations with Mrs. Cantor about Christian Science, which Sylvia enjoyed so much that she attended Sunday school, where she was proud, she wrote Aurelia, of knowing "all the right answers." A skeptical Sylvia

thought she was too much of a materialist to accept a doctrine that
proclaimed the material world was a kind of illusion, a human-
created evil that could be overcome by fealty to God's word. But
she did not dismiss the faith out of hand because she did believe
in the power of good thoughts, in mind over matter, to a certain
extent. After all, it was part of her artist's credo that she could reshape the world. Christian Science, moreover, draws on the Pla-
tonic nature of Christianity that posits an irrefutable realm of what
Sylvia called "absolute fact." Individuals by their very nature could
not have access to this ultimate source of truth. Sylvia sounds like
Saint Paul, echoing his remark on the fallibility of human knowledge when she alludes to the individual's own "particular gro-
tesque glass of distortion." In a fascinating journal passage, she
compares the individual's sensibility to a sounding board picking
up various intimations of immortality. Wordsworth, Berkeley—a
host of thinkers and artists—seem to suffuse Sylvia's synthesis of
her own experience, leading to a remarkable statement about the
"radio programs . . . all around us, clogging the air, needing only
a certain sensitive mechanism to make them a reality, a fact."
Sylvia would later write for the radio—the wireless as it was called
in Britain—realizing how powerfully this spoken medium could
penetrate the psyche, provoking the listener to create a simula-
crum of the world. She thought of Hamlet's line, "Thinking makes
it so." She thought of what she had made of her father's death.
Where Christian Science faltered was in its inability to distinguish
between truth and the individual's "dream-world," valid enough
for that person, for Sylvia herself, but was it near to the truth that
others imagined? She could not say. She could only observe that
these Christian Scientists certainly treated their beliefs as real—
just as real as her "dream-bubble of reality," a phrase that wonder-
fully captures the evanescence of perception. What was unchanging
fact? Could it be found in a laboratory? These questions recall
Dick's own certitudes, which Sylvia could not share. Sylvia seems
more comfortable with Wordsworth's notion that we half-perceive
and half-create our world; she was not willing to take the knower
out of what is known. Perhaps the best one could do is master what

she called the "counter positions," the dialectic between competing versions of truth.

What had especially pleased Sylvia about "Sunday at the Mintons" is that although she had started out simply modeling Elizabeth on herself, she ended by creating a world that was not merely derived from her own. That development seemed like a breakthrough, creating a work of art that transcended her own concerns—creating, in fact, a story that dramatized the very tensions between dream and reality that her journal passage probed.

On 2 August, Sylvia wrote to her mother about meeting Valerie Gendron, who wrote love stories for the pulps and ladies magazines. Sylvia wanted to spend the day talking to a writer who had been "through the mill." A subsequent visit with Val resulted in Sylvia's decision to follow her mentor's advice: Write fifteen hundred words a day, no matter what. Think of it as singing scales and doing warm-up exercises, Val told her during a five-hour talkfest that Sylvia treasured as one of her best adventures as a writer. It was a wonderful workout that included Val's critique of a Plath story, a gesture Sylvia regarded as exceptionally generous. Sylvia poured over this experience in her journal, describing in detail the bookmobile Val ran to help support herself in a sort of disheveled independence that to Sylvia seem scrumptious—as did the three hunks of cake she duly recorded eating. Suddenly Sylvia's journal brimmed with drafts of the kind of romantic stories that women's magazines preferred.

Pleasant dates with Dick may also have stimulated some of this boy-girl fiction. In the quiet, scheduled summer of 1952, Sylvia seems to have suspended her doubts about Dick. A day off from babysitting felt like the lid on her life was blown off. She needed the security of knowing that in a few weeks she would be back at Smith and immersed in the delirium of study. Mrs. Cantor treated her like Little Red Riding Hood when Dick called one night near 11 p.m. Where did Sylvia meet so many boys? Mrs. Canter wondered. Now the unregulated atmosphere of the Belmont, the midnight-to-dawn dances and beach parties Sylvia described to Enid Epstein, a Smith classmate, seemed preferable to the confining Cantors. The Belmont was like "college with the lid off."

A second encounter with Eddie before Sylvia began her junior year at Smith caused trouble. He judged her cold letters afterward as an indication that she did not think she had measured up to his expectations. If so, Eddie insisted she was quite mistaken. He had come away all the more impressed with her, although, according to Paul Alexander, Eddie became disturbed at Sylvia's tendency to pose, to pretend pleasure—like she did while listening to bad jazz in a Boston club. She was too studied, lacked spontaneity, and seemed *"all mask."* In her journal, Sylvia would later liken herself to Nina Leeds, a character in Eugene O'Neill's *Strange Interlude,* a play that experiments with the use of masks to dramatize the disparity between what people say and what they think as they withhold themselves from others.

On 23 September, Dick drove Sylvia, in a state of high tension, to Smith to begin the fall term. Now withdrawn and withholding, he upset her. Was she at fault? Did he sense, as she put it in her journal, that she was jealous of him? She turned to his more outgoing brother, Perry, always a favorite of hers, who reciprocated her warm confidence in him. He admitted he was anxious about Dick, who was "tough to take when he is 'that way.'" Perry wondered if Dick's emotional problems had to do with his conflicted views of his parents and the moral standards they set for him. Was Dick capable of love, Perry wondered, adding, "He certainly needs someone to believe in him." But Sylvia should not blame herself: "Syl— you are wonderful. You always are helping me, giving, never taking, never asking. What would I do without you. Love, love, Perry." He remained an openhearted admirer, and years later he assisted biographer Edward Butscher, who could not secure Dick Norton's cooperation.

For all her reservations about Dick, Sylvia felt bereft because of his coolness, and she depended even more on her affectionate correspondence with her mother, who sent news in early October that a story, "Initiation," had won a $100 prize from *Seventeen,* where it would be published in January 1953. "Initiation" deals with a high school girl's ambivalent feelings about the hazing ritual of the sorority she is pledging, feelings that are reinforced when the sorority spurns her best friend for not wearing the right clothes and not conforming to the group's sense of propriety. Sylvia herself had gone through her own "initiation," telling her mother that she had been required to ask everyone on a bus what each had for breakfast. One playful passenger replied, "Heather birds' eyebrows on toast," explaining that these creatures lived on "mythological moors." Put that in a story, Aurelia said. *Letters Home* contains a note explaining the circumstances of "Initiation"'s origin, yet another effort on Aurelia's part to counteract the merciless portrait of her that would later appear in *The Bell Jar*. In this case, Olive Higgins Prouty seconded Aurelia's suggestion. "Think of the material you have!" Prouty exhorted Plath. As Paul Alexander suggests, this was a pivotal moment in Sylvia's vocation as a writer, training her focus on the world in front of her.

In early November, Dick Norton told Sylvia he had been diagnosed with tuberculosis and would be staying in a sanitarium in Saranac, Massachusetts. Tests soon showed she had not contracted the disease, but their enforced separation depressed her. On 3 November, she wrote in her journal that this was the first time she had ever really considered committing suicide. She envied Dick's enforced leisure. His meals, the time he had to relax, and his freedom to read what he wanted riled her. Smith had become a cage. Thoughts of suicide, however, were just that: thoughts to be dismissed as the desire to annihilate the world by annihilating oneself. "The deluded height of desperate egoism," she opined, despising herself for blubbering in her "mother's skirts." Suddenly she understood how masses of people could succumb to Hitler, thereby alleviating themselves of the awful responsibility of thinking and doing for themselves. She was beginning to understand that for someone like herself, and like the women she admired—Sara Teasdale and Virginia Woolf—the idea of living happily ever after was the "fallacy of existence." In a telling journal passage, she admitted that because she did not know how high she should set her ambition, she was feeling especially low. More than ever, she missed Ann Davidow. Marcia had moved off campus to live with her mother, and Sylvia felt no rapport with her new roommate, Mary, a high-achieving science student.

Dick wrote on 8 November, virtually confirming Perry's analysis:

"I have become aware of a few of my shortcomings, especially a false superior smugness, an inflexibility, a childish search for sensuous pleasure, a certain degree of bewildered prudery, and an unwillingness to face facts honestly." The words sound a little like the "making amends" confessions and apologies of those undergoing treatment in Alcoholic Anonymous. Dick's letter did little immediately to ease Sylvia's distress.

On 14 November, after a tension-relieving night at Joe's Pizza in Northampton, Sylvia went to visit Marcia, who "touched the soft spot," permitting Sylvia to "let go" and drop her "tight mask." She cried and talked herself into working on her character. She had to stop playing the "spoiled child." The next day she received a letter from Dick. At Saranac, Dick had begun reading Virginia Woolf, Hemingway, Conrad, and other Plath favorites. He relinquished a good deal of his confident demeanor: "I am now unreservedly grateful, and acknowledging the blindnesses on my part in former frictions between us, I can say 'I love you' with no qualms and without flinching." He was not living in the "luxurious erotic Garden of Eden" Sylvia had invented for him.

A few days later, Dick attempted an even more direct approach: "How I would like to caress your warm, smooth, long back, slip apart the dutiful bra, press you away, and find those lovely large soft glandular breasts that cling to your chest wall and fall away slightly to be rounded and pointed with brown nipples . . . the curling soft hair . . ."

His erotic efforts seem rather forced and even clinical, and Sylvia's depression did not lift. On 18 November, she confided to her journal: "You are crucified by your own limitations."

On 19 November, an overwrought Sylvia wrote her mother, vilifying the science course that had undone her. In *Letters Home,* Aurelia observes that her daughter's tirade against studying "barren dry formulas" that were driving her to distraction—even to suicidal thoughts that made her wonder if she should see a psychiatrist—represented the first sign of her daughter's tendency to magnify a "situation out of all proportion." The recent suicide of one of Warren's classmates at Exeter set Sylvia off, Aurelia suggested, and was the subtext of her daughter's extreme state of mind. But Sylvia had not shared with her mother the drama with Dick. Sylvia's dread of becoming mired in what she called the nauseating, artificial absurdities of science might have been a displacement of her ambivalence about Dick. She still worried that she would have to settle down, like other Smith graduates, to a life supporting a husband whose interests were not her own. According to Aurelia, Sylvia returned to Smith after the Thanksgiving break, well rested and caught up in her studies. Evidently she made her peace with science, although her reprieve would be short-lived.

Sylvia wrote Eddie Cohen in late November suggesting they publish a version of their correspondence under the title "Dialogue of the Damned." He did not relish becoming one half of a Sylvia Plath enterprise, "material" for her imagination, and her notion that they could portray themselves as representatives of a generation struck him as absurd. They were two "hyper IQed eggheads," nothing like the masses. Unlike Aurelia, unlike Dick, unlike everyone else in her life, Eddie never indulged her. He never supposed he was anything like the brilliant writer he recognized in Sylvia Plath, but he also never acted as though he was any less intelligent than she—all of which meant he could often spot those times when she deluded herself with the egotism she herself had identified in her journals. Sometimes Eddie sounded like a voice inside of her, one that she desperately needed when she subsumed herself in negativity or in delusions of grandeur. He was not going to return the letters she had asked for until he was certain that she saw him as a "real person," not a "byproduct of your life." The clairvoyant Eddie already had a fix on the novelist who would, in *The Bell Jar*, do exactly what he suspected she would do: turn real people into byproducts of her imagination.

On 1 December, Sylvia wrote a cheerful letter to Warren about her struggles with joules, amperes, and other euphonious scientific terms. She was enthused about Myron Klotz, a brilliant Yale student and a pitcher for a Detroit Tigers minor league team. An impressed Sylvia wrote her mother that Myron had earned $10,000 in a single season. Perry Norton had introduced the "tall, handsome guy" to Sylvia. Myron was a product of Austrian Hungarian mineworkers who barely spoke English. She just loved this sort of combination, which was reminiscent of Ilo, the Estonian farmworker and artist. She knew nothing about baseball, but Myron sure was a "beautiful lug." Sylvia liked to think of herself as fitting into a world of immigrants and guys and dolls, as well as consorting with ladies and gentlemen. She wanted to speak the language of literary blue-bloods and of pulp fictioneers. She reminded Warren of their childhood treat, skalshalala meat (their term for "a morsel of meat that remains in your mouth no matter how long you chew it. Gristle, in other words"), even as she told him, "I love you baby, as Mickey Spillane would say." A few days later, Aurelia received a similar letter (which she did not include in *Letters Home),* which mentions Sylvia's thrilling meeting with Myron and also her disappointment in the poems and stories Dick sent her, none of which had much *"feeling."*

Myron turned out to be great fun, Sylvia noted in another report to her mother. They had pizza at Joe's and discussed baseball and poetry. On the way back to Smith, Myron played a gangster and Sylvia a gun moll, with the campus as their mise-en-scène. Sylvia later drew a fedora that Myron wore, a gift from his mother, who worried that he would catch cold. He also had a black gangster coat. It amused her that he also sported a Phi-Beta-Kappa key: "Such a mixture of vanity (how much is cover up I don't know) and real sweetness." She was touched that he had memorized one of her letters.

A letter from Eddie that arrived in mid-December pinpointed Sylvia's love of histrionics, which could be turned into a Henry James novel that fretted the action, worked it over, and projected it back into her sensibility. He noted, for example, how her attitude toward Dick had changed. Now she seemed keen to confect a melodrama out of ministering to the ailing hero. In fact, Dick told her that he was reading *A Farewell to Arms,* and it is tempting to see Sylvia imagining a role reversal in which it is not the dying Catherine, but rather Frederic Henry (Dick) who needs (Sylvia's) support. Eddie, never one to blink at the truth as he saw it, rendered a devastating verdict. Wasn't she creating a plot that satisfied her, rather than seeing the men in her life for what they really were? Wasn't it the idea of a love story that appealed to her, and not the actual men who courted her? At the risk of sounding "ungracious," he suggested that Sylvia remained more interested in the drama of these affairs than in the affairs themselves. Sylvia understood exactly what Eddie was saying, because she had noted as much about herself in her journal.

As if to show Sylvia that he was in love with *her* and not some conception of his own, Eddie described what he liked about her: her voice, her tan, the way she settled languorously into a booth, her trick of licking the air with her tongue as though savoring the ideas that spilled out of her delectable brain. He mentioned her sensuous face, though not specifically her most erotic attribute: the full lips that perhaps accounted for Dick's observation that she had "negroid" features. Eddie promised to return her letters, but he did not do so. Perhaps he was still concerned about the figure he would cut in her prose.

In effect, Eddie diagnosed Sylvia as a Henry James narrator. She wanted to be near the action, while never fully committing herself to it. Just two weeks after Eddie's pronouncement, Dick chimed in, reporting what his friends said about Sylvia: "You were an *observer* of life and not a *participator,* in some ways . . . you seemed interested in the crude, raw parts of life, in a sensuous fashion—and yet content to read, view, see, observe, and not enter in."

Sylvia could divert her depression, writing gamely to Aurelia about adventures in an airplane with Myron, flipping over Northampton and tilting right side up in ecstasy, but she was not sleeping at night. On 15 December, she announced to her mother she was going to see a psychiatrist about "my science." Whatever the outcome of that meeting, it did not result in a plan for long-term treatment, and Sylvia went away deluding herself that she had done enough to dispel her gloom.

On 28 December, while visiting Dick at Saranac, Sylvia broke her leg on the advanced ski slope. In *Letters Home,* Aurelia implies that Sylvia, eschewing professional instruction, had recklessly hurtled downhill. Sylvia's telegram announced a "fabulous fractured fibula," as though she had accomplished some sort of Hemingwayesque feat. To Myron, she described herself in typically Baroque fashion gaily plummeting straight down without having learned how to steer, and then encountering a moment similar to their plane ride: "a sudden brief eternity of actually leaving the ground, cartwheeling . . . and plowing face first into a drift. I got up, grinned, and started to walk away. No good. Bang." She signed the telegram to Aurelia, "Your fractious, fugacious, frangible Sivvy." It was a light-hearted way of saying she had snapped. In times of stress, she would run herself off the road, so to speak—as she would actually do later while driving after Ted Hughes had left her. Sylvia sought to assure her mother, though, that the accident had actually been salutary, shocking her into a realization that she had been foolish to succumb to self-made "mental obstacles." The accident, in other words, had broken through a self-demeaning pattern of behavior.

Sylvia wasn't joking, however, when she wrote Eddie, dropping her bravado and conceding the merits of his analysis. And she was not as sanguine as she appeared to Aurelia. Indeed, Eddie was so disturbed by what she wrote he advised her to see a psychiatrist. He noted a recurring pattern: the appearance of a "handsome stranger" with whom she established an "immediate and miraculous rapport," only to have him fade from her purview. Eddie did not want to say what this scenario meant, although it must have been tempting to do so, since in one instance the stranger had been a scholar familiar with Otto's Plath's work who seemed a sort of father-substitute, as well as a prospective lover. Perhaps reality was breaking through her illusions, Eddie speculated, showing her that prolonging the relationship with Dick only brought out her vicious, competitive side. But that "reality" could be as debilitating and even more dangerous than her illusions, which is why he urged her to get professional help.

In her journal, Sylvia rejected Eddie's advice, saying that all she needed was more sleep, "a constructive attitude, and a little good luck." She was determined to be more outgoing and get to know her fellow Smith students and the faculty better. In her junior year, Sylvia moved house from Haven to Lawrence, a dorm for scholarship students. Even casual friends say she seemed to take an interest in them. "Attitude is everything," she announced in her journal, sounding like a self-help pop psychologist—and also the mythologist of herself, declaring that her winter solstice was over, and the "dying god of life and fertility is reborn."

Nancy Hunter Steiner, who became Sylvia's roommate, explains in a memoir why Lawrence House was a more congenial milieu for Sylvia. As scholarship students, she notes, "we brought to even the most trivial activity an almost savage industriousness—a clenched-teeth determination to succeed that emanated from us like cheap perfume." No one expected Sylvia to stay up at night playing bridge. Lawrence House students did not make marriage to a wealthy man their first priority, recalls Ellen Ouelette. Judy Denison, a physics major inspired by the work of Marie Curie, vowed to emulate the Nobel Prize winner by marrying a physicist—who, unfortunately, later told her she should be happy ironing his shirts. "If you wanted to make me happy, you'd buy shirts that did not need ironing," Judy retorted. The marriage ended in divorce.

Ellen Ouelette remembered how different Lawrence House was from other dorms. At Christmas, the Lawrence House students were in the habit of writing poems to one another so that they did not have to buy presents, something not all of them could afford. They would each draw a name out of a hat and then write a poem to the person selected. Eileen drew Sylvia's name and was petrified. Eileen had received a D in freshman English, and she was well aware of Sylvia's status as a star on campus. What to do? She went to Sylvia's roommate, Nancy Hunter, and explained her dilemma. She learned from Nancy that Sylvia liked Modigliani's paintings. So Eileen wrote a poem that began, "To Sylvia Plath with her Modigliani eyes, / My Christmas gift will be a surprise." Sylvia made no comment on the poem but received it graciously.

Sylvia could sometimes appear nervous and high strung, but in the main she exuded considerable confidence. She had resolved her feelings about Dick, realizing her ambivalent attitude toward him had its origins in childhood. Even then, she said, she had been competing with him, panting after him on her bicycle. He was her childhood pacesetter. He was a projection of her "naive idealism"— and she had to admit, she did not want to kiss a man she feared was full of germs.

Meanwhile, Myron (Sylvia called him her Hercules) had no

trouble carrying her around, leg cast and all. And as if on cue—
Eddie would surely have smiled—another myrmidon arrived: Gordon Lameyer, an Amherst College senior, with whom Sylvia struck
up an "instant rapport." He was a James Joyce devotee, and Sylvia
had chosen Joyce as the subject of her senior thesis. Gordon
looked *"most promising,"* she wrote to her mother on 5 February, as
though sizing up another candidate for her praetorian guard. She
spoke of "the new Gordon," making him sound like the latest model
car. He was also "utterly lush." She loved talking religion with this
self-described "renegade Unitarian." They had similar mothers. Indeed, Gordon's mother, a Wellesley resident, had told him about
Sylvia, who had addressed the local Smith club. Mrs. Lameyer encouraged his desire to date this brilliant student, now first in her
class and a winner of several college literary awards. Gordon also
offered Sylvia something new. He was in the Naval Reserve Officer
Training Corps and already had the manner, as Edward Butscher
puts it, of an "officer and a gentleman in the grand old tradition."
Myron, with his "bad skin" and "barbarian parents," now seemed
second string, Sylvia declared in her journal.

Sylvia was ducking dates with Dick. She had not dumped him
yet. "In the Mountains," published in the *Smith Review* (1954), suggests why. When Isobel feels Austin's "warm and possessive" arm
across her shoulders, she experiences the "old hurting fear, just remembering the way it had been." As in "Sunday at the Mintons,"
the male is extravagantly confident of his prerogatives. Like Dick,
Austin is in a sanitarium and is uncharacteristically reading a novel
(it is obviously *A Farewell to Arms),* "worrying about the imaginary
man and the dying girl" because their story reminds him of himself and Isobel. Earlier in their relationship, Austin had lectured
Isobel about "how silly she was to feel sorry for people in books."
He now wants to prove he has changed, as he openly declares his
need for her. But to Isobel this change in him is a sign of weakness,
and though she cannot bring herself to tell him she does not love
him, she implies as much: "It is different now."

Unhappy that their last visit together had not relieved his anxieties, Dick was getting testy, writing Sylvia on 23 February, "Your
enthusiastic, career-oriented individualism sometimes chills the

onlooker and presents marriage in the light of a hurdle or an undesirable estate for the less-fortunate and plodding humans." If for no
other reason than his prose style, Sylvia Plath could never have
married anyone like Dick. Well aware that he was losing Sylvia, Dick
tried a more conciliatory approach, on 10 March adding, "One of
TB's associated diseases is an unsureness of one's essential value
with ones friends." He also wrote to her mother, trying to get a
read on what was going through Sylvia's mind. A tactful Aurelia
consulted with her daughter and sent Dick a carefully worded letter saying she was touched by his concern, adding that at the moment Sylvia was not "matrimonially minded." She tried to let him
down easy: "I have always found Sivvy to be very honest. Should
she hedge now, I am sure it would be because she was afraid of
hurting you at a time when it might do you physical harm. . . ."
But after more dilatory responses from Sylvia, a cranky Dick replied to Aurelia: "One should not worry about 'hurting' me, a concern better reserved for the five-year-old one is about to rob of a
toy. My interest is ever with the 'facts of the case,' even if they are
disturbing on first acquaintance. What is hidden from view generally is more dangerous to everybody than the transient discomfort of its discovery." Once again the stiffness in Dick's style
surely put off Sylvia, just then composing an O'Neill-type drama
of her life involving "the great God Gordon," as she referred to
him in a letter to her mother on 11 April.

If Sylvia had known more about baseball, she would have made
Myron Klotz part of her "deep bench," which included another
new acquisition, Ray Wunderlich, a Columbia Medical School
student she had met during her brief employment at the Belmont
Hotel. He escorted her to plays in New York (Arthur Miller's *The
Crucible* and Tennessee Williams's *Camino Real).* The trip to the city
revved her up for the *Mademoiselle* competition for aspiring young
writers who would be selected to spend June in Manhattan as
guest editors at the magazine. At the same time, she was thrilled at
sighting W. H. Auden, the reigning poet of the period, arriving for
a stay at Smith, telling her brother, Warren, that someday she
would like to touch the "Hem of his Garment," and present him
with a poem, "I found my God in Auden."

Sylvia was writing poetry again, always a difficult project while studying at Smith. She adored meter and verse formats like the villanelle, an elaborately rhymed and structured nineteen-line poem. She seemed encouraged when she received more than a form letter rejection from *The New Yorker* for "Doomsday," a work Harper's accepted a few months later that is included in the juvenilia section of *The Collected Poems*. It is a deftly composed and witty commentary on the vanity of human aspirations, including, no doubt, her own: "Our painted stages fall apart by scenes." The images of breaking, shattering, fracturing, blasting, and toppling are reminiscent of her careening ride down a ski slope, ending in another fall when Sylvia tried to arise from her accident. The actors in "Doomsday" that halt in "mortal shock" are emanations of a sensibility that had experienced just such a crash. And the renegade Unitarian emerges in the line, "Our lucky relics have been put in hock."

"Doomsday," despite its grim theme, has a jauntily mordant tone that reflects the exuberant Plath of this period. In letters to her mother she enclosed poems like "Verbal Calisthenics," which begins: "My love for you is more / Athletic than a verb . . ." She exulted in her election as editor of the *Smith Review* for the next year, her last at Smith. She seemed, in fact, to be winding herself up into a manic state, as the legend of Sylvia Plath spread on campus, transforming her in an apotheosis of herself. "Laurels for Recent Poem / Sylvia Plath Again Wins," the 16 April issue of the school newspaper announced, as if she were a racehorse and not the author of another story in *Seventeen*.

On 27 April, Sylvia noted in her journal that *Harper's* acceptance of "Doomsday" and two other poems marked her "first real professional acceptance," and that "things have been happening like a chain of fire crackers." At the home of Elizabeth Drew, one of Sylvia's teachers and one of the country's distinguished literary critics, Sylvia watched W. H. Auden sip beer and smoke Lucky Strikes while discussing *The Tempest,* commenting that Ariel embodied the creative imagination. Measured against her dreams of male greatness, even Gordon began to pale when she learned he was considering a career as an insurance salesman, and Ray seemed weak, physically and emotionally. He had not even made a pass at her. She wanted, she confessed, the impossible: a "demigod of a man," a "romantic nonexistent hero."

Writing to Warren on 12 May, Sylvia rejoiced at his acceptance to Harvard University, hoping that his scholarship would relieve Aurelia of a financial burden. In fact, Sylvia hoped that both of them would be self-financed for the next year, because she well knew how hard Aurelia had worked to give her children the best of everything: "Mother would actually Kill herself for us if we calmly accepted all she wanted to do for us." Sylvia was sincere, but she was also appalled at the extent of Aurelia's altruism—although Sylvia did not say so to Warren, or yet realize as much herself. Aurelia's self-sacrifice took an enormous toll on her daughter, who wanted to feel less obligated, but who also found the need to perform for her mother excruciatingly painful, a sore point that got worse as the summer of 1953 wore on. But just the opposite was the case in the spring, when all the world seemed to be opening up to Sylvia. It was time to start paying Aurelia dividends for all that she had invested in her children, Sylvia exhorted Warren.

CHAPTER 3

QUEEN OF THE DEAD

(1953–55)

June 1953: Plath experiences an intense period in New York City at *Mademoiselle* and finds it exhilarating, then exhausting—her first foray into the high fashion urban megalopolis of fame she later dissected in *The Bell Jar*. Returning home in late June, she becomes depressed, then receives electroconvulsive therapy; **24 August:** She attempts and nearly succeeds at suicide. She returns to Smith, apparently recovered; **1955:** Sylvia graduates *summa cum laude* and leaves for England as a Fulbright scholar at Newnham College, Cambridge.

By early May the news got even better: Sylvia was awarded the *Mademoiselle* guest editorship. She had been selected by the magazine's college board, headed by Marybeth Little. In "Your Job as Guest Editor," the magazine explained that this was an opportunity to learn more about its readership. The position also provided awardees with valuable training and counseling and a "behind-the-scenes" look at the publishing world. The competition for this prestigious internship took into account not only the student's writing abilities, but also her participation in extracurricular activities. These Sylvia listed as membership in the Studio Art Club, working on decorations for the freshman prom and charity ball, and on the editorial boards of the *Smith Review* and the *Campus Cat* (a humor magazine), serving as secretary of the Honor Board (one of the campus organizations dealing with honors students), and her experience as correspondent for the *Springfield Daily News* through the Smith College news office.

All guest editors would work a five-day week from 1 June to 26 June. A *Mademoiselle* editor wrote with suggestions about clothing: dark lightweight dresses, made of nylon, shantung, or other silks and cottons, and a bathing suit for weekends. "We plan to do one 'do dress' party, so you should bring along a gown, and don't forget hats—we're afraid they're necessary for all the public appearances you will make," wrote Marybeth Little on 5 May.

Sylvia was already preparing for one of her editor assignments: interviewing and being photographed with a famous author. She had sent the magazine her preliminary choices: Shirley Jackson, E. B. White, Irwin Shaw, and J. D. Salinger. Of course, she would have read them all in *The New Yorker,* the publication she most wanted to appear in herself. *Catcher in the Rye* would later serve as a model for *The Bell Jar,* but how different its author was from Sylvia Plath, who sought fame even as Salinger was developing a mystique as an elusive writer erasing himself from public view. In the end, even before leaving for New York, Sylvia had secured the requisite interview with British novelist Elizabeth Bowen.

Home for just two days between the end of her examinations at Smith and her departure for New York City, Sylvia frenetically packed and planned for her month at *Mademoiselle,* all the while urging her mother to do something for herself—maybe write articles, which Sylvia would love to edit, about her teaching for women's magazines. Out the door, Sylvia was carrying with her words of overwhelming gratitude for all her mother's sacrifices, which had resulted in so many opportunities for her children.

Betsy Talbot Blackwell, editor-in-chief of *Mademoiselle,* interviewed all guest editors on their first day. As her title denoted, she had final say over all copy and departments. She also sized up the guest editors and decided on their suitability for the magazine's various departments. The guest editors were then divided into small groups to lunch with the *Mademoiselle* staff. Sylvia soon learned that editing meant not merely writing and revising, but also functioning as errand clerk and typist, as a memo sent to her cohort explained. She put an exclamation mark in the left-hand margin next to the following statement: *"Magazine deadlines are as final as exam dates, and are to be observed religiously—no extracurricular activities will be scheduled until deadline crises are past!"* This may have been her first inkling of the pressures that would undo her, reminding her of the nerve-wracking build-up to exams. Crises? Sylvia had already had enough of those, and now, before the first day on the job, she was on notice to expect more. Like everyone else, she was required to "pitch in" on assignments in any department that needed help. Although the memo promised "lighter moments," it also declared this was no "glamor job." After such sobering words, the memo ended with a section on extracurricular activities, mentioning visits to designers, fashion shows, meetings with famous people, theater parties, dinners and dancing, and special screenings. Half-skeptical, half-hopeful, Sylvia wrote at the bottom of the memo: "Sounds like a fairy tale, doesn't it!"

"Citystruck Sivvy," as she dubbed herself in a letter to Aurelia, spent her month on the sixth floor at 575 Madison Avenue working late. In the evening, from her room (1511) at the Barbizon Hotel she could marvel at the sight of Manhattan lighting up, with glimpses of the Third Avenue El and the East River. Laurie Levy, another summer guest editor, recalled an outing with Sylvia: "We billowed about the steaming summer-festival streets trying to keep cool in below-calf cotton skirts." They passed one another in the *Mademoiselle* hallways, "our teeth white against the magenta lipstick of 1953." Sylvia was given all sorts of copy to read and rewrite, including submissions from Elizabeth Bowen, Rumer Godden, Noël Coward, and Dylan Thomas. She rather relished writing a rejection slip to a staffer at *The New Yorker,* but she also worried that she would not get into Frank O'Connor's much-prized summer writing class at Harvard.

Sylvia admitted to her mother that the end of semester rush and quick removal to New York had been both heady and daunting, and that she had trouble dealing with high-pressure situations. At *Mademoiselle* a handwriting expert had delivered this analysis of Sylvia:

STRENGTHS: Enjoyment of working experience intense; sense of form, beauty and style, useful in fields of fashion and interior design. Eager for accomplishment.
WEAKNESSES: Overcome superficiality, stilted behavior, rigidity of outlook.

Plath appreciated how much important work *Mademoiselle* managing editor Cyrilly Abels assigned to her. Sylvia signed herself "Syrilly" in one letter to Aurelia. Abels was, in the words of a *Mademoiselle* primer for guest editors, "boss of the deadline." She approved all copy. Owing to her wide-ranging contacts with writers, publishers, and agents, she was also the magazine's ambassador to the literary world.

Elation and exhaustion were compounded when Sylvia and several other guest editors came down with ptomaine poisoning. Even so, she was meeting well-known authors such as Vance Bourjaily, dating boys from all over who were working at the UN, and spending time in Greenwich Village. Then the cheerful letters dwindled. It would take years for the full story to come out.

During this busy month, the horrifying execution of the Rosenbergs, convicted of participating in a Soviet spy conspiracy to steal the secret of the atomic bomb, intruded with such force that Sylvia felt nauseated. The pacifist of "Bitter Strawberries," who had been shocked by the head picker who wanted Russia bombed off the map, reappeared in a journal entry on 19 June describing a stylish, beautiful "catlike" girl waking up from a nap on the conference room divan, yawning and saying with "beautiful bored nastiness: 'I'm so glad they are going to die.'" Everyone else went about business as usual, planning the weekend without a thought for the preciousness of human life. It seemed ironic to Sylvia that the prevailing mood deemed it right to execute the Rosenbergs for purloining the secret of her country's zealously guarded mechanics of inhuman invention. Too bad the electrocution could not be televised that evening, she remarked, since it would be so much more realistic than the crime shows. She imagined the country taking these deaths as nonchalantly as had that blasé beauty in her office.

More than twenty years later, in *The Public Burning* Robert Coover would publish a scathing portrayal of the Rosenberg execution that included the kind of spectacle Plath imagined. Like Plath, Coover believed the execution had tainted and degraded his nation. Both writers were concerned with the individual's connection to history and—like Rebecca West in the prologue to her masterpiece, *Black Lamb and Grey Falcon*—deplored the fact that people could be so idiotic as not to see how their fates were entangled with the lives of millions of others. No matter how much it meant to be working at *Mademoiselle,* Sylvia never lost sight of the world elsewhere, to which she was irrevocably connected by her consciousness of what it means to be fully human. The events of June 1953 became the basis of *The Bell Jar,* in which Plath transmogrified her traumatic month into a fable, a *Catcher in the Rye*–style story that captures all the glitter and gore of New York City, the abode of the brilliant and the phony, the predatory and the pretentious.

When Sylvia returned home in late June, Aurelia found her daughter unusually somber. That intense period in New York hit others hard, as well. Laurie Levy wrote, "We dispersed in different directions to have our letdowns alone." Aurelia dreaded breaking the bad news: Sylvia had not been chosen for Frank O'Conner's Harvard writing class. Like many ambitious people, Sylvia did not care how many awards she won, only that the acceptances kept coming. (O'Connor would later say that he thought Sylvia too advanced for his class). But Aurelia, expecting her child to be disappointed, was aghast to see that the news drove Sylvia to despair.

Even if it was the proximate cause of her depression, it is unlikely that one month in New York, however trying, had produced this humorless and even dull Sylvia. For well over a year, Eddie Cohen had been warning her that something was seriously amiss. During that year she wrote as though the power of positive thinking would pull her through. But working at a high-energy Madison Avenue magazine wore down her will to succeed, already severely weakened by doubts she could take her talent to the next level. To put it another way, Sylvia's stint in Manhattan accelerated the crackup Eddie had tried to head off.

Aurelia described Sylvia's "great change" in *Letters Home* as a fundamental break in the daughter who had always expressed such joie de vivre. Sylvia's journals suggest that her effort to maintain a brave front had collapsed. It was no longer enough to unburden herself by falling into Marcia's arms and crying out her fears and anxieties. Writing to Eddie would not relieve enough of the pressure. A summer writing course with a renowned writer was not available to help her overcome dejection.

Sylvia saw one way out of her predicament: Attend Harvard Summer School and take a psychology course, which she considered both a practical and creative way of developing her talent. Also, she would meet new people and have access to the library and other activities in Cambridge, which would give her life structure. She dreaded staying home alone with the awful burden of constructing her own schedule. She admitted in her journal that she was frightened and called herself a "big baby." Self-doubt sapped her creativity.

But the course would cost $250, not then a negligible sum for an undergraduate who calculated she had just enough to get by during her final year at Smith and had counted on making her mother's summer easier by selling stories generated in O'Hara's class. On balance, then, better to stay home, face her fears, learn shorthand from Aurelia as a practical skill (a woman at Smith's vocational office had suggested as much), start reading Joyce for her senior thesis, and try to "forget my damn ego-centered self."

In her journal entry for 6 July, Sylvia addressed herself as though she were a fairy-tale princess who had to be brought back to earth after the ball. Not to write at home would be a failure of nerve proving her unworthiness. She even held Dick up as a model. After all, he had been able to read and write while in the sanitarium. But how could she write when she equated living at home with returning to the womb, and when she had begun to think of suicide. She put it in these extreme terms: "Stop thinking of razors & self-wounds & going out and ending it all." By 14 July, Sylvia was sleeping no more than two hours a night and having homicidal thoughts about Aurelia. Confessing that she could no longer imagine an existence outside of her "limited self," she cried for God—or a god, some force outside herself that would lift her spirits.

Sylvia, as Eddie suspected, could not see that part of becoming an adult meant knowing when to ask for help. Sylvia told herself that her "negativism" was a kind of sickness, but like a Christian Scientist she thought she should heal herself, even though she was not able to place her faith in God. Thinking she could somehow control her emotions, she viewed her dilemma as an ethical or moral one, a matter of behaving according to a certain standard she thought appropriate for her age and competence. In spite of her interest in that Harvard psychology course, she did not see how compulsively repetitive her behavior had become, that her problem was her own psychology. She had escaped the crisis at the Belmont by finding refuge with the Cantors, and then had school to look forward to. This time she felt she could confront her demons at home with even less resilience in the aftermath of what she deemed O'Hara's rejection of her.

Aurelia's description in *Letters Home* of Sylvia's affect suggests all the signs of clinical depression. Not even sunbathing seemed therapeutic. She would sit, book in hand, but could not read. *Sylvia Plath could not read!* All her talk was of how she had let people down. Even worse, she could not write. Aurelia noticed gashes on her daughter's legs, and Sylvia responded, "I just wanted to see if I had the guts!" Horrified, Aurelia felt the hot touch of Sylvia's hand and heard her scorching cry that the world "is so rotten! I want to die! Let's die together!" Instead, Sylvia agreed to see a doctor and then a psychiatrist, although neither seemed to help much, other than prescribing sleeping pills and then submitting her to brutal electric shock treatments administered without sedatives or muscle relaxants.

On 24 August, a day when Sylvia seemed to be doing better, Aurelia went out with a friend, and then returned home to find a note saying her daughter had gone out for a long walk. Sylvia went missing for three days, until Warren heard what sounded like a moan coming from the basement. There he found Sylvia in a crawl space, half-conscious after throwing up some of the sleeping pills she had swallowed to end her life. She had a gash on her face that would leave a scar, but otherwise she seemed to recover rather quickly from her physical ordeal. In September, she began to recuperate under the supervision of Dr. Ruth Beuscher at McLean Hospital in Belmont, Massachusetts. Sylvia later described her therapist to Gordon Lameyer as "one of my best friends, only 9 years older than I, looking like Myrna Loy, tall, Bohemian, coruscatingly brilliant, and most marvelous."

Sylvia's disappearance and discovery were widely reported, and she became news in a way she never intended but which had a remarkable impact on her vocation as a writer. Eventually, she would realize that dying had become part of her true subject matter. The notion of living with thoughts of death would suffuse some of her best, most sincere material. She had meant to die and had felt more strongly about dying than about any other decision she would ever make. Suicide, a kind of ultimate commitment, repudiated deceit and her false facades. Whatever happened next would have to be measured against the authenticity of that act.

There was no easy way back from death, which has a sureness and finality to it that appealed to Plath. Recovery was a far less decisive process, fitful and fraught with confusion and doubts about her capacity to revive her creativity. Certainly she was in no shape to return to Smith. Literary critic Robert Gorham Davis, one of Sylvia's favorite professors, wrote Aurelia offering his help, mentioning that his daughter knew Sylvia well. He and his wife, whom Sylvia also admired, were taken aback because Plath had seemed so gay during her last semester at Smith: "Though we have both had some experience with upsets of this sort in other people, we did not notice in the Spring any signs of stress of this kind, though this may have been imperceptive of us." Indeed, Davis had once confided to his colleague, George Gibian, that unlike other neurotic creative writing students, Sylvia seemed entirely whole and healthy. He did add, though, that Sylvia had demanded "far too much of herself."

Professor Elizabeth Drew, another Plath favorite, wrote directly to Sylvia.

I know exactly how you felt, because once in my life I had a similar depression, though for a different reason, & it *seemed* the logical & the only way out. But now that is all over &

you must remember all the time how good life is & how much joy & adventure there will be in it for you. As to your work, you are by far the best student in English in the College & you don't have to *strain* to be. You could do it standing on your head or in your sleep! I suspect you were pushing yourself much too hard in the spring . . . You just burnt yourself out for a spell. Now you've got to let life flow in all over you again & it *will*, never fear.

Such letters testified to the powerful impact Sylvia Plath had at Smith, signaling how dearly she was missed and what a warm welcome she would receive on her return.

Gordon Lameyer's letter was perhaps just as important to Sylvia: "I admire you, Sylvia, I *admire* you more than any girl I know. More than anything I don't want you to feel differently about me now. I want to be your dearest and closest friend as you have been ever since June to me. Believe me, please believe me, I can *understand* anything. Your happiness is everything to me, so please get well as soon as you can." Lameyer would write her long letters while at sea during his service in the navy.

These letters do not seem to have had an immediate impact on Sylvia, judging by Aurelia's letter to Olive Higgins Prouty, who wanted to be informed about Sylvia's care and also to contribute to it financially. Prouty had suffered a nervous breakdown twenty years earlier and had recovered completely under expert care that made her "better equipped to meet life." She wanted no less for Sylvia. Aurelia wrote Prouty that the psychiatrists told her Sylvia had not confided to her mother just how insecure she felt. That Sylvia also craved the guidance of a father figure came as no surprise to Aurelia. To Sylvia, suicide seem preferable to years of incarceration in a mental institution, the kind of facility she associated with Olivia de Havilland's harrowing performance in *The Snake Pit* (1948). Prouty visited Plath in early October and wrote on the 14th to Dr. Beuscher, expressing concern that Sylvia was not mixing well with others and seemed disheartened because she was not coordinated enough to do the kind of handwork (sewing, in this case) that treatment programs often prescribed for patients. Sylvia tried weaving, and though her doctor thought it was well done, Sylvia disparaged her efforts.

In November, Sylvia received shock treatments—this time administered with more preparation and with Dr. Beuscher by her side—and insulin therapy, the latter the subject of "Tongues of Stone." In the narrative, a young girl watches her body grow fatter with insulin treatments, and in her dreary state she cannot read words that look to her like "dead black hieroglyphics." She has lost her tan and shies away from the sun, wishing she could shrink to the size of a fly's body. Day after day she reports that the insulin shots have made no change. She believes she is drying up and in the final stage of withdrawal from a preposterous life. She had been "pretending to be clever and gay, and all the while these poisons were gathering in her body, ready to break out behind the bright false bubbles of her eyes at any moment crying: Idiot! Imposter!" Like Sylvia, the young girl dreads another sixty years with a brain folding up like a "gray, paralyzed bat in the dark cavern of her living skull." In the story, the girl interprets her rescue as defeat, since she has been resuscitated into a zombie, sallow-skinned and bruised and "jolted back into the hell of her dead body." "Tongues of Stone" ends abruptly in a transition that seems forced, even if it is true to Sylvia's case: Suddenly, in her sleep the girl sees light breaking through her blindness, and every fiber of her mind and body flares with the "everlasting rising sun."

Sylvia treated her period at McLean as resulting in full recovery. Jane Anderson, a fellow patient and a Smith student who went on to become a therapist, doubted that Plath had worked hard on her therapy. She did not make "much of a commitment to it in terms of trying to understand what was going on in herself and she was angry about that." When Anderson commented on Plath's rather passive response to treatment, Sylvia seemed to become "less friendly and less willing to talk about things in depth." Aurelia would later write to Ted Hughes's wife Carol, "Anyone who did not know Sylvia *before* she had her first [electric shock] treatment (and that includes Dr B) *never knew the whole Sylvia.*"

By early December, Sylvia seemed to have emerged from her depression. Wilbury Crockett, her high school teacher, visited and reported to Aurelia that Sylvia seemed happy playing bridge with fellow patients and behaving sociably. Until her suicide attempt, he had never seen her depressed, and now she had recovered her sparkle. Sylvia told her mother she wanted to return to Smith for the spring semester, beginning in January 1954. At the end of December, she wrote a long letter to Eddie and then decided not to send it, entrusting what she wrote instead to her mother as a record of the summer of 1953. Aurelia duly included a part of the missive in *Letters Home.*

Essentially, Sylvia presented herself as a fraud who had wasted her junior year at Smith taking the wrong subjects and committing herself to a thesis on James Joyce, even though she had only a superficial grasp of his work. Depleted after her New York City ordeal, she had been dismayed that her friends seemed content with their accomplishments. Sleeplessness, futile appointments with psychiatrists, and writer's block all contributed to her suicide attempt. Her body had resisted her best efforts to drown herself, then she took too many sleeping pills and botched her bid for oblivion. Like the girl in "Tongues of Stone," she had been angry about her rescue. Then Mrs. Prouty intervened, and to Sylvia's surprise she had gotten better—just like the character in *The Snake Pit,* who had the benefit of a wise and compassionate therapist. Sylvia also mentioned Gordon Lameyer's letters. He continued to write and promised to return to her even though she had not sent him a word in four months.

In *Letters Home,* Aurelia identified Eddie only as "E" and omitted this crucial invitation: "I do miss you to talk to . . . please do write me frankly and fully what's been with you the last months or so . . . Aw, please, scold me, placate me, tell me your loves and losses, but do talk to me, huh? as ever, syl." If Sylvia did not send the letter she handed to her mother, some version of it did reach Eddie, who replied on 29 January that he had not been forceful enough in insisting that she get psychiatric help. He had even debated the issue with a psychiatrist friend, who told Eddie he had no standing in the case and could not intervene. After all, he was making assumptions on the basis of a few letters. To Sylvia's query about whether he had seen news reports of her attempted suicide,

Eddie admitted he had, but thought it best to wait for her to communicate with him. Then he told her what she probably wanted to hear most of all: She sounded like the old Sylvia, the one whose "easy flow of words" and "electric communication" had attracted him. When that Sylvia had disappeared from her letters, he had become alarmed. But now she had put herself together again, he insisted.

What mattered to Sylvia, Eddie understood, was her writing—above all, her style. When she had lost the ability to imagine, she was as good as dead, a point she explored in "The Wishing Box," published in *Granta* (1956). Agnes is envious of her husband's extravagant, literary, Technicolor dreams, which become a staple of his life. She dreams only vague nightmares—nothing like her wonderful childhood dreams of the "wishing box" and of Superman, who flew her over Alabama. She goes to the movies and watches television, but her imagination has shut down. She is in a panic and cannot sleep at night. Her mind, no longer able to form images, is condemned to a "perfect vacancy." She comes from a long-lived family and dreads the prospect of "wakeful, visionless days and nights." She takes the fifty sleeping pills prescribed for her all at once and commits suicide, an act that is presented as a kind of victory in the last lines of the story, which describe her "secret smile of triumph, as if, in some far country unattainable to mortal man, she were, at last, waltzing with the dark, red-caped prince of her early dreams." Such a story suggests that the act of suicide itself is neither shameful nor solely the response of a disordered mind. On the contrary, suicide, in certain circumstances, has an attractive inevitability to it when the human capacity to create a world has disintegrated. It is not such a stretch from this story to one of Plath's last poems, "Edge," in which the perfected woman reposes in a "smile of accomplishment."

Sylvia presented the first months of her return to Smith in idyllic terms, writing to Enid Epstein on 18 January describing a snow-laden sylvan scene. She also wrote about walking in the shadows of trees on the path into Northampton, playing bridge and other games with friends, hanging out in the coffee shop with Marcia Brown discussing Dostoevsky, and seeing good movies. To Sally Rogers, who considered applying to Smith, Sylvia wrote a letter extolling the college's intimate atmosphere. As a scholarship student, Sylvia did not feel out of place, since even the girls from wealthy families dressed casually. There were so many different kinds of residences, large and small, that Sally was sure to find her niche. The small classes and supportive faculty, who often visited the residences, suited Sylvia, who did not like the idea of large lecture halls. Sally could be as social as she liked, or remain studious and benefit from faculty members who took an interest in students, inviting them into their homes. Of course, there were times when Sylvia had been "blue," but it all depended on "you," she told Sally, to make what you would of yourself—not an easy task, Sylvia admitted, when "you're still growing up, the way we are."

You could not live in Lawrence House and not hear about Sylvia's dramatic suicide attempt. Several freshmen had read her work in *Seventeen*. Marilyn Martin, class of '57, recalls it was as if the walls were whispering, "Sylvia is back. Sylvia is back."

CB Follett ('Lyn), class of '58, later wrote a poem that captured the Sylvia Plath mystique.

We all knew, didn't know,
knew of her—
never pointed
just a flinch of our head
as she walked
cool and brilliant
along campus paths . . .

In Follet's poem, Sylvia's scar is one sign of her difference. She was one of them who had tried death and entered the "shock chamber," then returned, somehow whole again, making them feel fragile. She looked like other college girls in her pageboy June Allyson hair, and yet "she was, in her camouflage, / an exotic we added to our collection."

Outside of Lawrence House, though, what had happened to Sylvia was the subject of much speculation. Ravelle Silberman, a freshman with literary aspirations that included writing poetry and following Plath's example, thought, like other underclassman, that Sylvia had been pregnant and had gone away to have her baby. Unwanted pregnancy was usually to blame when Smith girls had to interrupt their education. Ravelle, who lived in Gillette House, did not get to know Sylvia well until Plath returned to teach at Smith. To a freshman like Ravelle, Sylvia and her cohort in Lawrence House appeared rather snobbish in their carefully groomed Smith outfits, as Ravelle shunned skirts for jeans. She steered clear of these scholarship girls, even though Ravelle herself was on a scholarship and shared many of their literary aspirations. Her fascination with Plath would later yield insight into Plath's marriage to Hughes, and also into the aura Sylvia began to establish for herself much later in London.

Several Smith alumni remember their freshmen fondness for Sylvia, an outgoing, friendly upperclassman. They were flattered by her attention. As she wrote in a letter to Phil McCurdy, she had picked out a freshman, Kathleen Knight, to date her brother Warren. Kathleen believed Sylvia picked her because Kathleen was tall, light-haired, and pale-skinned like Sylvia. Kathleen said Warren was shy and very sweet. Like Judy Denison, a promising physicist, Kathleen was a scholarship girl who welcomed Sylvia as a sort of alternative role model. "Freshman girls were told they should aim to be 'good members of the Junior League,'" Kathleen recalled. In other words, women were supposed to forsake careers and engage in volunteer work for charitable and educational purposes. "The scholarship girls looked at each other and said, 'What?' This is why they were going to college." Judy summed up the way lots of Smith girls felt: "Somebody was complaining about her boyfriend. He said he couldn't make any commitments because it would upset all his plans. And we said, 'We can't even make any plans until we have a commitment.'"

Helen Lane, then in her freshman year, remembered that students were instructed not to mention Sylvia's suicide attempt. In fact, it was not hard to treat Sylvia like a normal Smith student. She wore her shoulder-length hair in a popular pageboy style and tossed her head a bit when she laughed. She wore knee socks, Bermuda shorts, Shetland sweaters, and plaid skirts. "Very collegiate looking," remembered Judy Denison, another freshman. Judy mentioned that Sylvia had a dazzling smile, and Helen mentioned that Sylvia laughed easily. Sylvia counseled Marilyn, who was applying for an internship at *Mademoiselle,* and encouraged her to attend a symposium at which Alfred Kazin and *New Yorker* editor William Maxwell spoke. "Sylvia said there was more to Smith than attending classes. She opened that to me. I don't think I would have gone otherwise," Marilyn said. Sylvia sat beside Helen, then reading T. S. Eliot, and discussed "The Lovesong of J. Alfred Prufrock." It astonished Helen to discover that Plath was also an accomplished bridge player and played only with the best, as beginners watched her handle the cards. Later, Helen thought of Sylvia planning to take each trick the way she would strategically work out a line of poetry or prose.

On 25 February, Sylvia typed a cheerful eight-page, single-spaced letter to Jane Anderson. They were not especially close friends, but Jane had grown up in Wellesley and had dated Dick Norton. She had taken a special interest in Sylvia's case and had even presented Sylvia with newspaper clippings about the latter's three-day disappearance and Warren's discovery of her underneath the house. Like Sylvia, Jane traced a good deal of her suicidal feeling to her conflicted relationship with her father. She admired Sylvia's accomplishments, but she also believed that through electric shock treatments Plath had taken a shortcut, never really dealing with the underlying causes of her suicide attempt. In *The Bell Jar,* Jane is transmogrified into Joan Gilling, a rather eerie mental institution companion and a sort of upsetting double whom Esther regards with appalled fascination. In the novel, Esther recovers, but Joan commits suicide. But in her newsy report to Jane, Sylvia was sunny, telling Jane how well she had readjusted to college life—a message that seemed written for the benefit of Dr. Beuscher, since Sylvia urged Jane to show the letter to the therapist. Sylvia was pleased to have her old room all to herself, a situation made possible because the girls in Lawrence House made sure no one else took it. During her reading of Dostoevsky, the subject of suicide came up in class, and like Hester feeling the heat of her *A* in the *Scarlet Letter,* Sylvia "felt sure" her scar was "glowing symbolically." And yet, she discovered that not only could she discuss the subject openly, she felt like a sort of expert on suicide—although no one dared to question her about her own attempt. She had already gone on several dates, and even though she was a year behind and would miss some of her graduating friends, she seemed content and even happy to spend another year at Smith. She loved her course work, especially classes in American and Russian literature.

Sylvia also had a new "alter ego," Nancy Hunter, a freshman who lived in the room Sylvia had chosen for the fall semester of 1953 but never occupied because of her breakdown. Nancy had spent her first semester surrounded by the ambiance of Sylvia Plath, hearing stories about a student who had already become a legend. The first time Nancy caught sight of Sylvia, however, she was startled and blurted out, "They didn't tell me you were beautiful." Sylvia and everyone else laughed. Nancy wrote that Sylvia could have been "an airline stewardess or the ingenuous heroine of a B movie. She did not appear tortured or alienated; at times it was difficult for me to believe that she had ever felt a self-destructive impulse." Hunter believed no photograph she had ever seen of Sylvia did her justice, a remark that Ted Hughes would later second. Judging by Sylvia's 15 April letter to Phil McCurdy, Nancy held her own in discussions about sex, war, and capital punishment. A later letter described Nancy as "tall, slender, with an enchanting heart-shaped face, green Kirghiz eyes, black hair and a more than pigmentary resemblance to a certain Modigliani odalisque."

An exuberant poet wrote to her mother on 16 April that she had written her first sonnet in a year. "Doom of Exiles" details the descent from a cheerful world of green alleys into the "infernal haunt of demon dangers." Like a good deal of Plath's early verse, the poem stiffens as she works out an intricate rhyme scheme and stanza structure that is at once impressive but also too self-consciously poetic. This time she was trying to balance a sense of a defeated humanity against its indomitable desire to "crack the nut / In which the riddle of our race is shut." It is not hard to picture her—thesaurus in hand, as Nancy Hunter reports in her memoir—searching for the precise word in an agonizing, plodding process.

On 19 April, Sylvia announced to her mother that she had met

Richard Sassoon, whose father was a cousin of the British poet Siegfried Sassoon. She described Richard as a slender "Parisian fellow," even though he was a British subject and had family in North Carolina. She delighted in his outré conversation, which he would carry on in youthfully pretentious letters, large parts of which were written in French. Perhaps Sylvia enjoyed the wordplay of his rather decadent manner, so at odds with contemporary culture. She liked his "wicked laugh." He presented himself as an exile, and that surely appealed to her.

Richard was a Yale student, and Sylvia, familiar with New Haven after her outings with Dick Norton and Myron Klotz, appreciated just how much Sassoon stood out from his contemporaries. Constance Blackwell, Smith class of 1956, sometimes joined Sylvia and Richard on their Yale weekends. Blackwell recalls that Sassoon was "generally regarded as the most clever and worldly wise of all—he was very amazing and witty—it was he who belonged to the Elizabethan Club, where we went once or twice to have tea and smoke clay pipes. Richard was preparing himself to be a great literary figure." This social club housed sixteenth- and seventeenth-century books and Shakespeare folios, and promoted literary conversation while Irish maids in black uniforms and white aprons served the quintessential English beverage. In such a setting, Plath may have felt welcome enough to level with Richard Sassoon in a way that was not possible with other males of her generation. In the only "heart-to-heart" talk Blackwell ever had with Plath, Constance remembers Sylvia saying "how difficult it was to speak about our own dreams and ambitions with young men we adored—because they themselves had their own demons of ambition."

More than a decade later, in the fall of 1968, when Yale went coed, women still found the "maleness of Yale" overwhelming. "Male eating clubs, male-populated streets, even a male-oriented health program. Walking down a Yale street we became acutely aware of the staring. We were conscious of ourselves as objects, common objects to be looked over and appraised," Janet Lever and Pepper Schwartz write of their experience in *Women at Yale: Liberating a College Campus* (1971). "You were expected to be a mixture of Margaret Mead and Scarlett O'Hara," Lever told a *Time* interviewer. Well, Sylvia Plath, three-time reader of *Gone with the Wind,* was prepared.

Richard formed part of an unusual male grouping inspired by the charismatic Henri Peyre, described as a "quintessential Frenchman" in his *New York Times* obituary (10 December 1988). Author of more than thirty books, including *French Novelists of Today* and *The Contemporary French Novel,* Peyre told a *Newsweek* interviewer, "The only sport I enjoy is conversing with women. Most of life is a purely nuanced affair, and women help men realize this. Yale is much too masculine a place." For Peyre's acolytes, literature was a way of life. At Smith, Constance Blackwell suggests, literature was more of an acquisition, almost a commodity. Sassoon and his friends had an appealing vulnerability, she recalls, and were just the right antidote to hard-drinking Yale men. Sassoon & Co. were authentic. When they drank, Constance noted, they drank sherry, which put her, so to speak, halfway to England, where she wanted to study and mature as a writer.

So Richard Sassoon was a kind of literary dream come true for Sylvia Plath. He seemed magical, the kind of lover Plath describes in the refrain to her villanelle, "Mad Girl's Love Song": "I think I made you up in my head." On so many evenings out, Sylvia scorned men who did not know how to talk to her. She rued her own efforts to rid herself of any original expressions that might intimidate her dates. Even someone like the literary-minded Gordon Lameyer was a project Sylvia had to shape to suit herself. With Richard, she did not have to summon a compliant demeanor to mask her true emotions. The soigné Sassoon was also a master at planning dates, excursions to the city, and cultural events. He was too small for her physically, Sylvia would often say, and yet she found a man who exuded aestheticism very appealing. The story, as Constance Blackwell heard it, was that Richard's father had initiated his son into the delights of sex by taking him to a prostitute.

Sassoon had a Volkswagen, Constance Blackwell recalls, and was "a bit of a hypochondriac. We used to tease him that he and his Volkswagen got ill at the same time." Sylvia told Phil McCurdy about a gas station stop on the Merritt Parkway, where she enjoyed the spectacle of herself sleeping in Sassoon's Volkswagen, seated among wine bottles and books on Baudelaire and attracting attention that she greeted with "blithe abandon." To Aurelia, she almost apologized, describing Sassoon as a "very intuitive weird sinuous little guy whose eyes are black and shadowed so he looks as if he were an absinthe addict . . . all of which helps me to be carefree and gay." Sassoon was a decidedly bohemian corrective to her orthodox dates. Nancy Hunter thought Sylvia built Sassoon into a Byronic hero but also an "amusing toy." Sometimes Sylvia even seemed to find him repulsive, telling her roommate, "When he holds me in his arms, I feel like Mother Earth with a small brown bug crawling on me." The only way Nancy could explain Sylvia's continuing dates with Sassoon was to conclude, "She could not resist exploring the bizarre or ugly, even when it frightened or sickened her, and I could not help feeling that for a girl with a delicate equilibrium it was a dangerous pastime."

When a Lawrence House girl called Sassoon a worm, Nancy explained how powerful Sassoon made Sylvia feel. Marilyn Martin got a firsthand glimpse of what Nancy meant. Marilyn was used to seeing Sylvia with Gordon Lameyer, whom Marilyn described as "all American . . . such a handsome, charming person." Sylvia and Gordon looked wonderful together, like a poster couple. After a date with a guy from Amherst, Marilyn had returned with him to Lawrence House. They were on the porch, the make-out spot couples would repair to after the girls signed in and waited for the bells signaling they should return to their rooms. Marilyn watched Sylvia approach the porch with a date Marilyn did not recognize. He was small and swarthy. Later she learned it was Richard Sassoon. Couples usually looked for a dark corner. But Sylvia, in full view, virtually attacked her companion, leaning over Sassoon, who was sitting on a railing. "It was kind of embarrassing," Marilyn said. Sylvia was "very passionate, more passionate than most people on the porch would be." This was a "level of sexuality that I was not comfortable with . . . in literature, yes, but right here?"

Constance Blackwell thought Richard was a little afraid of Sylvia. To Constance's boyfriend, Alex Holm, a shocked Sassoon reported that Sylvia had said to him, "I wish I could take your penis back to Smith with me." Unlike the Catholic and Jewish girls Constance knew, the Protestant Sylvia seemed to have no guilt about sex. Yet to watch her cross the campus she looked like a typical Smith girl. With her flowing hair and robust health, you expected her to have a tennis racket in her hand. Blackwell's vision evokes Katharine Hepburn in her prime. "I think Richard knew he wasn't up to Sylvia. Charming as he was, he didn't have that private strong character. When I saw Sylvia with Ted, there was a man big enough for her," Blackwell concluded.

Sylvia admitted to Phil McCurdy she did not fully follow the French her "little expatriate frenchman" spoke to her, although she certainly understood "je t'adore." That Richard was a little wearing, though, is apparent in Sylvia's confession to Phil that she sometimes wanted "good healthy vulgar american sun, sweat, and song . . . entendu?" This was, after all, a Smith undergraduate who enjoyed bragging about climbing an 830-foot-high fire tower with three others to gape at the "circling crown of lights far far below," an all-at-once brave, scary, ecstatic experience. The arch and elusive Sassoon could be quite a trial at times. Here he is trying to placate Plath: "Please do not say you do not know me. That has depressed me a little. . . . And do you think I know myself well enough to tell you? . . . I have said *much* about the world—surely not without some self-revelation. And I have made you smile, I have made you laugh—perhaps I have even made you cry—was this not me! and me alone?"

Eddie Cohen seems to have been the only one of Sylvia's correspondents who did not take her recovery at face value. On 28 April, he wrote a detailed response to two of her letters describing her breakdown. Something was missing for him. Why did she descend into such a deep depression at the very moment when "life should have been at a peak"? He realized that he was probing experiences that were still raw, but he seriously doubted that Sylvia could go on for long without understanding why she had chosen that manner of suicide and why her initial therapy had been so ineffective. He was asking her, in short, to examine her reactions: "Attempting to cherish that old life when things were so relatively uncomplicated will do you little good, and when reality intrudes, as it eventually must, you will merely bounce back to where you so recently returned hence."

Back at it on 6 May, Eddie would not let go—this time pointing out how Sylvia tried to incorporate her male suitors into stories of her own making. Eddie proved to be intractable material when he showed up unannounced. Since Sylvia had not scripted the occasion, what "could have been an exhilarating experience turned into a stiff debacle," Eddie complained. The super-organized Sylvia had been overwhelmed by her experience at *Mademoiselle,* Eddie pointed out, because so much of her routine mandated that she respond to the demands of others: "You like to plot all the possibilities in your future as if it were a short story. When I first heard of your problems last summer, I could not but wonder what went wrong that you had not counted on."

Two days earlier, Sylvia wrote her mother, "Just a note in the midst of a rigorously planned schedule . . ." She seemed to revel in a ten-hours-per-day reading project that would take her through the end of May, writing Phil on 13 May after a "full day of rigid discipline" finishing *War and Peace* and *Anna Karenina.* She was looking forward to the summer—a little too exuberantly, as it turned out. Pace Eddie.

Sylvia went home with bleached blonde hair. A shocked Aurelia adjusted, admitting in *Letters Home* that the change was flattering. Sylvia told Gordon Lameyer that she thought her new hair color drew attention away from her facial scar. After a round of visits to New York and a short stay in Wellesley, Plath joined Nancy Hunter for a summer in Cambridge, studying German at Harvard summer school and attending many cultural events. They visited Olive Higgins Prouty on the way. The giddy and irrepressible girls ate two helpings of cucumber sandwiches in a most "unladylike display of gluttony," Hunter wrote.

Hunter has provided a striking portrayal of Sylvia's summer in a memoir that was first written in the 1970s to correct certain misapprehensions about Plath. For all her high-powered ambitions and her literary interests, Sylvia was in many ways a conventional Smith girl. She was no rebel and indeed disapproved of a Lawrence House contingent of nonconformists who spurned Smith proprieties. She took her world as it was, Hunter notes, not imagining that it would change much—or that she had any obligation to challenge its conventions. One of Sylvia's projects that summer, in fact, was to work on her cooking, an undertaking that impressed Nancy. Sylvia's tastes were sophisticated, and though they had a food budget, she tended to ignore the staples, expecting Hunter to take care of those, while Plath worked on her creations. Although Hunter complained that her roommate's penchant for specialty items was putting a strain on their limited resources, Sylvia brushed off this concern as Nancy's problem.

Plath did not seem at all sensitive about discussing her previous summer's breakdown. Indeed, she provided Nancy with a startling comment on Otto Plath (not surprising to readers of "Daddy"), calling him an "autocrat" and saying, "I adored and despised him, and I probably wished many times that he were dead. When he obliged me and died, I imagined that I had killed him."

The roommates agreed to accept all dates that included dinner, although a wary Nancy had second thoughts about a professor, identified as "Irwin," they met outside Widener Library, where Esther Greenwood meets her Irwin in *The Bell Jar*. According to Steiner, Irwin later called and asked Nancy for a date. She was surprised to learn on the way to dinner that he would be preparing it. She had not been alone with a man in such circumstances and only agreed to accompany him when he told her he would keep the door open and that his landlady was nearby. In the course of the evening, though, he made a pass and ended up chasing Nancy around his apartment. She escaped and told an intrigued Sylvia about her misadventure. When Irwin phoned, Sylvia took his calls and eventually agreed, to Nancy's amazement, to date him. The message was clear: Plath felt she could handle such a man, a "wolf" in the parlance of the 1950s. Indeed, she wrote to Gordon Lameyer about Nancy's tendency to overreact. Nancy was like "sun-silver on a dark, moody lake, and her calm is a result of tensions which break open at home in shrill, neurotic screaming." Learning to deal with Nancy had been good for Sylvia, she told Gordon, since she had been able to work on her own equanimity to compensate for Nancy's "eternal crises."

But Sylvia returned from her date in distress, bleeding copiously. She admitted Irwin had raped her. A terrified Sylvia—in

morbid fear of hospitals and of the kind of attention she had received after her suicide attempt—made Nancy call a doctor Irwin
had previously summoned to treat Sylvia, and on the phone Nancy
took his instructions as to how to treat the hemorrhage. When the
bleeding proved intractable, Nancy finally persuaded Sylvia they
had to go to the hospital. Nancy then called Irwin, insisting that
he drive them to the hospital to meet the doctor there and pay for
Sylvia's treatment. While there, Nancy heard the doctor say that
Sylvia would have no more trouble. And then he added that what
she had experienced was not surprising. He had treated other girls
in the same situation. To Nancy's astonishment, Sylvia continued
to see Irwin.

How to account for this seeming masochism? As the doctor's
parting comment suggests, the conception of sexual abuse in the
1950s was quite different from contemporary attitudes toward
such behavior. To the Irwins of Sylvia's day, women were fair game,
and the women themselves were blameworthy. How Sylvia saw her
culpability is not clear, especially since Hunter apparently was not
privy to her roommate's motivations.

Sylvia may not have been able to explain her behavior to herself. She seemed to be undergoing a transformation that had gone
underground, so to speak, provoking an irritated Eddie to com-
plain on 10 August that her letters were "too sparing." She was
dodging him, teasing and tantalizing, Eddie concluded. Nancy
noted, "Sylvia seemed to regard man as an object that could be
manipulated at will." Nancy and Sylvia remained friends but were
never again so close. Nancy believed that Sylvia "absorbed the
essence of people like doses of a unique psychedelic drug designed
to expand her consciousness. Sometimes she seemed to forget that
they had emotions and wills of their own."

Kay Quinn, one of the Smith girls who had shared the Cambridge apartment with Sylvia and Nancy, later told Helen Lane that
Sylvia sometimes acted "strange," prompting Kay to suspect that
she had not overcome the behavior that resulted in her suicide attempt. Kay also mentioned an incident in which Sylvia, bleeding
heavily from her vagina, asked Kay to hold her. Whether this incident is related to Irwin's rape is not clear. But Plath's reckless

involvement with Irwin—even after she had been warned by Nancy—seems a precursor of her later desire to take on the daunting Ted Hughes.

The accounts of Irwin in Nancy Hunter Steiner's memoir and in *The Bell Jar* are so similar that Plath scholar Peter K. Steinberg—after noting that Irwin is referred to as Edwin in Paul Alexander's biography—decided to track down the real man. In the Frances McCullough Papers at the University of Maryland, Steinberg discovered a letter, dated 11 January 1975, from the poet Donald Hall speculating that his friend, Edwin Akutowicz, was Irwin. Akutowicz had just written Hall a letter expressing surprise that the Sylvia Plath he had dated had become famous. Hall called Edwin "totally unworldly. He went around making love with women, at an extraordinary rate, without any affect at all, as far as anybody could tell." This description certainly fits the oblivious Irwin in the novel and the memoir, as does the fact that, like Irwin, Edwin (with a 1948 Harvard PhD) was a mathematics professor. On 10 March 1975, McCullough wrote to Akutowicz, explaining she had edited Plath's letters and was curious to learn his impression of Sylvia, who when he knew her was just beginning to reengage with the world after her suicide attempt.

On 25 March, Akutowicz replied, observing that he could hear Sylvia's "gently malicious laughter" at his superficial impressions of her. He did not detect any "deeper tensions" in her. In fact, at first glance one might suppose she was "beautiful and dumb." But she was hardly that, he added. In fact, he remembered not only conversations about poetry (Edmund Spenser in particular) but about probability, a subject that of course interested a mathematician. He remembered her hearty laugh and her unembarrassed description of crawling under the porch to take her own life. She was less neurotic than most young women he knew. What made her unusual, in his estimation, was her rather somber memories of her father, her intense dedication to poetry, and the way she "caught on to the idea of suicide as a reality."

At the end of summer, Sylvia returned to her family home in Wellesley. Sylvia wrote relentlessly upbeat letters to Aurelia, who had taken the summer off to join her parents on Cape Cod and to recuperate from a recurrence of bleeding ulcers. To others, Sylvia made passing references to her "very attractive, but nervous mother, whom I see as little as possible." Sylvia mentioned enjoyable weekends cooking for Gordon Lameyer. They had also seen Dr. Beuscher, on whom Sylvia still relied.

By the time Sylvia returned for her final year at Smith, she had decided to apply for a Fulbright scholarship to study at either Oxford or Cambridge. She was lining up her references: Elizabeth Drew, Mary Ellen Chase, and Newton Arvin, all distinguished Smith faculty, favorites of hers, and writers with national reputations. She thought a letter from Dr. Beuscher would be the best way to handle the story of her breakdown and institutionalization, which had resulted, in Sylvia's view, in a complete cure. She was also applying to graduate school, with Harvard, Yale, and Columbia heading her list. She had reverted to her naturally brown hair to highlight a demure, studious look.

In the fall of 1954, Sylvia made friends at Smith with Elinor Klein, who was expecting to meet a "shy spectacled, unattractive kid in the corner clutching her Dostoevski for dear life." But this was a willowy beauty with "great soft dark eyes," a "wide laughing mouth," and a "tumble of light hair." Sylvia immediately dispelled any "worshipful attitudes" by showing Elinor her rejection slips, which Sylvia seemed proud of because they were proof of her hard work. They talked nonstop on the first of many glorious afternoons. Klein fondly remembered her friend's humor, which bubbled up effortlessly, even during their "most serious conversations."

Jody Simon, Smith '55, knew Sylvia slightly. They shared a philosophy class, where Simon noticed that Plath's comments were particularly insightful and interesting. "She always seemed to me to be trembling slightly" and fidgeting with her hair, Jody remembers. "I recall it as an inner intensity externalized." Simon's overall impression, though, was of a calm and confident person. "I appeared shy and reticent, described as 'quiet' in our '55 yearbook, and I felt Sylvia extended herself toward me in a kind, interested and thoughtful way." In a German course, Darryl Hafter watched a very quiet, unassuming Sylvia gradually master the language, in class presenting a Rilke poem in a powerful English translation of her own devising.

Sylvia attributed her good spirits that fall to her bohemian summer, suggesting to her mother that she had needed a break from her practical self—the one who stuck to a schedule, budgeted her time and money, and expressed her conventional, unoriginal, and puritanical side. Dr. Beuscher had evidently encouraged acting out, to rid Sylvia of the "good girl" mind-set that had made her resentful of her mother, the embodiment of prim and proper decorum. To Nancy Hunter, however, Sylvia had gone too far in the opposite direction, forsaking not merely the traditional behavior of a Smith undergraduate, but showing a disquieting lack of sense. Sylvia rationalized her "blazing jaunts" as learning the "hard way" to be independent.

Sylvia was aware of her penchant for mythologizing herself as she turned to Dostoevsky, preparing a senior thesis: a study of the double in his novels. In what is perhaps the study's most revealing passage, Plath wonders whether Golyadkin, the protagonist of *The Double*, deals with a real alter ego or simply a projection of his imagination. She cites various critics who fault Dostoevsky for not clarifying his main character's sense of reality. Plath concurs, but obviously the issue itself—what is real—exercised her deepest emotions. What she wrote about her childhood in essays like "Ocean 1212-W" and "America! America!" formed part of her essential myth. Was not the "Plath" of her journals and letters also her double and alter ego?

Marilyn Martin remembers a conversation with Sylvia about Henry James's novel *The Portrait of a Lady* "and how we become what we read sometimes. We move into that world. Sylvia and I talked about this. The difference in reading when you had to write about it rather than step outside and criticize. Identifying with the characters." Like so many creative artists, Sylvia absorbed art into her bloodstream, and it took considerable effort for her to function outside of that assimilated sensibility and write as a literary critic. In fact, on her first English assignment at Smith, she had been dismayed to receive a B–. It is often said that her worries about doing well at Smith were a product of perfectionism, but such an analysis ignores how strenuous it was for a sensibility like hers to conform to the academic model of learning. Her thesis on Dostoevsky proves that she could learn to write a scholarly paper perfectly well, but her letters also show that doing so put a strain on her. Her switch from Joyce to Dostoevsky also suggests that she found a theme in the Russian author that resonated more deeply in her than anything Joyce wrote.

That Sylvia Plath perceived her mythologizing tendencies did not mean, of course, that she could control them, or that she would not make mistakes, misconstruing the dream for the reality, as Golyadkin does. Going to England on a Fulbright scholarship (if she was fortunate to be offered one) would be another test, she wrote her mother on 13 October. Taking up her scholarship would mean relinquishing the security of her native land, finding new friends, and attempting to succeed in a formidable, intellectually unfamiliar world. As she worked on the first draft of her senior thesis, she worried about having something new to say about an old topic. Isn't this also what England represented: daring to do well in a culture far older than her own and daunting to an upstart American? She did not consider, however, that England, too, would become a Sylvia Plath project, seen through her own special lenses, which could distort as well as discover reality.

The literary world became more palpable for Sylvia Plath when she encountered Alfred Kazin, author of *On Native Grounds* and a prominent American literary critic, teaching a course at Smith. Her description of a curt and aloof figure is apposite. In *New York Jew,* Kazin recalls that she looked like any other Smith student. When she showed him her work, he became suspicious, because it was so polished and professional. Suggesting that she was presenting him with plagiarism, Kazin named the magazines such work appeared in. "I know," Plath replied. "They've already taken them."

He warmed up when he realized that Plath was a published author and deadly serious about writing. He liked that she had worked her way through college. He had been disappointed with his apathetic students and at first assumed she was simply another "pampered Smith baby," Sylvia wrote her mother on 25 October.

He invited her to audit his class, which she did, vowing to learn as much as she could from "such a man," who told her the class needed her contribution. She did not elaborate, but what Kazin offered her was another version of independence. He took the money and the tributes from the academic world in stride, but unlike her other professors, he was not really part of it. The point was to write; there were no excuses for not doing so. "You don't write to support yourself; you work to support your writing," was his message to Plath, one she quoted to her mother. She soon became a Kazin favorite. Constance Blackwell can still hear him calling her: "Syl-via, Syl-via." In the letter he wrote in support of her application to graduate school, Kazin noted he was not in the habit of writing on behalf of students—and certainly not with the superlatives he used to describe Plath. "She is someone to be watched, to be encouraged—and to be remembered," he concluded.

Sylvia was still aiming at publication in *The New Yorker* and *The Atlantic Monthly*, and she enthused over Kazin's interest in her—which included a kind of command performance at his home, reading and discussing her story, "Paula Brown's Snowsuit." At the same time, she continued her impersonation of a "regular girl"—to quote from *New York Jew*, the "first to clear the dishes after coffee." Sylvia did not seem to mind building up her hopes because, she told Aurelia on 7 December, she loved living "in suspense." Kazin had invited her to an informal lunch and was writing a recommendation for her Woodrow Wilson fellowship application. Just how extravagant she could become is clear in her final comment on Kazin, "I worship him." Yet to Kazin, she appeared "guarded to an extreme. I knew nothing about her and never expected to know anything." She simply presented an image of perfection, the pet of what he called, in *New York Jew*, "the nervous English department."

Sylvia spent part of her Christmas break in New York City, with Sassoon playing Prince Charming to her Cinderella, as she described it in a letter to a friend. Gordon Lameyer, still very much in the picture, was in the navy's gunnery school in Virginia. In a typical description of her itinerary, she mentioned breakfasting on oysters in a scene that would not be out of place in a Hollywood

romance, and ending her day in film noir fashion, "talking to de-
tectives in the 16th squad police station."

Sylvia continued to write poetry for a creative writing class, and
she submitted a story to the *Ladies Home Journal,* which rejected
her work but wanted to see a rewrite—an encouraging sign, since
rejections usually included an invitation to submit her next story.
More rejections followed from *The Saturday Evening Post* and other
magazines, but always having something on the way to a publisher
seemed to drive her on. She fretted over what seemed to her the
slim chances of studying at Oxford or Cambridge, and kept calcu-
lating which graduate school would serve her best, considering
that, as she told Aurelia on 29 January, "writing is the first love of
my life."

Sylvia Plath's strongest inclination pointed toward study and
perhaps teaching abroad. Her pacifism and sense of international
solidarity put her at odds with Cold War America and McCarthyism, which she wanted to counteract, as she put it in a letter to
Aurelia on 11 February, by acting on her realization that "new
races are going to influence the world . . . much as America did in
her day." She considered teaching in Tangier. Then on 15 February,
Sylvia wrote that Cambridge had accepted her, and that the Smith
College English department was behind her in their rejection of
"machine-made American grad degrees . . . P.S. English men are
great!" Writing several poems a week, Sylvia was also thinking of
submitting a book to the Yale Younger Poets series.

More exciting trips to New York and an encouraging letter from
The Atlantic Monthly made the spring of 1955 seem a reprise of the
fateful 1953 season when the heady round of success and frenetic
activity had only served to panic Sylvia. This time, though, she
was nearing graduation and pleased with her senior thesis and her
advisor, her Russian literature professor, George Gibian. He had
been deeply impressed with her, describing Sylvia as the ideal student to Edward Butscher. Even a "lame" suggestion from Gibian
turned into a wonderful chapter of the thesis, Gibian remembered.
She also babysat for him and enthusiastically wrote to Gordon
Lameyer, "I was holding the deliciously warm twins and feeding

them bottled milk (after five glasses of sherry I felt an overwhelming impulse to strip and nurse them myself!)".

Sylvia remained under the steadying influence of Dr. Beuscher, whom she saw periodically, as well the sobering encouragement of Alfred Kazin and the kind attention of Professor Mary Ellen Chase, who made sure Sylvia knew, step-by-step, how her Cambridge application fared and what to expect next. Sylvia formed new friendships, purposely not isolating herself as she had done before her suicide attempt. Sue Weller had become a close friend as copasetic as Marcia Brown. Sylvia invited Sue to accompany her home for spring break.

Sylvia continued to see Gordon Lameyer and briefly considered an engagement to him. She decided against it because she did not want to cut off opportunities or be saddled with a commitment to supporting his career. She thus avoided another awkward involvement of the kind she had backed away from with Dick Norton. Richard Sassoon was another case altogether. He might write passionately, but he came nowhere near the subject of marriage: "I bear the name of love tonight and bear myself alone and alone to boredom's bed and bear my love like a cross—so cross you are not with me—a cross forever until you are with me—that's true, I swear—and swear madly because it is true—o god of the godly keep off the pidgins! Ah to conquer death—not to avoid it—but to have it now and then—in between the now and then—until then, all my love, Richard." These letters evidently amused Sylvia, who proposed taking Sassoon along on one of her visits to Olive Higgins Prouty.

Sylvia was beginning to meet major contemporary poets like Marianne Moore and John Ciardi. She did a public reading of her work for an intercollegiate poetry contest (she tied for first place) and enjoyed making the audience laugh. Later, the college radio station recorded her reading her work. Moore made a deep impression, appearing as a sort of fairy godmother and expressing a wish to meet Aurelia, Sylvia wrote in a 16 April letter to her mother. A letter from *The Atlantic Monthly* requested revision of a poem that Sylvia thought might ruin the work's spontaneity. She regretfully admitted, "I battle between desperate Machiavellian opportunism and uncompromising artistic ethics." The former won out.

Plath was thrilled to get a letter from Ciardi calling her a real poet. She was also hoping that May would bring further publication in *Vogue, The Atlantic Monthly,* and *Mademoiselle,* as well as several more prizes from Smith. Reading her letters is rather like making the rounds of perpetual desire. This time there were fewer disappointments. At pains to show how fulfilled Sylvia felt in the late spring of 1955, Aurelia noted her daughter's happy birthday call in *Letters Home:* "Thank you, Mother, for giving me life." In early May, Sylvia was invited to judge a contest at a writer's festival in the Catskills. She enjoyed the work and the attention—mistakenly thinking, however, that her well-received public performance meant that she would enjoy a teaching career.

The official award of a Fulbright to study at Cambridge was announced in late May at the same time as Edward Weeks, editor of *The Atlantic Monthly,* wrote Sylvia to say that her original version of "Circus in Three Rings" was better than the revision the magazine had requested. He would publish her work in the August issue. After his call for more new work, Plath practically chortled to her mother, "That fortress of Bostonian conservative respectability has been 'charmed' by your tight-rope-walking daughter!" In the same 21 May letter, Plath listed the eleven awards she had received that year, totaling $470. At graduation, Sylvia listened to Adlai Stevenson give the commencement address, watched Marianne Moore receive an honorary degree, acknowledged Alfred Kazin's wave to her as she accepted her degree, and whispered in her mother's ear, "My cup runneth over!"

The apotheosis of Sylvia Plath seemed perfected in June, when letters from Gordon Lameyer and Richard Sassoon arrived with breathtaking tributes—and, in Sassoon's case, a new, almost pleading eroticism that complemented Lameyer's earnest adoration: "From you . . . I have found a language, a way of looking at life, a beauty in the terrible paradoxes. You have given me courage to work in the dark, energy to concentrate on my work, vision to clear the shelf of the masters who sit starting down on me with their chilling jeer, confidence to act in the Hamlet play of life. I have taken all you had to give—and you gave more than anyone." Sassoon wrote his letter on 4 June, a day later, abasing himself even as he exalted her: "O my darling sweet clever Sylvia! You will make the heavens answer someday . . . if ever I am there . . . and I shall be."

A new note of urgency verging on panic enters Sassoon's letters that summer, as he realizes he may be losing her: "I do not believe I shall ever love another woman so deeply, so happily, so sadly, so confidently, so desperately, so fully . . . something in me has broken . . . Goodbye my very dearest Sylvia . . . love—it is a great thing, even when it has failed. And it was the love really that faltered or failed, was it? Because it lives."

The next day, 19 July, Sylvia mentioned to her mother that in Cambridge she had gone out to dinner and a play with Peter Davison, now another of her lovers. Alfred Kazin had introduced Plath to Davison, then twenty-seven and an editor at Harcourt, Brace. At Smith, Davison met a typical undergraduate, robust and ingenuous, but also driven to write and full of questions about the world of publishing. The conventionally pretty girl in the Smith sweater-and-skirt ensemble formed a "curious, even a disturbing alliance" with her intensity of expression, he pointed out in *Half-Remembered*. Davison asked Plath to show him her first novel whenever she wrote it. Davison seemed especially suitable for the summer before her departure for Cambridge because, she told her mother, his voice sounded "nice and Britishy and tweedy." He was a Harvard man who wrote poetry and had a Scottish poet for a father, she told Warren.

The affair began easily enough, with a dinner date and with Sylvia slipping into Davison's bed quite casually. He soon learned that she was hard on her lovers and suspected he did not measure up. Because they shared a certain "mutuality," only Richard Sassoon seemed to have satisfied her sexually. Like Eddie Cohen, Davison felt Plath held back. Only once did her mask slip, when she disclosed the horrifying details of her suicide attempt and her hostility toward her mother and scorn for her father, "a sort of fuddy-duddy professor who dealt with bugs down in Boston."

Davison found Plath an entrancing companion who shared her ambitions and experiences freely, as he did during their summer romance, which ended abruptly after a visit to the Plath home.

Davison met Aurelia for the first time and was struck by her formality and correctness when she greeted him as though she were greeting one of Sylvia's serious suitors. (Eddie Cohen had received a similar reception.) At home, Sylvia treated her mother with affection. In his walk with Sylvia later, it was another story—not only with regard to Aurelia, but also to himself. Sylvia let him know that their time together had ended now that she was off to England. She dismissed him in such a way that he felt used and rather callow, even though she had initially approached him with respect. In her journal, Plath explained that she was "too serious" for Davison, and that only Richard Sassoon understood the nature of her "tragic joy." Although the affair with Davison was brief, he would return later as an important figure in her publishing career—and still later in the biography wars involving the Plath estate.

Everything seemed under Plath's control. Gordon Lameyer wrote to say he would wait for her, and Richard Sassoon remained in the picture with his paeans: "Sylvia, you are a great big, healthy, powerful woman!" She should never forget it, even when she was not feeling so, Sassoon wrote on 9 August in a letter written in an extraordinary fatherly tone. In *Letters Home,* Aurelia mentions no strain between herself and Sylvia during this summer, but Sassoon's letter refers to his regret over "so much hatred and frustration in your home." Knowing that he was touching on a fraught subject, the wary Sassoon nevertheless ventured to advise her, "Believe me, it is no good to leave a home with a foul taste in the air. Particularly, as we never know what will happen in the absence. Please think about it, Sylvia. Just say she is one hell of a bitch and then determine to get along with her for the last month. It was after all your purpose in staying at home this summer, and you will feel better to have accomplished something there. . . ." Without Sylvia's side of the correspondence, it is hard to tell exactly what troubled her, or how she reacted to Sassoon's admonition—or what she did about it.

In other moods, Plath was just as likely to confess, as she did to

Warren on 28 July, that she was already feeling the homesickness that always began before she departed on trips. She wanted him to know how much she loved him. She hoped he would confide in her and write to her while she was away on her two-year journey. She had been wandering about in a "blue streak of incredible nostalgia." You had to pick your day with Sylvia Plath. She declared to Warren, "My wings need to be tried. O Icarus . . ."

CHAPTER 4

I AM NATURE

(1955–57)

September 1955: Plath arrives in England; **25 February 1956:**
First dramatic meeting with Ted Hughes; **16 June:** Plath and Hughes
marry and honeymoon in Spain; **1957:** Plath earns her Cambridge
degree, and the couple moves to America.

In September, Sylvia sailed to London, enjoying a short shipboard
romance and a stop in France, where "men know how to look at
one," she assured Elinor Friedman Klein. Sylvia reveled in London's centuries of tradition, suffused with the silvery, misty light
of a Constable painting. She walked for miles through the parks,
toured Soho, and visited the National Gallery in Trafalgar Square, a
Dickensian pub, and bookstalls. She was already assembling a submission list of British literary magazines.

Cambridge did not disappoint. She was still in that romance of
travel mood that made her digs seem charming, with a gas ring
and fireplace that meant, of course, no central heating. The formal
gardens, the "quaint crooked streets," the River Cam, and King's
Chapel were all part of an enchanting, cozy picture she presented
of herself. She was surrounded by her books and anticipating the
purchase of a tea set and prints for her bare walls. "Here all is to
begin again," she wrote Aurelia on 3 October. She studied the clas-
sics of the ancient and modern stage, philosophy and ethics, and
literary criticism. She described the controversial literary critic F. R.

Leavis lecturing: "a magnificent, acid, malevolently humorous little man who looks exactly like a bandy-legged leprechaun." She hoped Richard Sassoon would make good on his desire to study at the Sorbonne. She could not think of a better escort during her foray to Paris.

By mid-October, Sylvia had been to a Labour Club dance and was meeting men (they outnumbered women ten-to-one at Cambridge). First up was Mallory Wober, tall, dark, and handsome, a Londoner who had spent nearly a decade in India. He took her punting on the Cam and reminded her of Dmitri Karamazov, Sylvia wrote Elinor Friedman Klein. Indeed, Plath greeted Wober like a figure out of fiction as the "dark Dmitri Karamazov hewn out of the Himalayas," who would descend on her "in a dark cloud" and astound the "wearied mahomette who will probably be trying feebly to hang herself with yards and yards of holly-ribbon conveniently supplied by an invisible troll who lives under the staircase." Other "chaps" were taking her to tea, to meals, to concerts, and for long, picturesque walks. None of these dates seems to have been very passionate. Wober was good company, supplying her with phonograph records and entertaining her on an organ he brought up to her room. She regarded him as a substitute for the brother she missed. For Edward Butscher, Wober recalled Sylvia's stunning physical presence, how she could enter a room and turn heads. He found her energizing and empowering.

Sylvia successfully auditioned for the Amateur Dramatic Club, doing scenes as the clever and bold Rosalind in *As You Like It* and as Camille in *Camino Real,* based on Dumas's famous courtesan, who had been transfigured into Greta Garbo's dying goddess character in *Camille.* Sylvia had her audience laughing as she described her idea of the stage set, and afterward a male member of the audience complimented her on her wonderful voice, which filled the room. She wrote many playful illustrated letters to Wober, picturing herself awaiting his visits to her room, "languishing like Camille amid my withered yellow dahlias." She found rehearsals demanding and wrote to Wober about her dealings with "dramatic tyrants." She was joking, no doubt, and yet she seemed relieved to think of him as both her escort and her escape. She liked to say the name

Mallory, she told him. It had the right number of syllables to achieve a dramatic effect, which she would demonstrate for him sometime.

After a month in Cambridge, Sylvia announced that she was "living it up." She had two teas and a sherry party to attend on the day she wrote to Elinor Friedman Klein about her Cambridge "heaven." Plath called herself popular, although when Edward Butscher later interviewed several of her Cambridge contemporaries, they seemed to regard her as a pill—too methodical even in the way she cut her egg and toast into squares, and too shiny with Samsonite luggage that stood out against the shabbiness of postwar England. Sylvia herself stood out amidst the "oppressive ugliness" and "threadbare" dirtiness of even upper-middle-class homes in a country still recovering from the ravages of war.

Jane Baltzell Kopp, a fellow American student, cringed sometimes in Sylvia's company, because the latter was so brashly American and apparently unaware of the jokes that Cambridge students made about her. Actually, Sylvia was not as oblivious as Kopp supposed. She knew quite well that she put people off with her "emotional, irresponsible gushing," as she wrote in her journal, but often she could not help it. In her perfectly decorated room, she would enthuse about how she enjoyed a certain piece of furniture, and her English acquaintances mused over the oddity of using a verb like enjoy in connection with the decor. Out on the streets, Sylvia sometimes seemed like any other gauche American tourist. She was girlish, Kopp recalled, pedaling her bike with the frenzy of a small child. One of Plath's professors remembered that she wore "charming, girlish clothes, the kind of clothes that made you look at the girl, not the garments, hair down to the shoulders still, but ever so neatly brushed and combed, and held back in place by a broad bandeau on the crown." Kopp called Sylvia's style " 'Ivy League College Girl': jumpers, turtlenecks, skirts, and pullovers, loafers."

As Kopp admits, she had a rather fraught friendship with Plath, who regarded the similarly educated Kopp as her double—no doubt a conceit heavily influenced not only by a reading of Dostoevsky, but also by Edgar Allen Poe's story, "William Wilson," in which the eponymous hero's double turns up at the most inconvenient times. Kopp did not quite fit that role, and she rejected this characterization of her when Edward Butscher interviewed her. But something odd was going on between these two women, since Kopp kept doing things that set Plath off. Some instances seemed inadvertent—like Kopp leaving a key in the lock on the inside of a shared Paris hotel room door, preventing Sylvia from entering and sleeping off a late-night jaunt. But others—like writing in Plath's books—seem, consciously or not, provocations of the fastidious Sylvia. The refrain of Kopp's reminiscence is that Sylvia took herself too seriously, an attitude that always seemed, for some reason, to surprise Kopp. In her journal Sylvia wrote admiringly of Kopp's humor, good looks, and magnetic personality. She saw the two of them in frankly competitive terms: "It is a mutual grabbing for queenship; both of us must be unique." The solution, said Sylvia— sounding like Elizabeth fending off Mary, Queen of Scots—was to keep separate and not "overlap in too many places."

Belonging to a theater club made all the difference in Sylvia's adjustment to Cambridge, since she developed an immediate rapport with cast and crewmembers and joined them for socializing. "I have simply been treated like a queen!" Sylvia wrote on 29 October, two days after her twenty-third birthday. She seemed delighted to have been cast as a mad poetess in an eighteenth-century farce, telling Mallory Wober it was the producer's "stroke of intuition." On the same day, in a letter to Olive Higgins Prouty, Sylvia presented a somewhat sober persona to her patron, reporting that her fingers turned blue in her ill-heated room, and that she was attending fifteen hours of lectures a week, as well as sessions with a tutor each morning. She was less prone to want immediate success, and more inclined to perfect herself and her work gradually.

By early November, Plath seemed content that a small Cambridge literary magazine had accepted two of her poems. She was beginning to regard her drama club activities as a drain and decided she would drop out if she did not win any major roles. The next term, she confided to Wober, she would forsake the "riproaring life & become a sedate femme du salon." She was also working out a schedule that permitted her to write two hours a day, no matter what. Waiting for the perfect time, she told Wober, meant you became "paralysed from lack of practice." Although she enjoyed her studies, she concluded that an academic career was not for her. It seemed too confining and pedantic and static—in other words, not a real world. She described the small number of women dons as spinster freaks, unappealing models for a young woman who wanted the world and a mate, too.

Sylvia seemed exhausted by the newness of her environs, where she was without any of her old friends. The frigid Cambridge climate took its toll, too—not to mention the starchy, soggy, sludgy food, so different from the appetizing meals at Smith. Homesick, she stocked her room with fruit. Sinus attacks signaled stress. In her journal she declared that the English winter might do her in.

Sylvia admitted to her mother that she missed Sassoon, now at the Sorbonne. He seemed more mature than the Cambridge men she met, although David Buck, whom she had just dated, had some of the aesthetic and worldly qualities she treasured in Richard. Her first letter to Sassoon on 22 November reads like a parody of his style, a baroque and curiously abstract poetic set piece describing artificial fires reflected in goblets of sherry. For all its "culture," Cambridge was also stuffy and insular. "In the beginning was the word and the word was Sassoon," she said. To Mallory Wober, she wrote an opaque letter on 23 November, referring to her penchant for adopting various personae and closing with the admonition, "Watch out for schizophrenic women." She was playing a whore in *Bartholomew Fair* and wrote a note to Wober on the 24th thanking him for coming to her performance. It made her feel like a prima donna, or at least a "glorified & sublime tart."

Now experiencing full-blown nostalgia for home, Sylvia thanked her mother profusely for a Christmas box packed with large hazelnut cookies. Cooking and homemaking, she wrote to Mrs. Prouty, mattered a "great deal." Plath was not a "career girl," a term that denoted a woman alone, deliberately forsaking married life. She was jettisoning her former prize student, award-winning, collegiate self, she told her benefactor. Away from home at Christmas for the first time in her life, she felt like a female Ulysses, "wandering between the scylla of big ben and the charybdis of the eiffel tower." She engaged in an orgy of letter writing—thirty messages in all—to the wonderful people she knew. Some received cards and short notes with drawings. This burst of correspondence made her feel thankful and gratified.

To Elinor Friedman Klein and others, Plath made Cambridge into a setting for her misadventures. She enjoyed creating a sensation and then describing the consequences to friends—as she did with a horseback riding exploit that had left her black and blue. Her mount, Sam, had forsaken the sedate pleasures of a country ride and plunged her into a busy Cambridge intersection. Plath reveled in the chaos that ensued: "I find myself hugging Sam's neck passionately. old women & children run screaming for doorways as we heave up onto sidewalk. such power: like the old gods of chance: I felt like one human, avenging thunderbolt," she wrote to Elinor Friedman Klein on 14 December. Sam eventually wearied of his romp and came to a full stop. Twice before, she had careened her way toward destruction: toppling down a ski slope and breaking her leg, then floundering in a spinning car as Warren skidded into an icy Northampton on the day of Sylvia's return to Smith after her suicide attempt. She would soon set off for a Christmas holiday in France and seemed fixated on the hazards of departures and arrivals.

Sylvia enjoyed Paris and Nice, writing detailed letters to Mallory Wober about her travels—although she did not mention spending much of her time in the company of Richard Sassoon. In her journal, she described traveling together with him in a train compartment, with the "good weight of Sassoon, sleeping fitfully, on my breast." Her mention of the train rocking on the rails intensifies the maternal image. This moment seems a reprieve from the striving, frantic nature of her ambition, which manifested as early as the sixth grade, when she mapped her imagination with an image of Marseille—now visible from her train window—set against the moon shining on the Mediterranean. Her journal explodes with colors—red for the earth, orange for the villas roofs, yellow and peach and aqua for the walls, and green palms juxtaposed with a "screaming blue sea." She had returned to childhood, to her sea-girl reveries.

At the end of this seemingly idyllic holiday, Richard confessed that he had been seeing someone else, a Swiss girl who wanted to marry him. He wanted to be free to continue seeing her and perhaps others. His abrupt announcement struck hard at Plath's *amour propre*. She wrote a twenty-five-page story about her French sojourn, which *The New Yorker* rejected in late February, and which Sylvia herself came to regard as "absurd and sentimental." But she did not quite give up on Sassoon, confessing to Aurelia that he was the only man she had ever "really loved." She often dressed in black now, she noted in her journal, which contained passages addressing her lost love as though he were dead. Richard had brought out "the highest" in her, she confessed to John, one of her Cambridge pursuers. Plenty of "nice boys" had wanted to marry her, but she was holding out for a man equal to all of her. Sassoon had come closest to her ideal, and yet she worried about his health and his depressive nature. He did not look like the kind of man that should attract her, but he did anyway, she admitted to her mother. In another mood, she supposed that she loved Richard for what she wanted to make of him, and not for himself. Richard's desertion led to a culminating wail in her journal: She wanted a husband, lover, father, and son "all at once." She hoped that Richard would again have need of her. She sent a note to Mallory Wober on 8 February begging off a date because she was in a ferocious mood and, like Garbo, wanted to be left alone.

Marriage seemed to preoccupy Plath's thoughts, and she kept writing to her mother that she was not a "career girl." She missed the depth of connection that family life fostered. Apparently still thinking of Sassoon, in her journal she wrote about her desire to fight for the man she wanted. She envisioned a life abroad on the Continent, near the "moving currents of people." Not even her grandmother's terminal cancer could draw Sylvia back to America, which she now regarded as a dead end. She was hoping for a renewal of her Fulbright, so that she would not have to sell matches in Moscow or make a fast buck on the Place Pigalle.

Expectations about the future and a summer on the Continent were just enough to keep Sylvia going during an otherwise dreary period in her social and creative life. She had sold a superficial piece about Cambridge to *The Christian Science Monitor* and continued sending her work to *The New Yorker,* but her poetry struck her as "glib." She admitted to her mother on 25 February that she had seen a psychiatrist, whose welcoming manner made it comfortable for her to discuss her past and feel some continuity with the state-side life she had left behind. She realized that in Newnham, her home college, she had no equivalent of the older women who had guided her at Smith. She called the female dons "bluestocking gro-tesques." Even worse, each college within Cambridge was a closed society, making it virtually impossible for Sylvia to find a mature mentor outside of Newnham, where women professors knew only a "second-hand" sort of life.

Aching for a way to break out of her midwinter slump, Sylvia wrote her mother on 25 February that she was about to attend a party to celebrate a new literary review representing a departure from the staid college publications, which seemed amateurish to her. The new journal, put together by a group of American and British students, had a bracing, astringent, and "taut" style that she admired. At the end of her 3 March letter, Sylvia mentioned meeting an ex-Cambridge poet at a wild party sponsored by *St. Botolph's Review.* She had written a poem about him and noted he was the first British man she could be "strong enough to be equal with." She doubted she would ever see him again. "Such is life," she concluded, as though believing this time she would not be able to make her imagination and reality coincide.

Sylvia arrived at the party already drunk but in good enough shape to remember and recite the work of Ted Hughes, the *St. Botolph's* poet she most admired. According to her journal, she en-tered the room with "brave ease." Jane Baltzell Kopp, Sylvia's dop-pelgänger, watched Sylvia arrive and thought she looked "young and uncertain, which was not characteristic." Jane was at the party because she had read Hughes's "savage poems, powerful and con-temporary in content," so different from the "mannered, blood-less, facile style of the other undergraduates." As Hughes himself wrote to his sister, Olwyn, he rejected the "meanness and deadness of almost all modern English verse." Jane wanted to get a good look at Ted Hughes but decided not to accost the brooding, appar-ently misanthropic man leaning against a wall. "He was large and

alarmingly powerful, both physically and in psychological presence." His dark expression had a malign impact on the party, Kopp
suggests. Writing to a friend, Hughes showed no sign of having
been unhappy. He had a hand in organizing the party at the Wom-
en's Union, picking a well-appointed room with church-like stained
windows, some of which had been smashed in the revelry.

Kopp adds a detail that helps explain why Plath focused on
Hughes. His work, Kopp reckons, "came very near to carrying off
the audacity of the almost-Renaissance rhetoric in which they were
written." When Plath arrived at Cambridge, she almost immediately
realized that although Smith had prepared her well in Chaucer and
Shakespeare, she did not have a good grasp of the sixteenth- and
seventeenth-century literature she was now expected to master. And
here was Hughes, so young and yet, in certain important respects,
already an adept.

Plath's mood is best gauged by analyzing her journal references
to the "satanic Luke": Lucas Myers, nearly as tall as Ted and, to Sylvia, the only one at the party who rivaled Hughes as a writer. She
danced first with Myers, who later remembered her red shoes and
her "flash" ("rare among Cambridge girls of the period," comments
Elaine Feinstein, Hughes's biographer). The day after the party,
Plath wrote it up in her journal, glowing with excitement. Jazzed
up by the music, she sighted her prey and described what she saw
with a surprising turn of phrase: "Then the worst happened . . ."
She meant the "big, dark" and "hunky" boy she had been asking
about. He had spotted her. They were shouting to one another
above the noise, and the first words Hughes heard from her were
from his own poetry. "You like?" Hughes asked as he backed her
into another room and sloshed some brandy into her glass. Then
he kissed her—"bang smash on the mouth," ripping her hair band
and earrings while barking, "I shall keep." The curt wording Plath
records in her journal sharpens the sense of Hughes's ability to cut
through the party palaver, the politenesses of Cambridge he was
known to flout. When he kissed her on the neck, she retaliated with
a long, hard bite on his cheek that drew a line of blood. Hughes
might as well have stepped right out of a Brontë novel. She could
not stop obsessing about him. She had already been told he was

the biggest seducer in Cambridge. Thoughts of Hughes were almost enough to drive away her longing for Richard Sassoon.

Two days later, Plath had completed "Pursuit," the poem dedicated to Ted Hughes that sets out in one astonishing burst of insight all Plath needed to know about the love of her life. The image
in the first line of a stalking panther immediately segues to a startling conclusion: "One day I'll have my death of him." If she
dreads this denouement, she also seems to welcome it like a gift—or
rather, she seems to relish her death as something that she will
take from him. The line acknowledges a bond, a mutuality, between predator and victim. In Plath's own mythology, death by
whatever means—even suicide—could be poetic, a kind of aesthetic
completion and thus a desirable, if grisly, denouement, as perfectly
consummated as in a Poe story. As she confided to her journal, she
picked up the poetic identities of characters who died and believed
in them "completely for a while. What they say is True." Already,
Hughes, whose poems would so often feature wild animals, appears to be a figure out of Blake's tyger poem, with fire running
through his hot network of veins.

The poem empathizes with the ravenous panther, whose fierce
joy in the consummation of appetite becomes aestheticized in
lines that revel in the "sweet . . . singeing fury of his fur." The
panther as lover is a common trope among literary lovers such as
H. G. Wells (Jaguar) and Rebecca West (Panther), the latter just
coming into her own when she met her older lover. The Wells-
West letters also consider ravishment a mutual hunt. In "Pursuit,"
the panther "keeps my speed," the beloved says, as she hurls her
heart to "halt his pace." The poem ends on a note of fear, after the
beloved realizes that the panther demands "a total sacrifice." As he
treads the stairs toward her bolted door, the overwhelming mood
is one of horror and arousal, the theme of her journal reports that
"the worst happened." The poem's concluding lines, however, echo
another journal entry: "I listen always for footsteps coming up the
stairs and hate them if they are not for me." To quote Edward
Butscher, the panther can be read as an "aspect of herself," and as
an example of Plath's "masochism," according to Anne Stevenson
and Elaine Feinstein. But the panther is "emphatically male, and

women are his victims," Ronald Hayman rejoins. To put it another way: No other man had it in him to excite such a vehement, all-encompassing response, and Plath seems to have intuited the triumph and tragedy of mating with such a man. That Hughes was not physically violent, according to Anne Stevenson, is beside the point. He had a violent imagination, and Plath divined that it was her misfortune to meet such a man even as she dreamed of him as her salvation. As critic Margarot Uroff points out, "It would be several years before Hughes himself would write of an animal as ravenous as her panther."

After several days of mooning about Ted Hughes—a fantastical figure Plath really believed would not materialize again—she resumed brooding about the real Richard Sassoon, the man who got away. She had earlier written a poem with him in mind that seems as prophetic as "Pursuit." In "Circus in Three Rings," included in her *Collected Poems,* Sassoon emerges as a mocking Mephistopheles, vanishing with "devilish ease" in smoke that sears the speaker's eyes. In her journal, Plath wrote to him: "Break your image and wrench it from me." The "demon of doom" in her poem and the Sassoon of her journal seemed to have a magical impact, a Prospero-like power to appear and disappear both in her imagination and in her life. She wanted him, once and for all, to say he was "unavailable" to her—or that he was willing to save her from death. Insistent on his talismanic force, she urged him, "kill your image." Otherwise, she remained "frozen in the land of the bronze dead."

Sassoon's side of this fraught liaison can never be fully explained so long as he remains one of the fugitive figures of Plath biography, eluding her chroniclers just as he evaded her. He sent a letter that gave her no hope, although she confessed in a letter sent to her mother on 9 March that he had rebuffed her because he was not ready to marry—certainly not before he had established himself in a profession and was prepared to create the home and family she craved. Still, she would not relent in her love, even after rehearsing all his faults and weaknesses. Richard's rejection affronted her pride and sense of prowess, her boast that her love could "melt doors," as she put it in her journal. She wrote him again, conceding his point that she had demanded something of him that he

could not give. But now it was Richard and Richard alone that she
would consecrate. She had decided to visit him on her spring
break, no matter what he said. She had to face him in France even
if he was absent—and just maybe she could get over him, since she
had also been in contact with Gordon Lameyer, who was coming
over to investigate the prospect of studying in Germany. Gradually, Sylvia reconstituted her queenship, writing in her journal on
the night of 6 March after a very long Shakespearean performance,
"Come my coach. Goodnight, goodnight."

In a mythological mood, Sylvia's next journal entry, on 8
March, mentions a discussion of D. H. Lawrence's "The Man Who
Died" in Dorothea Krook's lecture. As Krook read passages from
the fable, Sylvia felt a chill, as though the "angel had hauled me by
the hair in a shiver of gooseflesh: about the temple of Isis bereaved,
Isis in search," she wrote in her journal, quoting the very words of
Lawrence's story. She recalled visiting Venice, where Lawrence
died. She had a "mystic vision with Sassoon; I was the woman who
died." In Sassoon's presence she had been reborn, flaming into life,
experiencing the "resolute fury of existence." She believed she had
lived what Lawrence wrote. "It matters," she declared.

Lawrence brought back to Plath the consequences of her suicide
attempt and recovery, which she had earlier attempted to explore
in "Tongues of Stone," but had not fully worked out. In "The Man
Who Died," Christ's resurrection is presented as a near-death experience, a loss of consciousness that he welcomes: "He had wanted
to stay outside, in the place where even memory is stone dead."
Nauseated at his return to consciousness, he yearns for the "nullity
of being dead." Lawrence's description of Christ in his tomb, enclosed by narrow walls of rock penetrated by chinks of light that
he leans toward as he awakens, brings to mind those woozy moments in the crawl space when Plath moved and struck her head
against a wall or a rock.

Christ is "filled still with the sickness of unspeakable disillusion." But of course he is not Christ—not the Christian Christ, for
Lawrence never uses his name, preferring instead to call him
throughout "the man who died," which is to say a mortal who
chose death, as Sylvia did, because of a sense of disillusionment, a

void that nothing in life can supplant. The man rises without desire, experiencing the very same lack of desire that beset Sylvia in the first days of her recovery. So profound is this "desireless resoluteness," the man prefers it to any form of consciousness.

It may seem odd to say that Plath was elated to read this disturbing story, but apparently it addressed her own psychological problems in ontological terms. The man is weary of existence, not merely of what he has been able to make of it. What brings him back to life is first the light, and then his awareness of the sun, "falling into the hollows of his neck, and his thin, colourless arms utterly inert." Like the protagonist in "Tongues of Stone," he experiences no wish to return to the world, and yet the world keeps breaking in on him.

Repeated references to the sun that bathes the man in light call to mind the many references in Plath's writing to sunbathing, which brought out in her a sheer joy in existence. The man lies in the sun, and it makes him sway as he hears a bird cry out the "triumph of life." Life seems as resolute as was his wish to die. Lawrence connects this gradual revival in the man to the cry of a cock, which in turn is compared to the "short, sharp wave of life," the sea of feeling that elated Sylvia even as a child. The cock, like the man, is caught in the "cord of circumstance" (it has been hobbled by a rope), but it continues to crow and rock "in the tide of the swaying ocean of life."

The man attributes his slowly emerging sense of himself to Judas and the high priests who "saved me from my own salvation." In effect, Christ repudiates any sense of divinity he once claimed, now regarding himself as merely a man. Sylvia's own near death, as she would say after she met Ted Hughes, had been necessary in order to transform her into the woman who attracted him. Her painful experience had prepared her to go on. She had rejected the supposed salvation of her summer in New York, just as the man who died rejects "my own excessive salvation."

Yet it is precisely his desire to free himself from this "excessive need for salvation" that attracts the wandering man to the woman who tends the temple of Isis. Indeed, she looks upon him as the lost Osiris who can fecundate the goddess's womb. Plath identified with Isis in her attraction to the mangod, the Isis whom Lawrence describes as searching and grieving for her beloved in "tormented ecstasy." The Plath of the journals realizes at this point that she has discovered in Lawrence's text the very dynamic of life she has painstakingly reassembled out of the fragments of a woman who died. Lawrence's description of Isis finding her beloved bit by bit, "heart and head and limbs and body," is the equivalent of Plath's experience on all those dates and drives with Myron and Richard, Dick and Gordon—each assignation undertaken in search of another piece of the man who would make her whole. "For she was Isis of the subtle lotus, the womb which waits submerged and in bud, waits for the touch of that other inward sun that streams its rays from the loins of the male Osiris," Lawrence wrote. " 'The goddess is great,' " the man says to the lady who tends Isis's shrine. Sylvia was awaiting the man who would, in so many words, say the same to her. In Lawrence's version of rebirth, the man may see himself as an Osiris-candidate, so to speak, but what he experiences is the "greater day of the human consciousness." And it is that sense of speaking to and for the world that Plath treasured in the story Lawrence had to tell. Perhaps the most thrilling moment for Plath was that when the man felt "his own sun dawned, and sent its fire running along his limbs, so that his face shone unconsciously."

No wonder Krook's class seemed to galvanize Sylvia Plath. To her mother on 9 March, Sylvia wrote one of those patented sunshiny letters. She describes how the light came flooding through her windows into a room she especially treasured for its window seat, where she often perched writing poetry. Full of affection and enclosing two poems, including "Pursuit," Sylvia effervesced. She noted the Blakean, hypnotic quality of "Pursuit," emphasizing the "terrible beauty of death," the result of having lived fully and intensely. Although Hughes was the primary inspiration for "Pursuit," biographers have overlooked Plath's disclosure that she associated the fires of pain in that poem with Sassoon's furious soul, which had also ravished her. She did not mention Hughes in this letter to Aurelia, but perhaps she thought of him when she yearned for a man who could "overcome" Richard's image. Sounding very much like Marilyn Monroe, who would soon wed Arthur Miller, Plath called herself a princess awaiting her white knight, employing the same imagery Monroe used in sessions with her psychiatrist.

Writing to Elinor Friedman Klein, on that same day Sylvia compared Rhett Butler's *Gone with the Wind* rejection of Scarlett O'Hara ("Frankly, my dear, I don't give a damn!") to Sassoon's desire to make his fortune and to give Plath her freedom—just when she had readied herself to surrender to him! The tone of this letter— "You have got to listen to this, because I am full of it"—is reminiscent of a late-night dorm room confession, as Plath spills out her confession of how Sassoon has set her raving, writing a letter that rivals Scarlett's plea that Rhett not abandon her. Sassoon was even talking about enlisting in the army, just as Rhett had forsaken Scarlett to join the retreating Confederates. Sylvia explained to her dear Elly that she had asked Sassoon if they could have a spring together in France and Italy before he got himself killed. She even imagined, as she was imploring him to see her, that like Rhett, Sassoon had a mistress on the side. In return, she received a postcard from her "noble" lover saying he would someday reappear, "crashing out of the ether."

At this point, Sassoon was not so much a real man as an obsession, an image that could be replaced only by "some big, brilliant combination of all the men I have ever met . . ." Ted Hughes is not mentioned in this letter; apparently he still seemed unreal so long as her relationship with Sassoon remained unresolved. Richard still loved Sylvia, as he would later make clear, but he refused to act on the urgency of her need for him. The more she pressed, the more he resisted. Before 9 March, the Sylvia Plath of the journal raved about Richard's retreat, but the Sylvia Plath of the letter to Elly shows some of that self-mocking talent that critic Caroline King Barnard Hall has traced in the poetry, early and late (including "Circus in Three Rings"), that sends up Plath's imagination of disaster.

The letters to Elly and Aurelia signaled that Plath was pulling out of her obsessive-depressive state. She was looking forward to a visit from Gordon Lameyer. Her Fulbright, renewed for another year, would give her enough money to host Aurelia for a visit, and in Dorothea Krook she had at last found a brilliant, attractive supervisor whom she could match her wits against. Gary Haupt, a Fulbright student from Yale, was a huge source of comfort, "sweet, if pedantic." He had stood by her through the ordeal of an operation to remove a very painful cinder from her eye.

For once, Sylvia's journal and her letters seem to be working in tandem as, having minimized her academic commitments, she confidently plotted her life as a writer in Europe. She wanted to write a novel that would include a story of love, suicide, and recovery, with perhaps a collegiate setting and incorporating her letters to Sassoon. Singing as she rode her bike, in a display of renewed appetite she picked up four sandwiches.

At first, Sylvia did not realize that Ted Hughes was on her trail. Then, while biking on 10 March, she learned from a Cambridge friend that the previous night Hughes had tried to look her up, throwing stones at the wrong window. Hughes, a recent Cambridge graduate, visited often. But he had a day job in London as, in his words, a "shit-shoveller" for the J. Arthur Rank film studio. He read scripts all day to determine which ones might be adapted for the screen. At the news of his reappearance, a flustered Sylvia mumbled to her friend that Hughes should "drop by, or something," and rode off. Her nearly speechless excitement is evident in a journal entry that sputters: "He. O he." She repeated, "please let him come" like a "black marauder." Let him play Ulysses to her Penelope. She even quotes lines from "Pursuit" as she awaits being taken. She was dressing in violent, fierce colors and working herself up into a state that she compared to writing "Mad Girl's Love Song" and "Circus in Three Rings." Those poems reflect just how intense her apocalyptic inner world could be, conjuring images of catastrophe—of the worst happening, as she described her first sight of Hughes. She reveled in straining her emotions to the utmost, even as she realized that by imagining disaster she might also find a way to save herself. Unless brought to the brink, she would never know just how great she could become. The previous night she dreamed of herself as "Isis bereaved, Isis in search." She finds the suave "dark one" grinning behind a newspaper. The dark man turns out to be Richard Sassoon. Then another dark man, thinking she is a whore, accosts her in the street as she runs after Richard. Waking from her dream, Plath waited again for his tread on the stairs, all the while dreading what would become of her in Paris, since she was still determined to have one more showdown with Sassoon. She even imagined that without his protection she would be raped.

The next day Plath learned that Hughes and two other chaps had again thrown clods against the wrong window. She seemed fated never to meet him, and this time imagined herself as Blanche Dubois in *A Streetcar Name Desire,* becoming mired in the mud with drunken soldiers seeking her company. She thought of herself as a woman of the night whom Hughes and his cronies would not confront in daylight. She ached, though, to make him real, since he existed now simply as a figure of her imagination, a panther on the "forest fringes of hearsay."

On 18 March, Sylvia wrote her mother, "I'd be happiest writing, I think, with a vital husband." A good deal of her angst over Sassoon surely had to do with her rush to implement the next phase of her literary career: Husband, home, family, write. She would be all set, but not so Sassoon. That same day, Hughes wrote to his close friend, Lucas Myers, asking Myers to arrange for Sylvia to meet him in London.

On 21 March, as Sylvia was about to embark on her Easter vacation, she wrote a cheerful letter to Marcia Brown, omitting any reference to the drama with Sassoon and her first encounter with Hughes, except to say that she was on her way to London to meet "two erratic" poets. Lucas Myers, cousin of poet Allen Tate, she mentioned by name, but Hughes remained anonymous in this ebullient depiction of life at Cambridge, where world politics got debated and America now seemed so provincial that Sylvia dreaded her return, dreaming instead of spending a year writing in southern Europe. And yet, just a day earlier she had been dreaming of a home in the Connecticut Valley and summers on Cape Cod. This nostalgia was what her mother wanted to hear, but it was also what Sylvia wanted to write. America/Sassoon, Europe/Hughes—Sylvia seemed to be sidling in two very different directions.

On 23 March, on her way to France, Sylvia Plath ran up the stairs to Ted Hughes's grimy flat at 18 Rugby Street. Three days later in her Paris hotel, she noted their "sleepless holocaust night" in her journal. Even as she was preparing to beard Sassoon, she mentioned the marks Hughes had left on her "battered" face, including a purple bruise, and her raw and wounded neck. For his part, Hughes wrote her a short note, saying the memory of her smooth body went through him like brandy. He would be in London until 14 April, he informed her, and would see her there or come to her in Cambridge after her holiday in France.

But Sassoon, not Hughes, had Plath's full attention. At his apartment, prepared to deliver her plea, she learned from the concierge that Sassoon was gone and would not return until after Easter. Her journal describes a scene worthy of a weepie. Outside, an old beggar woman is singing in a "mournful monotone," while inside the radio blares, "Smile though your heart is breaking." Through her tears, Sylvia writes and writes a long disorganized missive, as she gazes at her unopened letters to Sassoon, "lying there blue and unread." The color of aerograms and her mood coalesce. In a reaction shot, a black poodle pats the disconsolate lover with a paw. A stunned Sylvia notes, "Never before had a man gone off to leave me to cry after." Gamely, she patted the poodle and set off wandering the Paris streets.

There is no indication that Plath was writing parody or sending herself up. Her self-dramatizing was real enough to her, but at the same time it bears all the marks of the popular romantic melodrama of her time, the kinds of films that starred Merle Oberon and Susan Hayworth in the late 1940s and early 1950s. Sassoon may well have debouched from the melodrama of her passion to avoid just this kind of scene.

Sylvia compounded her misery by imagining that Ted was regaling his Cambridge cronies with tales of his Plath conquest. One of his friends, Michael Boddy, had come upon her and Ted in the Rugby Street flat. Now the word would be out that she was Hughes's mistress, she imagined. Ted himself became an object of suspicion: In the height of their lovemaking he had called her Shirley, making Sylvia feel like one of his interchangeable lovers.

Plath's journal makes it seem as though Boddy had caught the couple in the act of love. But Boddy told Hughes's biographer that the two were simply sitting in chairs, leaning forward, whispering, and "virtually oblivious of me." After walking Plath to her hotel, Hughes returned to awaken Boddy, who recalled that his friend was deeply agitated in a way that Boddy had never witnessed before. Sylvia Plath, in fact, had made a profound impression upon Ted Hughes. Sylvia, however, was still very much immersed in her fantasy world. She took long walks through Paris streets and was accosted by men in much the way she imagined in her dreams, although she was not raped and decided to forego the risk of a chance sexual encounter. She might be mourning her loss of Sassoon, but she ate heartily and saw plenty of friends, including one from Cambridge, who seemed to grow more attractive hour-by-hour, until she had him in bed, only to be disappointed when he decided he better not—a result, she opined, of his too proper breeding and desire to be associated only with distinguished families.

Sylvia sent her mother a letter emphasizing the "gay side" of her Paris excursion. A journal fragment for 1 April 1956 refers to her "Sally Bowles act." Sounding also like the *Americaine* Doris Day, Sylvia loved her room in a small hotel that had accommodating people in charge. Her lovely little garret overlooked rooftops and gables and was crowned with an artist's skylight. The journal and the letters to Aurelia jibe in expressing Sylvia's newfound delight in being on her own without the male escorts she had always relied on. She gazed in shop windows and decided that as a wealthy woman she would indulge in a closet full of colored shoes, a rainbow array of princess opera pumps. Back in her room in the "blue wash of moonlight," she succumbed to crying once again over Sassoon. The next day, though, she recovered her spirits with a big lunch of onion soup, a chateaubriand rare, two glasses of wine, and an apple tart. Sylvia rarely did without dessert—or without fantasies of the "black marauder" who had "split into many men" lurking on stairs, streets, under beds, at her door, on a park bench. She seemed frustrated that Hughes had not pursued her to Paris in order to become the one palpable man, instead of the several that she had to conjure up. One night with him had not been enough.

Four days later, Sylvia met Gordon Lameyer in Paris for their trip to Germany. While not exciting, their reunion might be safe and soothing like her times with Gary Haupt, she thought, now that she and Gordon were just friends. Still, she resented the idea of looking forward to leaning on a man. She would have put off leaving Paris if Sassoon had suddenly appeared. She even thought of cutting short her trip and returning to London and Ted. Switching moods from one sentence to another, she monitored her own life the way another person obsessively checks a wristwatch. In yet another move, Sylvia dollied back for a panoramic shot: "It is the historic moment," she records in her journal entry for 5 April, "all gathers and bids me to be gone from Paris."

Sylvia's irritation with herself would be taken out on Lameyer, who began, even as a "friend," to give her a wide berth. In Edward Butscher's *The Woman and the Work,* Lameyer's remembers shying away from his erstwhile showboating almost-fiancé. Their time together was a fiasco. They quarreled incessantly.

On 9 April, Hughes sent Plath a note and a love poem, the latter containing an exquisite line about a bird gathering the world in its throat in one note. "Ridiculous to call it love," the poem began, but there it was. He felt haunted by the "true ghost of my loss." He awaited her arrival. A fragment of Plath's journal indicates her return to Ted Hughes on Friday, 13 April, expecting a welcome—if rough—ride as she submitted herself to his "ruthless force," which had stabbed her into accepting his "being." She seemed struggling still for some kind of perspective, since she enjoined herself not to forget others, like Dorothea Krook (who reminded her of Dr. Beuscher) and even the memory of Sassoon, who could be tender as well as virile. But Hughes had a sun-like energy that she decided to absorb for as long as their time together lasted.

It was not easy. Sylvia still craved what she called in her journal "older seasoned beings" who could advise her in a loving way. Her grandmother, dying of cancer, made Plath feel especially vulnerable and worried that her overtaxed mother, who suffered repeatedly from gastric ailments, would be so weakened that she, too, might die. Cut off from the "ritual of family love," Sylvia blamed Sassoon for the "hell" that seemed to overtake her suddenly, and seemingly without warning. She wrote a long letter to Warren reaffirming her love for him and more letters to her mother that counted on a visit from Aurelia soon.

Hughes's biographer believes that he had already decided to make Sylvia Plath a part of his life. He now dropped his plans to join his brother, Gerald, in Australia. In late April, the couple set off on long walks. He learned of her suicide attempt and quickly perceived, as he later wrote to his sister, Olwyn, that Sylvia's sometimes gushing and brash Americanism resulted from her eagerness to make a good impression. Indeed, in a journal fragment written on 1 April, she had exhorted herself to "be more subdued" and quiet. *"Don't blab too much."* In other words, "listen more." In sum, "be nice but *not too enthusiastic."*

Hughes's friends were baffled by his interest in Plath. They disliked her polished and engineered poetry, which was nothing like his vivid and vehement verse, and they deplored her forwardness. In *Crow Steered/Bergs Appeared,* Lucas Myers mentions telling Hughes that *Varsity,* a Cambridge magazine, had commissioned Sylvia to write about Paris, owing to the entertainment value of her florid style. Hughes appeared hurt and clearly wanted to spare Sylvia ridicule. Such comments made Ted want to take hold of Sylvia and protect her. Just as important, though, he valued her supportive and perceptive reading of his poetry. He was an amateur compared to her, especially with regard to the tectonics of the publishing world, but Sylvia had as much to learn from Hughes, whom she regarded then as the superior poet.

Ted quit his shit-shoveling job and hurried to Cambridge to be near Sylvia in order to imbibe exactly what his friends drew back from: all that American vibrancy. As he put it in a *Paris Review* interview, "She was not only herself, she was America and American literature in person." Sylvia's version of these first days with Ted is told mainly in letters to her mother and brother. She presented Hughes as one of the wonders of the world. She held back nothing from him, and their partnership resulted in some of her most forceful writing. That announcement alone, sent to Aurelia on 19 April, suggests how swiftly Sylvia Plath and Ted Hughes had aligned their stars to form a constellation out of reach of his friends or hers. Of course, she *made* Hughes huge, just as he *created* her.

If Hughes associated Sylvia with his discovery of a new world, she associated him with her sudden discovery of "all nature," as she put it in a 21 April letter to Aurelia. Sylvia enclosed "Ode To Ted," a portrait of man in nature, out crunching oat sprouts as he walks in woodland, naming creatures and splitting open the earth to reveal the habitats of moles and worms, even as birds seem to chorus his arrival. He moves through fen and farmland among grazing cows and onto a bed of ground where, "I lay for my love's pleasing." The poem refers to "this adam's woman," and an unembarrassed Sylvia invited Aurelia to visit the shining Eden her daughter had made for herself with Ted.

Eden included a thoroughly domesticated life. Ted taught Sylvia how to cook on the gas ring in her fireplace, bringing her shrimp that he helped her peel. When she received the terrible news of her grandmother's death, she and Ted "consecrated" their May Day to her memory. He seemed, in all things, at her disposal. He spent all afternoon on a couch reading her copy of *The Catcher in the Rye,* while she wrote up her thrilling meeting with Nicolai Bulganin, the Russian premier, at a reception that *Varsity* reporters attended (*The New Yorker* rejected her report, and then the *Smith Alumnae Quarterly* published it in the fall of 1956). The couple planned to spend a summer in Spain, during which she would begin her novel about Cambridge while writing short stories for *The New Yorker* and *Mademoiselle.* On 4 May, Sylvia mentioned marriage to Ted for the first time in a letter to her mother. By 9 May, Sylvia was proposing a trip home the following year to give Ted his coming-out party, a barbecue in Wellesley. Sylvia believed that her stay in McLean Hospital had prepared her for this new life. All she had suffered was building toward this denouement with Ted. He was her reward for waiting. She wrote her mother in tones that suggested she had settled down for good. She was at peace. He had become her life's work. She predicted greatness for both of them.

On 22 May, Ted wrote Olwyn that both his life and work were "peaking" in the company of a "first-rate American poetess" he wanted his sister to meet. This American believed that his work was as good as he thought it was. She knew the top American journals and was busily sending his work to them. But he did not mention just how close they had become or that they were planning to marry.

Sylvia's sessions with Professor Krook had been so brilliant, Sylvia told Aurelia, that Krook was revising her student's lecture notes on Plato. Sylvia described their sessions as fierce and thoroughly enjoyable arguments, suggesting she was putting nearly as much energy into her time with Krook as she was into her relationship with Ted. Wendy Campbell, a friend of Krook, sat in on Plath's sessions with Krook and saw Sylvia at her best: brilliant and charming, "so alive and warm and interested." Campbell's memoir leaves an indelible impression of Plath, one that no photograph has ever quite captured: "She seemed to be entirely collected and concentrated and in focus . . . Tall and slender and delicate wristed, she had pale honey hair, fine, thick, and long, and beautiful dark brown eyes. And her skin was pale gold and waxy, the same even colour." Campbell observed that Sylvia and Ted "seemed to have found solid ground in each other." She found their company heartening. She felt "understood and received," which meant a good deal, since she found the conventional expressions of sympathy after her husband's death nearly unbearable. But Sylvia and Ted had a "spontaneous empathy with my state of mind which was very liberating to me."

In a visit to Cambridge, Mary Ellen Chase, one of Sylvia's mentors, strongly hinted that there might be a position open at Smith. Plath began considering the possibility of a teaching post, although she would not accept it without a husband to accompany her. She did not want to be another one of those spinster professors with no real role in the social life of the campus and community. It may have been Chase's visit that galvanized Plath into moving up the marriage date, even though a letter from Olive Higgins Prouty advised Sylvia to slow down.

In early June, Sylvia's patron wrote a sobering letter, treating Sylvia's over-the-moon description of Ted as a sign of infatuation with a new love. Ted sounded too much like Sylvia's poet-hero,

Dylan Thomas, Prouty pointed out. She was not merely skeptical, as Sylvia suspected she would be. Prouty was downright dismissive of Ted as a potential husband and father. She predicted he would be unfaithful. Would Sylvia be able to tolerate his love affairs, as Thomas's wife had tolerated her husband's? Sylvia's obsession with Thomas had been upsetting to the levelheaded Gordon Lameyer, who was distrustful of the poet's flamboyance and Sylvia's defense of him. Now Prouty detected a similar recklessness in Sylvia, which the older woman attempted to restrain. After all, Prouty was exactly what Sylvia supposed she wanted: an older advisor to steer her past the pitfalls. Prouty astutely fastened on the distressing words Plath used to praise Ted. "You don't really believe, do you, that the characteristics which you describe as 'bashing people around,' unkindness and I think you said cruelty, can be permanently changed in a man of 26?" Wasn't Sylvia just going through another round in her perpetual building up of the men she loved? This was a warning that Sylvia chose to ignore as she wrote letters to her mother designed to cast Ted as the kind of overpowering man Aurelia herself had submitted to. The letters Sylvia wrote to her mother in May seem like briefs for Ted, overwhelming accumulations of superlatives that would make it virtually impossible for Aurelia to do anything other than support her daughter's choice.

But did Sylvia have misgivings? On 4 June, Jane Anderson, having received a warm invitation in March from Sylvia to visit Cambridge, arrived to behold a very "pressured" Plath. Anderson later recalled in a sworn deposition (she was suing Ted Hughes because of a character in the movie version of *The Bell Jar* based on her) that Sylvia confessed she was in love with a poet who was also a "very sadistic man." Although Sylvia was concerned about Ted's relationships with other women and his sadism, she believed, "I can manage that." To Anderson, Plath appeared to remain anxious over her decision. And Anderson did not know what response to make: to second Sylvia's decision or to ask her to reconsider it? So Anderson just listened. After a brief tour of Cambridge, the two women parted, leaving Anderson with the impression that Plath, still under considerable tension, was relieved to see her go. They never communicated again. Anderson interpreted the caricature of her as Joan Gilling in *The Bell Jar* as revenge for her lack of a response to Plath's momentous plans.

On 13 June, an enraptured couple welcomed Aurelia to London, and at dinner that night they broke the news that they wished to marry immediately. In person, Hughes seemed to be the superman Plath had portrayed with an almost comic book flourish in her correspondence. Tall, dark-featured, and powerfully built, he also seemed in the presence of these two adoring women a gentle giant who had swept down on Sylvia like a god, an Osiris to her Isis. For all his strength, he seemed—then—a pliable consort. He had apparently forsaken the rather dissolute life Sylvia had earlier imagined for him in her journal, and he seemed to have become thoroughly domesticated. He had opened his heart to Sylvia and identified with her dreams and ambitions as no other man had done. Richard Sassoon had thwarted her, Gordon Lameyer had quarreled with her, Eddie Cohen had questioned her, and Myron Klotz and all the rest had let her down by failing to set the bold course of a writing life that Ted now held out to her. All those men were dead to her—or rather pieces of them, like the pieces of Osiris, had now been reconstructed into the stalwart and scintillating figure of Ted Hughes.

Even with Aurelia's predilection for powerful men, it is still somewhat surprising that she took so quickly to Ted Hughes, whom her daughter had known for just a few months. To be sure, it would have been devastating to deny Sylvia her joy of Ted, especially when the couple put their plans to Aurelia in person. That they had done so, rather than simply announcing their decision in a letter, probably carried weight with Aurelia, who had, in effect, been summoned by this royal couple. She was the queen mother, who would accompany them on the first phase of their European honeymoon and then proceed to visit the sites of her own mother's early years in Austria.

But didn't Aurelia wonder whether Sylvia was rushing into a momentous undertaking? Aurelia was never able to tell in print the full story of what she thought of Ted Hughes. Wanting to remain a part of her grandchildrens' lives, she feared alienating their father. He held the copyright to Sylvia's letters, which meant that in order to publish *Letters Home,* Aurelia had to secure his permission. As a result, she scrupulously avoided direct comments on Ted and his marriage to her daughter. But even in private, according to Aurelia's friend, Richard Larschan, she maintained a deep respect for Ted and a sober awareness that her daughter's troubled psyche had contributed to the couple's breakup.

In *Letters Home,* Aurelia introduces her daughter's precipitous behavior with a sweeping sentence: "To my complete surprise, three days after landing at Southampton on June 13, 1956, I found myself the sole family attendant at Sylvia's and Ted's secret wedding in the Church of St. George the Martyr, London." Why secret? Sylvia thought that by openly announcing her marriage to Ted she might forfeit her Fulbright scholarship, since she assumed the award was meant for single students. Why surprise? After all, Sylvia had talked up marriage in letters to her mother. But initially the marriage was to have been put off until Sylvia completed her studies, when she would have the opportunity to return home and present her noble man. Now, however, Aurelia had been invited to join in their intrigue, just as Sylvia had always shared with her mother notes and reports about her gentlemen callers and their relative merits and deficiencies. Now, Aurelia was part of her daughter's conspiracy, one that not even Ted's parents knew about. And Ted played his own part very well, confiding in Aurelia his concerns about having to teach in order to generate an income. Aurelia had been doing that much of her life, and she candidly told him that sometimes she felt like no more than a jailer.

Why Hughes did not inform his parents or Olwyn, in whom he was wont to confide, has been a puzzle for biographers. Was his sudden involvement with an American student so overwhelming that he wanted more time to figure out what to say? His first letters to Olwyn sound like those of a younger brother with a lot of explaining to do. No one—certainly not Ted's Cambridge cronies—ever expected him to become a conventional husband, let alone marry an American who seemed to have such a different sensibility from his own. Lucas Myers, profoundly skeptical of Sylvia, saw the secrecy about the marriage as a way for Plath to take complete control, making sure no one could come between her and Hughes. Ted let Sylvia take charge and seemed at no point resistant—even to the idea of setting off on a honeymoon with his mother-in-law. How better to demonstrate his biddable side than to ease himself into Sylvia's energetic arrangements? This passive side of Hughes (if the couple had any quarrels before their marriage, neither of them vouchsafed as much to others) permitted, indeed encouraged Plath to project an idealized picture of their marriage.

Two days after the marriage, Sylvia wrote to Warren, presenting her union with Hughes as a predictable result of their three months of togetherness, reading and hiking and cooking and writing, side by side. Aurelia had endorsed her daughter's commitment, and Ted already loved and cared for Aurelia "very much," said Sylvia, who later told Marcia Brown that her mother behaved "like a young girl—taking pictures, drinking wine etc." To Warren, Sylvia presented the secret marriage as a necessity. She seemed to revel in the exclusivity of this match: The couple kept to themselves and liked it that way, she wrote her mother on 4 July, shortly after Aurelia had said good-bye to the newlyweds in Paris.

From Madrid on 7 July, Sylvia wrote a letter to Aurelia describing her procession through Europe with Ted as a kind of royal tour: "Wherever Ted and I go people seem to love us." Working people were drawn to this unaffected couple in a landscape of bold colors and brightness. For the first time in her life, Sylvia felt her sinuses clear. Like Rebecca West in Yugoslavia, Plath claimed to find a paradise in which she was no longer clogged with the factitious burdens of Anglo-American modernity.

On the same day, Ted wrote to his brother in Australia, once and for all renouncing his dream of starting life anew there. It was not the right country in which to develop his writing. Neither was England. Like Plath, Hughes believed Spain had set him free. In the company of an "American poetess" (he seemed to use the word as though describing a princess), he was writing better than ever and more continuously. Sylvia astutely analyzed his work, he reported, and found the faults that he had not yet been prepared to acknowledge. In fact, as part of the Plath program of submissions, he had been successfully published in *Poetry* and *The Nation*.

Sylvia continued to write her mother about a fairy-tale honey-moon in Benidorm, a sparkling Spanish coastal town beside the blazing blue Mediterranean Sea. Sylvia was delighted with their quarters in a house even closer to the sea than Grammy's place in Winthrop. They had a balcony terrace overlooking a seascape that stimulated Sylvia's sketching and writing. Ted was working on ani-mal fables, while Sylvia plotted stories about Americans abroad that she hoped to place with women's magazines. The same day (14 July) she wrote to Warren, describing Ted as the "male counter-part" of herself.

In her journal, Sylvia luxuriated in descriptions of the living room they had "consecrated" to their writing. They built their days around composing stories and poems, Ted working on a big oak table and Sylvia on a typing stand. They went out early to shop, she reported to Eleanor Friedman Klein, and in the peasant market picked out live rabbits that they were obliged to slaughter for dinner. Sylvia and Ted then returned home to write for the rest of the morning, breaking for lunch and a siesta, then a swim and two hours of writing in the late afternoon, followed by a few hours of reading before bed. Travel, adventure, and romance—her life had turned into a movie, Sylvia wrote her mother.

Still involved in Sylvia's intrigue, Ted wrote his parents after the couple arrived in Benidorm that he intended to marry Sylvia and would do so by the time he visited them in September. He swore them to secrecy, mentioned Sylvia's concerns about losing her scholarship if the truth were known. As he later made clear to Ol-wyn, they needed the scholarship money to live on. He had al-ready signed on to Sylvia's plan to spend a year teaching in America, followed by a return to Europe. His parents should not worry, he added, because not only was Sylvia a good cook, she was great with money and a better earner than he was. He had met and liked her mother.

Ted devoted most of a long letter to his parents to describing a bullfight the young couple had seen in Madrid. It was a sorry affair that nevertheless commanded his full attention. Hughes's fascina-tion with the violent ceremonial aspects of this gruesome contest overshadowed any repugnance he may have expressed to Sylvia, although the forthrightness of the unflinching description he gave his parents compels disgust. His analytical, even cold comment on the entire episode is simply an expression of surprise at the bull's ability to adapt to the duel, although in the end the beast died, drained of its blood.

Sylvia had sickened at the sorry spectacle, and in "The Goring" evokes the rather sordid atmosphere of the truculent crowd, the picador's awkward stabbing and artless, unwieldy maneuvers. Only in the final moments of the deadly duet between bullfighter and bull did the grim ritual take on the look of a kind of ceremonious art redeeming the "sullied air." The poem's restrained tone disguises how ill at ease Sylvia was in Spain. To her mother she wrote about the "horrid picador" and the messy slaughter. Although she tells Aurelia that Ted shared her feelings, her language reveals a markedly different sensibility. Hughes would later write a poem, entitled "You Hated Spain," about her reaction. As his biographer Elaine Feinstein observes, Ted was at home with the primitive side of Spain, whereas the sort of blood consciousness that had thrilled Sylvia in D. H. Lawrence's writing repulsed her in person.

The idyllic aerie by the sea gradually became a battleground between the landlord and a wary, cagey Sylvia trying to outmaneuver this witch-like presence, who kept barging in to lecture her renter about how to operate the freakish petrol stove, and against taking interruptions of electrical power and running water "too seriously." "That Widow Mangada" provides a virtually verbatim version of Sylvia's journal entries, which recorded her growing disillusionment with her Spanish heaven.

That Sylvia ignored or did not appreciate Ted's different take on the bullfight suggests some of her exultant happiness was a rather forced affair. This, at least, was Richard Sassoon's conclusion after he received a letter announcing her marriage to Hughes. Sounding rather like Eddie Cohen, the reserved Sassoon replied that he saw no reason why Sylvia should not be as happy, or happier, with Hughes than she had been with him—except that what she had written did not appear to him to be the letter of a "happy woman. At least, not to me, and as you know me extremely well and are a good letter writer I may accept my reactions as feasible." The sinu-

osity of his prose reflects how fraught and convoluted their relationship had become, but also, perhaps, how conflicted and
unresolved Sylvia's feelings really were, in spite of her protestations
to the contrary. He did not doubt he deserved her harshness. But
she was "woman enough to know that I—above all I—am not one
who needs to be blamed. . . . Long before I was your *bien aimé,* I was
something else to you, and I think always I was somewhat more
than a paramour, always. . . . You tell me that I am to know that
you are doing what is best for you; it is so if you believe it, Sylvia,
and if it is so—then it is—'very simply' it. Even though I might wish
it otherwise . . ." And so Sassoon exited, refusing to allow himself
to be wrapped up in her version of their affaire de coeur.

A mysterious passage in Plath's journal for 23 July, written after
an encounter with Hughes that left her dreading the "wrongness
growing, creeping, choking the house," hints at the twisted nature
of her affections, which Sassoon had detected. She could suddenly
turn a personal disappointment into a cosmic sense of disenchant-
ment, declaring that the "world has grown crooked and sour as a
lemon overnight." Her estrangement, moreover, was not resolved
but merely dispelled by a visit from Marcia Brown and her husband, Mike, and by delightful exchanges with a group of Spanish
soldiers on a train to Madrid, as they learn to drink wine from a
leather flask.

On 25 August, approaching the end of their summer sojourn,
Sylvia and Ted met up with Warren in Paris, a rendezvous that Sylvia did not say much about. Warren had spent a summer in Austria
and was returning to the States for his final year at Harvard. Sylvia
and Ted were on their way to visit his family in what Sylvia referred to as their *Wuthering Heights* home. For all her rapturous
references to Spain and plans to write about it, the results were
meager. Except for "That Widow Mangada," a handful of poems
and stories that are unremarkable, and notes in her journal, she
produced only a bland travelogue sort of article that was published
in *The Christian Science Monitor.*

On 2 September, Sylvia wrote to her mother about her stay at
the Yorkshire home of Ted's family. As she put it, she was now part
of the "Brontë clan." Her journal reveals that this was more than a

casual allusion for a writer who immersed herself in literary lives so that she could live one. The bare hills, black stone walls, wicked northern winds, and coal fires that she describes in her letter evoke the atmosphere of *Wuthering Heights,* with Sylvia cast as the interloper entering the mysterious, ineffable world that perplexes and frightens Mr. Lockwood. She climbed the wild and lonely moors, just as Catherine and Heathcliff had. Did she recall the Hollywood version of *Wuthering Heights* (1939), with its iconic shot of Laurence Olivier and Merle Oberon huddled together on a hill rise, two passionate souls bound to one another, yet doomed to part?

In her 2 September letter, Sylvia continues in her guise as Mr. Lockwood, calling Ted's parents, William and Edith, "dear, simple Yorkshire folk." She loved them both. They liked her. Nothing untoward had happened yet. William, judging by what his son said about him, would have been quiet, even subdued. He had gone through the trauma of the trenches of World War I and now owned a tobacconist's shop. Edith, as portrayed by other Plath biographers, had a deep interest in magic and the occult—although Olwyn later chided Diane Middlebrook for saying so. (Actually, Ted's fascination with astrology and necromancy far outstripped anything his mother could possibly have known or cared to impart to her son.) She was quite conventional and genuinely appreciated Sylvia, who obviously relished the domestic side of life and brought with her a high-spirited and romantic embrace of the land.

Sylvia would soon be returning for her second and final year at Cambridge. Ted would go to London, where his reading of poetry for the BBC was successful and remunerative (they had spent nearly all their money in Spain). Hughes had one of the finest voices in modern poetry. He believed that only part of the brain registered the impact of poetry when it was not read aloud. He often read Shakespeare to Plath and encouraged her to spend part of her day reciting poetry. Her own recorded voice grew in authority and power, as did her awareness of audience, and for that Hughes deserves considerable credit.

Sylvia prepared to write a novel based on her Cambridge experiences. She and Ted were hoping to get teaching positions for a year, and perhaps do a reading tour as well when Sylvia brought Ted home to America. Her hopes were high. *The Atlantic Monthly* had bought "Pursuit" for fifty dollars. More good news followed on 2 October, when *Poetry* accepted six of her poems for another seventy-six dollars. And Peter Davison, now at *The Atlantic Monthly,* was encouraging her to submit more of her work. She wrote him a long letter explaining her plans for a novel, as well as touting Ted's poetry. He gratified her with a quick response that included his wish to see Hughes's work.

In her 2 October letter to Aurelia, Sylvia made a point of saying that she and Ted were not part of an "arty world," and that all they needed was one another. But the very sense of their uniqueness also put pressure on her. Thinking she had missed a rendezvous with Ted in London, she panicked and gave way to a "fury of tears," she told Aurelia. Although he turned up soon enough, Sylvia's extreme reaction showed how much he meant to the equilibrium of her everyday life.

Ted was well aware of Sylvia's investment in him, and from London, where he often stayed overnight or longer when employed by the BBC, he reinforced their bond with frequent affectionate and encouraging letters, as well as expressions of anxiety that jibed with her own moods. On 1 October, he wrote about how restless he felt without her. He wandered about like "somebody with a half-completed brain-operation." He enjoined her to "keep watch" on their marriage as he was doing, saying that way their happiness would be preserved. He had nicknames for her ("Puss-Kish-Ponky," for example) that served to intensify their intimacy and exclusivity. Anticipating a rendezvous with Sylvia, Ted announced that he would kiss her "into blisters." The man who had cared nothing about clothes, and was known to stuff newly caught fish in his jacket pockets, extolled a suit Sylvia had bought for him, saying he could now descend on London "sleek, sleek, sleek."

A day later Ted wrote about how he missed Sylvia's "ponky warmth." He sent her plots that she might use for her fiction. One involved a young newly married couple that set off for the country to avoid the distractions and complications of urban life. "They want to keep each other for themselves alone and away from temptation," Ted wrote, without a sign that he was basing this story line on their own lives. In an eerily prophetic twist, Hughes has friends of the couple visit and urge them, so good at entertaining, to open an inn. Although the inn is successful, the upshot of their venture is that they have brought the city, so to speak, back into their lives. Even worse, the wife turns jealous and suspects the husband's involvement with an old girlfriend. The story has a happy ending, in that the couple sells the hotel and buys another cottage closer to the city, reflecting their awareness that they cannot entirely escape modernity, but they can work on keeping their marriage solid. Hughes called it a "rotten plot," but was that all it was? "Can you pick any sense out of that?" he asked Sylvia. Was the question directed toward the meaning of the story, or the meaning of their lives? At any rate, Hughes was happy to say in a later letter that he was glad she liked the "inn-plot."

In "The Wishing Box," a story about the woman who is envious of her husband's fertile imagination as expressed in his dreams, Plath may have been articulating her concern that at this point Hughes seemed way ahead of her as a writer. At least that is one way—the Edward Butscher way—of looking at Sylvia's response to Ted's teeming creativity, so fecund that he was sending his newborn ideas to a half-grateful, half-resentful collaborator. Sylvia's letters, though, not only do not begrudge him, they positively exult in his productivity.

Hughes certainly gave Plath no reason to doubt her desirability. Hughes bid her good night, thinking of Puss's "little soft places" and how he wanted to kiss her "slowly from toe up," sucking and nibbling and licking her "all night long." Missing her, he felt like an amputee, dazed and shocked, because he had lost half of himself. Sometimes he just baldly broke out with: "I love you I love you I love you." Only her "terrific letters" comforted him. If more than a few days went by and Ted had not heard from Sylvia, he grew uneasy: "No letter from my ponk. Is she dead? Has half the world dropped off?" He imagined the desirable Sylvia welcoming the charms of knaves, while he sat staring at the skyline "like an old stone." Unable to work, he consoled himself by reading Yeats aloud.

In his letters, Hughes predicted greatness for Sylvia, just as she had for him. Without her, he wrote on 5 October, he could not sleep and was wasting his time. He walked about like a strange beast, and had even been stopped by the police because he looked like a suspicious character. Somehow, he wrote Sylvia, they had to turn all their "lacks" into good poems. He advised her on studying for exams at Cambridge, sensibly saying, for example, that the six books on Chaucer she had to read each contained some value but they surely overlapped, and there was no need to give them more than a note or two for each chapter she read. Similarly, he critiqued her poetry, offering straightforward advice—one professional to another—and praise. "Your verse never goes 'soft' like other women's," he wrote on 22 October, although he seemed to worry a bit that she might be searching for a formula that magazines like *The New Yorker* followed. But he wondered if such a formula existed. How to account for Eudora Welty or J. D. Salinger, two originals quite dissimilar, and yet both published in *The New Yorker*. If she wrote about what really attracted her, she could not miss, Ted told Sylvia. Like Plath, Hughes seemed to take rejections in stride, saying that at least *The New Yorker* might remember his name, even if they rejected his animal fables.

To Olwyn that October, Hughes touted Sylvia's successful publications in *The Atlantic Monthly* and *Poetry*. She was not a "blah American." Indeed, she was very like an indefatigable German, without affectations, and had a "startling poetic gift." He plotted her horoscope, which he drew in the letter for Olwyn's benefit. He was now showing Plath's poems to his contacts at the BBC. Ted clung to Sylvia as a renewing force, even as he spurned London, calling it "murderous," a ghost of itself, and so depleted that it had no "aura" left. It seemed utterly exhausted, he wrote to her on 23 October.

In late October, in a near state of collapse because Ted spent so much time in London that they could not live as husband and wife, Sylvia confessed her secret to Dorothea Krook, who rightly predicted that if Plath consulted the Fulbright advisor on campus and the Fulbright committee in London and made a full and contrite confession of her marriage, she would be allowed to keep her scholarship. And it was so. An elated Sylvia told Krook that no criticism whatsoever had been forthcoming; indeed, she had been congratulated on her marriage. But Krook, who still did not feel she knew her student that well, felt a twinge of concern because Sylvia seemed to depend on her marriage for so much of her own well-being. "I am living for Ted," Sylvia had written her mother on 22 October. In "Epitaph for Fire and Flower," a poem she enclosed in a letter to Aurelia, one line says it all: The lovers have a "touch" that will "kindle angels' envy." Well, not quite all, since the concluding lines evoke the "ardent look" that "Blackens flesh to bone and devours them."

By early November Ted had found a job near Cambridge teaching secondary school students, and the couple moved into a flat only five minutes from Newnham. He did not like Cambridge very much, and certain of his professors there apparently felt the same about him. The dons regarded Ted as a rather louche character and seemed surprised that the cheerful and well-scrubbed Sylvia would be attached to such a ruffian. Residing in Cambridge indicated that he was doing everything possible to allay Plath's easily aroused anxieties. They played out their evenings with tarot cards.

The Suez crisis and Britain's ill-fated invasion of Egypt after Nasser nationalized the Suez Canal brought out Plath's innate disgust with militarism and materialism. Even more importantly, her reaction reflects a sensibility that rejected narrow nationalism. She viewed politics as she did poetry, in cosmic terms. That Britain was in league with France and Israel only demonstrated to her that the world was out of joint. She cared nothing for the British Empire, for face-saving measures, for the niceties and duplicities of diplomatic negotiations. She did praise Hugh Gaitskill, leader of the Labour Party, for eloquently opposing the invasion, but she really had no interest in political parties as such. She was the same person who had written to Hans about world peace. It made her feel no better that her country held nuclear superiority. Other British policies on Cyprus and the emerging African states were no better, and she hoped America would put pressure on her ally to withdraw from Suez. She now regarded her own land as the proper place for her and Ted. Britain was dead. In a rare chauvinist moment, she declared to her mother on 1 November, "God Bless America!" Six days later she wrote again to say she was sickened at the news of the Soviet Union's invasion of Hungary. She continued to reiterate her opposition to all war, saying she hoped Warren would become a conscientious objector.

Sooty old England had become a drag, and Sylvia primed Ted with pictures of a sumptuous summer on Cape Cod. She had also set him up for a poetry contest sponsored by *Harper's* and adjudicated by Stephen Spender, W. H. Auden, and Marianne Moore. Winning the prize and publication of his first book would be the making of Ted Hughes in America and Britain. He wrote his friend Lucas Myers on 16 November about the contest, expressing "small hopes" for his success, although he was obviously a writer who thought of himself as in the running. He and Sylvia tried to work out their future on a Ouija board, with mixed results. Strenuous efforts on their part put them in contact with a spirit, who rightly predicted which magazines would accept their work. But relying on the Ouija board to predict the winners of football pools did not yield the fortune they anticipated.

Sometime in late November, Sylvia Plath had her first encounter with Olwyn Hughes, who visited her shortly before Sylvia relinquished her Cambridge room for the flat she would share with Ted. Olwyn was then twenty-eight, tall and strikingly "handsome," to borrow Elaine Feinstein's word. Olwyn had served in various secretarial positions in Paris and may have struck her sister-in-law as the very type of career woman Sylvia abjured. The confident Olwyn, single and with a hearty laugh, seemed utterly self-contained and without a permanent male companion. Olwyn found Sylvia to be somewhat reserved. But, according to Anne Stevenson, nothing much happened in this first meeting that would have given either woman pause.

On 15 December, Sylvia wrote to Marcia Brown to tell her all about the magnificent Ted, a "roaring hulking Yorkshireman." As usual, she described him as "looming" and ferocious. This time, though, she also associated Ted with the "sound of hurricanes," a neat way to absorb him into her earliest memories of a mythological life by the sea. She positively reveled in reporting that she could not boss him around, declaring he'd bash her head in if she tried. Even when she discussed his teaching, she said he terrified his pupils into admiration. She described Ted as "staunchly British," but she hoped he might consider settling in America, since Britain was a country that had no future.

Sylvia now believed she had overcome her demons. When Aurelia wrote at the end of the year about a young man in a suicidal state, Sylvia replied on 29 December with a heartfelt description of her own six-month ordeal, when she could not bear to read or write and detested the optimism of her doctors. Sylvia wanted her mother to tell him about Sylvia's case and what Aurelia had said to her at the time: that it was most important to open yourself to life, to be easy on yourself, to get out in nature, and to see that you are valued for yourself, not for your achievements. Tell him, she urged Aurelia, that Sylvia had thought her case was hopeless, but she had nonetheless recovered. But, she warned, do not minimize what he feels; agree with him even if he thinks his plight is dire, she reiterated. She wanted her mother to give him as much time as she could afford. "Adopt him for my sake (as the Cantors did me)" and make no demands, Sylvia instructed.

In end-of-the-year letters to Aurelia and Warren, Ted mentioned that he was encouraging Sylvia to get started on that novel she kept announcing. She was pouring a good deal of energy into her cooking, he noted. The film *Sylvia* suggests meal preparation and baking were the diversions of a blocked writer. And it is true that over the next year Sylvia would produce relatively little prose or verse. But her energies had to go somewhere, and it is hard to see how forcing the novel at this point would have done her much good. She needed more time to work out a major project than was available while studying for her courses; her interrupted writing routine induced considerable anxiety and even depression.

Sylvia began 1957 by adhering to her two-hour-a-day writing regimen, beginning at 6:00 a.m., before Ted went off to teach at a nearby secondary school. At his urging, she memorized a poem a day while working on love stories for women's magazines. She also typed some of Ted's work and assembled poems she planned to submit to the Yale Younger Poets series. For the first time, in a letter to Aurelia on 9 January, Sylvia mentioned "violent disagreements" with Ted, but she assured her mother that he was kind and loving and so good about bringing discipline to her work. Ted resisted the idea of teaching on a permanent basis, as some poets were now doing, securing sinecures that would, in his view, stifle creativity. Writing came first. He taught, temporarily, to earn an income. Sylvia sounded less sure about renouncing an academic career, confiding to her mother on 19 January that she would not argue with her husband about it, mainly because she had such confidence in his future.

On 21 January, Ted wrote to Aurelia and Warren to thank them for Christmas presents and to extol Sylvia's poetry—especially the cumulative power of the poems in the book she was putting together. Evidently he really did terrify his pupils into submission, since he mentions beating their heads for their "insolence." Terror tactics, even rages, got the attention of boys who actually had good hearts, Ted insisted, although he seemed less confident of his methods than Sylvia had suggested. He thought he lacked authority and behaved more like an older brother than the father figure they needed. Teaching these recalcitrant lads was a sobering experience, he admitted, evincing none of the all-conquering hero aspect Sylvia liked to tout.

Teaching at Smith for a year was no sure thing, but Mary Ellen Chase's visit to Cambridge buoyed Plath, who had thought that without a PhD she would get nowhere, judging by the first responses to the inquiries she sent to colleges. But Chase said Plath's publications more than made up for the lack of a PhD. Sylvia worried, however, about Ted, then not well known in the United States. He would probably have to settle for teaching in a private preparatory school, Chase suggested. Hughes had not changed his mind about teaching, but the idea of voyaging to America and earning a tidy sum to support them through a year of full-time writing seemed desirable. And they both wanted to get away from "stuffy" and "cliquey" England, as Sylvia put it in a letter to Aurelia on 3 February.

Less than three weeks later, on 23 February, Ted received a telegram at 10:30 a.m. telling him he had won the New York City Poetry Center/*Harper's* prize for his first book, *The Hawk in the Rain*. Now his hopes for a proper reception in America soared. They put in a long-distance call to Aurelia, forgetting it was not yet 6:00 a.m. in Wellesley, and in a follow-up letter the next day Sylvia gloated, dismissing the "frightened poetry editors" who had been rejecting his work. The major poet-judges recognized Ted's talent. "Genius will out." She was sure his book would be a bestseller.

Characteristically, he wrote Olwyn to tell her about his good fortune, even as he regretted the poems were not better. As Sylvia told her mother, Ted was modest about his work. Sylvia, as his agent, loved to talk him up. Her sense of destiny overwhelmed her as she noted 23 February was the first anniversary of the "fatal party" when she first met him. She took a proprietary pride in his work, declaring that she had typed and retyped those poems, and felt no sense of rivalry—only certainty that their award-winning output would increase. She believed that, in fact, she had made Ted as keen on competition as she was. In *Letters Home*, Aurelia commented that all her life Sylvia had sought such a man, and that from the age of four she had boosted male egos, always choosing boys who deserved her cheers. While Ted Hughes certainly did not lack confidence, Sylvia's "unshakable" (to use Aurelia's word) faith in him may well have accelerated his ambition. Intellect, vigor, grace, moral commitment, and a lyrical style, "O, he has everything," Sylvia concluded. In a letter to his brother, Gerald, and Gerald's wife, Joan, Ted simply said, "Sylvia is my luck completely."

Hughes's sudden success in America coincided with a tirade against his native land. In an aside that does not appear in the published collection of his letters, he gave Gerald and Joan his contemptuous opinion of a declining England, declaring the Anglo-Saxon "less worthy to live than any evil thing on earth." Hughes decried the British Imperial Army, in which he had served, and the public schools that produced a uniformity typified in the blazers worn at weekends, and in "cut glass accents" resulting in a "complete atrophy of sensitivity and introspection. You can never correct them, because you can never wound them into seeing how foolish they are."

Sylvia was beginning to torment herself about her unwritten novel, tentatively titled "Falcon Yard." Where was her plot? Why had she not made more of her travels to Cambridge, London, Yorkshire, Nice, Benidorm, Madrid, and Munich? Basing the protagonist on herself, a sort of femme fatale who "runs through several men," and featuring characters derived from Gary Haupt, Richard Sassoon, Gordon Lameyer, Mallory Wober, and others, she wanted to explore a character torn between playing it safe and a "big, blasting, dangerous love." Other female characters, based on Nancy Hunter and Jane Kopp, would serve as foils or alter egos, apparently providing the kinds of alternatives the protagonist confronted. But then her journal breaks off to consider life with Ted, and her concern that she may "escape into domesticity."

Sylvia turned to Virginia Woolf, whose diary comforted Sylvia because Woolf, too, got depressed. Indeed, Sylvia thought that in the dark summer of 1953 she had been channeling Woolf and emulating her suicide by drowning. But Sylvia had been resilient and had bobbed to the surface. Although she had dreamed of a traditional, grand wedding in Wellesley, she now reveled in the memory of the simple and spare ceremony in the "church of the chimney sweeps with nothing but love & hope & our own selves." Ted had worn his old black corduroy jacket and Sylvia a pink knit dress Aurelia had bought for her. In Sylvia's ecstatic prose, she and Ted were now the first couple, and like a new Adam and Eve they were destined to people the world with brilliant offspring. The marriage to Hughes transformed all that had gone before, so that earlier suitors would appear in her projected novel only to be dismissed as weak, flabby, and lacking in purpose.

For all her professions of pride in Ted, his success did take its toll on Sylvia, as she recounts in her journal, saying his criticism of her work came at a bad time. She seemed blocked, unable to write the novel. She did grind out three pages a day, but what she wrote was "blither." Part of the problem derived from studying for her June exams. She tried to relieve the pressure by biking, but she still beguiled herself with her novel about a self-destructive young woman who is redeemed by the power of love. Sometimes it sounded to her like she was producing a potboiler, a true-confession story, and not the "noble, gut-wrenching" account she had dreamed of writing. Part of Sylvia's problem, she realized, was her earnest heavy-handedness. The antidote, she confided to her journal, might be a style resembling Joyce Cary's in *The Horse's Mouth,* a delightful, informal, foray into an artist's mind that was vivid, funny, and yet an entirely serious aesthetic effort. She envied his popularity and wanted to emulate his other supple novels, such as *Herself Surprised.*

On 12 March, an elated Sylvia Plath learned that she had been offered a teaching position at Smith with a salary of $4,200, then a respectable yearly income for a college instructor. Although Sylvia had all along had reservations about teaching at Smith, now she could not imagine anything she would rather do, she told Aurelia. Teaching three courses a semester might prove daunting, but Plath supposed she would do well with good students and have lively discussions.

On 29 March, Olive Higgins Prouty replied to Plath's good news, sending along what Aurelia deemed in *Letters Home* "intuitive remarks": "There is no end to the thrilling things happening. It frightens me a little. I am very proud of you, Sylvia. I love to tell your story. Someone remarked to me after reading your poem in *The Atlantic,* 'How intense.' Sometime write me a little poem that *isn't* intense. A lamp turned too high might shatter its chimney. Please just *glow* sometimes."

A week later Plath completed a poem, "All the Dead Dears," an extraordinary meditation on the skeleton of a woman in a stone coffin the poet had seen in Cambridge's archeological museum. The poem's speaker notes that "this lady" is no "kin" of hers, and yet "she'll suck / Blood and whistle my marrow clean" to prove otherwise. What would Henry James have given to imagine a character like Sylvia Plath, so steeped in the past that she could sometimes feel it was eating her alive? The speaker imagines this figure of the ancient past hauling her in and making her feel the presence of other old souls who usurp the armchair—that is, make themselves at home in a kind of death-in-life scene that drives the speaker to think of humanity as "each skulled-and-crossbones Gulliver / Riddled with ghosts." The living will lie with relics like the woman in the stone coffin, "deadlocked with them, taking root as cradles rock." This extraordinary Gothic evocation of recurrence and continuity has the kind of brooding, brilliant, and haunting acuity that disturbed Prouty.

Sylvia now had written eighty single-spaced pages of "Falcon Yard" and hoped to complete a first draft of the novel before departing in June for America. Only fragments of the work survive, including a page titled "Character Notebook." She was trying to work out a trajectory for her heroine, Peregrine, a "Voyager, no Penelope." Another character, Lisa, is called a "male-woman" and is associated with Nancy Hunter and Olwyn Hughes. Kate, described as an older passionate woman and a priestess, seems derived from Dorothea Krook. A Mrs. Guinea would be introduced as a sort of Wife of Bath figure. Jess, an "honest dowd," would be comforting in a sort of stodgy Victorian way. This would be a novel about a woman of the world, an "Isis fable," Plath noted.

The women would be set against the Dionysian Leonard, a hero, a "God-man," who is "spermy" and creative. Adam Winthrop, a version of Gordon Lameyer, a mama's boy (Sylvia said as much in her journal), is dominated by women. She had it in mind to create a Cambridge fop based on Christopher Levenson, an acquaintance, and another frail suitor, Maurice, was a ringer for Sassoon, "a dark, sickly, lover-type." Warm and intuitive like Mallory Wober, Maurice is too cerebral, and like Sassoon, too worried about money (he had, in fact, rejected marrying Sylvia before he had earned a fortune). Why the title "Falcon Yard"? This was the place on the Cambridge campus where Sylvia and Ted first met. Apparently love would be portrayed as a "bird of prey," with "victors and victims." The novel would be characterized by "depravity and suffering" that would give rise to "a fable of faithfulness." The auras of the Brontës seem to preside over this work.

Even in its truncated form, "Falcon Yard," is a revelation. Peregrine is clearly the dominant, even prey-driven woman that ruffled Eddie Cohen, who deplored Plath's disdainful treatment of men. In her notes for Peregrine, Plath makes her character a goddess born out of a "perfect dream of love." Like Isis, she roams the world assembling the parts of the god-man who will fulfill her love. The god-man becomes for Peregrine/Isis a father, lover, and

priest, promising the "perpetually possible." Plath, however, realized Peregrine's plight: How can she accept the "fallible man as
divine"? It is the question D. H. Lawrence asks in "The Man Who
Died," when the priestess of Isis wishes to believe that the man
who died is Osiris. Unlike the Plath of *Letters Home* and correspondence with her closest friends, Peregrine expresses doubt in the
god-man she has made. Peregrine identifies herself not only as
Isis, but also as Lamia, the "sperm-sucking serpent" of Keats's
poem, and with Medusa, the "Mother of Madness, the Mother of
Death." Eventually Ted Hughes would flee Sylvia Plath, declaring
she had a kind of "death ray."

If Plath had trouble actually writing the novel, it may be because of its monumental nature. How to live the perfect life in a
fallen world? Peregrine asks. The question of how to write the perfect female epic was evidently just as daunting. No wonder Plath
responded with elation to Doris Lessing's Martha Quest, the very
epitome of the heroine Plath wanted to create. Sylvia broke off
writing the novel as she prepared for exams, then worked fitfully
on it while teaching at Smith. And she returned to it again after
completing *The Bell Jar.*

On 9 April, Sylvia wrote Elinor Friedman Klein and Marcia
Brown to catch them up on the news. While dreaming of the summer cottage on the Cape that Aurelia had rented as a wedding present, and anticipating her arrival on 25 June in New York—to be
followed by a gala reception for her and Ted on the 29th in
Wellesley—Sylvia was preparing for her grueling five days of exams covering two thousand years of "tragedy, morality, etc. etc."
She regarded her appointment at Smith as both exciting and terri-
fying. And oh how she relished her return to the land of modern
appliances after two years of dealing with dodgy British models.
Good-bye to coal stoves and wretched dental care.

To Marcia Brown, Sylvia described Ted teaching forty Teddy
boys (gang members), who carried chains and razors but could not
remember their multiplication tables. This was her English version
of *The Blackboard Jungle* (1955), the film starring Glenn Ford as a
neophyte English teacher determined to teach in a violent inner
city school. As always, in her letters to American friends, she gave

Ted Hughes the Hollywood treatment. He could not teach school without Sylvia making it a "moving, tragic, & in many ways rewarding experience."

To both Elinor and Marcia, Sylvia spread the news of Ted's prize, which had his publisher, Harper's, wondering if success would spoil Rock Hunter—yet another allusion to a film, this one released in 1957 and starring Tony Randall as an ad executive, whose first success involves pretending to be the lover of a movie star in a campaign to sell lipstick. Only Sylvia Plath could glamorize Ted's receipt of a publishing prize as though a new Clark Gable had suddenly been discovered and relieved of his obscurity. As for her, she drew on a sports metaphor, calling herself a "triple-threat woman: wife, writer, and teacher"—although she said she would trade in that epithet for motherhood.

London Magazine's acceptance of poems by both Plath and Hughes had Sylvia dreaming of catapulting to fame, as she wrote her mother on 13 April. Ted now had a British publisher for *The Hawk in the Rain*. Faber & Faber had taken the book on the recommendation of T. S. Eliot, who had passed on a complimentary message to Ted, Sylvia reported to Aurelia on 10 May. At the same time, Plath was still hoping to "break into the slicks," since a sale of several commercial stories could earn them a year's income.

Sylvia's ecstatic letters to her mother might be discounted, except that Ted's to his brother, Gerald, were almost as rhapsodic. "Marriage is my medium," he declared. He wrote about his and Sylvia's working and walking about in incandescent terms: "We strike sparks." He described them sitting by the river and watching water voles. The "unconscious delight" he attributed to her makes Sylvia seem very much like the sensitive Marilyn Monroe that Arthur Miller described in his memoirs and stories. "She's the most responsive alert creature in the world, about everything," Hughes concluded. And like Sylvia, he enthused about an America taking him into its embrace. Even when it came to family, he really did sound like Sylvia's male counterpart, saying that his prize and the praise for him were all the more pleasing because they had fulfilled his mother's dreams for him.

CHAPTER 5

QUEEN OF THE OCEAN

(1957–59)

1957: Plath and Hughes summer at Cape Cod before Sylvia begins teaching freshman English at Smith, while Ted obtains a part-time teaching position at University of Massachusetts, Amherst; **1958:** The couple moves to Boston, and Sylvia resumes treatment with Dr. Beuscher; **1959:** Sylvia befriends Anne Sexton in a poetry class taught in the spring semester by Robert Lowell. Sylvia and Ted spend a summer at Yaddo, the writer's colony in Saratoga Springs, New York, and then sail in December for England.

In early June, after the ordeal of exams that earned Plath the equivalent of about a B+ and a master's degree, the couple headed for Yorkshire to stay with Ted's parents before sailing to America. On 8 June, Sylvia described for her mother's benefit a cozy family get-together with Olwyn, who had just arrived from France. Sylvia had cast aside what she thought of as the false, artificial world of Cambridge with T. S. Eliot's line about "preparing a face to meet a face." The couple took long walks on the moors.

A letter Ted wrote to Olwyn on 20 June aboard the RMS *Queen Elizabeth* on the way to America suggests that not everyone was as simpatico as Sylvia said they were. "Don't criticize Sylvia too badly about the way she got up and came after me," Ted exhorted Olwyn, who thought Sylvia had been rude to John Fisher, Ted's old and beloved teacher. When Sylvia abruptly rushed out of the room, an awkward silence ensued until Ted said he'd better look after her. Then, as he returned to his company, she had rushed down the stairs after him. Olwyn was clearly impatient with Sylvia's moods, which shifted from high-pitched animation to sullen silence. Ted expatiated: A "nervy" Sylvia was still recovering from her exams and found company disturbed her need to rest. The "smarmy" behavior Olywn despised was Sylvia's response to panic, when she was trying too hard to be "open & too nice." Ted had seen a carefully hidden side of Sylvia that moved him to say apologetically, "She says stupid things then that mortify her afterwards. Her second thought—her retrospect, is penetrating, skeptical, and subtle. But she can never bring that second-thinking mind to the surface with a person until she's known them some time." Ted could have been Arthur Miller apologizing for Marilyn Monroe, whose erratic behavior often placed him in the same embarrassing situations. Both men felt deeply protective of the women who had inspired them far more than anyone in a superficial social setting could imagine. On the surface, it seemed to Olwyn that her brother had married a woman unworthy of him. Ted worked hard to bring Olwyn round: "You saw how much better she was the last day. Don't judge her on her awkward behavior." Like Miller, Hughes made his excuses, mentioning Sylvia's "miserable past," which he would in due course tell Olwyn about. Sylvia could be a harsh judge of people, Ted told his sister, but his wife had already developed considerable respect for Olwyn and prized her. How much Hughes was placating his sister, and how much he believed what he said, is impossible to tell.

The letters to his sister Hughes wrote aboard the *Queen Elizabeth* mention a period of depression, although aside from his complaints about the sumptuous food and boring sea, the reasons for his dejection are not clear. Of course, he was embarking on a new phase of his life, which in itself could have seemed daunting. But when Sylvia so often referred to him as her male counterpart, she may have been acknowledging a similar arc of mood swings that could make living together both wondrous and fraught.

Her journal entries written aboard ship focus mainly on the other passengers, whom she was sizing up as characters for her stories. She did mention, however, the "coffin-like bunks" and her difficulty sleeping in their cold cabin. A dreary sort of sameness seems to have overtaken Sylvia and Ted, who did not really have much to do on a ship monotonously rolling in the waves. Sylvia's journal does not do much with the rather conventional fellow travelers she described.

Writing in late June to his brother, Gerald, and Gerald's wife, Joan, Hughes described his first impressions of Wellesley and of the party Aurelia had arranged. He produced a classic description of 1950s conformist America, where everyone was expected to "mix," join the "rat-race," and put on a happy, "well-adjusted" face. The opulent food dismayed him, the meet and greets wearied him, and the fastidious surroundings made him want to engage in "private filthiness." This world had too much glaze for him. "But I'll learn my position," he noted, as though these new surroundings constituted a sort of game. "It's good for me to be surrounded by a world from which I instinctively recoil. I mightn't waste quite so much energy here." He enjoyed observing new birds, and he was on the lookout for the skunks he had heard about. And there was always fishing, one of his favorite pastimes. The huge cars—the materialistic culture of what he called "85ft long Cadillacs"—amused him. But what really pleased him was the lack of cruelty in literary life. Even the literary reviews, a notorious haven for the nasty, were "surprisingly honest, outspoken, but not venomous," as they were in London, where Hughes despised the vicious, inbred, and underhanded clubbishness of literary life. As Sylvia approached with more abundant food—chicken and lobster sandwiches—Ted marveled that he had landed in the lap of luxury. Like Sylvia, he believed in his own destiny, which he had charted in horoscopes. "There is no explanation for it," he said in a concluding line to Gerald and Joan, "though astrology, of course, explains it all."

Accounts of Hughes's behavior at the party differ, with some remembering a generally friendly, if taciturn, Ted, and others depicting a somewhat condescending, aloof figure. Of course, such impressions of him that survive have been refurbished with retrospection—not to mention suffused with the personalities of those who met him and later reported on his behavior. His letters suggest mixed emotions capable of sustaining nearly every available version of his American debut.

In *Letters Home,* Aurelia remembers a radiant Sylvia greeting her seventy guests and introducing her husband to them. Warren then drove the pair to the summer cottage Aurelia had rented so that they could have seven weeks or so of rest and quiet and time for their writing. A week later, Sylvia wrote to Marcia Brown, describing their "small gray cabin hidden in the pines" and their "easy living, no phones, simple meals," which allowed them to dress like hermits in dungarees. They wrote in the morning, biked in the afternoon to the beach, and read a good deal in the evening. For Sylvia, this meant Virginia Woolf's novels. Sylvia had trouble resuming "Falcon Yard," although in late July she had better luck writing stories, which she regarded as warm-up exercises for more serious work.

Ted's version of the Cape summer in a letter to Gerald and Joan was a little different. He attributed his own writer's block as well as Sylvia's to a paralyzing response to Aurelia's generosity: seventy dollars a week for the cottage. Although Ted did not explain himself, it seems that the couple's sense of self-sufficiency attenuated. And what Sylvia regarded as simple meals seemed to Ted virtual banquets, as she plied him with Himalayan heaps of food. Sylvia cooked to relax. She was a "princess of cooks" who delivered "fairy palace dishes," a bemused Ted noted, regarding eating only as a necessity. But he grew to enjoy browning on the beach and even appreciated the kitchen, with all its modern conveniences. He liked the verandah, where they took their meals. And when Sylvia really got going with her writing, they actually did eat rather simply.

Sylvia loved walking on the beach and imagining Ted as a sea-god, the perfect consort to her as earth goddess, she avowed in her journal. Plath associated her newfound maturity with her marriage to Hughes, just as Monroe, likewise married in June 1956, linked her yearlong break from Hollywood and journey to New York to be with Miller with her fulfillment as an actress. Just 160 miles southwest from Ted and Sylvia and at virtually the same time, Arthur Miller and Marilyn Monroe were walking along Amagansett beaches near the tip of Long Island—he treating her as a goddess to be cherished, and she looking up to her tall husband as her towering hero. Sylvia and Marilyn, both survivors of suicide, saw their mates as saviors. Having produced no notable work in the previous six months, Sylvia was sure that without Ted's constant support, she would have gone mad. Marilyn, in virtually the same downward cycle and deeply disappointed over the outcome of her last picture, *The Prince and the Showgirl,* wanted to believe, as did Sylvia, that she was storing up energy for a new burst of creativity. But Sylvia Plath, like Marilyn Monroe, could in a matter of a few days, or even hours, execute a reverse angle shot of her marriage, or complaining in her 18 July journal about a "lousy day . . . No more dreams of queen and king for a day with valets bringing in racks of white suits, jackets, etc. for Ted & ballgowns and tiaras for me."

A brooding Sylvia worked on a story about a troublemaking mother who wants her daughter to be a social success. The plot might as well have been stolen from *Stella Dallas,* although Plath made no mention of her mentor or her work. Ultimately, the mother is redeemed in the story, just as Stella is, both in Prouty's novel and in its radio serial. Living in the wonderful cottage for the summer, how could Sylvia help but be grateful to Aurelia? At the same time, though, she hated the feeling of obligation, the sense of being beholden that Ted, too, disliked. The story, which seemed to her slick but good—exactly what a magazine like *The Saturday Evening Post* would publish (they later rejected it)—apparently did wonders for Sylvia's mood. Ted reappeared in her journal as the salt-air seagod, smelling as fresh as a newborn.

But what followed was a horrifying two weeks during which Plath thought she was pregnant. She had been rather casual about contraception, she admitted in her journal, and now her period was overdue. How could she possibly handle her writing, teaching at Smith, and the responsibilities of motherhood? She wanted children, but not now! The energy they would have to devote as parents would put them into debt, robbing them of the time they needed to hone their talents. Even worse, they would regard the infant as an intruder. Ted referred to this period as their "black week" in a letter to Gerald and Joan, without specifically mentioning the dreaded pregnancy. Then all Sylvia's worries dissipated in the "hot drench" of blood, two weeks late, that relieved her misery, and they both began writing at great speed, applying their brains "like the bits of electric drills," a relieved Ted told Gerald and Joan.

On 6 August, Sylvia wrote her mother in some excitement over a short verse play, "Dialogue Over a Ouija Board," later included in the notes section of *The Collected Poems*. She was suggestible and skeptical, indulging Ted in his occult occupations, which often had a materialistic motivation. He was a poet, like Sylvia, who thought a good deal about money and how to get it. To say that he had made an investment in Sylvia, this go-ahead American, may sound crass, but he loved her no less for it, and for being a canny woman who could figure out how to make five pounds go a long way toward paying their rent in Cambridge and feeding them as well. The Ouija board, in other words, became for both of them a conversation about how to generate capital, as it does for Sybil and Leroy in "Dialogue Over a Ouija Board." Sybil is resigned to Leroy's obsession with a "bare board" that has yielded contradictory results. Leroy wonders if perhaps Sibyl will be included in her white-haired benefactress's will—a revealing gloss, perhaps, on why Sylvia was so assiduous about keeping open lines of communication with the wealthy Olive Higgins Prouty, and making sure that Prouty was among the first to meet Ted when he alighted on the American shore. "She was very amusing though she's old now and her mind wanders a bit—still she's plain and direct. I got on with her well," Ted wrote to his sister, Olwyn.

"Dialogue" reveals a good deal about Hughes, who often portrayed himself as an amateur Plath shaped up for worldly competition. As Leroy, though, he is the one who wants to know from the Ouija spirit if he is to have his "fling at fame." For Sibyl, the future is best left unknown. She is fixated on the afterlife and asks about her father, but she receives a garbled transmission. Though Leroy seems the more credulous of the two, Sibyl doubts his fealty to the supernatural, saying that if a bush began to speak to him he would kneel but then check for the wiring. "Dialogue" marvelously captures the playful, querulous strain in the pairing of these two sensibilities, who seem to agree in this instance that they are in thrall to imps, since neither Sibyl nor Leroy can believe that any major gods would come at the call of a glass maneuvered over a board. As Sibyl shrewdly points out, Leroy has no real need of spirits because, "You'd presume your inner voice god-plumed enough / To people the boughs with talking birds."

Leroy teases Sibyl about her "inklings" of "doom." He accuses her of opportunism—even when it comes to calling spirits, which she will placate if they prognosticate what she wants. It "pays to be politic," Sibyl replies. The overlay of heroic lavender Plath used to scent Ted's entrance into her life—not only in letters, but also in personal introductions of him to friends and family—is stripped away in the hard, if still good-natured give-and-take of "Dialogue." Sylvia Plath had plenty of illusions about Ted Hughes, but she also had startling insights into the real man. After all, Sibyl calls the Ouija board "our battlefield."

The piece ends with Sibyl and Leroy returning to the reality of their daily life. "[T]he dream / Of dreamers is dispelled," he concludes. She wishes for the "decorum" of their days to "sustain" them, and he wants their actions to reflect that they mean well. As the lights go out, they make the same wish: "May two real people breathe in a real room," perhaps a recognition of just how powerfully Sylvia and Ted could project their imaginations so as to create an unreal world. "Dialogue" confirms Oscar Wilde's adage that art is a lie that tells the truth. Sylvia's play seems so much more revealing than the performances Plath and Hughes put on in their letters.

Sibyl is, of course, the name of a prophetess, and Leroy is the cognomen of a king. Together the names signify the way these two poets mythologized themselves. With no evident trace of irony, Hughes remarks in his notes to *The Collected Poems* that his wife "mentioned flashes of prescience—always about something unimportant." Did he not see the predictive value of "Dialogue"? Critic Jacqueline Rose notes that Plath "situates quite explicitly" in Leroy's lines the "male invocation of poetry" associated with violence entering their room like an earthquake, turning Sibyl "ashen." Like

Hughes, Plath both venerated and dreaded the eruptive nature of his poetic gift and her own rage, which could erupt in response to it. In "Dialogue" Sybil ends their colloquy with spirits by smashing the glass.

About a week before the couple left Northampton for the fall semester at Smith, Ted wrote Olwyn the first of many scornful descriptions of an America wrapped in cellophane, "crapularised" into processed food that reflected a more general lack of texture in a "boundless" suburban uniformity, in which everyone was friendly in a facetious sort of way, but no one knew anyone's else's family history. He thought better of Northampton, which he had visited earlier in the summer when they were looking for lodgings. With its main street full of shops "huddled together," it was "fairly English." This letter and others demonstrate that Sylvia's hope that Hughes would open up to America—which would in turn expand his poetic sensibility—was sadly mistaken. He associated affluence with inauthenticity.

In September 1957, Sylvia and Ted settled into an apartment in Northampton within walking distance of the Smith campus. On the surface (which is what Sylvia presented to her mother on 23 September), Ted was a considerate husband, making breakfast and doing the dishes. Sylvia had three classes and a total of sixty-five students, each of whom she would also be seeing in individual conferences. This work, plus department and general faculty meetings, would fill out her schedule.

Sylvia still found time to mull over in her journal ideas for several stories, including one about a woman who is shocked to discover that her poet-husband has not been writing about her, but about a "Dream Woman Muse." Another story, set in *Wuthering Heights* country, is cryptically linked to Ted as a poet associated with decay and "aloneness." This is perhaps Plath's first recognition of his estrangement from an American scene that had separated him from the ghosts and spirits of his native land. Hughes's letters reflect a sensibility ill at ease in surroundings that had no resonance or texture for him. Smith girls had a sort of machined beauty—"Chromium dianas," he called them. "I sit for hours like the statue of a man writing," he wrote to Lucas Myers in early

October. "Two years will be our stretch in America," he wrote, as though describing a prison sentence. Not even a visit to the Poetry Center cheered him, judging by his dismissive remarks about the dowagers and maidens who accosted him about his work.

By 1 October, Sylvia's anxiety level seemed to peak. She had trouble sleeping, doubted her teaching abilities, deplored her lack of experience, obsessed over the perplexed expressions of her students—but most of all decried the demon in herself that demanded excellence when, in fact, she was "middling good." Correcting papers exhausted her. She was ashamed to admit that she was afraid of not measuring up to Smith standards. She counseled herself to face reality, adopt a stoic face, and do her job as best she could. But of course, she could not leave it at that, admitting, "Not being perfect hurts." Ted, more resigned to his teaching and unproductive writing regimen, admitted to Olwyn that life was pleasant, and he was in good humor, whereas Sylvia was "creaking under her burdens." Sylvia complained to Warren on 5 November of a "rough class of spoiled bitches." Her funk, she admitted, arose out of wanting to create her own metaphors, not discuss the ones in Henry James and D. H. Lawrence. Reading them was one thing; teaching them seemed to diminish her own creativity.

These words to Warren may have provoked Sylvia to take herself in hand. In her journal, she dismissed her complaints as those of a spoiled little girl. She deserved a good slap. She vowed not to weigh Ted down with her woes and to learn to live with her anxieties. Gradually, she pointed out to herself, she had learned to cope with her students, get enough sleep, write letters to friends, and finally do some baking. These small victories were confidence builders.

Sylvia's initial disappointments as a teacher, and her eventual acclimation to the classroom, seem confirmed in the reminiscences of her students. As a Smith freshman, Barbara Russell Kornfield "struggled mightily as we read William James, no doubt why my first paper was a D+. She was a tough teacher for a 17 year old." Of course, Kornfield did not know about her own teacher's struggles to improve, or about what the sudden appearance of Hughes, a stranger to the class, meant to Plath. "I do remember quite clearly,"

Kornfield adds, "we had no compunctions about asking her who he was. In an ethereal voice, she replied: 'That is a man from heaven sent.'"

Part of Plath's problem during her first months at Smith stemmed from her decision to adopt the Socratic method of her Cambridge tutorials. She had reveled in the hard give-and-take of her sessions with Dorothea Krook, which were quite unlike anything she had experienced at Smith—or her own students were prepared to endure. Anne Mohegan Smith remembers one of her Smith classmates, Merrill Schwartz, explained that in her freshman English literature section Plath began the year

> singling out students as foils in class, challenging/ridiculing their comments and more than once reducing them to tears. I heard this from Merrill who was one of the students singled out in this way; she came to the Wilder House dining room with swollen red eyelids, and told our table about it. She was a lively girl with a heavy, nasal Brooklyn accent and a high-pitched cackle of a laugh, but however irrepressible she might seem, she could be wounded, and was. After that day, I heard about this behavior once again from another student in Plath's class who lived in a different college house from mine.

Before beginning her year at Smith, Sylvia had written letters worrying about how she would establish her authority in the classroom, especially since she was only a little more than six years older than her students. Her resort to Cambridge pedagogy was a way to exert power in precisely the place where she felt most vulnerable. But "then, suddenly, about halfway through the semester, the behavior stopped," Smith noted. "Florence Dalrymple told me years later that Plath . . . was told (probably by our class dean) to stop it at once—students perceived it as abuse."

Whatever start-up problems Plath may have had at Smith seem to have been resolved quickly. By the end of November, she reported to Warren, she had been asked to teach for a second year, but she had already decided against it, since teaching had put a stop to her writing. She and Ted were planning to move out of Northampton by the end of the summer and settle in Boston, where Sylvia hope to find some kind of part-time employment that would not sap her writing energy. They would rent a flat on the "slummy side" of Beacon Hill, as far from an academic environment as they could get.

Whatever Ted's qualms about America, he had lost none of his charm. His latest conquest was Olive Higgins Prouty, who had, if Sylvia is to be believed, become "obsessed with Ted." It was a common enough experience. Ted only had to say hello to you, recalled Ravelle Silberman (a freshman when she met Hughes), and he was already flirting with you. He enjoyed watching women compete for him, recalled writer Marvin Cohen, who met Hughes many years later and became a friend of Olwyn.

On 7 December, Sylvia wrote to Aurelia with considerably more confidence about her teaching, saying she was making the best of a bad job. Several faculty members had relayed comments from students who had called her a "brilliant teacher." But that accolade did not mean Sylvia inspired much affection—certainly not like one of her mentors, Alfred Fisher, whom Smith undergraduates adored, and who appears in CB Follett's poem about Sylvia as "our druid king."

By the end of the fall semester, Sylvia had exhausted herself, and by the time she reached Wellesley for her Christmas break, she had developed a fever and then came down with pneumonia, which was successfully treated with antibiotics. Over the holidays, Sylvia nursed her ambition, dreaming "too much" of fame, she admitted in her journal. Thoughts of "Falcon Yard" as a "rich, humorous satire" flitted randomly among ideas for stories, the fate of the book she had submitted to the Yale Younger Poets series, and plans to apply for a fellowship that would fund their return to Europe. A certain estrangement had set in: "You can't go home again," she wrote, noting that her beloved memories of her seaside childhood in Winthrop had "shrunk."

Plath also experienced pressure from Smith faculty, who urged her to stay a second year. Alfred Fisher said her failure to do so would be deemed "irresponsible." She resisted overtures from her former thesis advisor, George Gibian, too, commenting in her journal that her colleagues meant well but really had no idea of what was good for her. Winters were often hard for her, and she contracted a cough in early January. Her aches and pains seemed of a piece with her dread of preparing for class, attending department meetings, and dealing with her writing almost like an onlooker whose troubles Alfred Fisher dismissed with, "It's all in your mind." *Citizen Kane*—especially the famous scene with the glass globe that contains Kane's grieving memory of the snow scene, which signals the end of his childhood, and the parade of Kanes in the mirror shots—appealed to Sylvia as emblematic of her own haunted retrospection. To her surprise, sometimes classes went well, but teaching still exhausted her. Knowing this was her last term had freed her to take more pleasure in her students, whom she now regarded "as really *good* girls," she told Aurelia on 13 January.

But Sylvia thought mostly of June and her return to full-time writing. It seemed so long since she had achieved anything notable, and now she learned she had not won the Yale Younger Poets prize, and she would not have her first book published—not yet. And how infuriating, she wrote in her journal, to see that she had not been included in an anthology of six "new poets of england and america." Only two of them, May Swenson and Adrienne Rich, seemed any good, and they were not "better or more-published than me," Plath observed. She needed a tougher, freer voice, she told herself, anticipating work still years beyond her reach. She regretted her diaries, "spattered with undone imperatives, directives."

At the end of January 1958, Ted commuted eight miles to teach literature and creative writing at the Amherst campus of the University of Massachusetts, a position he obtained through one of Plath's contacts at Smith. He was teaching two classes three times a week. Milton, Goethe, Keats, Wordsworth, Yeats, Thoreau, and Molière were on his syllabus for a great works course. He also taught freshman composition. This job helped to pay for what Sylvia's salary did not cover and contributed to the savings they would rely on when they returned to their writers' lives.

Sylvia had moments, she confided to her journal, when visions of cozy academic life beckoned. They could easily earn eight thousand a year teaching, making a living off of classes on Joyce and James. She could become a teacher/writer like Elizabeth Drew, one of her mentors, queening about as a beloved campus icon. But she remained true to Ted's antiacademic attitudes and to her own ambition to overtake poets like the "facile Isabella Gardner & even the lesbian and fanciful & jeweled Elizabeth Bishop in America." Teaching did not allow her to live her own self, as she put it in her journal. She needed to sweat out her novel next summer. With "Falcon Yard" behind her, perhaps by the fourth year of their marriage it would be time to begin conceiving children. An academic career would have meant years of graduate school to earn a PhD and a very junior position at Smith. Yet the faculty thought, as George Gibian put it, that to teach at Smith was the "very highest thing an intellectual woman could do, and to give THAT up was very odd."

Never at her best in bleak, blustery cold seasons, Sylvia groused about even good friends, like the Roches. Paul, an Englishman, was teaching at Smith, and his wife, Clarissa, befriended Sylvia, although their greatest period of intimacy would come later in Britain. Paul, Sylvia noted, had lost his Adonis-boy looks and was no poet—for all his connections to William Carlos Williams and Marianne Moore. Ted held a similar critical view, describing his fellow countryman as "tall, thin a rapt shelleyan look, bright blue eyes that he holds wide open and slightly glazed, but withal utterly seedy . . . an old lady charmer, with his beautiful hushing voice, and wonderful English manners." Clarissa seemed "naive and likeable" to Ted, but in Sylvia's journal she appeared as a sullen blonde figure in a "silken pout" over a cup of coffee.

Sylvia and Ted also socialized with the poet W. S. Merwin and his British wife, Dido, then living in Boston. Bill Merwin embodied a cliché: the man's man. Poet Grace Schulman remembered that Bill and Ted formed a sort of men's club. Their utterly self-sufficient maleness seemed to impress her, inspiring a wonder at the masculine gravitational pull that Sylvia herself felt so strongly. At this early stage, though, the Merwins mainly represented to Sylvia the admirable urbanity of a couple on their own, in a high-rise apartment with windows so wide they reminded her of a ship deck.

Campus life bothered Sylvia because it subjected her to men like the poet Anthony Hecht, a notorious misogynist who plied her with patronizing pleasantries about her earnest, energetic manner. She was a grader for critic Newton Arvin's lecture course, a job she enjoyed, which nevertheless made her feel like a drudge, dealing with assignments and students in a sort of mopping up operation. She would return home and give everything a thorough cleaning—and then bake a lemon meringue pie, taking immense satisfaction in her own realm. In a better mood, she described a party and her enjoyment of "blond witchy dear Clarissa" and a cherubic Paul, looking "Rossetti-like" with his blue eyes and blond curls. Department gossip amused her, especially tales of Alfred Fisher, who had married three of his students, and other tales about which faculty members had "the Power." Sylvia preened when told how good her freshmen classes were. She exulted in a "dangerous enjoyment from shocking" her students, she wrote to Olwyn on 9 February, describing a memorable class that had stimulated "laughter & even tears, the occasion of the latter being a snowy Saturday spent evoking the bloody & cruel history of the Irish whiteboys, potato famines, mass hangings, etc." Such interludes broke up the otherwise discontented winter that had Sylvia holding on with visions of June, dreaming of trading her Smith "girl-studded" past for the anonymity of Boston.

It was Ted's turn in mid-March to be brought down with stomach upsets and fevers, as though he were putting himself in Sylvia's place. They argued about his clothes and about Sylvia's need to sew on buttons that went missing from his jackets. Reading the autobiography of a male friend, she objected to his notion that a man could eternally love a woman, even after he left her. She mused, "loving, leaving—a lovely consonance. I don't see it: and my man doesn't." Or so she thought.

Plath sought inspiration in the work of Paul Klee, Henri Rousseau, Gauguin, and De Chirico, and on 22 March, at the beginning of spring break, she reported to Aurelia that the poem-drought had ended. Work was beginning to shoot out like a geyser. She was also writing Dole Pineapple jingles for a contest. After all, they could use a car. Even just a few cash prizes would help. Commerce and art intermingled easily in the poems she enclosed for her mother's perusal. In "Battle-Scene from the Comic Operatic Fantasy *The Seafarer,*" her whimsical work on Klee, she evokes a "little Odyssey" of battles in bathtubs such as children can create with extraordinary intensity. The child's ability to fashion a fully functioning world separate from what Plath calls "meat-and-potato thoughts" in "Departure of the Ghost (After Paul Klee)" suggests how sorely she wanted to escape from the all-too-material world of her Smith routines.

By 28 March, Plath had produced eight new poems—her best ever, she thought, vowing not to waste "poem-time" on people she did not like. In a self-described arrogant mood, she pictured herself as the "Poetess of America" and Ted as the "Poet of England." Ted, likewise, was touting himself to Olwyn, writing in late March about selling a poem to the "high-heeled" *Mademoiselle,* and extolling Sylvia's recent productivity, the result of twelve-hour writing jags.

But a return to teaching brought out Sylvia's complaints. Ted's nose picking and scratching were getting on her nerves, even as she realized her petulance hardly made her an appealing companion. Right on schedule, she developed a cold and began her own irritating round of twitching and sneezing, only to be heartened by Ted's comforting closeness and willingness to cook for her when she felt ill. Thank God she had a man who understood the demon in her. At Easter she filled Ted's slippers with a chocolate rabbit and eggs, and he ate them all.

At a poetry reading arranged for Ted at Harvard by his friend Jack Sweeney, Sylvia was surrounded by the people who populated her journal: Mrs. Cantor, Gordon Lameyer, Marcia Brown, Phil McCurdy, Peter Davison, Aurelia, Olive Higgins Prouty—a veritable rollout of an audience she had made for herself and Ted. The group now also included Adrienne Rich, one of Plath's chief rivals, cut down to size as "little, round & stumpy," but also endowed with "vibrant short black hair" and "great sparking black eyes."

Sylvia had to admit that Rich seemed perfectly genuine, if opinionated. In the end, Sylvia felt distant from the company, as though the whole affair, like the novel she still could not command, was out of her control. She had the end-of-term blues, a syndrome familiar to seasoned academics, but a dreary period for a poet dead tired of reading scholarly studies of the writers she loved. It always seemed to surprise her when a class went well, since her mind was elsewhere, on what she would write when no longer shackled to the academic bench. She scoured her apartment in a fit of spring cleaning. During this period of furious tidying up, she noted in her journal a quarrel with Ted, who objected to her throwing out parts of his ratty old wardrobe. Later, she went out looking for him and spotted him on the street, staring at her with one of his killer looks.

By the spring of 1958, Ted, like Sylvia, found the whole academic enterprise enervating and apparently sometimes took his disaffection out on her. Eileen Ouelette remembered the time the couple attended one of the Lawrence House Wednesday night dinners. Sylvia sat at the head table with Ted, who belittled her throughout the evening, much to Eileen's dismay. Then in her senior year, Eileen disliked this thin, tall Englishman. But Sylvia seemed very happy and very much in love, ignoring his disparaging commentary. Indeed, Sylvia wrote about him in her journal as the kind of man women looked for in romantic novels and when they scanned the pages of the *Ladies Home Journal*. When he was out, and they separated for as little as an hour, Sylvia wrote that she missed his heat and smell.

Like Hughes, Plath rejected any allegiance ancillary to her art. "The Disquieting Muses," conceived as she was forsaking her teaching career, is an answer to the cautious mother who appears in Sylvia's 11 May 1958 journal entry. A reserved Aurelia seemed not to rejoice when her daughter told her on Mother's Day about the poems accepted for publication. Aurelia worried about the insolvency of poetry, but Sylvia remained stubbornly loyal to the muses that fostered her genius. She addressed her mother directly in the poem's last lines, which renew Sylvia's dedication to her troubling muses: "no frown of mine / Will betray the company I keep." She seemed to take almost a perverse satisfaction when *The New Yorker* rejected the poem. In her journal, she comforted herself with the thought of Henry James, writing often without much of an audience, and with the wish to tell him about his posthumous reputation, a reward for all the suffering he had endured. She had no intention, however, of waiting to be discovered. "I am made, crudely, for success. Does failure whet my blade?"

Sylvia described her last day of teaching (22 May) in a letter to Warren, reporting rounds of applause, ranging from tepid to thunderous in direct proportion to her own reactions to each class. Daniel Aaron, who observed her teaching earlier in the semester, described her as "rather schoolmarmy, prim and neat," but overall, an effective instructor. To Warren, she confessed her disillusionment with her colleagues, a weak, vain, jealous, and petty lot. She called Smith an "airtight" community of gossipy, pot-bellied tenured males, sparing the women any specific epithets. She had adopted Ted's scorn for go-ahead Americans with their ten-year plans—even though she was surely one of them and would find the next months of freedom a trial precisely because she had no long-term, institutionally based program or regular job. She rather prided herself on having no charge accounts, TV, car, or other items purchased on the installment plan. Ted did not need immediate signs of success, she told Warren. But Sylvia always did, despite what she told her brother. For all their scorn of American appetites, Sylvia and Ted seemed very American indeed in their assurance that they would become wealthy and famous.

By late May, the ghost of Sylvia Plath, withdrawing from her all-too-terrestrial time at Smith, saw herself and Ted as practiced, smiling liars—he the vain and navel-gazing male, penis proud. He was going out alone, telling her not to come along. She was sure he was ashamed of something. Another day, as told in her journal, she spotted him near Paradise Pond on the Smith campus, smiling broadly in the company of a grinning undergraduate, whose appearance assaulted Sylvia in "several sharp flashes, like blows." This was a man seeking adulation, and the girl served it up like soup, then bolted when she saw Sylvia bearing down on her. Ted wasn't even sure of her name. Was it Sheila? Just like him, thought Sylvia, who remembered their first long night together when he called her Shirley.

No biographer has identified "Sheila," except to say that she was a student Ted had taught on the University of Massachusetts Amherst campus. What, then, was she doing at Smith? No biographer has been able to establish that Hughes was unfaithful to Plath during this period of her marriage, although A. Alvarez, who often talked about women with Hughes, has no doubt that Hughes was constitutionally incapable of fidelity. At any rate, Sylvia now believed she understood why Ted had been arriving home late. She rejected his explanations and got angrier when he snored and snorted in his sleep—another complacent male—while she remained awake. In her journal tirade, she admitted that she had divined this side of him when they first met, but had capitulated to the vulgar heat of their coupling. Why had she tidied up this messy man, now sulking in her disapproval?

Plath left a blank of nearly three weeks in her journal, not resuming until 11 June with the admission that she had taken that much time to deal with her last "nightmarish entry." They had fought. Sylvia had sprained her thumb and had scratched and bloodied Ted. He hit her hard enough that she saw stars. Hughes would later tell his American editor, Frances McCullough, that he tried slapping Sylvia out of her rages, "but it was no good," McCullough wrote. "And once she turned into his slap and got a black eye, & went to the doctor & told him Ted beat her regularly." To Warren, Sylvia described, with typical hyperbole, "rousing battles every so often in which I come out with sprained thumbs and Ted with missing earlobes."

Ted rejoiced in finding a flat in the Beacon Hill section of Boston (they would not move in until September). The narrow streets and cobbles appealed to his sense of human scale. Better, evidently, to live in a cramped two-room apartment than in the indulgent luxury of the suburbs or the brassiness of New York City, with its "pathetic Bohemian district, called The Village," he wrote Olwyn in early June. The robust Ted Hughes found America at midcentury too tame, undoubtedly influencing Sylvia's aside to Warren on 11 June that she was working on "overcoming a clever, too brittle and glossy feminine tone."

By 20 June, Sylvia's journal records her battle with depression. She simply did not have the sense of self-sufficiency that she so admired in Ted, who she compared to an iceberg with a depth and reality that constantly surprised her. She admitted that the thought of having a child was tempting, since caring for a baby would divert a reckoning with her demons—which in better days she called her muses. Summoned to writing, she nevertheless quaked at the wide gap that now opened up between her desire to write and the anxiety that desire provoked. She hoped to relieve her paralysis by revisiting the site of her early childhood, Winthrop by the sea, which she always associated with a life-giving power and creativity.

Then on 25 June, a miracle. After years and years of rejections, *The New Yorker* had accepted two poems, "Mussel-Hunter at Rock Harbor" and "Nocturne." Sylvia positively yipped with joy, exclaiming that the good news would carry her through the summer like the "crest of a creative wave." That same day she wrote to Aurelia announcing her good fortune, which would amount to something like $350. That would pay for three months' rent.

The *New Yorker* poems showed the vulnerable side of Plath, somber and overwhelmed with composing a life outside of the academic boundaries that protected her. "Mussel Hunter at Rock Harbor" moves relentlessly toward the husk of a fiddler crab that has wandered out of its element to high ground among grasses. This stranded creature stimulates an inquiry: Is this the fate of a recluse, a suicide, an intrepid discoverer of new worlds? These alternatives occur to a poet seeking to renew her inspiration by returning to the seashore, figuring out her options, and trying to become her own woman, her own poet. "Night Walk," published in *The New Yorker* and later retitled "Hardcastle Crags" in *Collected Poems,* brought Plath back to a "deep wooded gorge" in the Yorkshire valley of Hebden River. The landscape looms at night like the "antique world" that overwhelms the walker, who turns back toward the "stone-built town" before she is broken down into the quartz grit of the stones and hills. Sylvia was trying to save herself, even while wondering what kind of fate might pulverize her hopes. Could she build her work, like the town, out of the hard material of existence? Her haunting journal passages about a wounded bird she and Ted tried to nurse—and their failure, which ended in Ted gassing the bird to put it out of its misery—read like an unintended forecast of Sylvia's own fate. She marveled at how beautiful, perfect, and composed the asphyxiated bird looked in death.

During this period, "my father's spirit" (as Sylvia put it in her journal) seemed to preside over the poems she was assembling, once again, for a book that would eventually be called *The Colossus*, its eponymous poem dealing with her mythologizing of Otto Plath. If Sylvia had become an actress, she would have been attracted to the role of Hamlet, beseeched by his father, a spirit "doomed to walk the night." Reckoning with her powerful father's image was gradually becoming a Shakespearean struggle with existence itself, with the claims of the past upon the present. Even as Sylvia tried to liberate herself from her father's call, she was also suffocating. That sense of becoming bereft of and haunted by a father who will not let go, experienced by a child grown strong in the dominion of the father, bedeviled Sylvia Plath as she sat down beside Ted at the Ouija board during the summer of 1958, half-believing she really was in communion with Otto Plath, who appeared as "Prince Otto."

Sylvia could not sleep. She felt paralyzed, her novel appearing in her mind's eye like a ghost that could not materialize. For the first time, she regarded Ted as an obstacle. He was powerfully didactic about his own ideas, as she began to see when they were in the company of others. They were still remarkably compatible, she confided to her journal, but she had to admit that she enjoyed herself during those times he was away from her. He liked giving orders, making him sound like the peremptory Otto Plath. Ted's stiff neck, resulting from too much exercise, seemed indicative to Sylvia of his rigid personality.

In letters to Aurelia and Olywn, Ted revealed no hint of Sylvia's summertime funk. On the contrary, he pictured her as a poet on the go. Did he not see the suffering of a soul who said marriage to him was like sharing one skin? Was Ted keeping up appearances, or writing in wish fulfillment? Judging by Sylvia's journals, he was so absorbed in his own routines that he did not take in her torment. And she did not let on to her mother, writing instead that she was reading about the sea for poetic inspiration and resuming her study of German because of her attachment to her roots.

By late July, Sylvia began producing poems again, breaking a ten-day drought. This cycle reprised the summer before on Cape Cod, when it had taken two weeks or so for her to settle down to a writing regimen. Prose remained an obstacle. With plenty of ideas for stories, she was stymied when it came to plots, as well as feeling she had been spoiled by the early success of her fiction in *Seventeen* and *Mademoiselle.* Even on the level of slick magazine pieces, she thought she had to step up her game.

Although Sylvia had always supposed she would wait to have children until after the publication of a novel or a first book of poetry, she began to yearn for motherhood. On 2 August, she complained to her journal that her life with Ted had become "ingrown." In *Letters Home,* Aurelia describes Sylvia and Ted's reaction to a visit on 3 August with friends and their three children. The two-year-old girl latched on to Ted, while Sylvia reverently examined the one-year-old as though discovering some treasure she had been seeking. Aurelia imagined what it would be like to be a fairy godmother waving a wand, producing a home, and greeting her daughter with all she needed to have a family and her writing, too.

To Sylvia, though, having children in America meant capitulating to an overwhelming complacency. She hated the way her Aunt Dot looked down on Ted because he did not have a job and was not career oriented. Having those solid, middle-class achievements meant succumbing to the desperation that Sylvia disliked in her mother. Better the anxiety of the artist than the neurosis of the conformist. Sylvia averred that security was inside herself and Ted. She had the confidence of seeing "Mussel Hunter at Rock Harbor" in the 9 August issue of *The New Yorker* and imagining readers all over the world marveling at her work.

The move from Northampton to Boston in early September cheered Plath, especially since she now had a good view of the

Charles River. City noises took some adjusting to, she wrote to Elinor Friedman Klein. Plath sometimes suffered from painful menstrual cycles that could exacerbate her moodiness and discomfort with how little she had accomplished. On 11 September, she was suffering through cramps and a fever. She tried to distract herself with compulsive behavior: arranging the new apartment, scanning job ads in the paper—all the while telling herself she had to get on with her writing. Instead, she brooded over Elizabeth Taylor taking Eddie Fischer away from Debbie Reynolds. She asked herself in her journal why this should matter. And yet it did, because Sylvia Plath seemed wired into what critic Leo Braudy has called the "frenzy of renown." Ted Hughes was along for the ride, but Sylvia Plath drove herself just as wildly as the movie stars she read about.

Three days later, Sylvia noted in her journal that they were both in a "black depression." That their moods coincided so perfectly seemed yet another proof to her that he was her male counterpart—this time, though, she saw a dark side. Were they, like vampires, feeding off one another? She was in a suspicious mood and admitted her confusion. No longer part of an academic regime, she felt like a dilettante. If she got a job, at least she would be earning something and taking pleasure in a day's work. On 16 September, Peter Davison, a former lover and publishing contact, visited her and observed a "tense and withdrawn" Sylvia. His visit, however, was good for her. Two days later she was writing again, beginning with an analysis of Davison's character. She got a few "well-turned" sentences out of him. It was ever thus with her: relieving her depression with writing that converted her anxieties into satirical fiction. Davison preferred the "simpler, less poised," woman who had told him touchingly about her suicide during the summer he dated her. He disliked the overly controlled narrative she later produced in *The Bell Jar,* deploring her "clumsy irony, the defenses, the semifictionalized characters, the nastiness of temper that mar the novel for me." But this was genuine Sylvia Plath, too: astringent and happiest with a cudgel-like writing instrument in her hands.

By mid-October Sylvia had a job at Massachusetts General Hospital typing up records in the psychiatric clinic, answering phones, and performing all sorts of office work. The job was a tonic that resulted in, by critical consensus, her best work of short fiction, "Johnny Panic and the Bible of Dreams." In the story, a secretary/narrator obsessively types up other people's dreams. Although Plath believed she had profited greatly from her sessions with Dr. Beuscher, the story scorns modern medicine. Patients are "doomed to the crass fate these doctors call health and happiness." The demented narrator becomes the scapegoat for "five false priests in white surgical gowns," who place a "crown of wire" on her head and the "wafer of forgetfulness" on her tongue. In the psychologized 1950s, in the era of electric shocks, Plath imagines votaries protesting this crucifixion, chanting, "The only thing to love is Fear itself." Electric shock therapy robs the patient not just of memory, but also of the dread that is debilitating but also essential to the fully human, fully creative self. And yet the machine betrays the technicians, and "Johnny Panic," who embodies the fearful dreams the narrator has faithfully recorded, appears overhead in a "nimbus of arc lights" charging and illuminating the universe. Such an ending would seem to imply that fear is an ontological condition that cannot be medicalized—that is, cured. Plath was not endorsing fear per se—she knew too well how much it had immobilized her—but she regretted the bogus superiority of medical institutions that supposed they could manufacture a sense of health and well-being. The story is compelling and intriguing in large part because the narrator herself is unstable and yet commands a certain aura of authority—the kind of countercultural rebuttal to the establishment and to institutional psychiatric treatment reflected in novels like Ken Kesey's *One Flew Over the Cuckoo's Nest* (1962).

Sylvia did not, however, present a bold front to the poets and publishers who saw her socially. In his memoir, *The Fading Smile,* Davison reports poet Stanley Kunitz's observation: On visits Sylvia seemed to make a ritual of taking a chair and sitting slightly behind Ted, who took the main stage, so to speak. She played the adoring, "very mousy" spouse in Kunitz's memory. This is the same role Sylvia assumed during her year of teaching at Smith, when, according to Daniel Aaron's recollection, she was "very deferential . . . to her husband" and wanted him to be "included in everything."

These impressions accord with Sylvia's journal entries, which portray Ted at this time as the superior poet. Unsure of herself, Sylvia resumed weekly meetings with Dr. Beuscher.

We know what was on Sylvia's mind because she recorded Beuscher's words in a 12 December journal entry: "I give you permission to hate your mother." It was time, in other words, for Plath to acknowledge openly her loathing of the "smarmy matriarchy of togetherness." It was such a relief just to tell the permissive Beuscher whatever she was really thinking. Unlike Aurelia, the therapist did not "withold [sic] her listening." Similarly, Sylvia reveled in the battles with Ted, in those rough-and-tumble arguments, seeking what Aurelia had absolutely no appetite for. Wasn't Sylvia, in her own estimation, the mouse that roared? Wasn't her therapy all about how when writing to her mother—and even more so in her mother's presence—Sylvia surrendered to the role of dutiful daughter? Above all, this Sylvia wanted to please her mother, but in that very pleasing—that need to be good, that unquenchable craving for approval—she had betrayed herself and her urge to assert an entirely independent self, one that only got exercised in her fictional critiques of others. Why did she take an almost perverse pleasure in her rejection slips? Surely it was because this is what the world did: It *rejected you.* When a poem, story, or article did get accepted, Sylvia always reacted to her good fortune as if it were a kind of miracle, a momentary victory against overwhelming odds.

Beuscher's therapy provided no permanent solution to Plath's anxieties—or to her sense of her mother as a "walking vampire," sucking the life out of her. Sylvia might have been happier about hating her mother if Aurelia had not been so self-sacrificing, so saintly, that it enraged Sylvia when she thought her behavior worried her mother. She despised Aurelia because she had subjugated herself to the autocratic Otto, who wouldn't go to a doctor when he was sick, who died because he could not deal with disease. Yes, her mother had genuinely suffered, but the agony was also a lie, because Otto's tyranny had never been opposed or even admitted. Instead, Aurelia just gave herself over to her children. Aurelia's long battle with ulcers revealed how her children had bled her dry. Otto, with his gangrenous leg, would have been a "living idiot" if he had survived longer, Sylvia thought. Lucky for him that a blood clot had gone to his brain, so Aurelia could assume the role of mourning angel, telling her children that Daddy was gone. A disgusted Sylvia ended her journal rant with "Men men men." Sylvia told this tale about herself and her family in the third person, with scathing fairy-tale energy that ended in a sarcastic portrayal of Aurelia's "honey sweet" version of her innocent children's happy lives.

Sylvia hated her mother as one hates the messenger arriving with bad news. It felt like Aurelia had killed Otto and played the noble grieving wife, when, in fact, he, "an ogre" like all men, "didn't stay around." Sylvia's dismissive treatment of men exacted her revenge, she admitted in her journal. Men left and had fun; women stayed behind and mopped up. And Sylvia, still telling the tale of her life in the third person, pictured herself as the good girl who had gone mad and had been locked in a cell. The daughter had tried to kill herself as the only way to rid herself of her mother. This had been her golden rule: to do to herself what she wanted to do to her mother. She vowed to do everything her mother said not to do. She no longer wanted her mother's sacrifice, so she had sacrificed herself. Now, Sylvia slipped back into the first person, resenting her mother worrying about her and Ted. "She wants to be me: she wanted me to be her: she wants to crawl into my stomach and be my baby and ride along. But I must go her way," was Sylvia's summary judgment.

Dr. Beuscher associated Sylvia's writing block with hatred of her mother. Not writing withheld the very thing that excited Aurelia's approval, which would also be a form of appropriation, making Sylvia's achievement Aurelia's. Sylvia's suicide had been an effort to punish her mother and to show that her kind of love was inadequate. Sylvia had felt better about her mother while living in England, because letters could function as a way for both of them to keep their desired images intact.

Sylvia did not seem to realize the danger of relying on Ted to be absolutely everything her father and mother were not. With him, she believed, she had rejected the compromises, the settling for less with smaller men. Dr. Beuscher had identified the risks: Would Sylvia have the courage to admit she had chosen the wrong man?

Plath said the question did not scare her. Instead it prompted another aria about her husband's virtues. A bad sign.

Indeed, the compulsion to lionize Ted drove Sylvia to obsessive thoughts about motherhood and family, to experience the same kind of dynamic that Marilyn Monroe was playing out with Arthur Miller. The adoring, virtually simpering persona that Monroe affected in her public appearances with her big man reappeared in reports of Plath's obeisance to her master. Thirteen December: a girl appears at the door of their apartment, selling Christmas arrangements, and Sylvia calls to Ted, telling the girl, "The man decides in this house." Dr. Beuscher might have pointed out that Sylvia no longer felt the need of a father for reasons quite different from what Sylvia supposed. Or rather, Sylvia would need and yet reject that father once again when she saw that Ted was not so different from Otto after all. Such thoughts did occur to Sylvia in moments when an angry Ted accused her of behaving just like her mother. She was mulling over a story about a man with "deep-rooted conventional ideas of womanhood." Talking with Ted about jobs—their money was running out—may have turned Sylvia's attention to the notion of a story about Dick Norton and the doctor's life she had renounced when she rejected him. Such a marriage would have deprived her of the very experience she needed to become a writer, she reasoned. Moreover, as a doctor's wife she would have resented his opportunities. But the story went nowhere, and Sylvia diverted herself with looking up the requirements for a PhD in psychology.

The sessions with Dr. Beuscher became more stressful, reducing Sylvia to tears as she admitted to jealousy of Ted and suspicion of his appeal to other women—and, at last, confessing that she identified him with her father, their faces and bodies becoming interchangeable in her dreams. Ted became the missing man, the father out with the girl on the Smith campus, a scene that had enraged Sylvia and fueled her dread about her husband leaving her. Sylvia's journal entries about her colloquies with Dr. Beuscher resemble a cathartic Greek play, with Plath worrying that perhaps like others in her life, Dr. Beuscher would abandon her. Sylvia had not been paying for treatment and was relieved when her therapist suggested a fee of five dollars an hour. Like Marilyn Monroe, who also was undergoing psychiatric treatment at the time, Sylvia Plath wondered why she could not count on even those closest to her, why she suspected their motives—while at the same time she puzzled over a sense of guilt that resulted in punishing herself. And like Monroe, Plath read Freud in hope of understanding her rages at herself and others that led to her suicide attempt. Both women wondered if bringing another child into the world might somehow redeem them, make their lives worthwhile by grounding them in the continuity of existence. But birthing a child was also a frightening prospect. Sylvia dreamed of losing a month-old baby. She had trouble rising in the morning and was slipping into passivity, "going sloppy," she wrote.

Sylvia tried to keep her doubts to herself, knowing how much they would upset Ted. Judging by his letters home, he had worked up a good writing schedule by January 1959, while Sylvia still struggled. He had it all settled in his mind that they would return to England by the end of the year. For both Ted and Sylvia, a dinner party with Robert Lowell and his wife, Elizabeth Hardwick, proved rewarding. Lowell was a great admirer of Hughes's poetry, and Sylvia made a point of recording how tenderly Lowell kissed his wife. Such displays of affection, on which Sylvia put a high premium, present a very different picture from Hughes's fond but also cavalier recollection of meeting Lowell, the mad poet, who from time to time had to be institutionalized when his behavior became erratic and sometimes even violent. Sylvia, for her part, looked forward to Lowell's poetry class at Boston University, which would begin shortly.

In the afterglow of the Lowell-Hardwick party, Plath wrote "Point Shirley." Set in her grandmother's back yard after the great hurricane of Sylvia's childhood, the poem evokes the image of a spit of sand slowly eroded by the sea—an apt image of her own memories wearing out over time, suggesting the grief of loss, which is emphasized by the blood-red sun sinking over Boston. Sylvia remembered her grandmother's love, which she now wanted to get from "these dry-papped stones." Although motherhood and birth are never mentioned, they seem present in the poet's yearning to generate a new life that arises out of her love for the old. She had Dr. Spock on her reading list. She enjoying visiting a friend and playing with her children, feeling a part of "young womanhood" absorbed in "women and womentalk." She was even keeping her poems away from Ted because his opinion might paralyze her. After a visit to Stanley Kunitz, she concluded that Kunitz did not like women poets. Listening to him, she could only think about having a baby, and of her disappointment at the arrival of another menstrual period.

It helped a little to attend Robert Lowell's class and hear his response to her poems, but in truth, she did not feel very inspired by his ineffectual teaching and was hoping to do more with her prose. This is the class that included Anne Sexton and another well-known poet, George Starbuck. Sexton later wrote an unrevealing memoir about her jaunts with Sylvia and Starbuck. Lowell recalled Plath as "willowy, long-waisted, sharp-elbowed, nervous, giggly, gracious—a brilliant, tense presence embarrassed by restraint. Her humility and willingness to accept what was admired seemed at times to give her an air of maddening docility that hid her unfashionable patience and boldness. . . . I sensed her abashment and distinction, and never guessed her later appalling and triumphant fulfillment." Although Lowell was beginning to enter his confessional poetry phase and Sexton proved an apt acolyte with her flamboyantly self-referential poems, the greater influence on Plath was Theodore Roethke's brilliantly controlled self-revelatory poems, full of fecund metaphors of growth. Her reading of Faulkner, especially of *Sanctuary* and "The Bear," would have a long-term impact on her own violent, apocalyptic verse. Sylvia Plath gave Anne Sexton her due but also thought her contemporary's work "loose."

On 9 March, Sylvia, accompanied by Ted, visited her father's grave in Winthrop, just a flat stone near Azalea Path. She wanted to dig him up as proof of his existence. She felt cheated, probably because seeing the site resolved nothing. His dying while she was so young seemed a swindle. The poem commemorating her visit, "Electra on Azalea Path," is, as she realized, overdone. She did not yet have the capacity to strip down her emotions into the taut lines of her later work. Still, the poem does capture the sensibility of a daughter who tells her father how she has dreamed his "epic, image by image," and in the poem's concluding line confesses, "It was my love that did us both to death." Discussing her father and this visit in therapy made Sylvia feel she was regressing. But then Ted won a Guggenheim Fellowship, Sylvia received another acceptance from *The New Yorker,* and the couple was invited to spend two months at Yaddo, the writer's colony in Saratoga Springs, New York, where they would repair in mid-September. Their concerns about money would be relieved until the end of the year, and in Yaddo's bracing, pampered climate, perhaps Plath would finally achieve a breakthrough.

For all her complaining about stunted creativity, Sylvia arose on 31 May to realize that since the beginning of 1959 she had written six stories, including some of her best: "Johnny Panic," "The Shadow," "Sweetie Pie and the Guttermen," and "Above the Oxbow." "The Shadow" re-creates the ambiance of the war years, when Sylvia listened to radio programs and read comic books featuring Superman, the Green Hornet, and The Shadow, with their messages that crime doesn't pay. In the story, a young girl learns about the atrocities committed in Japanese prisoner of war camps and dreams of an evil that is not so easily defeated: "The hostile, brooding aura of the nightmare seeped out, somehow to become part of my waking landscape." Even worse, her father is ostracized in their neighborhood because he is German. And the young girl further implicates her father in evil by biting a boy: "In some obscure, roundabout way" she has betrayed her father to the neighbors. When he is forced to leave home on government orders, the girl cries out at the unfairness and declares there can be no God if such injustice is permitted. What had seemed to be the externality of evil in programs like *The Shadow* is now brought home to her: "The shadow in my mind lengthened with the night blotting out our half of the world, and beyond it; the whole globe seemed sunk in darkness." Such a story debunks American exceptionalism and foreshadows Sylvia's return with Ted to Europe.

Sylvia continued to publish poetry in top-rated journals like *Partisan Review, The Sewanee Review,* and *The Hudson Review,* but her first book of poetry had just missed winning the Yale Younger Poets prize that went to George Starbuck, whom Sylvia dismissed as a light verse writer. In a letter to Ann Davidow, she confessed she did not have the confidence to commit herself to a novel, the long-delayed "Falcon Yard," which she could perhaps resurrect when she and Ted headed for Yaddo in September, now that she had thought of a name for a heroine, Sadie Peregrine, a stand-in for herself. In the interim, they were setting off on a cross-country adventure as soon as they found a summer sublet for their Boston apartment.

By 25 June, Sylvia had purchased camping equipment. Out of the summer sojourn, she produced one memorable story, "The Fifty-Ninth Bear," which makes for fascinating reading when set beside the long letter Hughes wrote to his parents about the adventure that inspired the tale, and beside Sylvia's contemporaneous report to Aurelia and Warren. Ted described how he and Sylvia woke up in the middle of the night to the sounds of bears foraging through garbage in Yellowstone Park, sniffing around their tent, and then apparently breaking into their car's trunk, prompting him to look out and discover that a bear had broken the rear window to get at their food—all details Sylvia put in her story. Later they learned a bear had killed a woman who had shone a flashlight on it. Ted counted sixty-seven bears during their stay. Sylvia's account emphasized their fear that the bear would eat them. She described looking out of the tent at the bear, not mentioning what Ted did at that moment. Later, he did get up to have a look. Sylvia said they were "quite shaken."

In Plath's story, the husband is hectored by his passive-aggressive wife into shooing the bear away, an effort that results in the husband's death. This death is the culmination of tensions between the couple, centering on his rather condescending efforts to placate her. She is portrayed as a hysteric who depends on her husband and resents him at the same time. According to Lucas Myers, when the story was published in *The London Magazine,* he and others were troubled by Plath's willingness to kill Ted off in a story. But the husband's name in "The Fifty-Ninth Bear" is Norton, and he does not resemble Ted Hughes so much as he does Dick Norton, whose sense of male prerogative deeply offended Sylvia. Neither Plath's journals nor her letters offer any support for the kind of animosity toward the male protector that is portrayed in the story. Moreover, the wife, named Sadie (like the protagonist of Sylvia's projected novel), is an unflattering portrait of Sylvia herself—or of the Sylvia she would have become as Dick Norton's wife, subordinating herself to a doctor's practice and neurotically relying on him to cosset her. Ted's own commanding presence, and his affinity for the natural world, are entirely absent from this story. Indeed, as critic Tracy Brain observes, "The Fifty-Ninth Bear" is all about tourists on trips who "do" nature while having no real connection with it—and pay for their errant stupidity with their lives.

And yet, how can one read "The Fifty-Ninth Bear" and not wonder if in fiction Sylvia Plath was owning up to her anger about her husband, which she could not yet express in a nonfictional voice? After all, Norton sings a ditty about the "wanderin' boys of Liverpool," although he is not explicitly identified as English. In this reading, the name Norton is merely a way to disguise an attack on Ted. Still, the man who is killed is foolish (to use Ted's word from the letter to his parents) to shine a flashlight at the bear. And Ted Hughes was no fool. With his profound rapport with wild creatures he could not be more different from the hapless Norton of the story. What Sylvia might have been getting at in the private mythology of her life is unrecoverable, but the story seems nevertheless self-congratulatory, in the sense that it was her way of explaining why she rejected Dick and opted for Ted.

Plath had her usual trouble settling into a new environment. She loved Yaddo's traditional furnishings and the sumptuous meals, but she spent the balance of September reading Eudora Welty and Jean Stafford and writing story ideas in her journal. She sent three stories to Peter Davison, now an editor at *The Atlantic Monthly*. She doubted this weak-willed male, as she deemed him, would accept her work. Sylvia put in a good seven hours a day on her writing, enjoying her top-floor view of the "dense pines." Ted had his own writing studio in the woods. Sumptuous breakfasts and box lunches kept them going for a whole day.

Sylvia read Arthur Miller while Ted was writing a play, which is perhaps why in early October she dreamed of Marilyn Monroe. Aurelia had wished she could be the fairy godmother in her daughter's life, and Plath was working on a "mummy" story when she dreamed the fairy godmother scene with Marilyn. Only with Monroe could Plath unbend, even though Monroe and Miller "could, of course, not know us at all," Sylvia noted. And she still could not write her novel. And she still called Ted her "salvation." Maybe in England, she confided to her journal, she would have more luck. Harcourt had just turned down her first book of poetry.

Sometime during her stay at Yaddo, Plath realized she was pregnant, although her journal is surprisingly silent on the subject. In early November, in her fourth month, she sped up her creation of new poems. "It's wonderful how the prospect of such responsibilities concentrates one's mind," Ted wrote to a friend in early December. But then Sylvia's output abruptly stopped, and she wondered what had happened to the confident writer of "Sunday at the Mintons." She worried that in spite of all efforts to the contrary she had relied too much on Ted. Now Yaddo seemed like a nunnery that locked her away from the world, and she thought of beating it back to Boston before settling in London—or perhaps in the English countryside, not far from the city. She was terribly confused, alternately elated and enervated, reflexively thinking that a baby would prevent her from being herself, and then spending a happy day with a stomach that felt fat with life—only to have another disturbed by a dream of dying in childbirth.

The couple decided Sylvia would give birth in England, where they arrived in mid-December. An ebullient Ted, writing to Daniel Huws, declared he had escaped petrification and was already renewing himself in England. In her journal, Sylvia welcomed her return to a country that had been receptive to her poems and stories and seemed to share her sensibility. On 9 December, Ted wrote to Lucas Myers that Sylvia, now six months pregnant, had written a dozen spectacular poems that reflected an entirely new phase— all done as wild monologues. "I've already stolen several things from them," he boasted.

CHAPTER 6

THE UNIVERSAL MOTHER

(1960—62)

1960: Plath and Hughes rent a London flat; **1 April:** Frieda Rebecca, their first child, is born; **October:** *The Colossus,* Plath's first book, is published; **6 February 1961:** Plath suffers a miscarriage; **28 February:** Plath undergoes an appendectomy; **March:** Plath begins writing *The Bell Jar;* **July:** the couple purchases a manor house in Devon; **17 January 1962:** Nicholas Farrar Hughes is born; **May:** David and Assia Wevill visit Court Green.

On 3 February, Sylvia sent a round-up letter to Marcia Brown, explaining what it had been like to move back to England. She and Ted had stayed part of the time with Hughes's parents in Yorkshire, but with Olwyn visiting and other relatives dropping by, Sylvia had little time to herself or space in which to read, let alone write. Ted's mother, a messy housekeeper who left greasy pans in the oven and cupboards, got on Sylvia's fastidious nerves. Sylvia wanted to help out, but Mrs. Hughes resisted. Sylvia felt hurt, she later told her friend Elizabeth Compton. Mrs. Hughes, Compton felt sure, did not want to exclude Sylvia, only wanting to pay respect to this well-educated woman of a different class.

Then there had been a ghastly three-week search for a furnished flat. The awful rainy, cold, and windy weather—always sure to depress Plath—and the appalling, dingy condition of the housing stock that cost more that twenty-five dollars a week (out of their price range), made her feel adrift in the large city, especially since she wanted to be near a good doctor and hospital. The American poet W. S. Merwin and his English wife, Dido, tried to be helpful, making phone calls and using their contacts, but they also agreed with Sylvia that the English were the "most secretly dirty race on earth." Even new items in department stores looked shabby to Sylvia. To get anything decent seemed to involve "key money," a form of large bribe to a real estate agent or landlord. Welcome to England, which had yet to boom itself out of its postwar blues.

Thanks to the Merwins, Sylvia and Ted finally found a flat on Chalcot Square near Primrose Hill, a very pleasant, almost country-like setting. The place needed a lot of work (Sylvia was applying her third coat of paint), but they were happy to have a home on a three-year lease—and relieved, since the baby was due in late March. They had a sunny kitchen and a view of the square, where Sylvia watched birds and children playing. They had to buy appliances, but the Merwins lent them some furniture. At the equivalent of eighteen dollars a week, plus charges for gas and electricity, they could budget enough using Ted's Guggenheim Fellowship money. And of course the National Health Service would cover all costs associated with childbirth. Ted's letters share Sylvia's enthusiasm for their new home, as well as her dismay over what he called the "frightful competition for flats." Sylvia reported to her mother on 7 February that Ted had just finished painting the living room walls in white over textured paper, and that they intended to have an engraving of Isis, enlarged from one of his astrology books, mounted on one wall. To Olwyn, Ted wrote that he liked "the feel of living in London. My stay in America seems to have greatly objectified my sense of England."

Sylvia decided to have her baby at home with the assistance of a midwife, not an unusual practice in England, but one forced on Sylvia because it was too late to register at a hospital under the National Health Service. She could be admitted as an emergency patient, but Sylvia preferred to plan ahead. She was comforted to have the assistance of Dido's obstetrician. Natural childbirth—still an unusual choice for a woman in the States—had the blessing of her English doctor, who promised to be on call should there be complications. Sylvia was also practicing relaxation exercises, and although she did not mention it to Marcia, Ted had also experimented with hypnotizing her and with teaching her self-hypnotic states that relieved stress. She was counting on him to be on hand, to cook and generally to bolster her—although she wished a friend like Marcia could also be around. Sylvia, probably more fearful than she let on, wanted to know what Marcia thought of this setup.

Dido Merwin, Lucas Myers, and other British friends of Ted Hughes have portrayed Sylvia as rigid, self-absorbed, and hopelessly American. And yet here was an aspect of her that they did not seem to appreciate. Her American doctor had advised against natural childbirth. And indeed, everything in Sylvia's suburban background cried out against this old world way of doing things. For all her nightmares about childbirth gone wrong, Sylvia showed considerable flexibility and courage in approaching this momentous change in her life. Her husband seems to have had qualms. To Lucas Meyers, Hughes showed the first sign that not all was well. Out for a drink with his friend from Cambridge days, Ted "confided to me what seemed not to be manageable in the marriage," Myers recalls in *Crows Steered/Bergs Appeared*. To Myers, Hughes had never before been critical of married life with Sylvia, and like many of his friends, Myers perceived Hughes to be a "mostly willing prisoner" of the marriage. But in one instance, he told Myers, he had decided to count the number of times Sylvia had interrupted his work in the course of a morning: The total had reached 104.

Although Sylvia told Marcia that neither she nor Ted could get any work done during the previous two months, in fact, as letters to Aurelia reveal, Sylvia was working on a new book of poetry that would find a publisher in February. She was also typing some of Ted's work. As usual, Sylvia treated her mother to an anodyne version of events, emphasizing the coziness of the Hughes home and socializing with his family—especially with the beautiful Olwyn, blonde, as tall as Sylvia, and at thirty-one looking no more than twenty-one. Ted's sister already loved her, Sylvia declared in her fairy-tale version of her stay with her in-laws. Sylvia's first pregnancy, she assured her mother, was going well. Other than some backaches, heartburn, and a kicking baby, she felt surprisingly comfortable, perhaps because she gained relatively little weight. She estimated she walked three to five miles a day. She wondered if the birth of her child would coincide with the publication date (18 March) of Ted's second book, *Lupercal*.

On 18 February, Sylvia wrote optimistically about living in England to Lynne Lawner, a friend acquired during a poetry contest several years earlier. Heinemann had accepted her first book of poetry for publication: "I think I shall be a very happy exile & have absolutely no desire to return to the land of milk & honey & spin-dryers." A Somerset Maugham award for Ted (about $1,400) had them dreaming of a writing holiday the following winter somewhere in southern Europe. Sylvia was still cooking a full meal the day after her official due date of 27 March. A. Alvarez's positive review of *Lupercal* in the *Observer* seemed to add to their anticipatory excitement on 31 March, when Sylvia predicted in a letter to her mother that the baby's arrival could not be much more than a day away. Sylvia had swelled to 155 pounds, about twenty more than her usual weight.

Sylvia went out for an evening walk, watching a thin moon hover over the magical landscape of Primrose Hill, strewn with daffodils, and then retired for the night. She awakened just after midnight, when, as she wrote her mother, "everything began." The first labor pains started at 1:15 a.m. The doctor arrived around 4 a.m., but without anesthetics, since no one had anticipated the rapid birth, which Sylvia called violent and painful, but also amazing. It was all over by 6:00 a.m., a remarkably easy first birth, nothing like Sylvia had anticipated. By the next day, she was sitting up in bed typing letters to her mother and Marcia Brown, detailing the epic event and describing Frieda Rebecca Hughes, "dozing and snorkeling" since dawn and already bathed by the midwife in Sylvia's largest Pyrex baking dish. Ted had held her hand throughout the ordeal. She had avoided the horror of a hospital stay, a fear of Sylvia's that Nancy Hunter Steiner has described in her memoir. Even though Sylvia had been advised to stay in bed, she got up to call her mother, announcing the birth of "Ein wunderkind, Mummy.

Ein wunderkind!" Months later she would write a beautiful poem, "Morning Song," that began with Frieda's "bald cry," announcing herself to the world, and ending with a tribute to a child already shaping a language for herself, "clear vowels" that "rise like balloons."

Sylvia gave Ted full credit for all his support. For weeks he had been putting her to sleep in trances, predicting an "easy, short delivery." At a time when squeamish men paced hospital corridors removed from the anguish and complications of childbirth, Ted Hughes was on the spot, relishing the moment when the baby crowned and began to emerge from Sylvia's body. He told Lucas Myers all about it three weeks later in a long letter. Ted praised Sylvia's active participation in the birth, unlike passive, immobilized mothers, "stupefied with drugs," worked over by doctors in American hospitals. He likened her pushing the baby out of herself to "backing a lorry around a tight bend in a narrow alley full of parked cars." Sylvia had absorbed Ted's rejection of American know-how. A week after Frieda's birth, Sylvia reprimanded her mother for taking a chauvinistic attitude: "No more about growth hormones and growth stopping, please! I'm surprised at you. Tampering with nature! What an American thing to feel measuring people to ideal heights will make them happier . . ."

On 21 April, a weeping Sylvia watched what became known as the Aldermaston marchers line up in a seven-mile-long column with "Ban the Bomb!" banners and signs, heading toward Trafalgar Square. She was proud that her baby should be part of this protest against the poisoning of the atmosphere with fallout from nuclear tests. Sylvia never wavered in thinking of the atomic bomb as civilization's great misfortune. Politically and culturally, she felt much closer to England than to America, especially when she watched friends like the Merwins join the march. She hoped that neither Aurelia nor Warren was thinking of voting for the Machiavellian Richard Nixon. She wondered what they thought of Kennedy, expressing no opinion of her own about him.

"Frieda is my answer to the H-bomb," Sylvia wrote Lynne Lawner. Plath was a very happy mother. She looked forward to having a large family. Wendy Campbell came from Cambridge to visit and saw a radiant Sylvia taking to motherhood with impressive assurance. Jane Truslow, a friend at Smith who had married Peter Davison, also visited the Chalcot Square flat, after which she expressed her astonishment that a prima donna like Sylvia had adapted to family life with such aplomb. Truslow told Edward Butscher that it was the first time she saw Sylvia able to get outside of herself. Peter Davison, always apt to see the negative side of his former lover, noted her intense restlessness. Dido Merwin, up to then a warm supporter of Sylvia, began to withdraw her affection, appalled at what she saw as a virago who hounded her long-suffering husband, who did everything possible to placate her. It seems true that Ted almost never complained to his friends about Sylvia and went out of his way to excuse her moody periods and rudeness. It troubled Sylvia that she did not have "a good American girlfriend," and Ann Davidow's visit in early May was more than welcome. They took up where they had left off ten years earlier. Plath felt an instant rapport with Ann's husband, Leo Goodman, and noted that his astrological sign was Leo, just like Ted's.

After a month at home, Sylvia relished a dinner party with T. S. Eliot, who had first recommended that Faber & Faber publish Ted's work. Ted described Eliot to Olwyn as "whimsical" and yet "remote." He kept staring at the floor, looking up only to smile at his wife, Valerie. But Sylvia enjoyed drinking sherry with the "wry and humorous" poet near a coal fire. He immediately put her at ease, even though she thought of herself as in the presence of a "descended god." Valerie, just as welcoming, showed Sylvia her husband's baby pictures: a handsome man right from the start, Sylvia wrote Aurelia. Then Stephen Spender and his wife arrived. Intimate gossip ensued about W. H. Auden, D. H. Lawrence, Virginia Woolf—virtually all of Sylvia's favorites got the full treatment. Sylvia did not walk, she "floated" into dinner. Spender admired Ted's "craggy Yorkshire handsomeness combined with a certain elongated refinement." He remembered that Sylvia talked more than her husband and that he liked this pretty, intelligent woman, later writing her and apologizing for talking too much at dinner when Eliot's conversation began to lag.

During this period, Sylvia met A. Alvarez for the first time. As poetry editor of *The Observer,* he had accepted both her work and Ted's. He was, in biographer Elaine Feinstein's words, a "king-maker," a critic who could establish reputations. He held a position of prominence on a major daily paper that no one else occupied— then or now. When he first visited their flat, Sylvia played the part of proper wife so well that he was embarrassed to learn that Mrs. Hughes was the Sylvia Plath he had published. She had to bring up the subject of her work when she realized he did not recognize her. But Alvarez detected no note of grievance or resentment in her be-havior.

On 21 June in a letter to Olive Higgins Prouty, Hughes called Sylvia a marvelous mother who calmly fed her baby and exhib-ited endless patience. Sylvia returned the compliment three days later in a letter to Aurelia, extolling Ted as a "marvel of under-standing" who was "wonderful with the baby." They took turns working in the Merwin study—mornings for Sylvia and afternoons for Ted. Both poets gave public readings, and Ted continued to earn good fees for reading his poems and those of others on the BBC, which also produced two of his verse plays. He had also be-gun selling his manuscripts to dealers and to Indiana University. In this way, the couple cobbled together an income. They attended a Faber & Faber cocktail party, where a proud Sylvia watched while Ted was photographed next to W. H. Auden, establishing Ted's place in the next generation of Faber poets. That her destiny seemed bound up with London seemed confirmed on the day she hap-pened to walk down Fitzroy Road and saw a freehold house for sale, an unusual occurrence since most dwellings went for ninety-nine year leases. This was the street on which Yeats lived, Sylvia told her mother. The couple, still relying on Ted's Guggenheim money and a thousand dollars she drew out of their Wellesley bank account, could not afford to buy a house, but she hoped that someday they would find just such a residence to own.

On 22 August, Ted wrote Aurelia and Warren a chatty letter about visiting his parents in Yorkshire. He needed a respite from the hurly-burly of London. He described a fetching Sylvia, who had been reading Alan Moorehead's book about the Gallipoli cam-paign and eagerly questioned his father, a survivor of that catastro-

Otto, Aurelia, and Sylvia Plath, July 1933.

Courtesy Mortimer Rare Book Room, Smith College.

Sylvia and Warren Plath on a sailboat in Winthrop, Massachusetts, August 1940, three months before Otto Plath's death.

Courtesy Mortimer Rare Book Room, Smith College.

26 Elmwood Road, the home of Aurelia, Warren,
and Sylvia Plath, Wellesley, Massachusetts.

Courtesy Peter K. Steinberg and Mortimer Rare Book Room, Smith College.

Sylvia Plath sunbathing in the backyard, 26 Elmwood Road, June 1946

Courtesy Mortimer Rare Book Room, Smith College.

Sylvia Plath, c. November 6, 1954.
Courtesy Judith Denison. Glenda Hydler: Restoration.

Sylvia Plath, April 1954, in front of
Lawrence House, Smith College.
Courtesy Mortimer Rare Book Room,
Smith College.

The River Cam in Cambridge,
where Sylvia studied during her Fulbright years, 1955–57.
Courtesy Peter K. Steinberg and Mortimer Rare Book Room, Smith College.

Sylvia Plath and Ted Hughes in Concord, Massachusetts, December 1959.
Courtesy Marcia Brown and Mortimer Rare Book Room, Smith College.

Chalcot Square, London, near the flat where Sylvia Plath and
Ted Hughes settled after moving from America to England in 1959.
Courtesy Peter K. Steinberg and Mortimer Rare Book Room, Smith College.

Court Green, Devon, the home Sylvia and Ted Hughes purchased in 1961.
Courtesy Peter K. Steinberg and Mortimer Rare Book Room, Smith College.

Sylvia and Nicholas Hughes in Devonshire, December 1962.
Photographer unknown. Copyright estate of Aurelia S. Plath.
Courtesy Smith College archives.

23 Fitzroy Road, London, the flat where Sylvia died.
Courtesy Peter K. Steinberg and Mortimer Rare Book Room, Smith College.

Primrose Hill, near both Chalcot Square and 23 Fitzroy Road,
and a favorite of Sylvia's because of its country air and walkways.

Courtesy Peter K. Steinberg and Mortimer Rare Book Room, Smith College.

Aurelia Plath, January 1961.
*Courtesy Mortimer Rare Book Room,
Smith College.*

Frieda (top left) and Nicholas (bottom right) with Elizabeth Compton's children, Hester (top right), Emma (lower left), and James (middle), 1967.

Courtesy Elizabeth Compton Sigmund. Glenda Hydler: Restoration.

phe. Father and son rarely spoke about this traumatic episode from William Hughes's youth, so watching his usually taciturn father open up to Sylvia proved quite entertaining to Ted. Long walks and time spent in Edith Hughes's garden soothed Sylvia, she reported to her mother.

Returning to London a fortnight later, Sylvia received a BBC invitation to read her work on the radio. With Ted's work in demand and her hope that he might write a popular play, they dreamed of a car and a country home, complete with a loom, a kiln, a book press, and other items of handcraft. They both thought they might strike it rich if he could write a play to suit the volatile spirit of the times, as Arnold Wesker and the other "angry young men" were doing. Sylvia even had Ted read Clifford Odets to absorb the working class, proletarian ethos.

On 17 December, just as the couple departed for another holiday in Yorkshire, Sylvia and Ted wrote separate letters to Aurelia and Warren. Ted confirmed Sylvia's reports of the significant attention his work continued to receive. He also made a point of saying that fatherhood was as much an adjustment for him as motherhood had been for Sylvia. He welcomed the change to family man, but seemed quite taken aback at his status as a public figure. He spoke of his fame as though a great cruelty had been done to him and showed no sign of the exultation that Sylvia experienced in the wake of his literary celebrity. He felt depleted, while Sylvia felt more full of herself. Literary life imprisoned Hughes even as it liberated his wife, but she honored his desire to reject certain kinds of media attention. He turned down, much to his mother's regret, an invitation to appear on a television program featuring the "poet of the year." He did not like the idea of being watched. But in the main he believed he had escaped the worst effects of his renown and had emerged, as out of "battlesmoke," still his own man. In the last month, Sylvia had recovered her momentum, writing five superior poems and energetic stories aimed at the women's magazine market, Ted reported. He thought these commercial outlets would be good for her, ridding her once and for all of the "arty" mood pieces her Smith professors had promoted. Sylvia really needed to put more action into her stories with killings, births, marriages—stories, in other words, in which things actually happened and were not just thought about. They were working together on plots that would get her stories going. As for his own work, he provides quite a long précis of a play, *The House of Aries,* which sounded very much in the vein of D. H. Lawrence: an exploration of the tensions between the logical, rational mind and the instinctive animalistic self which, if in conflict within the individual, lead to malaise and yearning for an undaunted savior, a dream figure, an "ideal accomplisher." Ted worried that his play was excessively abstract. It is, but it also projects precisely the kind of sensibility that moved Sylvia to write that notorious line in "Daddy": "Every woman adores a fascist."

The Christmas visit did not go that well, as Sylvia related in part of a letter Aurelia chose not to include in *Letters Home.* According to Anne Stevenson's biography, the trouble started when Olwyn expressed dismay over Sylvia's highly critical commentary about someone Olwyn did not know, but who was a poet she admired. To Olwyn, her sister-in-law's furious reaction only proved the "unwritten rule": Sylvia was not to be criticized. But surely another interpretation occurred to Sylvia: Why was Olwyn judging her, when Olwyn did not even know the party concerned? Wasn't Olwyn the one who was too quick to judge? Stevenson, working under the heavy burden of Olwyn's hectoring letters expressing exasperation with the biographer's handling of events, cut short this acrimonious scene. But the unauthorized Paul Alexander dilates upon it. Sylvia accused Olwyn of degrading her and Ted. An enraged Olwyn called Sylvia a "nasty bitch," and apparently disgusted with Plath's hearty appetite, made remarks about her overeating at Christmas dinner. And why had Sylvia not put Olwyn up at the Chalcot Square flat when Olwyn has visited London in the spring? Referring to Sylvia as "Miss Plath," Olwyn announced that *she* was the "daughter of the house." A silent Sylvia took Frieda out of Olwyn's hands, even as Ted's sister was evidently trying to calm down.

Olwyn later told Alexander that Sylvia had "overreacted to their charged dialogue." But anyone not beholden to Olywn, anyone who had observed her over many years—and who was willing to speak to a biographer (as Marvin Cohen did with me)—can readily observe that even years after Sylvia's death, Olwyn still hated her brother's wife. Indeed, anyone Olwyn perceived as standing in the way of her close connection to Ted was bound to be rejected. Edward Butscher reports that Sylvia told Clarissa Roche that the bond between Olwyn and Ted amounted to "intellectual incest." In her angrier moments, Sylvia omitted the adjective, Roche confided to Butscher. The higher Sylvia stood in Ted's estimation—especially after the publication of *The Colossus*—the more jealous Olwyn became. Never again, Sylvia vowed, would she stay in the same home with Olwyn Hughes.

Sylvia attached great importance to A. Alvarez's review of *The Colossus,* which *The Observer* published on 18 December. "She steers clear of feminine charm, deliciousness, gentility, supersensitivity and the act of being a poetess," Alvarez wrote. "She simply writes good poetry." Welcome praise indeed for a poet who believed that, like Ted, she had broken through the constraints that Alvarez thought crippled a good deal of postwar British poetry. That she was holding her own in the intense competition of London literary life (from which Ted Hughes was now retreating, as he dreamed of a country refuge) emboldened her and may have accounted for her caustic expression of superiority that set Olwyn off.

Reviews of *The Colossus* were outstanding. Critics in prestigious journals and newspapers praised the "virtuoso qualities of her style," calling her "clever" and "vivacious," poised and cool, and deserving to be ranked with Ted Hughes and Theodore Roethke. Some of these adjectives could be interpreted as condescending, but read in full the reviews reveal respect and admiration. Of course, even supporters like Alvarez saw certain faults—a desire sometimes to indulge in rhetoric for its own sake, for example— but in the main Plath attracted the approval of important poet-critics like John Wain, Roy Fuller, and A. E. Dyson. A scene in the film *Sylvia,* in which an English critic dismisses *The Colossus* as merely the product of a wife married to a more important poet, does not do justice to Plath's place in the literary world of her time. Ted Hughes, writing to Lucas Myers on 21 January, expressed his satisfaction with Plath's excellent reviews. Both Ted and Sylvia wrote to Olive Higgins Prouty about their successes, and she, in turn, wrote back warmly, enclosing a check for $150.

Sylvia was pregnant again, and besides her usual wintertime colds and flu, she suffered from appendicitis. Surgery, she was advised, could be done safely long before the baby was due in late August. She would probably enter the hospital in early February, but in the meantime she started on a part-time copyediting job at *The Bookseller,* a trade organ. And she and Ted appeared in a BBC program, "Two of a Kind," in which they described their lives and work. He depicted a couple so in sync with one another that they had become almost one sensibility. Sylvia, calling herself "more practical," provided a soberer account of their collaboration.

Then on the morning of 6 February, Sylvia had a miscarriage. There seemed to be no explanation, she wrote her mother, assuring her that Ted was taking wonderful care of her. Sylvia felt especially awful, because she had asked Aurelia to change her travel plans so as to be present around the time of the child's birth. Undaunted, however, Sylvia was looking forward to her next pregnancy after scheduling removal of her appendix for late February. Given her horror of hospitals and concerns about the pain and recovery from surgery, she did remarkably well, enjoying Ted's hospital visit and substitution of rare steak sandwiches and Toll House cookies for the frightful hospital food. To the adoring Sylvia, he looked like a giant, trolling the hospital corridors next to people half his size. He seemed to be courting her as in their first days together.

The first of March marked an epic day, because Ted had delivered to her the much-coveted *New Yorker* first-reading contract. This development meant she would send her poems to *The New Yorker* first, and only to other publications if her work were not accepted. She received a one-hundred-dollar signing bonus, plus a 25 percent increase in the rates they paid her. The renewable one-year contract had cost of living raises built into it as well. Even though Sylvia had yet to write her greatest poetry, all signs pointed to her ascension to the pantheon with her beloved Ted.

Except for the food, Sylvia had no criticism of the National Health Service. Indeed, the facilities were brighter and the staff more cheerful than what she had seen in Wellesley when her mother had been hospitalized. Sylvia also enjoyed listening to her fellow patients. She began taking notes of their conversations. She greatly admired their hardy, uncomplaining natures. She enjoyed chatty visits with the vivacious "Bunny," the goiter lady, and "the Duchess." She was treated more like a guest than a patient. "Will I have an enema?" a solicitous nurse asked. The doctors were handsome and reassuring. Indeed, everyone was so amiable, saying goodnight to one another, that Sylvia felt no need to indulge in "the mopes" or any sort of self-pity. Turning in for her first night, she was delighted to discover she had her own set of flowered curtains affording her some privacy.

As she recovered from surgery, Sylvia began to notice petty annoyances: getting bumped in the hallway, feeling uncomfortable in a drafty room with a cracked window, and—the worst—the "ward-snorer." And why were there no bells to call nurses? By 5 March, on her way to recovery and managing her pain quite well, Sylvia could feel herself departing from the company of sufferers, who lost interest in you as soon as you returned to health. But she loved all the gossiping—good story material—and realized that Ted was having a much harder time of it at home trying to work and take care of Frieda. Her feelings of camaraderie in hospital are reminiscent of her days at camp. In both cases, these tight-knit, closed-in communities brought out her compassion, as she consoled homesick girls and later cheered up other patients. And as she did during her work in the psychiatric ward and her time spent aboard an ocean liner, she enjoyed studying cases of the afflicted and the eccentric, writing them up in her journal. Sylvia reported that only one person, one of her fellow patient's daughters, noticed her books, telling her mother she was bedded next to an "intellectual."

Returning home on 8 March, Sylvia still had to rely on Ted for baby lifting and laundry. Between her miscarriage and her hospital stay, it had been a terrible month for him, Sylvia told her mother. And yet he never complained. She felt badly about what she had put her "saintly" spouse through. Women in the hospital marveled that a husband would take on so much. Ted had some help with babysitting, but in the main he took over because he wanted Sylvia to recuperate as fast as possible to rejoin him in their writing regimen. In a letter to her Aunt Dotty, Sylvia reported that under Ted's care she had regained her energy by the end of March. With the thought of more children to come, Sylvia told Aurelia that by 1962 they just had to find a house, although they hardly had the income that would qualify them for a mortgage. Ted kept winning cash prizes, though, and his BBC work would net him something like $1,500 in the course of a year.

By 1 May, Sylvia was buoyed by the news that Knopf would publish *The Colossus* in the United States. Ted had written Aurelia a few weeks earlier to say Sylvia was in top form and much in demand. From her recent work he singled out "Tulips," a poem derived from her hospital stay, and a work that reflected Sylvia's surrender not only of her day clothes and her body, but also her sense of self to the surgical staff. Looking at the photographs of her husband and daughter, she describes herself as a "thirty-year-old cargo boat," letting slip things that "sink out of sight." The poem says what Sylvia could not quite articulate in her journal and letters: The hospital stay had been a welcome letting go, a relaxation of nerves and an abnegation of family responsibilities. In the hospital she feels like a nun, white and pure. The stay is also, however, a kind of death, "the white of human extinction," in critic Marjorie Perloff's words. The red tulips, rude with life, arrive as an intrusion, an invasion of the patient's pleasant anesthetic daze. The flowers seem like that roaring snorer Sylvia mentions in her journal, bringing the world back to her. But the tulips also come to symbolize the opening and closing of her blooming heart as she tastes water (her tears?) that reminds her of the salty sea in a "country far away as health."

The persona of the poem, like Plath herself, seems to be emerging out of her passivity, becoming a person again, although she is not yet well. In *The Collected Poems*, Ted Hughes includes a note suggesting "Tulips" was *the* breakthrough poem, marking the moment when Plath threw away her thesaurus and spoke with spontaneity and clarity in her own poet's voice. Certainly after her miscarriage and hospital stay, both of which left her feeling like someone done to, "Tulips" seems to presage a rebirth in the classic fashion—in this case with a heroine, rather than a hero, reluctantly, then inexorably moving toward a seagoing quest, a type of female Ulysses.

Ted looked upon Sylvia's hospital stay as a detoxification. He believed that her appendix had been slowly poisoning her for five years. So the rest had done her good, giving her respite from taking care of Frieda as well, a comment that could be taken as a gloss on "Tulips." That Ted, as he told Sylvia, had genuinely enjoyed taking care of his daughter seems apparent in his delighted descriptions of her standing up in her pen and laughing at everybody, then throwing her ball and bawling at them. He announced to Aurelia that they were buying a new Morris station wagon. He promised to take her on a tour when she arrived in June.

Sylvia did not mention in letters to her mother that she was already about a third of the way through the novel that would become *The Bell Jar,* the story of a college girl, as she told Ann Davidow, "building up and going through a nervous breakdown." The book was full of real people, Sylvia admitted, and would have to be published under a pseudonym. The confident tone of her letter, written on 27 April, suggests that Sylvia had overcome the false starts and abrupt stops that had inhibited her previous attempts to write a long narrative. "I have never been so excited about anything," Sylvia wrote—even though she predicted lawsuits. She found the book by turns funny and serious. It made her laugh. And indeed, the novel's mordant humor is superbly conveyed in Maggie Gyllenhaal's audiobook narration.

Early June brought yet another sign of Sylvia's burgeoning reputation. The BBC devoted a twenty-five-minute program exclusively to her poetry, a mark of distinction, she told her mother, that put her in the company of Robert Lowell and Theodore Roethke, poets whose work had received similar treatment. The next week Aurelia arrived to mind Frieda, now just beginning to toddle, so that Sylvia and Ted could join the Merwins on their French farm for a two-week holiday. Ted said nothing at all about the Merwins' negative reactions to Sylvia's behavior, continuing his policy (as Dido Merwin described it) of *never* taking issue with his wife's behavior.

In July, the couple joined Aurelia in Yorkshire, uniting with the

Hughes family while Sylvia and Ted began looking for a country home, preferably in Devon, for their expanding family. Sylvia was now four months pregnant. The couple wanted easy access by rail to London, but also a more southerly climate—especially for Sylvia, who found Yorkshire cold and grim. By the end of July, the couple had discovered their dream home in Devon: Court Green, a nine-room house that included a wine cellar and an attic. It had a thatched roof, a cobbled court, and a lawn, making it a virtual picture-book English estate. At one time the home of Sir and Lady Arundel, Court Green is situated on land that had been farmed since the eleventh century, with a tumulus signifying the remains of even earlier Roman occupation. The three-acre walled estate included a two-room cottage and a stable that would serve as a garage. The grounds also included a vegetable garden, an apple orchard, cherry trees, and blackberry and raspberry bushes. An abandoned tennis court could be made into a yard for the children to play in. And there was a village, North Tawton, nearby. It was all quite grand, but also quite dilapidated. And it was not anything Ted and Sylvia could afford. An enthusiastic Aurelia wanted to foot the bill, taking out a mortgage for the whole property, but Ted resisted this proposal, ultimately agreeing instead to loans of $1,400 each from Aurelia and his parents, which greatly reduced the mortgage.

Busy planning their move to Devon, Sylvia and Ted sublet their London flat to a young Canadian poet, David Wevill, and his German-Russian-Jewish wife, Assia, both of whom made a strong impression and inspired a sense of identification, Sylvia told her mother. After all, Sylvia and Ted were just a few years ahead of this other twosome trying their luck in literary London. Writing to Lucas Myers shortly after moving into Court Green in early September, Ted observed that England gave Sylvia the leisure to "develop naturally" for a "more & more appreciative audience whereas America would be cramping & stunting & distorting her with that dreadful competitive spotlight, to which Sylvia is so susceptible, when she's under it, as any Easterner over there."

Sylvia luxuriated in her new home, swept clean by the Arundels. The coal stove warmed the first floor, and an electric heater took care of upstairs. As he always did when they moved into a new place, Ted built bookshelves. Sylvia had festooned the house with flowers from the garden and served breakfast with freshly picked blackberries. She had located a prenatal clinic nearby and seemed entirely pleased with her peaceful surroundings, which Frieda also found delightful. She was evidently taking after her mother, picking up every little crumb in her playroom. Sylvia had also lined up a midwife and doctor (his surgery was just three houses up and across from Court Green), and she was looking forward to another home birth in January. A local woman was engaged to do some cleaning and washing up. Warren visited in early September, and Sylvia loved the way he pitched in, mowing the lawn and chopping wood. He also sanded an elm plank that she used as a desk in the best front bedroom. Ted's study was in the attic, a room of his own that had him joyously leading the kind of life he always wanted, Sylvia assured her mother.

Sylvia's received gifts of money from Olive Higgins Prouty and her grandfather, which covered many of the moving-in expenses. Sylvia had sold a story, and Ted was doing some work thirty-five miles away at the BBC studio in Plymouth. From Exeter, about an hour away, he sometimes took the train to the BBC London studios. His descriptions of Court Green and its surroundings were nearly as ebullient as Sylvia's, although he found their little village "grim." Still, he had banished the "headache" of London and felt as though he had removed an ant's nest from between his ears. He counted seventy-one apple trees, one less than Sylvia's total, and was busy with strawberry plants, imagining there was money to be made out of their produce. He took pleasure in picking his own fruit and eating it atop his own prehistoric mound.

Writing to Daniel Weissbort, an old Cambridge friend, Ted congratulated him on his marriage, an institution Ted recommended. But he also made an oblique comment that reflects, perhaps, what it was beginning to feel like settling into a fully domesticated life without urban distractions, but also without the outlets the city provided. "Marriage is a nest of small scorpions, but it kills the big dragons," Ted wrote. For all the couple's talk about sharing the same wavelength, it is inconceivable that Sylvia could have written such a sentence—at least not then.

Unlike Ted, Sylvia really wanted to settle into village life, and she contacted the Anglican rector about attending church, even though, as she explained to him, she was a Unitarian. The broad-minded and well-traveled clergyman was most welcoming, although Sylvia found the Sunday service a rather tepid affair. The rector appears, along with other local characters, in Plath's charming story, "Mothers," revealing how curious she was about the lives of her neighbors, whom she invited into her home, bestowing on them the respect that her husband would not have thought of expressing. Sylvia's satisfaction did not mean, however, that she did not miss her homeland. In mid-October she asked Aurelia to send a few issues of the *Ladies Home Journal*. She missed "Americanness" now that she was in exile. And she did not section herself off from what was happening in the rest of the world—especially the atomic testing that she feared would raise the levels of strontium 90 in the milk supply. Expressing herself just like a Brit, she declared the American fallout shelter craze "mad." She wrote to Marcia Brown, hoping to coax her into a visit. As was usual with a close friend, Sylvia was more candid than she was with her mother, admitting the village was rather ugly and the rector dull and stupid. He had taken one look at the books on Sylvia's shelves and called her an "educated pagan." Still, evensong in the Anglican chapel soothed her. She realized that to the locals she was a curiosity, but they treated her with warmth and generosity.

During the autumn of 1961, Sylvia made occasional visits to London to see editors and publishers, attending the occasional party and meeting writers. But she never remained long and was always anxious to return to Court Green. Village life, including a hunt meet, continued to intrigue her. Red-jacketed, brass-buttoned foxhunters paraded through the village tooting their horns, accompanied by "sulphurous dogs." Such events, she told her mother, were "oddly moving," although she sympathized with the foxes.

Sylvia wrote reviews of children's books for the *New Statesman*, assembling quite a collection for Frieda, and soon, Nicholas. Repairs to the house continued. She enjoyed peaceful interludes in the Anglican chapel and long walks with Frieda. On 9 November, she was elated to learn that she had won a $2,000 Saxton grant to support her proposed novel, the subject of which Sylvia still did not share with her mother. Instead, she reported to Aurelia that *The New Yorker* had just accepted her poem, "Blackberrying," clearly based on one of her jaunts with Frieda, when they picked juicy ripe fruit that made them part of a "blood sisterhood." Indeed, the blackberries are described in terms of Plath's body, "big as the ball of my thumb." The simple pleasures she described in letters to her mother become in this poem an unflinching evocation of rapacity—both hers and nature's—suggesting the way humans eat and are eaten by the natural world. Blackberrying takes her down a sheep path that opens out "on nothing," just a great space and the "din" of what sounds like silversmiths "beating at an intractable metal." Even as Sylvia told her mother that her world was coming together, her poems offer an alternative vision of futility.

By mid-November, Sylvia had a draft of *The Bell Jar* in hand and was busy fiddling with details that would disguise her all-too-literal rendering of people and places. Her publisher worried about libel, an especially vexing problem in England, where the onus is on author and publisher to prove they have not libeled the plaintiff, whereas in America the burden of proof is on the plaintiff. At least Aurelia was not going to sue her daughter, Sylvia said: In the novel, the mother is "dutiful" and "hard-working," with a "beastly" and "ungrateful" daughter. With the novel virtually completed, Sylvia swore her editor to secrecy, since the Saxton grant was supposed to be for fiction she had not yet finished.

With *The Bell Jar*, Plath was finally able to put her own experience in perspective as the story of what success meant in 1950s America to her alter-ego, Esther Greenwood: "I was supposed to be the envy of thousands of other college girls just like me all over America who wanted nothing more than to be tripping about in those same size seven patent leather shoes I'd bought in Bloomingdale's one lunch hour with a black patent leather belt and black patent leather pocket-book to match." Esther looks the part, with her perfectly put together ensemble like those of the other magazine guest editors with their "all-American bone structures." The term all-American, usually reserved for superior college athletes, here suggests the conventionality with which this all-star team is assembled. Plath reduced the number of actual guest editors from twenty to twelve, the number of the apostles—in this case, devotees of American drive and energy. Only Esther has lost her ambition, and what troubles her is that very lack of aspiration. She cannot simply *be*. She has to become something more, and when the zeal to be great deserts her, she is left with nothing.

With children, a home, and a husband, Plath was able to confront her earlier self. But as Ted Hughes wrote in his introduction to her journals, while a "new self" had created her mature poetry and her novel, it could not "ultimately save her." If one interprets *The Bell Jar* as, in a sense, Sylvia turning her back "on an enemy who seems safely defeated, and is defeated," her victory may well be, Hughes speculates, the "most dangerous moment of all." Not always the keenest reader of his wife's mind-set, here Hughes seems to have got it right. She mistakenly thought that with *The Bell Jar* she had put her trauma behind her.

Esther is demoralized, in part, by the standardized America that Hughes so detested. She rejects Buddy Willard, modeled after Dick Norton, because he has no intuition. She scorns his "good marks," but then turns this hostility upon herself, noting that after "nineteen years of running after good marks and prizes and grants of one sort and another, I was letting up, slowing down, dropping clean out of the race." Unlike Doreen, who does have intuition and does take chances, Esther suffers from a failure of nerve and a paralyzing indecisiveness that she tries to remedy with reckless behavior, resulting in a nearly successful rape she has invited in a desperate effort to "go the whole way."

Esther makes it through her time of trial, rejecting the facile advice of Joan Gilling, whose false recovery from a mental breakdown ends when Joan kills herself. Esther is not cured, any more than Plath's demons had been banished. Indeed, as Esther observes in the novel, "How did I know that someday—at college, in Europe, somewhere, anywhere—the bell jar, with its stifling distortions, wouldn't descend again?" Indeed, Ted Hughes would use the metaphor of the bell jar more than once in *Birthday Letters* to suggest the return of Plath's furies.

"Frieda moos & baas & peeps back at cows, sheep & birds," Sylvia reported in a holiday card to Ann Davidow and her husband, Leo. In fact, Sylvia sent out most of her Christmas cards by 7 December by "ordinary mail" at considerable savings. It might be good for Frieda, Sylvia supposed, to attend Sunday school, even if she was bound to reject the dogma. Plath suggested it was better to have a religious background to rebel against than no background at all. Writing to Aurelia, Sylvia confessed that she found Cold War politics deeply disturbing and criticized the harsh, threatening rhetoric President Kennedy aimed at Nikita Khrushchev. She feared for Frieda, growing up in such a self-destructive atmosphere. The work of right-wing organizations like the John Birch Society and the growth of the military-industrial complex convinced her that America was on the wrong course. She thought the British misguided to ally themselves with the United States. She would have preferred a neutral United Kingdom. Even so, Sylvia rejoiced in receiving the *Ladies Home Journal* from her mother—especially the recipes in the magazine, since the English equivalents were "things like 'Lard and Stale Bread Pie, garnished with Cold Pigs Feet' or 'Left-Over Pot Roast in Aspic.'" The lack of central heating was taking its toll, even though they had four electric heaters now in addition to the coal stove. But Frieda thrived, and on balance Sylvia believed they were better off than in an overheated American home. She reveled in a traditional Christmas, complete with tree trimming and a display of fifty Christmas cards.

Near term, Sylvia stopped writing in January 1962, contenting herself with baking and performing other household routines while awaiting the imminent arrival of her second child. Finally born a few days late on 17 January, Nicholas was a big baby. At over nine pounds he was more than two pounds heavier than Frieda had been, and he felt like it, Sylvia reported to her mother. Even though her labor took longer this time, she seemed perfectly at home with her midwife and a gas cylinder she tapped into by applying a mask to her face. Sylvia described the birth as an epic event, with the bluish-looking boy shooting out of her onto the bed in a "tidal wave of water," drenching her, Ted, the midwife, and the doctor. Frieda stood by, safety pins in hand, kissing the baby. Ted thought he had taken it all in stride, but the next day, he admitted in a letter to a friend, he was exhausted. Births, he assured his correspondent, took as much out of the father as the mother.

Sylvia emerged from her "cow-state" and resumed writing in February, relieved that she could give Ted a respite from so much childcare. Although the night feedings depleted her, having babies, she told her mother, was wonderful, and she wished she could just go "on and on." She felt reborn. Nicholas seemed more docile than Frieda had been as a baby. Frieda was now the household terror, tearing off pieces of wallpaper when she found a niche that fit her fingernail and uprooting bulbs. Sylvia tried to keep her daughter busy by showing her how to garden, a "pacifying pastime," as she put it in a letter to Ann and Leo Goodman. Nicholas was proving to be a "true Hughes": "craggy, dark, quiet & smiley." Too much wet and windy weather in March, however, had Sylvia yearning for a full spring. Finally, her letters to Aurelia began to mention a novel, "something amusing."

After a cold and sunless March, Sylvia, afflicted with chilblains (as she wrote the Roches on 12 March) and busy with expensive repairs to the house, looked forward to the spring and visitors, including (she hoped) the Roches and a BBC crew coming to interview her. Ted was taking day trips to London to see publishers and work on BBC programs. She was picking six hundred daffodils a week and taking them to market. Baby Nick, as Frieda called him, was sleeping in his pram among the daisies. Sylvia could not have presented a more idyllic picture for her mother, who was preparing to visit that summer. To the Roches, she offered a more sobering report on the toll the winter, which produced temperatures lower than forty degrees inside parts of the house, had taken on her. She was working, she told them, on a "grossly amateur novel" (*The Bell Jar*).

Ted sent an enchanting May Day letter to Aurelia and Warren, likening the array of thousands of daffodils on their property to a "perpetual court-ball." Sylvia, he said, was staggering with delight. Away from the "panic pressure" of the American poetry world, she was in her own element, writing extremely well. The house had given both of them a grounding utterly lacking in the unreality and fantasies of literary life, he concluded. Sylvia's calendar shows that she was painting moldings and other items in the children's playroom, baking, working in the garden, reading Dr. Spock, writing reviews for the *New Statesman,* and working on a dramatic poem, "Three Women." She was also developing a warm relationship with Elizabeth Compton and her husband, David, both admirers of Ted's work who were beginning to read Sylvia's as well.

Besides working on the house and in the vegetable garden, Ted took off twice a week to fish on the Taw River. He surely would have done so whatever the state of his marriage. But his participation in Sylvia's all-consuming domesticity—especially after the initial excitement over Nicholas's birth and refurbishing of the house—may have given way to his sense of marriage as a "nest of small scorpions." Writing to his brother, Gerald, in early May, Hughes went into considerable detail about his fishing expeditions, reminiscent of the boyish hunting days he had spent with his older brother. Ted did not mention the weekend visitors he and Sylvia had just entertained, David and Assia Wevill. To Aurelia, Sylvia described David as a "nice young Canadian poet," and Assia as his "very attractive, intelligent wife." Accounts vary as to what happened that weekend. To Sylvia, however, the attraction between Ted and Assia was palpable. Ted later told Olwyn his affair with Assia began in June, although David Wevill later told Olwyn he was not aware of the affair until Sylvia wrote to him in October.

Just the faintest hint of trouble may have been signaled in Ted's 24 May letter to the Merwins, in which he confessed he had "written nothing." He said he was "quite content" to let the tension smooth itself out instead of "writing purely out of nerves." Taking it easy that way, he hoped he might be able to "hear myself speak." It is a common enough idea—the writer awaiting the arrival of his own voice—but the words, in retrospect, seem also to convey an undertow that perhaps Hughes himself did not yet appreciate. He may have exaggerated his dry spell, since his letters to Olwyn are full of news about his writing projects, but perhaps he meant "nothing" in the sense that he had not produced anything worth being called writing. Certainly nothing in the tone of Ted's letters approaches Sylvia's avowal in a 7 June letter to her mother: "This is the richest and happiest time of my life." Apparently, her husband was beginning to see married life as an engulfment.

A. Alvarez visited the couple during this period and noticed that Sylvia no longer seemed the subordinate wife he took her for when they first met. Now, as he puts it in *The Savage God,* she appeared "solid and complete, her own woman again." She was sharp and clear and in command of her household. The power, in short, had shifted to her. As she showed him around Court Green, Alvarez had the distinct impression that this was "*her* property."

Sylvia wrote to Olwyn sometime in June, describing Nicholas's birth, his pacific demeanor, and his "Buddhalook," which she found "endearing." During a lunch, Elizabeth Compton remembered, Sylvia bounced Nicholas on her lap and said, "Just watch those eyes. He's such a greedy little boy. He wants his fair share." To Olwyn, Sylvia described mowing and scything "like a black," and being preoccupied with many other household tasks. In a letter to Elizabeth Compton a few months after Sylvia died, Aurelia evoked the scene: "the cobbled Court, the giant elms—the front and rear doors open so that one can see through from the court to the green—where Sylvia mowed her bit of lawn and planted the flower beds and Frieda brought her toys out on the green to play."

Sylvia was quite excited about, "Three Women: A Poem for Three Voices," set in "a maternity ward and round about," suggesting that what occurs is as much in the mind as in a tangible place. Performed on BBC radio on 19 August 1962 "to great effect," Ted thought, this haunting piece incorporates several aspects of Sylvia's psyche: a woman with child who feels a part of the world, as though she is a "great event"; a mother who in giving birth rages against the world of "flat" and "formless" men who plot destruction, bulldozing and guillotining their way to death, which becomes the woman's lover like a disease she carries with her; and a woman who wonders what it is she misses and feels "solitary as grass." How shocking this prophetic piece is to read when set against the benign letters Plath and Hughes were writing at the time. While the calm and contented voice of Sylvia's correspondence is represented in "Three Women," so, too, is her anguish and her anxiety that her life was about to miscarry. The "second voice" insists she can love her husband and that he will understand her and love her "through the blur of my deformity." But she cannot be sure that, like starfish who can grow back missing arms, she can be "prodigal in what lacks me." She remains suspended between hope and doubt. And for Sylvia, it would only get worse.

CHAPTER 7

QUEEN ALSO OF THE IMMORTALS

(1962–63)

July 1962: The call that kills a marriage—Plath discovers her husband's infidelity; **October:** The couple separates, and Hughes moves to London; **December:** Plath moves to a London flat with her two children; **January 1963:** *The Bell Jar* is published in England under a pseudonym; **11 February:** Plath commits suicide.

9 July 1962: The double ring of doom—Sylvia raced to catch the call before Ted could intercept it. To American ears, the harsh doorbell-like sound seemed insistent—not like the plodding, monotonous tones of an American phone. She recognized the woman asking for Ted, even though Assia lowered her voice, pretending, Sylvia thought, to be a man. She had been on edge ever since David and Assia Wevill's May visit to Court Green. Sylvia would later mythologize Assia as a Jezebel, a harlot queen, an evil woman bent on taking away her Ted.

Aurelia, then staying at Court Green, saw her daughter clutch the phone, blanch, then turn it over to Ted. This was the moment Sylvia's life sped up, the second her poetry erupted like a Greek necessity and became palpably autobiographical. Two days later, she could still write to Clarissa Roche, asking her to come for a visit as if nothing had happened. But in her poetry she described her defilement by words pouring out of the phone like mud. Court Green, the Devon home she had created as a haven for their family and their writing, now seemed polluted: "O god, how shall I ever clean the phone table?" Aurelia watched her fastidious daughter, a homemaker who believed in a spotless house—the same way she believed in impeccable poetry—rip the phone line out of the wall, treating it like a monster's threatening tentacle. It was too late, and the poet felt infected, sensing the caller's words were like a monster's spawn percolating in her heart.

Ted talked into the phone briefly and hung up, but Sylvia believed he had summoned this speaking abomination: "It is he who has achieved these syllables," she declared in her cryptic poem, "Words heard, by accident, over the phone." "Now the room is ahiss," wrote Sylvia, transforming the vowels and sibilant s's of Assia's name into a threatening noise. It is a scene from a 1950s science fiction movie, the imagination of disaster that Susan Sontag saw as a prevalent theme of the decade. The awful horror of being swallowed up resonates in the poem's last hysterical lines: "Muck funnel, muck funnel— / You are too big. They must take you back!" The nameless "they," Sylvia's being dragged into this swamp of feeling, dramatizes her engulfment by the terror of her decomposing marriage.

The typical criticism of Plath then held her poetry to be overwrought, both in terms of technique and of temperature. The reader who withdraws from her work cries out, as she does, "They must take you back!" But Plath's great achievement is precisely her refusal to be temperate, to exercise the restraint the British deem "good form." Just as understatement can be a powerful literary tool, overstatement, like an optometrist's overcorrection, can compel greater perception.

Charged words were a tonic for Sylvia Plath—no matter whether they expressed her highs or her lows. What Sylvia said on the day of the phone call—that she had never been happier with her husband, her children, her home, and her writing—was neither a ruse, nor wishful thinking meant to deflect the tension between the couple that troubled Aurelia. Sylvia's moods rose and fell, day-by-day—sometimes moment-by-moment, like the voices in "Three Women." Words were how she persuaded herself. Words—as her poems reiterate—were the very stuff of life to her: "[T]he blood jet is poetry." Using words, she could create that blissful union with Ted, and with words she could demolish it. She could not, however, permanently secure herself with words, and her recognition that poetry was only a momentary stay against confusion undid her. She wanted more than words could give her.

The magical property Sylvia ascribed to words is evident in the bonfire she proceeded to make of Ted's papers—adding for good measure her second novel, in which he figured as the hero. All these words had to be destroyed in order for her to continue composing her life and work. That her immolation of his writing did not disturb Hughes suggests he understood what words meant to her. To see burning of the papers as merely an act of revenge—or even as the act of a disturbed woman—does not do justice to the kind of writer Sylvia Plath was. As her husband knew, she could live again only if she destroyed those words, which now seemed a lie. In "Burning the Letters" (13 August), Plath wrote of flaking papers that "breathe like people," deriving a savage sort of energy from the fire in veins that "glow like trees." This ignition of rising flames mingles with the sound of dogs tearing apart a fox, the image of a life consumed, its oxygen supply depleted. The papers memorializing the life were now merely particles of immortality, seeming to satisfy her even as her rage reddened the very air.

Sylvia demanded that Ted move out. The next day he decamped for London. He returned occasionally to see the children. An angry, humiliated Sylvia hated to see her mother witness her disintegrating marriage. Confiding in her friend Elizabeth Compton, Sylvia called Ted a "*little* man." This sounded to Elizabeth like an anguished cry over a fallen idol. Sylvia had trouble sleeping. "Poppies in July" reflects her exhaustion and search for relief. The flowers appear as "little hell flames" and seem to emit a dark energy that the poet craves, picturing a mouth unable to "marry a hurt like that!" Sylvia had drawn blood when she first kissed Ted Hughes, and she had married a hurt like that. Now she craved an alternative, "liquors" that would dull and still her. During this time of turmoil, Al Alvarez wrote her two letters (dated 21 and 24 July), responding to her demand that he tell her frankly what he thought of her new poems. She could take any criticism he wished to offer, she emphasized. But all he could say was, "They seem to me the best things you've ever done. By a long way."

On 21 July, Sylvia wrote to Irish poet Richard Murphy, asking if perhaps he could help arrange for a visit in late August for her and Ted. Apparently she still hoped that the marriage could be repaired. She "desperately" wanted to be near the sea and boats and away from "squalling babies." The ocean had been the center of her life, and its appearance in Murphy's poetry attracted her. "I think you would be a very lovely person for us to visit just now," she added, without explaining the crisis in her marriage.

Aurelia left for home on 4 August. She recalled in *Letters Home*, "There was a great deal of anxiety in the air" as the conflicted couple bid her a stony good-bye, an epilogue to the "oppressive silences" between Sylvia and Ted that Aurelia had noticed from the beginning of her stay. Yet the couple continued to speak to one another. Indeed, they continued to fulfill their professional commitments in London and elsewhere, not keeping their breakup a secret, exactly, but behaving like amicable husband and wife when they appeared in public.

Sylvia puzzled over what to tell people. A mid-August letter to her mother did not even mention the troubles with Ted. But on 27 August, she wrote in the hope that Aurelia would not be too shocked that Sylvia wanted a legal separation agreement. She did not believe in divorce, but she could not abide the degrading and agonizing days that had destroyed her well-being. Her language is melodramatic, evoking the doomed romances and marriages that her mentor, Olive Higgins Prouty, memorably portrayed in *Stella Dallas* and *Now, Voyager*. Made into films starring, respectively, Barbara Stanwyck and Bette Davis, Prouty's works belonged to Plath's store of tearjerker tales like *Jezebel* (another Bette Davis vehicle) that she could call up without irony.

Evidently Ted could not abide this side of Sylvia, for she reported to Mrs. Prouty at the end of September, "He says all the kindness and sweetness I loved & married him for was mere sentimentality." To Aurelia, Sylvia added, "He now thinks all feeling is sentimental & womanish." That Plath scorned Prouty's sentimental novels is beside the point; they infected the poet's temperament the same way a tune you do not like keeps playing in your head. Culture is fixed in the human psyche like the grooves of a long-playing record.

Ted's mood can be gauged from the letter he sent to Olwyn in the late summer of 1962. The "prolonged distractions" of the previous nine months had depleted his bank account and diminished his productivity. So he was grateful when his sister offered her help. "Things are quite irrevocable," he added. He had deferred too long to "other peoples' wishes." But now he seemed to feel a new burst of energy, with several promising projects in the works. The problem, his letter indicates, had been the "awful intimate interference that marriage is." The language is startling, especially after reading so many earlier Hughes letters conveying just the opposite sentiment. But with Olwyn he could express himself without the need for excuses or rationalization. He was appalled at how he had circumscribed his existence.

During the second week of September, Sylvia left the children with a nanny to join Ted on an excursion to Ireland. Was the journey an effort to settle the terms of a separation or divorce? Ted wasn't sure, he told Olwyn. The trip ended abruptly when he disappeared. Afterward he wrote to Olwyn, claiming, in contradictory fashion, that Sylvia had reverted to the immature state he had observed when he first met her, and that she reminded him of Aurelia, whom he said he detested. It wouldn't hurt for Sylvia to grow up, he concluded. An unsympathetic Murphy did not know what to make of Sylvia, who wrote him upon her return home that his sudden coolness perplexed her, since he had shown her some cottages she might wish to rent. She assured him her interest was only in finding a place to write and to care for her children, accompanied by a nanny. The idea that she might be invading Murphy's literary territory in order to write about it was preposterous, she assured him. "Please have the kindness, the largeness, to say you will not wish me ill nor keep me from what I clearly and calmly see as the one fate open. I would like to think your understanding could vault the barrier it was stuck at when I left," she concluded. There is no record that he replied.

After Sylvia returned to Court Green, her midwife, Winifred

Davies, wrote to Aurelia. Davies had placed her hopes on the Irish holiday, which to her dismay went awry. Sylvia had returned upset that Ted had not come home, and she resolved to seek a separation. Sylvia said her decision had lifted her spirits. But Winifred thought Sylvia had a "hard hill to pull." Talking did seem to ease Sylvia and bring some clarity, Winifred assured Aurelia. Winifred found it hard to "judge fairly," since she had heard only Sylvia's side, but it seemed to Winifred that Ted had "never grown up," and that "paying bills, doing income tax, looking after his wife and children" were beyond him. So Sylvia had to be the practical one in their partnership. Ted desired the freedom to go to parties, to travel. He might tire of this in time, but then it would be "too late," in Winifred's estimation. "It seems to me that success has gone to his head, and he is not big enough to take it." Winifred summed up her sad conclusion: "I feel awfully sorry for them all, but I do not think Sylvia can go on living on a rack, and it will really be better for the children to have one happy parent rather then two arguing ones . . ." Ted's mother also wrote Aurelia, expressing her sorrow over the ruptured marriage, but noting that Sylvia had Court Green, a car, and the ability to "write for a living." Aurelia took the letter to mean the break between Sylvia and Ted could not be repaired.

On 17 September, responding to Sylvia's plea for help, Dr. Beuscher was uncertain how to proceed. So much of their therapy had centered on Aurelia and on Beuscher as an alternative source of authority. Was Sylvia consulting her as a "woman (mother) (witch) (earth goddess), or as a mere psychiatrist?" In truth, Beuscher could no longer be objective. Too much of Sylvia's plight as a daughter and as a woman paralleled Beuscher's own experience. The psychiatrist admitted she was furious with Ted, who was acting like a "little child." His talk of starting over every few years was not the mark of a mature man. He was like a child in a toy store who wants everything, and then throws a tantrum when his wishes are thwarted. Making choices, even if that limited your scope in some ways, is what every adult had to do. Isn't this what Sylvia had done? Beuscher was afraid that Sylvia might pin her well-being on this one man, rather than on her own "oneness." The poet had not exhausted her possibilities by picking one man "for life." All was not lost if Sylvia lost Ted. Sylvia had to remember that her husband was suffering an identity crisis. She should not, Dr. Beuscher admonished her, go down in a "whirlpool of HIS making." This meant resisting the urge to suffer in his company: "Do your crying alone." Sylvia was in danger of repeating Aurelia's role: playing martyr to a "brutal male." If Ted really wanted a "succession of two-dimensional bitchy fuckings," then Sylvia should get a lawyer to hit him in his pocketbook for child support, reminding him of his responsibilities. Play the lady, the psychiatrist urged her, and resist the temptation to go to bed with him. In closing, Beuscher dismissed Sylvia's offer to pay for therapy: "If I 'cure' no one else in my whole career, you are enough. I love you."

Beuscher's follow-up letter on 24 September advised a divorce, since Sylvia evidently told her that she was not "moping" and had grown to detest Ted. Collect the evidence and get a divorce now, while he remained reckless, the psychiatrist urged her. It would be harder later, especially if in a fit of remorse he proposed a reconciliation. If Sylvia could find happiness, whether or not she found another man, her children would be happy. Just stay out of Ted's bed, Beuscher reiterated, apparently concerned that Sylvia would backtrack. Read Erich Fromm's *The Art of Loving,* the psychiatrist advised. She wanted to hear from Sylvia that she had done so. No love could really survive, Fromm argued, without the fundamental self-confidence that Beuscher wanted to see in Plath.

Right up to the end of September, Sylvia described herself as trying to hold on to the last vestiges of what she had with her husband. Yet during this period she also saw a lawyer and seemed about to make peace with the idea of life without Ted—reclaiming her own freedom is what she called it. On 24 September, she wrote her mother that she realized Ted "wasn't coming back." This realization seemed to liberate her: "My own life, my wholeness, has been seeping back." Seeping? She had used this word in her poppy poem to describe the slow dulling of her emotions. Was she escaping, or just entering the trauma of her breakup with Ted? "For a Fatherless Son," written two days later, is full of foreboding: "You will be aware of an absence, presently." Her happiness was temporary, her son's smiles appeared as "found money." Two days later, in another note to Aurelia, Sylvia concluded that she had to exert control over what little life she had left. She did not tell her mother about her crying jags and weight loss. She succumbed to the flu. She started smoking.

Sylvia steadied herself with routines: breakfast with Frieda and the religious taking of tea at 4:00 p.m. in the nursery; invitations extended to visitors; outings with the children; and riding lessons twice a week. Having a nanny also helped. "I don't break down with someone else around," Sylvia assured her mother. Clarissa Roche, on a four-day visit, listened to Sylvia vilify Ted: The "strong, passionate Heathcliff had turned round and now appeared to her as a massive, crude, oafish peasant, who could not protect her from herself nor from the consequences of having grasped at woman-hood."

The nights were so awful that Sylvia resorted to sleeping pills. They took her somewhere deep, she said, and waking up with plenty of coffee stimulated her to write both prose and poetry in the early morning hours. No matter how much Sylvia blamed Ted, the idea of divorce revolted her. She believed in the sanctity of marriage. She suspected Ted had a bachelor pad in London. Not Sylvia—no man on the side. She treasured the proprieties: "Measuring the flour, cutting off the surplus / Adhering to rules, to rules, to rules," she wrote obsessively in "A Birthday Present" (30 September 1962). Without that sense of order, life did not matter: "After all I am alive only by accident," she admitted. "I would have killed myself gladly that time any possible way."

Plath was referring, of course, to the attempt to kill herself after her traumatic stint at *Mademoiselle*. Suicide was always a genuine option. She had said as much to Anne Sexton during some of her happiest days with Ted Hughes. The two women poets discussed their suicide attempts with aplomb. They wanted to take life on their own terms, and though suicide can be regarded as the action of someone out of control, the suicidee might regard the act in quite a different light. In "Lady Lazarus," Plath boasted that to her dying was an art: "I do it exceptionally well."

Plath's poems and extant journals show that death itself held no horror for her. They also reveal that as important as writing was to her, it could not, ultimately, salve her. She confessed ruefully: "A story, a picture, can renew sensation a little, but not enough, not enough. Nothing is real except the present, and already I feel the weight of centuries smothering me." Her last poems are burdened with this sense of history and mortality. The passage of time imposed an unremitting pressure, and losing her father when she was so young made her consciousness of death inescapable. This mindfulness of mortality is probably why she said she lived every moment with intensity.

When she felt alone, nothing seemed real, and the present appeared an empty shell. Might as well commit suicide, she confided to her journal: "The loneliness of the soul in its appalling self-consciousness, is horrible and overpowering." She did not believe in life after death—not in the literal sense. She thought instead of recently deceased writers such as Edna St. Vincent Millay and George Bernard Shaw, who "left something—and other people will feel part of what they felt." Approaching her own denouement, she was confident of her own pitch to posterity. Life after death meant "living on paper and flesh living in offspring." Or so she thought, pulling back with a "Maybe. I don't know," in a journal entry written in her nineteenth year.

By the autumn of 1962, Sylvia Plath was probing her connection to eternity. How would it come for her? Like an annunciation? She pondered the question in "A Birthday Present." "My god, what a laugh" she heard the voice of immortality mocking her. This Pauline poem, with its references to veils, to what shrouds the human perception of a world elsewhere, built upon the superstructure of her fascination with what comes after death—not so much an end in itself as a transit to another realm. Death, in fact, is a seductive presence in this poem: "Only let down the veil, the veil, the veil." Has the coming of death ever been more grandly welcomed than in the final three stanzas of this poem, which evoke the "deep gravity of it," as pristine as the "cry of a baby," as the universe slides from her side. The scene is reminiscent of Brutus falling on his sword, rendered glorious in the Greco-Roman accents of "Edge," perhaps Plath's last poem, resulting from her re-cent reading of Greek drama.

In October, Sylvia experienced a burst of inspiration resulting in two dozen of her most powerful poems. Critics have been awed by their intensity and craft, but they have not done justice to their mordant humor. Even a poem as serious and daring as "Daddy" provoked raucous laughter when Sylvia read it to Clarissa Roche. To be sure, Sylvia remained angry and sometimes confused about her broken marriage and about what to do next. She could seem hysterical, reporting that Ted had told her about his and Assia's speculation that Sylvia would commit suicide. Could Ted Hughes be quite that cruel? William Styron has noted in *Darkness Visible* that clinical depression often brings on overwhelming tendencies to create melodramatic scenes that express feelings, not facts. And the onset of depression is often not detectable by the afflicted one or by others because the depressed individual continues to func-tion—at least on a basic level. Sylvia was doing better than that. Even at her worst, she continued to write.

Depression is a mysterious disease, Styron emphasizes, and so its origins and generalizations about it are both problematical. In-dividuals respond to the disease . . . well, individually. The litera-ture on the subject, he concludes, contains no comprehensive explanation of the disorder. Why one person survives depression and another does not is a mystery, although Plath's poetry reveals an attitude toward death that made suicide, in certain conditions, desirable—even just.

Death and dead bodies populate her poems. In "The Detective," written on 1 October, she spoofs the detective story's presentation of clues and explanations that wrap up a mystery. The confident detective tells Watson that they "walk on air" with only the moon, "embalmed in phosphorus" and a "crow in a tree. Make notes." Existence is an enigma; the evidence is evanescent. Observation is all. Clearly Plath's droll sense of fun—fun of a very high order—had not deserted her. And this is surely what is so thrilling about her life and work: its witty persistence, no matter the impedi-ments.

Sylvia took to beekeeping, one of her many ways of honoring her father's memory and feeling close to him, and in the first part of October she wrote her famous sequence about an insect world that had fascinated Otto Plath. The poems, like beekeeping, provide an all-encompassing experience—surely a welcome activity for a distraught writer, who had "seen my strangeness evaporate," as she puts it in "Stings" (6 October), finding comfort in announcing her control of "my honey-machine." In "The Arrival of the Bee Box," the noisy swarm becomes Shakespearean, clustering in "unintelligible syllables . . . like a Roman mob." Sylvia addresses herself as the "sweet God" that will set them free. More than one friend observed a more cheerful woman, still angry, but also liberated and thriving on animosity toward Ted and the ecstasy of composing poetry. Sylvia said that working on a poem gave her greater pleasure than any other activity. She lived for it and—she eventually realized—she was willing to die for it.

The bee poems also reflect a sense of powerlessness overcome. Sylvia knew this work was a triumph, but she knew she had a long way to go. Writing to her mother on 9 October, she wanted to believe that in a return to Ireland "I may find my soul, and in London next fall, my brain, and maybe in heaven what was my heart." The last phrase echoes what she had told a friend, that she had given Ted her heart, and there was no getting it back—not in this life anyway. Ireland, the land of her hero, Yeats, she regarded as a fount of inspiration. London was "the city," where poetry became commerce, where Al Alvarez at *The Observer,* now an indispensable reader of her work, published it.

Sylvia's letter of 9 October can be taken as a kind of relapse. "Everything is breaking," including her dinner set and her dilapidated cottage, she told Aurelia. Even her beloved bees stung her after she had upset their sugar feeder. But in that same letter she refused her mother's invitation to come home, to be financially supported and looked after. The daughter demurred. She had made her life in England. If she ran away, she would "never stop." Surely this refusal was a courageous act, especially since she recognized, "I shall hear of Ted all my life, of his success, his genius . . . I must make a life all my own as fast as I can . . . I am a fighter." This was taking Ted on in his homeland, and given the superiority of the work she was now creating, her statement cannot be discounted as bravado. In retrospect, it is difficult not to see her suicide in terms of this letter, as a turning of the tables: "I shall hear of Sylvia all my life, of her success, of her genius."

Sylvia signaled the fragile equilibrium of her life to Aurelia, expressing the hope that Warren or his wife or some other family member could come for a visit by the spring. Aurelia herself would not do—as an uncompromising Sylvia vehemently pointed out: "I haven't the strength to see you for some time. The horror of what you saw and what I saw you see last summer is between us and I cannot face you again until I have a new life; it would be too great a strain."

And so Sylvia regrouped, three days later writing her most famous poem, "Daddy." A new life meant coming to terms with the old one. The autobiographical references are inescapable: The speaker is thirty, mentioning she was ten when her father died and twenty when she attempted a suicide that would reunite her with him; the father is German, and like the pontificating Otto, stands before a blackboard; a heavy marble statue has one gray toe (one thinks of Otto's amputated leg). And, of course, the poem definitively addresses the longing to recover a father who presided with such authority over his household that he seemed, as the poem has it, "a bag full of God." Anyone reading Sylvia's vituperative letters about Ted would be hard put not to identify him as one of the poem's "brutes."

"Daddy" reverberates with twentieth-century history, especially echoes of the Second World War, and reflects the poet's desire to imprint herself on world-shaping events—to insert herself into history like one of those Jews sent off to concentration camps. The child who vowed when her father died that she would never speak to God again includes a father in her list of rejected authority figures. Only by forsaking what she has loved and yearned for can she be her own person. The image of the victim identifying with her persecutor, the "panzer-man," anticipates the thesis Hannah Arendt's propounded a year later in "Eichmann in Jerusalem." (Eichmann was put on trial on 11 April 1961, more than a year before "Daddy" was conceived, and he was executed on 31 May 1962, a little more than four months before the poem's composition.) As critic Judith Kroll points out, Plath also anticipates Susan Sontag's analysis of fascist aesthetics—especially the desire to exalt "two seemingly opposite states, egomania and servitude."

Plath's identification with victims of the Holocaust has offended some readers. But it is very American of Plath to appropriate the history of others and welcome that history into her heart. Rather than reducing history to the confines of her personal agon, she regards her own experience as a chapter in a story larger than herself: "Every woman adores a fascist." This is the great gift of "Daddy": its amalgamation of the provincial and the international, the personal with the mythology of modern life. References to the "rack and screw" expand the poem's reach to the Middle Ages, and with an image of a father sucking the blood out of his child, to the vampire myth. A reader of Plath's generation might well conjure up Bela Lugosi, the fatherly middle-aged man engulfing his victims in his black cape. Photographs of the hulking, wolfish Ted Hughes, invariably dressed in black, also come to mind.

Plath's ironic, bitter poem draws on—even as it debunks—popular songs such as Cole Porter's "My Heart Belongs to Daddy" (1938), sung by Marilyn Monroe in *Let's Make Love* (1960). In the film, "Daddy" is slang for a woman's older lover, who treats her so well. In the poem, child and adult merge in the disturbing closing line: "Daddy, daddy, you bastard, I'm through." Through with Daddy? Through with the idea of an idealized daddy? Or through in the more complete sense of just giving up? Has Plath triumphed, or just destroyed what gave her life meaning? The poem is perfectly pitched to pivot either way.

But why did the poem make Sylvia and Clarissa Roche laugh? Was laughter a way to master the demons let loose in the poem, a therapeutic whistling past the graveyard? Certainly Sylvia's mood lifted, for on the very day she composed "Daddy," she wrote apologetically to her mother, "Do tear up my last one. It was written at what was probably my all-time low, and I have had an incredible change of spirit; I am joyous, happier than I have been for ages. . . ." Sylvia bustled with plans to remodel the cottage, Ted seemed amenable to a divorce, and she was writing every morning at five, a poem per day completed before breakfast. And these were "book poems. Terrific stuff. . . ." A novel was also in the works.

This revival turned her toward London: "I miss *brains,* hate this cow life, am dying to surround myself with intelligent, good people. I'll have a salon in London . . . I am a famous poetess here—mentioned this week in *The Listener* as one of the half-dozen women who will last—including Marianne Moore and the Brontës!" Such letters could only have been written to a mother—not just to impress Aurelia, but also to perform for the one person who could utterly identify with this victory. Aurelia had given up her own literary ambitions to serve her husband and would clearly empathize with a woman rebuilding her life after the loss of a spouse.

To Warren and his wife, Maggie, Sylvia wrote on the same day, "The release in my energy is enormous." She still believed in Ted's genius, and it hurt no less to be "ditched," but she was planning a London season full of freelance work, including broadcasting and reviewing. She still had to regain her health, she admitted, mentioning the black shadows under her eyes and a smoker's hacking cough. She hoped she might join them on a trip. Their letters meant so much to her, she assured them, and as she had done with Aurelia, she spoke delightedly about her children, adding that she wanted Warren and Maggie to consider themselves Frieda and Nick's godparents. In all, it sounded very much like Sylvia was reconstituting both her personal and professional worlds.

But at the same time, Sylvia emphasized to Warren and Maggie that she could not face her mother yet. Written four days later, lines in "Medusa" read like a companion piece to "Daddy"—this time an exorcism of the mother, the epithet "God-ball" recalling the "bag full of God." Aurelia appears as an ancient "barnacled umbilicus" and "Atlantic cable." Images from horror films again haunted Sylvia's imagination: "Off, off, eely tentacle!" Instead of shouting "I'm through," the poem ends on a flat, defiant note that seems less than convincing: "There is nothing between us." Or is the last line less emphatic because it can also mean there is no longer anything separating mother and daughter, that the daughter has thrown off her mother's hold on her only to reestablish a bond on the daughter's terms? The aim of both poems seems clear: to reinvent Sylvia Plath the poet, an act that entailed putting her parents in their places. In reality, Sylvia could not reject her mother, but in poetry her creative survival depended on the conceit that she had done just that.

Even though Sylvia's flu appears to have returned on the morning of 16 October, with her fever reaching 101 degrees, she remained ecstatic, writing her mother, "I am a genius of a writer; I have it in me. I am writing the best poems of my life; they will make my name." She anticipated finishing her novel in less than two months and was already inspired to write another. *The Bell Jar* had been accepted for British publication, and she looked forward to her "leap to London." But she fretted over household arrangements and an unsatisfactory nanny, and she still hoped that her Aunt Dot or Warren's wife, Maggie, could come to help with the children. Sylvia needed a respite, especially since she also had the ordeal of the divorce to confront. Although full of plans, she admitted she was struggling against "hard odds and alone."

In another letter to her mother written the same day, Sylvia pressed her case for Maggie, suggesting her sister-in-law join her for a six-week convalescence in Ireland. It was asking a lot, Sylvia conceded, for Warren's new wife to embark so soon on a trip abroad. Almost delirious from her 4:00 to 8:00 a.m. writing regimen, Sylvia pleaded, "I need someone from *home.*" Aurelia, for her part, was holding out for her daughter's return, although she sent money to procure household help.

Sylvia's grimmer mood emerged the next morning in "The Jailor," in which a nameless man poisons the feverish speaker, who declares she has eaten "Lies and smiles." Sylvia had condemned Ted many times for his lies, although the poem seems more about betrayal per se than about her disloyal husband. "Lesbos," written the next day, was even more explicit about her misery, mentioning a "stink of fat and baby crap . . . The smog of cooking. . . ." Yet neither of these highly allusive poems seems fully developed, as if in deciding not to be so explicitly autobiographical she had truncated her art.

Plath's dilemma was not much different from that of her contemporary, Marilyn Monroe. Each of Monroe's screen performances, beginning with *Bus Stop* (1956) and concluding with *The Misfits* (1961), was built on scripts that blatantly exploited many of her own characteristics and experiences. In those films, Monroe gave her greatest performances, but like Plath, she did so at great cost to her psyche. To make yourself your own material is both exhilarating and exhausting. The exposure can be gratifying but also denuding.

Writing on 18 October, Sylvia expressed shock at what she had sent her mother two days earlier. It had been the fever speaking. After a visit to the doctor, effective medication, and a good night's sleep, she was feeling better and taking back her plea for help. She felt strong enough to write Paul and Clarissa Roche, announcing that Ted had left her and that she would divorce him. He had confessed to a want of courage in not telling her earlier that he had never really wanted children. She was disgusted because it was his idea to move to the country, and now she was stranded, hoping they would have an opportunity to visit her.

Sylvia was gradually building up a persona, one she loosed in her next hectoring letter to her mother (21 October 1962): "Don't talk to me about the world needing cheerful stuff! What the person out of Belsen—physical or psychological—wants is nobody saying the birdies still go tweet-tweet, but the full knowledge that somebody else has been there and knows the *worst,* just what it is." For Plath, the Holocaust was both literal and metaphorical—she did not want the two separated in her poems. She wanted to feel like a Jew and like the cigarette-tortured "negress with pink paws" in "The Jailor." Sylvia was a cynosure for suffering, "going through hell," and her agony would mean far more to people than *Ladies' Home Journal* "blither" about happy marriages.

Emerging from another cycle of sickness two days later, Sylvia wrote yet another apology to Aurelia, asking forgiveness for her grumpy, fever-induced letters. She now could count on Susan O'Neill-Roe, "dear to the children" and a love to Sylvia. The next day, Sylvia would dedicate "Cut" to Susan. Sylvia wrote in gushing tones about wanting to "study, learn history, politics, languages, travel. I want to be the most loving and fascinating mother in the world," she declared to Aurelia. To Clarissa Roche, on 25 October, Sylvia wrote an equally buoyant letter announcing, "things were calming down," and that she was happily planning her future now that Ted with his scornful comments about her novel writing was no longer in the way.

Sylvia Plath not only aggrandized her life, she also made her body into a historic and mythic battleground, the site of an epic contestation. Perhaps better than any poem she wrote, "Cut" exemplifies her grandiosity of purpose, the thrill of cutting her "thumb instead of an onion." These lines bespeak a persona intent on watching itself with excited yet clinical detachment. The shocking accident becomes a vignette of a pilgrim scalped by an Indian, and then—like a CinemaScope feature—the landscape broadens outward to encompass the image of a million soldiers, "Redcoats," an allusion, apparently, to the blood flowing from the thumb Plath almost cut off. This virtual severing of a digit makes her wonder whose side these Redcoats are on, as if some treachery is involved in what she has done to herself. Thus she allegorizes her digit as a homunculus, a saboteur, a kamikaze man (a curious locution reminiscent of "panzer-man" in "Daddy"). Even more outlandish is the gauze bandage reddened with blood, which looks like a Ku Klux Klan hood over the thumb. The poem ends in a salute to the "trepanned veteran, / Dirty girl, / Thumb stump," the poet's yoking of the literal to the metaphorical, the personal to the political, and the moment to history. Allusions to mutilation, war, subversion, and persecution echo what she said in more prosy terms about wanting to study history, politics, language, travel. She had to bring it all to bear on the stuff of her life, the material of her writing, and present it on a world stage. It is not difficult to imagine Plath, with electrodes on her head and undergoing electroconvulsive therapy, identifying with the "trepanned veteran"—a "head case" with a hole in her skull.

Such poems emboldened Sylvia. She looked forward to cutting a figure on her way to the city. As she wrote her mother the day before writing "Cut," she planned to use the money Aurelia had sent to buy a Chagford dress (a reference to a clothing shop in

Devon, which today still advertises "snazzy" dresses). She was going to put her hems up and get a fashionable short haircut. "Just wait till I hit London," she announced. Sylvia Plath had to present a certain "look." She was as acutely conscious of appearance as a public figure, as Marilyn Monroe, and like the actress, she craved public display of her prowess after the failure of her marriage. In a sense she was a mad girl who could not help herself, but she had the confidence to give in to her torment. As a result, she was now giving the performance of her life, going from strength to strength as she built up to a crescendo of poetic outpouring.

Sylvia mentioned to her mother that her "riding mistress" had said she was "very good." A woman riding a horse named Ariel appears in a poem by the same name, one in a series produced in late October culminating in the hard-won triumph of "Lady Lazarus," in which the female protagonist exclaims, "I eat men like air." Sylvia would show these verses in London, she told her mother. She would be announcing to one and all her intention to divorce Ted. She refused to play the "country wife" he had left behind. A woman betrayed was also a woman avenging herself. Or as the speaker in "Ariel" puts it, "I / Am the arrow." Yet just two lines later, the word "suicidal" is attached to this same speaker, so that as in "Lady Lazarus," near-death experience is deemed vital to rebirth. The late October poems building toward Plath's birthday on 27 October enact an ascent, Lady Lazarus rising "out of ash," the flames of rebirth suggested by her red hair. As grand as the poem sounds, Sylvia prefaced a planned reading of this poem on the BBC with a comment mixing the mythic and the down to earth: "She is the phoenix, the libertarian spirit, what you will. She is also just a good, plain, very resourceful woman."

In Plath's poetry, in her letters to her mother, in what she was telling others she wrote and spoke to, Sylvia declared her need for an audience. On 29 and 30 October, she met in London with Al Alvarez and read him her recent poems. He seemed then the only editor who could appreciate her bold new work. When Alvarez encountered *New Statesman* editor Karl Miller on the street, a stunned Alvarez learned that Miller had rejected Plath's new work, including "Daddy" and "Lady Lazarus," as "too extreme." Many years after

Sylvia's death, Olwyn, who had access to her sister-in-law's so-called lost journal, would imply in a letter to Alvarez that Sylvia began to think of him as more than a supporter of her work. Olwyn didn't make the connection, but perhaps Sylvia did: As Sylvia's lover, Alvarez would also represent part of her new life, just as Ted Hughes had done after Richard Sassoon had rejected her.

Sylvia's powerful new voice emerged in a program produced by Peter Orr of the British Council. She sounded older than her thirty years and gave a commanding performance. The poems she read were designed for the ear, she had insisted to Alvarez, who championed her as a bold new voice that shattered the English sense of propriety. Sylvia Plath dared to be intense and violent, the "dirty girl" of "Cut." Like Plath, Alvarez had attempted suicide. Like her, he was a risk-taker, a rock climber and vigorous athlete. He was a fellow poet who likened the force of her work to "assault and battery."

By coming to London, Sylvia was going to best Ted Hughes at his own game. Peter Porter, a poet in the Hughes circle who also knew David and Assia Wevill, concluded that Ted really left Sylvia because he could all too clearly see her rising star:

> It has always seemed to me that Hughes, though formidable, was not as strong and imaginative a force as Plath. . . . Leaving Plath must have been not just an imperative for someone who wished to love other women whenever it suited him, but also a move to defend his own talent from competition with a superior one. Such a notion might seem doubtful given the greater recognition he enjoyed than she did, but it is one which has begun to convince readers of her poetry since the true scale of its achievement has become known. Judging the completed course of the two poets' productions, it is tempting to see Hughes's attitude as resembling Alexander Pope's Turk, who will suffer no rival next to the throne.

In *The Savage God: A Study of Suicide,* Alvarez mentions that in June 1962, even before Assia's call to Ted at Court Green, the balance of power had shifted to Sylvia. But Alvarez, mistaking the amity the couple showed him, supposed that Ted did not mind this turn of events.

From the moment Sylvia ripped the phone cord out of the wall, she was declaring open hostilities. The wife who had put her husband first, made sure he entered poetry competitions, cooked and cleaned for him, held her career in abeyance and raised his children—all that was over for Ted Hughes, and he knew it. He knew it because he had seen how Sylvia could turn on people, and he knew she was merciless—caricaturing even mentors like Mrs. Prouty and her own mother. The question was, "What wouldn't Sylvia do to Ted now that she was aroused?" This was, after all, the woman who had drawn blood the first time they kissed. Sylvia could play the victim, but no victim writes the kind of poetry she mustered in her last seven months.

Sylvia returned to her Devon home on 30 October only long enough to make preparations for her flat-hunting trip the first week of November. Although very much on her own, she accepted monetary support from Hughes, and he joined her on 4 November in the search for London lodgings. These fitful meetings upset her. Friends saw her cry and then surmount her grief with rage over his treachery. This behavior, like the poems she was then writing, played like a piece of music, the descending and ascending notes reflecting a huge emotional range. At parties, events, and various get-togethers, Sylvia, a prodigious performer, orchestrated her break with Ted, making it an operatic public affair. Like her urge to publish, to make herself known to the world, which had begun at such an early age, the compulsion to brand her husband in the open got the best of her.

Ted was behaving in a similar fashion, announcing his separation from Sylvia and attracting the attention of other women. On 1 November, he met anthropologist and poet Susan Alliston, who recorded in her journal his declaration that "Marriage is not for me." Alliston thought he had "got it in for Anglo Saxon women, perhaps too cold. He's now with a non-Anglo-Saxon"—a reference, no doubt, to Assia. He was already sizing up Alliston, though, admiring her long legs, which he later mentioned in his romantic introduction to her poems and journals. He told her that marriage was not for her either (she had recently separated from her husband). Two weeks later, she was at The Lamb, a Bloomsbury pub, trying to "beautify myself up a little" and hoping Ted would turn up.

On destiny's doorstep, Sylvia discovered her dream home: 23 Fitzroy Road in Primrose Hill, not far from Dr. John Horder, who was treating her infected thumb. She was alone as she read the plaque noting that W. B. Yeats had lived there. This was *it*. She immediately got to work securing a five-year lease and raced home to open her edition of Yeats's *Collected Plays,* which obliged her with this passage: "Get wine and food to give you strength and courage, and I will get the house ready." Although the obstacles for a single mother obtaining a flat that others wanted were formidable, and negotiations would prove complicated, the flat represented the assertion of a new, insurgent self. She contrasted herself with Ted, whom she now portrayed as an establishment man caught in "petty fetters" and "bribes," the world of London silks he had always scorned—a rather prophetic vision of a man who would become poet laureate.

On 7 November, readying herself for the move to London, an exultant Sylvia wrote Aurelia from Court Green about the new flat, which included "two floors with three bedrooms, upstairs, lounge, kitchen, and bath downstairs *and* a balcony garden!" As usual, she could not help overdoing it, vowing to be a "marvelous mother" who regretted nothing. She spent more than a page on domestic details, including her discovery of a "*fabulous* hairdresser." She loved her look, and it had cost her only $1.50. She liked to measure out her happiness in monetary terms, an aspect of the practical Plath that Hughes had deplored but depended upon. Ted had not even recognized her at the train station. No longer in his "shadow," she would make it on her own and be recognized for her own genius. She even felt magnanimous, if dismissive, about Assia, who had only her well-paid ad agency job and her vain wish to be a writer. Sylvia envied Ted and Assia "nothing." Men now stared in the street at her new fashionable self. She would appear a "knockout" at the Royal Court summer theater program devoted to poetry. Ted had disdained her love of stylish clothes and thought spending sums on ensembles extravagant. Sylvia, on the other hand, was a center court poet. She dreamed of eventually buying a London home if she ever published a "smash-hit novel."

Sylvia was hard hit in the second week of November when *The New Yorker* and *The Atlantic Monthly* rejected several of her recent poems—the very ones that would appeal to posterity. But she rebounded, assembling forty of her best works into a manuscript with a title that would make her name, "Ariel, and other Poems," a seeming tribute to Shakespeare's freewheeling and enchanting androgynous sprite. The poems reflected a fiercely feminine spirit abetted by a regiment of women, including her old friend Clarissa Roche, her nanny Susan O'Neill Rowe, and Ruth Fainlight (a writer and the wife of novelist Allen Sillitoe). These women stimulated Sylvia to write about motherhood as in itself a courageous, life-affirming choice—precisely the decision that a woman like Assia, so Sylvia believed, had avoided.

That fraught telephone call in July continued to gnaw at the poet, who in "The Fearful" (16 November), brooded on a woman who would pretend to be a man, hollowing out her voice so that it sounded dead. The woman thinks that a baby will rob her of her beauty (Sylvia had heard Assia, worried about losing her beauty, did not want children). "She would rather be dead than fat," so fearful is this woman who has turned her body over to a man. Plath would have made an excellent biographer. She had scoped out Assia and had a shrewd understanding of her rival's tastes and temperament. Later, after Plath's death, Assia would have access to Plath's journals and see firsthand how the poet had nailed her.

When Clarissa arrived the next day at Court Green for a visit, Sylvia embraced a friend she had previously called an "earth mother," exclaiming more than once, "You've saved my life." "The Fearful" had brought on another round of rage against Ted. Clarissa caught her at a weak moment, when the burdens of caring for Frieda and Nicholas, for all Sylvia's bravado, were wearing her out. And yet Clarissa also recalls their raucous laughter. Plath had a hearty laugh. By the time Clarissa departed on 19 November, Sylvia was again in high spirits, writing to her mother that same day as a busy professional woman, assembling her book of poetry and dealing with all manner of correspondence related to her work. She had time, however, to deck herself out with several new outfits and jewelry that she described in detail. These items were essential, making her feel "like a new woman," although she remained in suspense about the London flat, since her references and financials were still being reviewed.

On Thanksgiving Day, Sylvia wrote again, mentioning her bad cold, made worse by chores such as lugging coal buckets and ashbins. She still worried about obtaining the flat, since she had "so much against me—being a writer, the ex-wife of a successful writer, being an American, young, etc., etc." She was working like a navvy to prepare for her move, and that activity had disrupted her writing schedule, except for production of potboiling stuff that brought in some income. She was reviewing children's books for *New Statesman,* but also reviewing Malcolm Elwin's *Lord Byron's Wife,* which seemed to reflect her state of mind. Although she acknowledged that "Byron the lion was undeniably poor husband-stuff," she attributes the trouble in his marriage not only to his insufferable wife, Anna Isabella Milbanke, who always had to be "in the right," but also to Byron's sister, Augusta, with whom he had an incestuous relationship not unlike what Sylvia had insinuated (without any proof) was the case with Ted and Olwyn. Did Sylvia see that in her more self-righteous moods she resembled Anna Isabella—as Sylvia memorably put it—fixed in the "ego-screws of pride"? Sylvia, who would drop as much as twenty pounds during her separation from Ted, quotes Augusta's account of Annabella's wasting away in Byron's absence: "She is positively reduced to a Skeleton—pale as ashes—a deep hollow tone of voice & a calm in her manner quite supernatural."

Sylvia's description of Augusta as a "hectic if unsuccessful Pandarus" seems eerily prophetic of the role Olwyn would later play vis-à-vis Assia Wevill (see chapter 8). Sylvia deplored Annabella's "refusal to grant her spouse an interview (she never saw Byron again), let alone try to make a second go of it." Is it too much to suppose that Sylvia, seeing the unfortunate consequences of Annabella's adamantine attitude, decided not to cut off contact with her own lion simply because he was in the wrong? Trevor Thomas, who occupied the flat downstairs, would later observe her rages, which were an "ambivalent blend of blame, jealousy and wanting him back. She had not entirely given up hope of paradise regained."

It never seemed to occur to Sylvia that it would be difficult to replicate the support group she could call on at Court Green. Neighbors, a nanny, and visits from friends had done nicely for her, but she was bent on this London adventure and expected, as she told her mother, to be "self-sufficient." She was lining up readings and broadcasts, phone service for the flat (she had now reached the final stage of contract negotiations), a stove, and other amenities. During this period she impressed Ted Hughes, who while still decrying her "death-ray quality," also told his brother, Gerald, that they had worked out a more amicable relationship after she arrived in London. Did Sylvia's attraction to Alvarez also figure in her resurgence?

Between 12 December, the day Sylvia moved out of Court Green, and the end of January, she wrote little poetry, concentrating instead on a novel, "Doubletake," that dealt with Ted's desertion. She read biographies and contemporary women novelists, including Doris Lessing, whose new novel, *The Golden Notebook,* had just been published. When Plath met Lessing, the latter retreated from her importunate admirer. A better match was made with Emily Hahn, a *New Yorker* writer treasured for her ebullient, welcoming attitude. Hahn, a single mother and a shrewd survivor of hardship, a world traveler and a hardy raconteur, would have been a tonic for Plath, who was searching for new role models.

As Plath told interviewer Peter Orr in late October, she was shifting her attention to prose, wishing to engage with a broad range of subjects—stimulated no doubt by the historical biographies she had been reading. Some of her greatest poems were yet before her, but she seems to have sensed that this phase of her career might be winding down. She awaited the appearance of *The Bell Jar,* to be published in mid-January as the work of Victoria Lucas. Owing to the novel's autobiographical nature, Plath thought it best to use a pseudonym.

Sylvia had reason to believe her London life would be a success.

It was easier than ever for friends to visit, she had the trusted Dr. Horder close by, the zoo minutes away for the children's amusement, and proximity to the BBC, where she had good connections. Delays in furnishing the flat, acquiring phone service, and finding an au pair did little to dampen her enthusiasm. She happily painted and cleaned her new home. The weather had not yet turned against her, and Ted's visits to the flat to see the children had not yet riled her up. Even so, her life seemed to take on a relentless, unremitting quality that she tried to interrupt with lively letters home.

On 14 December, Sylvia wrote to her Aunt Dot about the children's delight at the zoo, and the shopkeepers who remembered her from the days she had spent in the neighborhood with Ted just a few years earlier. It was like a village really, but with all the conveniences of London. She made even the hassles of moving seem elevating. Sylvia sounded English, but she craved connection with her homeland. "You have no notion how much your cheery letters mean!" she told her aunt. Aurelia sent chatty letters about family and friends and assured Sylvia she was updating Mrs. Prouty about recent developments.

That same day Sylvia wrote her mother that she had never been happier. Even dashing about to get the electricity and gas connected, while her door blew shut with the keys inside, was transformed into a "comedy of errors." At the time, though, locking herself out had undone her, according to her neighbor Trevor Thomas, who recalled Sylvia's hysteria. Yet she spoke as though having a five-year lease guaranteed five years of happiness. She imagined Yeats's spirit blessing her. And why not? Al Alvarez had just told her that *Ariel* should win the Pulitzer Prize. She had a study that faced the rising sun. At night she joyously watched the full moon from her balcony. Everyone, it seemed, was a darling—or at least obliging—in her catalogue of good fortune.

A week later nothing had changed, as Sylvia detailed for Aurelia the new furnishings and furniture and flowerpots, and more new clothes (made possible by Aunt Dot's generous seven hundred dollar gift and a one hundred dollar check from Mrs. Prouty). "You should see me nipping around London," she assured her worried mother. Aurelia suspected that all this frenzied activity simply masked her daughter's depression—or so Aunt Dot had confided in a letter to Sylvia. Sylvia amped up her enthusiasm: "The weather has been blue and springlike." That would change.

Then came Alvarez's devastating Christmas Eve visit, which he has written about in *The Savage God*. Sylvia wanted more than supportive criticism from him. His understated published account suggests she wanted an affair. But other evidence suggests that the bond between them was much deeper than that. In a letter Olwyn Hughes wrote to Alvarez on 9 June 1988, in an effort to secure an interview for Anne Stevenson, Olwyn mentions reading Sylvia's journal, written just before her Christmas encounter with Alvarez. Olywn tells Alvarez about a journal entry in which Sylvia cautions herself to relax so as not to "scare you [Alvarez] off." Sylvia's admonition to herself, as Olwyn reports it, is remarkably similar to the poet's 1 April 1956, journal entry, in which she exhorts herself to "be more subdued" and quiet. *"Don't blab too much."* Olwyn refers to the "lost" journal, full of Sylvia's suffering but also her "jubilation" over her work, including two chapters—one of which recounted the traumatic Wevill weekend visit in May 1962—she had drafted of a new novel. Then Olwyn mentions the "episode with you [Alvarez]" and Richard Murphy's failure to respond to Plath's plans to secure a cottage in Ireland for the winter. Olwyn clearly alludes to Plath's romantic attachment to Alvarez, which Olwyn regards as "one of the keys" to understanding Sylvia's final days. In effect, Olwyn complicates the story considerably, making it not just about her brother Ted, but also about Alvarez. What exactly is Olwyn saying when she adds that she could understand why Alvarez "wouldn't want to descend to such indiscretion"? Olwyn assures him that Sylvia told no one about her personal relationship with Alvarez—although how Olwyn could know this is not clear, unless Sylvia said so in that lost journal.

In his reply of 10 June 1988, Alvarez adamantly refused to see Stevenson and "tell all," expressing disdain for her "languidly researched" work. What else is there to tell? When I put the question to him for this book, he replied, "She was in love with me." He would say no more, except to repeat what he has already written: He could not sleep with Sylvia because he was then involved with

Anne, his future wife. Alvarez regarded Ted as a friend he would not betray; in fact, Ted had slept a few nights on Alvarez's sofa, talking over his troubles with his estranged wife. And Sylvia wanted more from Alvarez than he was willing to deliver and more than he is willing to say, even now.

Sylvia's response to Alvarez's relative coolness was surely more than just disappointment. Like Hughes, Alvarez had championed the poet and the woman. In the most searching study of the Plath/ Alvarez *affaire,* an article that Alvarez himself endorses, William Wooten writes: "Alvarez was now appreciating poems Plath's husband had not read. Sending poems to Alvarez had become both an intimate act, making the editor a confidant in a marriage breakdown, and an act that defied intimacy, first of the marriage, then of the confidence." That Plath could no longer draw near to Alvarez made the last six weeks of her life all the more agonizing.

The children had colds when Sylvia next wrote to her mother on 26 December after Christmas dinner with friends. The holiday made her homesick. Snow was falling, a winter scene she compared to an "engraving out of Dickens." At first, this change from the soggy, wet winter she had anticipated cheered her. But by 2 January, the snow began to pile up. Everything had turned to sludge and then frozen. No snowplows swept through streets in a land that rarely saw appreciable snow. Still no phone. Still 103 degree fevers for Sylvia. No central heating. Dr. Horder prescribed a tonic for Sylvia, who had lost twenty pounds over the summer. "I am in the best of hands," Sylvia assured her mother. But the chill had set in. It seemed like England had been engulfed in a new ice age. That same day, Sylvia wrote dejectedly to Marcia Brown that she felt "utterly *flattened*" by the last six months of life without Ted. As she had done with Warren and his wife, Maggie, she wrote to friends, urging them to come for a spring visit. She was lonely in London and feeling like a "desperate mother."

And yet Sylvia was not without resources. Her urge for order asserted itself. On 3 January, Clarissa Roche arrived for a visit to find the flat tidy—although soon Sylvia admitted it was all too much for her. Still, she refused Clarissa's invitation to accompany her to Kent for a stay with the Roches. No, Sylvia said, she would manage somehow. Trevor Thomas saw the other side: the look of terror in Sylvia's face and her helplessness, which was becoming a nuisance, since she expected Thomas to help her cope with household crises. But his son said, "Can't you see Daddy, she's very sad? It's in her eyes." Children are often more observant, Thomas wrote in his memoir about Plath.

Sylvia continued to write, finding time by putting Frieda in nursery school for three hours a day and catching moments for composition while Nicholas napped. It was a virtuoso performance that kept her going—for a while. She had something to prove. To go home, to go to Clarissa, spelled doom, because in Sylvia's mind writing on her own had become a lifeline. To give up the flat—even temporarily—when the writing was going so well meant becoming a patient again, the Sylvia of ten years earlier.

Sylvia stumbled her way to local shops, afraid of falling on the ice. Lacking snow shovels, shopkeepers resorted to using boards to scoop out narrow paths. In her flat, Sylvia was besieged high and low, with a stain creeping along her freshly painted white ceiling and her bathtub filling with murky water (the result of a frozen waste pipe). She pondered the mysteries of British plumbing. The wallpaper sagged. Busted pipes, she was told—and not a plumber to be had when everyone suffered the same plight. Roofs could cope with rain, but not the heavy weight of the snow. Workman pitched the snow off the roof but left behind a faulty gutter right by Sylvia's bedroom window, resulting in a drip, drip, drip that she compared to Chinese water torture. It soon became apparent that this historic house had, in foul weather, revealed itself to be in an abysmal state of disrepair.

Sylvia blamed no one for deceiving her—after all, her neighbors were putting up with the same problems—but she had a nagging suspicion, never far from the thoughts of someone brought up in middle-class America, that the insalubrious British climate fostered a defect in the British sensibility, which like Ted, was all too willing to tolerate the haphazard. Americans plan for this sort of eventuality, she told the workmen. No American handyman would have stood with a bucket trying to catch the water cascading from the ceiling with the "embarrassed air of covering an obscenity."

Outside, Sylvia contemplated the maze of different pipes—really quite an extraordinary puzzle to an American used to plumbing that was out of sight, behind walls or underground. She was advised to plug her drains every night to prevent more freezing. The agent in charge of her property asked: Had no one from the water board told her as much? No, she replied, perplexed. He advised heating the pipes by any means (including candles!) and running hot water through them several times a day. When she poured a bucket of hot water on pipes outside her balcony, Trevor Thomas shouted up to say there was a puddle on his kitchen floor. "The agent is a fool," Thomas told her.

Miraculously, a plumber showed up. But then came the power cuts. It was just like the Blitz—a doughty time for hardy survivors of the war, but no pleasure for Sylvia Plath. The lights went out. Trevor Thomas told her the interruption of service had been announced in the newspapers. Hadn't she read about it? With the gas still working, she managed to cook meals, while she wrapped her children in winter clothes.

Midway through this winter siege, Sylvia wrote her mother, admitting her flu-induced exhaustion, but claiming she was pulling out of it. Day nurses had helped with the children, who were also afflicted with colds and fevers. She called the weather "filthy"— a good word to describe her overwhelming sense of disgust and gloom, made worse by the two-month wait to get her phone service installed. Finding an au pair was another trial. Sylvia had done her best to make fun of her plight in a commissioned article, "Snow Blitz." Trevor Thomas, not a very sympathetic observer of Plath's last days, resented the gloss she put on her plight by removing the expressions of sheer panic he witnessed.

Sylvia leveled with Aurelia: She realized she had lost her "*identity* under the steamroller of decisions and responsibilities of this last half year, with the babies a constant demand." Sylvia did not say, but it almost did not matter what she thought of Ted at this point. He was not there to help her, and he had come to represent the man who was not there, not the man she had dreamed of in an early Smith College journal, the man who "admired me, who understood me as much as I understood myself." How awful to realize that she was *"starting* from scratch" in this "first year" of her new life.

Ted would later say that in Sylvia's last weeks they were planning a reconciliation. Susan Alliston, now in Ted's confidence, recorded in her journal her surprise at how much he talked about himself and Sylvia, "so personally." She noted his remark that the "exclusivity of the relationship killed something—the keeping always on the same plane, and that she is an absolutist—will not accept a compromise." But now that Sylvia was on her own and had to do everything for herself. . . ? Alliston does not complete the thought, instead observing that she did not think Ted wanted a divorce. "It makes no difference," she adds cryptically.

Sylvia sounded wistful when she wrote of earning enough from writing to support herself. She yearned for a "windfall" that "a really successful novel" would bring to relieve her "ghastly vision of rent bleeding away year after year." The temporariness of it all after such a long decade of hard work defeated her. Time was running out. "But I need *time,"* Sylvia told her mother. Sylvia prescribed an antidote for herself, but it does not sound convincing: "I guess I just need somebody to cheer me up by saying I've done all right so far."

An alarmed Aurelia had no trouble reading the signs and got word to a friend in London to contact Sylvia. Pat Goodall sent a reassuring letter to Aurelia, reporting that on 19 January, a "bitter cold day," she went to see Sylvia and was met by a "bright and eager American expression" that immediately made Pat feel at home. The visit was worthwhile. Unfortunately, Pat mistook the point of this animation. Sylvia insisted that Pat and her husband stay for tea, while she "NEVER STOPPED TALKING!" The bright and cheerful children seemed well. They had all recovered from the flu, Sylvia assured Pat. They had a doctor who was "an absolute Saint." Sylvia seemed all the more remarkable to Pat, because "Saturday was the dreariest of winter days, yet inside her flat life seemed warm and cheery." Plath, a magnificent performer, loved to put on a show. Visits cheered her but did nothing to change her predicament. This bleak period is palpable in a poem completed on 28 January. "Sheep in Fog" envisages a heaven "Starless and fatherless, a dark water." The same day this dreary season made its appearance in "The Munich Mannequins": "The snow drops its pieces of darkness"—such a stark line annihilates the prosy pleasantries of "Snow Blitz."

Respectable to mixed reviews of *The Bell Jar* began appearing and did little to hearten Plath, especially since the novel had not found a publisher in America. In an introduction to the first publication of Plath's journals, Ted Hughes recalls, "If she felt any qualms at the public release of this supercharged piece of her autobiography, she made no mention of it at the time, either in conversation or in her diary." Although he concedes that certain reviews exasperated and dismayed her, "they did not visibly deflate her." But Sylvia confided to her friend Jillian Becker that the British reviews were discouraging, a real blow because when Sylvia saw the book in proof, she realized it was no potboiler and had high hopes for it.

To Trevor Thomas, Sylvia complained about her incarceration in a flat with two children, while Ted was free to enjoy his affair with Assia and travel. Thomas tried to console her, and she said he reminded her of her father. Thomas never knew which Sylvia he would encounter: charming, stylish, distracted, or even downright rude. By late January, the lightning shifts in Sylvia's moods accelerated. Between 28 January and 4 February, she managed to write ten poems, a surprising revival after such an appalling month. But she seemed to be turning in on herself: "People or stars / Regard me sadly, I disappoint them" ("Sheep in Fog"). Similar expressions in "Totem," "Paralytic," and "Mystic" constitute terse expressions of futility, relieved only briefly by poems like "Child," "Kindness," and "Balloons," which show she could still take great joy in her children. "Contusion," completed on 4 February, ends with the portentous line: "The mirrors are sheeted." The sense of closing up, of not seeing oneself reflected in the hopes of others, and the covering of objects in rooms no longer used—as if after a death—is pervasive.

On Sunday, 3 February, Sylvia called Ted and invited him to lunch. His diary notes, written the week after Sylvia's death, record that he remained with her until 2 a.m. They had not enjoyed such a good time since July, he remarked, as he listened to her read her new poems. Sylvia seemed to have regained her equilibrium, although she wept when he played with Frieda and embraced both of them. When Sylvia repeated her conviction that he was looking for someone else, he "kept denying it absolutely." He wanted to return to the marriage, but on terms that would no longer include what he deemed his slavish devotion to her. He was beginning to feel like his own man again.

The next day, according to Ted's diary, Sylvia rang him from a public call box in bitterly cold weather and demanded that he promise to leave England in two weeks. She could not work so long as she had to hear about him. Ted demanded to know who was talking about him. She would not say. And he was startled to see how the calm Sylvia of the day before had given way to this distressed woman. Even when he said he could not afford to leave England and had no place he wanted to go, she extracted his reluctant agreement to depart the country. "She wanted me never to see her again," Ted wrote. He talked over her phone call with Al Alvarez, who described his own divorce and regret that he had continued to see his wife after they were irreconcilable. Alvarez advised him to do as Sylvia said. Ted decided he would leave as soon as he could.

The same day, Sylvia wrote her last, disconsolate letter to her mother, confessing, "I just haven't written anybody because I have been feeling a bit grim—the upheaval over, I am seeing the finality of it all, and being catapulted from the cowlike happiness of maternity into loneliness and grim problems is no fun." She saw no way out: "I have absolutely no desire ever to return to America. Not now, anyway." Work for the BBC and other outlets had no equivalent in the United States. Aurelia's idea to take the children for a while seemed only disruptive to her daughter, likely to upset Frieda who was so close to her father, who visited once a week. Sylvia also counted on the National Health Service. She simply did not see how she could support herself back home. "I shall simply have to fight it out on my own over here," she insisted. A new, flighty, and persnickety German au pair bedeviled Sylvia, but still gave her some peaceful mornings and a few free evenings. This letter strained to mitigate the bad news. It is a crushing final testament because, in effect, Sylvia was saying that *all of it* now depended on her. Aurelia was right to think that her daughter had put up a gallant effort.

Sylvia's last two poems, "Balloons" and "Edge," completed on Tuesday, 5 February, perfectly express the plight of someone who seemed poised between life and death—between the airy buoyancy of the balloons her children played with, a world of wish fulfillment, and the finality of "Edge," in which the inevitability of death is articulated with profound satisfaction. "Balloons" ends with a burst balloon, "A red / Shred" in the child's "little fist." "Edge" expresses a bitter but nevertheless peaceful acceptance: "We have come so far, it is over." Was it over? In the end, Sylvia Plath gave herself less than a week to decide. It is a common pattern in suicide, these swings between euphoria and despair. The energy Sylvia expended in her early morning writing sessions stripped her of the power to deal with the rest of her day. Writing can become a regular part of an insomniac's routine, but waking up from a drugged sleep at 4:00 a.m. every day inevitably weakens an already vulnerable constitution. How much life can be left after writing so intensely?

Like Marilyn Monroe coming to a similar endpoint, Plath's displays of herself became more extreme. Sylvia could not root herself in her London flat, anymore than Marilyn could anchor herself while furnishing her new Hollywood home. They share the same inability to maintain a new life, while obsessing about the failure of the old one. Sylvia wrote hyperbolically to Marcia Brown, her college roommate: "Everything has blown and bubbled and warped and split." She felt "in limbo between the old world and the very uncertain and grim new."

Friends coped with multiple Sylvias and Marilyns, confident and full of doubt, happy and horribly angry. These women weighed upon themselves. Like Marilyn, Sylvia was entering her middle years, which are, in Leslie Farber's words, the "most vulnerable to the claims of this sickness of spirit, which now radically questions all we have been, at the same time scorning the solace formerly

sought in the future, making who we are to become the most oppressive of questions."

William Styron has eloquently described the unremitting pain
of depression that led to his own suicidal period, an agony that
Leslie Farber has succinctly articulated in his writings about the
suicide who feels that "one *is* a body one *is* mortal, and since, by
definition, mortality is crumbling, its claims are imperious." In
Sylvia's case, as in the life of many suicides, a terrible isolation enclosed her every move. She complained of having no friends, even
though the facts demonstrate otherwise. She felt *alone*—as Styron
did even when receiving an international award for his work. And
just as his medication (Halcion) may have contributed to his depression, so the drugs prescribed for Plath may have hastened the
onset of her dark thoughts. Even today, the pharmaceuticals used
to treat depression have widely varying impacts on different individuals. It can take weeks—sometimes months—to find the right
dose, and for some individuals that dose is never adequate.

Nothing changed in Sylvia Plath's last week of life, and perhaps
that is what bothered her, the dread that nothing would change. On
Wednesday, 6 February, still angry that Sylvia's friends were spread-
ing tales about his ill treatment of her, Ted wrote her a note and
visited her, announcing that he was going to engage a solicitor to
stop the lies. She implored him not to do that. She was very upset,
but not more so than on previous occasions, he vouchsafed to his
diary. But she kept asking him if he had faith in her, and that
seemed "new & odd."

On Thursday, another phone conversation between them settled nothing. Sylvia briefly entertained the idea of a reconciliation,
but then reverted to her demand that Ted leave the country. Her
mood, however, seemed better to him. That same day, she sacked
her au pair—why is not clear, although one version has Sylvia discovering the woman in bed with a man. Sylvia became so distraught
that she actually struck the woman. By 8 February, her trusted Dr.
Horder concluded that the drugs were not working and made plans
to hospitalize her. She could not have had a more sympathetic or
understanding physician. Horder himself suffered periodically

from depression. Without other help at hand, Sylvia phoned her friend, the writer Jillian Becker, and asked if she and the children could come over.

In *Giving Up,* Becker describes Sylvia's last wracking weekend. The desperate visitor arrived at the Becker home around 2:00 p.m. on Thursday afternoon and announced, "I feel terrible." Sylvia asked if she could lie down. Jillian led her to an upstairs bedroom, while Frieda and Nicholas played with Jillian's youngest daughter, Madeleine. At 4 o'clock, Sylvia came downstairs and said she would "rather not go home." She gave Jillian the keys to the Fitzroy Road flat and asked her to retrieve a number of items for a weekend stay.

Sylvia seemed to settle down after a steak dinner, just as she had done days before when Clarissa Roche visited and prepared a meal. Then Jillian watched her friend down several sleeping pills and waited until Sylvia slept. By 3:30 a.m., Sylvia had awakened and was weeping. For two hours she catalogued her woes—her father's death and Ted's betrayal of her with Assia. Jillian remembered Sylvia saying that when she and Ted moved to Court Green, they thought their "ideal life was starting." Aurelia also became a target. "Sometimes we mentioned our mothers, each of us unforgivingly," Jillian recalled. "In her case a need to impress her mother had been a driving force. She'd had to present her with success after success. The breakup of her marriage, she believed, was surely seen by her mother as a failure; and even though Aurelia Plath voiced no such judgment, the thought of it infuriated Sylvia. She hated the shame it would require her to feel." The women remained awake until 5:30 a.m., when Sylvia took an antidepressant and dozed off.

Friday morning Sylvia ate heartily and called Dr. Horder, who was also Becker's friend. Sylvia turned the phone over to Jillian when he asked to speak with her. "How does she seem to you?" Horder asked. "Depressed," Jillian replied. He wanted Jillian to make sure Sylvia took her pills. It was also important, he emphasized, that Sylvia look after her children. She needed a sense of purpose and responsibility.

Becker's own account of what happened next is far less dramatic than the versions reported elsewhere. Sylvia seems to have had a tranquil Friday and Saturday after her troubling night on

Thursday. She went out Saturday evening, but did not tell the Beckers about her plans, and she returned without disturbing their sleep. But according to Ted's diary, he met Sylvia at the Fitzroy flat Friday night after receiving a note from her that had arrived about 3:30 p.m. He called it a "farewell love letter." In just two sentences, she announced that she was leaving the country and would never see him again. But what she really intended to do baffled him. This time an unruffled Sylvia Plath confronted an agitated Ted Hughes. When he demanded an explanation, she coldly took her note away from him, set fire to it in an ashtray, and ordered him to leave. She refused to say anything more than that she had to go out. He left.

On Sunday morning, Sylvia enjoyed an ample lunch with the Beckers, commenting that the soup, meat, salad, cheese, dessert, and wine were "wonderful" (or "marvelous"—Becker could not remember the exact words). Sylvia seemed "a little more cheerful, a little less tense," and more focused on her children. She then announced that she wanted to return home that evening. Jillian wondered what had provoked this "suddenly purposeful" behavior. Was it her outing the previous night? Had it resolved something for her? In hindsight, Becker probed the moment: "Was it a decision to change her life—or . . . to die? Can a decision to die flush one through with a sense of excitement and urgency? Or was the bustle of commitment a deceptive performance, concealing a plunge into deepest despair? If so, it was an amazingly successful effort of will. She seemed invigorated, mildly elated, as I'd seldom seen her before." As she watched Sylvia packing with deliberation, apparently in full command of herself, Jillian reminded her friend about taking her pills. "Yes, I'll remember," Sylvia assured her.

Becker felt relieved: "The truth was she had tired me. Her need for my attention had begun to seem relentless." Jillian would have gone on taking care of Sylvia, but "she wanted to go, and nothing I could have done or said would have kept her against her will. And then there was Dr. Horder's injunction: 'She must look after the children, feel she's necessary for them.' " Jillian's husband, Gerry, drove Sylvia home. On the way she began to cry, and Gerry, an empathetic man who liked Sylvia, importuned her several times to return to the Beckers' home. But she refused, and he left her around

7:00 p.m., after she had fed the children and put them to bed. Then Dr. Horder called to make sure she was all right.

Near midnight, Sylvia rang Trevor Thomas's bell and asked him for stamps. She wanted to airmail some letters and get them in the post before morning. As he gave her the stamps, she asked him when he left for work in the morning. He asked why she wanted to know. Just wondering, she replied. Not long after closing his door, he noticed the hall light was still on. And when he opened the door, there was Sylvia. She had not moved. He told her he would call Dr. Horder. She did not want Dr. Horder, she answered. She was just having "the most wonderful dream."

It is likely that the Sylvia seen last by Trevor Thomas was on an antidepressant. The euphoric sense of wholeness that is common in drug-induced states wore off perhaps around 5 a.m., when Thomas could hear Sylvia still pacing above as he fell asleep. That wonderful but evanescent moment of transcendence, akin to what she experienced when writing poems, seeped out of her. Knowing that a nurse was coming in the morning, it is just possible Plath expected to be saved. Was she seeking a temporary state of oblivion to assuage her agonies? A near death to be followed by yet another rebirth? No one can say. Perhaps Alvarez is right in suggesting suicide, like divorce, is a confession of failure, an admission, in Sylvia's case, that "all one's energy, appetite and ambition have been aborted."

Mothers all over England tended to favor gas as a way to end their lives. They often took their children—extensions of their identities—with them, perhaps as vengeance against husbands and lovers, or because they had turned against a world that would treat their offspring cruelly. Sylvia seems to have considered this option in "Edge," which describes a mother folding her children back into her body, just like petals "of a rose close. . . ." But always, she had returned to suicide as a singular act and death as a kind of deliverance.

Sylvia understood losing consciousness as a kind of death. The sensation fascinated her, as she recounts in a journal entry written after a tooth extraction. As the gas enters her, she feels her mouth crack into a smile: "So that's how it was . . . so simple, and no one had told me." Death itself she imagined as everything fading to black, like a fainting spell, but with "no light, no waking." "I know a little how it must be," she wrote prophetically more than a decade earlier, to "feel the waters close above you . . . To have your mind broken, and the contents evaporated, gone."

It was now 11 February, and Sylvia Plath prepared to die. She left food and drink for her children in their room and opened a window. In the hallway, she attached a note with Dr. Horder's name and number to the baby carriage. She sealed the kitchen as best she could with tape, towels, and cloths. She turned on the gas and thrust her head as far as she could into the oven. A hired nurse, arriving around 9:30 a.m. to begin her day heard the children crying at the window and called on a workman to break into the flat. They found Sylvia Plath lying on the kitchen floor with her head in the oven. It was far too late to revive her.

It may seem perverse—or at the very least paradoxical—to say that by her suicide Sylvia Plath finally found a way to recover herself. By all accounts, including her own, she had been writing the poetry that would make her reputation, but she knew that no human being could sustain such a peak of perfection and perform all the normal functions of existence in the "kitchen of life," as Martha Gellhorn used to call day to day existence. When Sylvia Plath put an end to herself, she had reached one of those crisis points, exhilarated and exhausted by all she had accomplished—and by all she had left undone. This state of beatitude, this descent into the lower depths, is Shakespearean in its sublimity and tragedy and seems worthy of what Menenius says of Coriolanus, who had a nature "too noble for this world."

CHAPTER 8

IN THE TEMPLE OF ISIS:

AMONG THE HIEROPHANTS

(1963–)

The candidate for initiation has now been taken by the High Priestess (the Gnosis) within the Temple and she has transformed herself into the Goddess Isis . . . He learns from her the secrets of nature . . . He learns the true meaning of Black Magic . . . The fact that the Empress precedes the Emperor in the pack is perhaps a relic of matriarchal rule . . .

—Basil Ivan Rakoczi,
The Painted Caravan: A Penetration into the Secrets of Tarot Cards
(in Sylvia Plath's library at Smith College)

She had free and controlled access to depths formerly reserved to the primitive ecstatic priests, shamans, and Holy men . . .
—Ted Hughes

A priestess emptied out by the rites of her cult.
—A. Alvarez

Ted Hughes wrote the awful news to Olywn, tersely admitting that Sylvia had asked for his help. Too "jaded" by her entreaties, he had miscalculated just how desperate she had become. "Please don't make this business gossip of any sort. It was gossip—faithfully reported by her ratty acquaintances that drove Sylvia over & I don't like it." To Daniel and Helga Huws, he wrote, "No doubt where the blame lies." Ted tried to explain himself to Aurelia, adverting to the "psychic abnormalities" that afflicted both him and Sylvia. He presented their troubles as a form of mutual blindness and thought Sylvia had become a victim of bad timing, beset by "hellish details." He believed they were coming to realize the marriage could have been repaired. But Sylvia did not hold on. Neither her final letters nor her poems suggest a reconciliation. To spare his children's feelings, he said, he destroyed her journal recounting her final days, and this act surely does not indicate that Sylvia wished to resume her marriage. Ted told Aurelia that he was damned and did not want to be forgiven, presumably because of his role in destroying what he called "one of the greatest, truest spirits alive" and a "great poet." Although he acknowledged that Sylvia could be hard on the people she loved, he was unable amidst his own grief to take the measure of her Dostoyevskian rage. Sylvia Plath hated Ted Hughes with "that hate which is only a hair's-breadth from love, from the maddest love!"—to quote from the passage she asterisked in Mark Slonim's introduction to *The Brothers Karamazov*.

What could Aurelia say to Ted's postmortem? She wanted Warren and his wife, who went over to England for Sylvia's funeral, to return to America with her grandchildren. When Ted balked at that idea, she resigned herself to placating Hughes and those around him so that she could maintain contact with her grandchildren. She tried to enlist the help of Dr. Horder, who responded on 17 October 1963, "Ted's behavior is disappointing . . . I feel completely impotent because I never had any relationship with Ted and it has become fairly clear, only three weeks ago, that no relationship of a constructive nature between us is possible because of what happened."

Hughes worried, as he wrote Aurelia three months after Sylvia's suicide, that she would "mourn" over the children, especially Frieda, as a substitute for her daughter. He dreaded Aurelia's overwhelming love, which would engulf them and distort their sense of reality at a time when they were much too young to understand what was happening. He noted that because his feelings and

Aurelia's no longer had a "worldly object," their attachment to Sylvia freed them to regard her with an "unearthly" and even "religious" intensity. He did not want to deny Aurelia opportunities to visit her grandchildren, but he bluntly told her that her "watchful anxiety" had made life much harder for Sylvia, and he did not want to see the pattern repeated in the lives of his daughter and son.

Angrily, Ted told Aurelia that friends had informed him about her efforts to learn more about his marriage to Sylvia. Warren had gone to see Sylvia's lawyer, Aurelia recalled for Frances McCullough, who edited *Letters Home*. The lawyer was "very sympathetic. He discussed matters very freely . . . Sylvia was dead serious about the divorce until shortly before her death when her strength gave out. . . ." Already, years before biographers were on his case, Hughes said he felt "under investigation." And he resented the implication that he was holding back anything that Aurelia was entitled to know. Certain questions from Warren had put Ted on his guard. Already, he was declaring that only his public "self-immolation over Sylvia's name" would suffice. And yet when he vowed that his love for Sylvia remained, and that he would never marry again, what was he proposing but a kind of self-sacrifice? Even as he was writing letters to Assia Wevill, declaring himself wholly hers, he was insisting on his own form of consecration for Sylvia Plath. His behavior when Aurelia arrived to check up on him (this is how he put it) signaled the first phase of his dogged but futile effort to dictate the gospel of Sylvia Plath's biography.

Hughes envisioned a life in which his children would not "succumb back into Sylvia's Magnetism." He was also determined to spirit his family away from the "curators of the past." In other words, only Ted Hughes would officiate at her temple. He found it utterly fantastic that Aurelia supposed he would hold on to Court Green, the "site, in fact, of my crime against her, against myself, and against every human thing." Yet a month later, he wrote to Gerald, "I've been thinking I'll hang on to Court Green." Money was often a serious consideration for Hughes. He expected the property to appreciate in value, and it would make a good "country resort" for his children. Aurelia was now in England, which meant, Ted told his brother, "four weeks of nerves."

Ted had installed Assia in Sylvia's Fitzroy Road flat over the objections of his Aunt Hilda, who described Assia as a

> reincarnated Cleopatra. At first I couldn't bear the sight of her and told her to clear off and leave Ted in peace for a while until the Plaths had gone and I had gone. But of course she took no notice & Ted told me to mind my own business. . . . Ted is simply bewitched and I have told him he has only left one bondage for another, and she will turn into a devil one day. . . . I have come to the conclusion wherever Ted is there will be women, so it is no good being a hanger on. . . . I am concerned about the children.

Al Alvarez and his wife, Anne, shared this view of Assia, whom they saw in Ted's company during this period. She seemed manipulative—and very pleased with herself.

On 2 September 1963, Edith Hughes wrote to Olwyn, preparing her for the current situation at Court Green. Elizabeth Compton ("very nice & will be useful until you get settled") had told Edith that Sylvia had called Assia a "devil. Just watch what she will do to Ted." Edith cautioned Olwyn to go easy with her brother, but also to be firm about Assia: "Don't be conciliatory . . . or she will be wanting to come. For the children's & Ted's sake this must not happen." With Olwyn and Aunt Hilda installed at Court Green in October, Ted promised Assia he would find another home for them, but he never did let go of Court Green.

In a letter to Aurelia, he was full of news about the children, especially Frieda, whom he favored. He seemed relieved that they had adjusted in their old home. He reported that he was well treated by everyone, including Elizabeth Compton, who had been close to Sylvia. He was negotiating with publishers about the appearance of her poems. With full control over Plath's estate, and not yet the object of public scrutiny for his role in her death, Hughes seemed especially heartened to trumpet her work, "written in blood," he told poet Donald Hall, taking issue with reservations about certain poems that Hall had expressed in print.

Everything was about to change—or rather intensify—in Ted Hughes's life with the publication in March 1965 of *Ariel,* the book that confirmed Sylvia Plath's position as a world-class poet. Assia Wevill, wearing badly under the strain of coping with Plath—who had become, in Hughes's words, a "spectacular public figure"— gave birth on 3 March 1965, to a child by him, called Shura. A wary Hughes accused Assia of saving his letters, perhaps to use later against him—such was his reaction against the siege of "bloody eavesdroppers & filchers," even though the first biographer had yet to arrive. He instructed Assia to burn his letters, lest they be "intercepted." Anne, Alvarez's wife, thought of black-haired Ted and Assia, so often dressed in black, as two panthers hissing at each other: "It was very unpleasant." Anne remembered visiting Assia, ailing with the flu: "She was in Sylvia's bed all dressed up and glamorous and it really gave me the creeps . . . All she talked about was Sylvia."

Enter Lois Ames, a friend of Sylvia's, bent on writing the first biography. She had secured Aurelia's approval. Hughes was willing to cooperate only in so far as the book would provide a short and superficial view of Sylvia's life, based mainly on reminiscences of the "right people." He declared his intention to thwart any full scale, modern biography, the kind that inevitably proved reductive, he assured Aurelia and Warren when he wrote to them in March of 1966. Although Ames labored for several years on the biography, she gave it up in 1974, saying much later in an interview that it "became increasingly difficult for me to do this, as other biographers have found out. And I finally decided for the sake of my own sanity and my family that it was better to pay back the advance to Harper's. I always felt it was a wise decision." Her "Notes Toward a Biography," which appeared in *Tri-Quarterly* 7 in 1966, reads like a work of Victorian circumspection. Sylvia's last year is described as "difficult," and Ames does not even mention the separation from Hughes, saying only that Plath moved to London, and that "despite the care of a doctor and prescribed sedatives, she was unable to cope."

Hughes contributed biographical notes to the same *Tri-Quarterly* issue, excusing himself to Aurelia on 19 May 1966 by saying Sylvia had already become a "literary legend"—without assessing his own part in making her so. He rated her far ahead of Robert Lowell and even better than Hughes's touchstone, Emily Dickinson. His fervor belied his disclaimer that he did not want to portray himself as the "high priest of her mysteries." But that, of course, is exactly what he had done by claiming total control not only over her work, but also over the manner in which her life should be revered.

After Sylvia had been given demeaning and malicious treatment in *Time,* Hughes commiserated with Aurelia in a 13 July 1966. The magazine's 10 June issue reviewed *Ariel,* focusing on "Daddy," printing it in full, and labeling it an example of Plath's style, as "brutal as a truncheon." The poem was "merely the first jet of flame from a literary dragon who in the last months of her life breathed a living river of bale across the literary landscape." Leave it to *Time* to come up with "bale," the archaic meaning of which is associated with misery, woe, misfortune, evil, and harm. In Britain, *Ariel* had sold fifteen thousand copies in ten months, figures often associated with a bestselling novel, *Time* reported.

The remorse Hughes suffered over his part in Sylvia's suicide was now overshadowed by his outrage over her posthumous denudation. He regretted publishing *Ariel* in the United States—although how he could square his misgivings with his desire to promote her greatness is baffling, especially since he jiggered publication of the book with Robert Lowell's attention-getting introduction. Hughes deplored the too easy equation between Plath's poems and her suicide. Indeed, the poems had "cured" her, he argued.

In December, Aurelia wrote to Elinor Epstein, thanking her for publishing a memoir that honored her friendship with Sylvia without disclosing the intimacies they shared. Epstein's anodyne memoir, emphasizing what a cheery person Sylvia was, only served to launch a spate of reminiscences, pro and con Plath. Already, on 3 December 1966, Aurelia was writing to Epstein, "I am so sick of the 'legend,' the 'image.' "

Even as Hughes indulged himself in degrading the efforts of anyone—other than himself—who dared to depict Sylvia Plath, he was replicating the very domestic disarray that had contributed to her demise. A disheartened Assia Wevill began to conclude that not only could she never compete with the legend of Sylvia Plath, she could not even secure Hughes's commitment to find a permanent home she could call her own. Instead, she coped with a series of makeshift domiciles, beginning with the Fitzroy Road flat, then Court Green, followed by a brief period in Ireland—and then back to Court Green to confront the hostility of Hughes's parents, installed there as caretakers whenever Ted's marauding sensibility sent him off to the city and other locales that welcomed this controversial celebrity poet. By the end of the year, Assia was back in London with Shura, brooding over what to do about Hughes's broken promises.

To Daniel Weissbort in December 1966 Hughes revealed the mocking side of himself that revolted Sylvia Plath: first the bracing tonic of distraction-free country life, then the momentary sense of equilibrium it engendered, and then the flight to the city to "get the family lice combed out of you." Plath understood the need to be off to London—she experienced the need herself—but to couch that need in such loathing, and to revel in dispatching the domesticity she treasured enraged her, especially since Hughes could turn from pliant to disdainful in a trice. Much has been written about Plath's mercurial moods, but Hughes in his own way could cut her a new one.

On 25 May 1968, Olywn wrote to Aurelia broaching the idea of publishing *The Bell Jar* in the United States—even though, as Olwyn admitted in her letter, Ted had told her that Aurelia was adamantly against such publication. Think how much more money a novel would bring in for the children's benefit than the poetry would, Olwyn argued. Aurelia's response, which she decided not to send to Olwyn, was a terse rebuttal: "Surely the children will respect their father, when they are grown, for having refused to make money for them at such a price to their mother's people!"

Olwyn persisted for the next two years, writing a series of letters Aurelia later deposited in her daughter's Smith College archive. On 2 July, Olwyn argued against exaggerated fears of publicity over publication of *The Bell Jar*. No one would care much about the real-life figures Sylvia had turned into her characters. Sylvia herself was disappointed that Knopf had not wanted to publish the novel. And as a capper, Olwyn suggested Aurelia was depriving Sylvia of her place in "our literary heritage." A skeptical, infuriated Aurelia annotated this letter, noting what a ruckus "Daddy" had caused. She wrote Olwyn a week later that she had no idea of the "cupidity" of the American press and motion picture industry, which would only be interested in the sensationalistic aspects of *The Bell Jar* and Sylvia's suicide. Aurelia had obtained legal advice, which only confirmed her concerns. In an unsent note, dated 29 December, Aurelia let Olwyn have it: Aurelia was not only expected to suffer the publication of the novel, she was supposed to "sanction it!" Olwyn backed off, temporarily, even as she cited the opinions of writers like Alan Sillitoe, who deemed the novel a distinguished work. Olwyn's subsequent letters to an obdurate Aurelia asserted that the estate could control publicity about Sylvia by funneling all queries about her life to Lois Ames—who became, in effect, not merely the authorized, but also the proprietary biographer.

Then Frances McCullough announced that Random House planned to issue an American edition of *The Bell Jar*, capitalizing on the copyright law then in effect: "Plath or her publisher in England would have had to publish the book in the U.S. within 6 months, but because she never intended to publish it here, and because it was published under a pseudonym, that never happened." McCullough contacted Random House and "managed to make an ethical case that they shouldn't do this because Ted Hughes had promised Sylvia's mother it would never happen." Aurelia, worried about her deteriorating health and financial security, realized that nothing would stem the interest in all facets of her daughter's life and work. As a result, she went along with Frances McCullough's advice that to "protect the book," they had to publish it. "Later it became possible to amend that copyright provision and it was registered in Frieda and Nicholas's name," McCullough explained to Beth Alvarez, an archivist at the University of Maryland.

On 23 March 1969, Assia Wevill gassed herself and her daughter. In the past year, her life with Hughes had become a desperate affair. She had written to Aurelia on 4 January 1968: "Ted told me that I was no use to him as an invalid (this was during my post-flu depression and sinus and bronchitis and things), and I thought that was the most brutal thing he'd ever said to me, when I nursed him and his mother for three weeks of his slipped disc. I thought suddenly that that degree of brutality would slowly dement me. That I must perhaps think of living without him completely." Hughes's reaction to the news was the same as it had been when Sylvia killed herself: "I cannot believe how I never knew what was really happening to her." To Celia Chaikin, Assia's sister, he claimed that as a couple he and Assia were one, which is why her constant testing of him—right up to her telephone call shortly before her suicide—had not unduly troubled him. He had been too distracted and too exhausted to offer her the hope she craved. He might as well have copied the letters he wrote to Aurelia after Sylvia's death.

Writing to Aurelia on 14 April, an anguished Hughes alluded to the hellish atmosphere of Court Green, treating his home like a haunted Gothic castle. What could Aurelia have made of his insensitive comment that he and Assia had hoped they could make "some atonement" for Sylvia? And how did it help to tell Aurelia that since Sylvia's death his nature had turned "negative," prompting him yet again to make a fresh start. It was exactly this notion—that he could just move on—that had so devastated Plath.

On 2 May 1969, Olwyn rang up Al Alvarez to talk about Assia's suicide. He noted in his diary: "According to Olwyn—who is scarcely impartial and probably lying—Assia was drunk . . . and had taken sleeping pills." When Alvarez said the real crime was killing her little girl, Olwyn replied, "She could hardly have left Ted with *another* motherless child." An aghast Alvarez listened as Olwyn said that it had been a particularly trying week for Assia. She was probably looking ghastly and was probably thinking, "I've lost my beauty. Ted will never love me." In his diary, Alvarez wrote, "Olwyn could scarcely contain her triumph and contempt." Writing to Peter Redgrove, a friend, in the spring of 1970, Hughes might as well have said he had become a ringer for Byron's Manfred: "I seem to have been populated by the deceased who go on requiring God knows what of me & permit me very little."

In August 1970, Hughes married Carol Orchard, the daughter of a Devon farmer Hughes had befriended. Like certain other women who enter during the latter stages of a famous writer's career— Elaine Steinbeck and Mary Hemingway come to mind—Carol became the ideal consort. As caretaker of her husband's myth, she was anxious to make sure she did everything in her power to keep out of print the negativity that Hughes had identified in himself. From this point on, Carol and Olwyn joined forces to make certain their Ted was well defended and shielded from having to deal directly with the legend of Sylvia Plath. For his part, Hughes felt perfectly free to pursue love affairs, advising Marvin Cohen, one of Olwyn's writer friends, that the best way to get over the heartbreaking loss of a lover was to make sure that one always had another woman on hand as a replacement. Writing to Gerald and Joan Hughes, Ted announced that he had been leading a false life from about the age of sixteen and now had to start "from scratch."

In September of 1971, Hughes wrote to Lucas Myers about the "Sylvia mania," mentioning articles by A. Alvarez and Elizabeth Hardwick, and noting that in New York Plath was *the* topic of literary conversation. What Hughes did not say is that his decision to publish *The Bell Jar* in the United States had set off this passion for Plath. Alvarez boldly broke the silence, not only discussing Sylvia's suicide, but also refuting Hughes's claim that Plath's last poems had been analeptic. As Alvarez wrote in 1971 in *The Savage God,* "Art is not necessarily therapeutic . . . the act of formal expression may simply make the dredged-up material more readily available to [the artist]. The result of handling it in his work may well be that he finds himself living it out. For the artist, in short, nature often imitates art."

In November 1971, Hughes wrote to Alvarez "as a friend," asking him to stop contributing to popularization of Plath's suicide for an audience titillated by such revelations. Excerpts from *The Savage God* had just been published in *The Observer*. This humiliating exhumation, as Hughes put it, would only degrade discussion of Plath's poetry, and Alvarez well knew the work had to stand by itself. Such intrusive speculation was offensive to Hughes and to a few others who really knew the circumstances of Plath's suicide.

But what did Hughes know? Did he even know about the role Alvarez had played during Plath's last months? Over the years, what he knew would change as he developed his own theories and rationalizations for her actions and his. Like everyone else, Hughes had no access to her final hours and was not privy to her thoughts. Hughes also suggested that because Alvarez had supplied so many details, his version had become the "official text"—a preposterous notion, surely, since it is in the nature of biographical inquiry to be eternally provisional and subject to correction and revision. Hughes had demanded the right to vet Alvarez's work before publication. On what basis, then, could Alvarez have claimed an independent authority? But Hughes believed that Alvarez had no rights in the matter and should only feel ashamed that Plath's children now had to deal with what Alvarez had put into print. Alvarez had poisoned Frieda's and Nicholas's minds with words that entered their brains like electrodes, Hughes wrote in a frenzy of contumely. Alvarez responded in *The Observer* (15 November) to Hughes's complaining letter that it seemed better for everyone, including her children, to have a forthright and considerate account of Plath's life and death than to put up with a "cloud of vague and malicious rumours."

In 1972, Random House published *Monster,* Robin Morgan's radical feminist collection of poetry, which includes her all-out assault on Ted Hughes. In "Arraignment," she labels him Plath's murderer. Her charge sheet includes lines that suggest Hughes had mentally and physically abused Plath, brainwashed her children, profited from her literary estate, and driven Assia Wevill, as well, to her death. And he had been supported in his nefarious deeds by a complicit literary establishment. Even Alvarez and other male critics and poets sympathetic to Plath were accused of patronizing her. As a credo for the women's movement, *Monster* attracted considerable attention, selling over thirty thousand copies, a remarkable success for a poetry collection. After Ted Hughes's threats of a lawsuit, however, Random House decided not to publish the book abroad. As critic Janet Badia observes in the most extensive account of Morgan's book and its aftermath, *Monster's* hyperbole and irony—ending in the evisceration and murder of Hughes by a gang of feminists disguised as his groupies—epitomizes the militant feminist writing of the 1970s. Pirated editions turned up among women picketing Hughes's public readings and even his home. Morgan herself, as she relates in her memoir, *Saturday's Child*, received a call from Doris Lessing asking her to call off the protestors and to withdraw *Monster* from publication. But, as Badia points out, the more Hughes and his supporters sought to suppress the book, the more attention it received. Although Badia found remarkably little evidence of a widespread boycott of Hughes and his work, the press repeated the generally accepted story that he had become the victim of an unremitting feminist attack.

In March 1972, Plath scholar Judith Kroll journeyed to London to confer with Olwyn about establishing definitive texts of Plath's poems. After she had written to Rainbow Press about textual discrepancies in an edition of Plath's work, Kroll was surprised to hear directly from Olwyn. Kroll then discovered that Olwyn and Ted were the founders of the firm. Kroll found Olwyn "formidable," tall and copper-haired, and by turns friendly and imperious. Olwyn was easily distracted by an affair with a rowdy fellow Kroll identifies as "Richard," who often interrupted their work, and during Kroll's second visit in June even threatened to destroy the papers they were working on. Kroll had trouble reading Olwyn, who seemed to say things meant to get a rise out of the cautious scholar. "I think Sylvia just wrote those poems to dazzle Ted and win him back," Olwyn averred. It was hard to maintain one's equilibrium in the company of this mercurial personality: Olwyn allowed Kroll to take away valuable papers for several days, only to turn condescending and outraged when the scholar, who was performing considerable editing work, brought up the subject of payment (none was forthcoming). The erratic nature of the whole enterprise—often interrupted by the demanding Richard, who could turn violent and cause Olwyn to "call it a day"—cut short the hours Kroll had planned for her work. "Some of the men were rough on her [Olwyn]," said Marvin Cohen, one of Olwyn's friends.

"Sloppy and casual" are the words Kroll uses to describe Olwyn's custody of Plath's work, which resulted in a number of errors in *The Collected Poems* that could have been avoided. Both Olwyn and

Ted thought nothing of rearranging the order of Plath's work, even when Plath's own design was clear. Ted spent several hours with Kroll when she visited Court Green. He complimented her work, saying he thought she had got it right most of the time. From Hughes, this was praise indeed, since he scorned the academic study of literature. (He had forsaken his own literary studies at Cambridge for anthropology, believing that, as critic Janet Badia puts it, literary criticism "destroys not only the poem but the poet too.") Because of Kroll's ability to identify the biographical sources of the poems, though, Ted felt sure that she had been talking to Plath's friends. Kroll, in fact, had come by her knowledge through intense study of Plath's work, which led her to identify Aurelia with Plath's poem "Medusa." Ted and Olwyn told her that to publish the poem's connection with Aurelia would kill Sylvia's mother. When Kroll answered Olwyn's question about her astrological sign, Olwyn exclaimed that one of Kroll's planets was on a "collision course" with one of Aurelia's. In short, Kroll was "fatal for Aurelia." When Kroll insisted that sooner or later the background of "Medusa" would be public knowledge, Olwyn reiterated her question: "Do you want to be a murderer?"

In 1978, Kroll decided to visit Aurelia, who announced she had not read Kroll's book because the publisher had not bothered to send her a copy. The visit went well, and some weeks later, Aurelia wrote to say she had read and learned a good deal from Kroll's book, which she deemed "brilliant." Then Aurelia added that the identification of Aurelia and Medusa had been a " 'private joke' between her and Sylvia." In Aurelia's annotated copy of Kroll's book, now in the Sylvia Plath collection at Smith College, Aurelia comments on the discussion of "Medusa," noting that Sylvia used to "tease me about this!" To Kroll's comment that the poem "presents an exorcism of the oppressive parent," Aurelia replies, "And I worked constantly to free her & encouraged every act of independence!" An agitated Aurelia then read that, as in "Daddy," Plath created in "Medusa" "a scapegoat laden with the evils of her spoiled history, a source and sustainer of her false self, who therefore deserves to be expelled." At the bottom of the page Aurelia wrote: "I worked to be free of her & at least live *my* life—not to be drawn into the complexities & crises of hers. I loved spending time with the children—but wanted freedom which Sylvia refused to grant. *She,* in summer '62 showed me a house where she wished me to retire—in Eng!!" Elsewhere in Kroll's book, Aurelia reproduced the evidence of her wish to foster an autonomous Sylvia: "I sent her to camp, let her go to Smith instead of Wellesley College, rejoiced in her Fulbright!! *I* wanted to be free at last!"

No less than Ted Hughes, Aurelia Plath wanted to rebut various accounts of her daughter, especially in relation to *The Bell Jar.* In August 1972, she wrote to the novel's American editor, Frances Mc-Cullough: "For me, the book itself will always remain unbearably painful for the record of suffering it embodies and for the decent, loyal friends it hurts. Also, being very human, I resent being iden-tified with 'mother,' whose sanctimonious utterances and insipid personality make me want to retch!" Aurelia believed a collection of letters would demonstrate how loving Sylvia had been to her, as well as reveal Aurelia's own efforts to provide her daughter with every possible means of support. But Ted Hughes held the copy-right to his wife's correspondence, and Aurelia feared that Olwyn would block publication of what came to be titled *Letters Home.* On 16 August 1972, Aurelia wrote to Ted: "Olwyn, of course, doesn't know me as you do. Frankly, she frightens me. I am, I believe, a direct, uncomplicated person—now pressed to the wall financially because, in good faith in connection with this project, I've burned my bridges behind me [she had given up teaching]. I depend on you, Ted, to free me to do this very difficult work, which I am do-ing for your and Warren's children." How could Hughes deny her, when so often he and Olwyn argued for publication of Plath's work on grounds that it would benefit Frieda and Nicholas?

Hughes agreed to publication so long as Aurelia abided by his censorship of Sylvia's references to him. He wanted the book con-siderably shortened so as to read like a novel, which he thought would silence detractors and become a bestseller. In other words, he remained unable to see he was part of the very process of bio-graphical inquiry and popularization that he condemned. Even though he had praised Frances McCullough as a perspicacious edi-tor, he was taken aback at her objection to the extensive cuts he wanted, and he wrote a mollifying letter to Aurelia (after she had engaged lawyers to insure Ted abided by his agreement with her). She was upset at his butchery of her book, but he argued he was saving her from the "mob"—a favorite term of his, used to describe virtually anyone interested in anything having to do with Plath other than her work.

In September 1972, Harriet Rosenstein published "Reconsidering Sylvia Plath" in *Ms.* magazine, part of her work on a Brandeis University doctoral dissertation. Already Plath had become a flashpoint, her every line the focus of biographical discussion and critical debate. Rosenstein is mentioned several times in Olwyn's correspondence as someone who had been interviewing Plath's friends and associates, even though Olwyn had told her Lois Ames had the estate's exclusive cooperation. Indeed, Rosenstein's research experience survives in the lore of Plathists as an exemplar of what biographers have suffered as a result of the Plath estate's embargo.

In the Frances McCullough collection at the University of Maryland, the indefatigable Rosenstein makes repeated appearances as "Harriet the Spy," securing Sylvia's letters on the sly, interviewing Dr. Beuscher, hiding recording devices under a sofa, and in general "running circles around" Lois Ames—so much so that McCullough proposes that Olwyn make a "truce" with Rosenstein and name her the authorized biographer after deposing the author of the "idiot licensed biography." But Olwyn objected, noting that Rosenstein had been telling people that Ted's sister was the "great big monster in the wood pile" and a "witch (black)."

In her *Ms.* article, Rosenstein employs religious language in describing the already fractured audience of "apostles" and "infidels" that clashed over Plath. "Sects" and "schisms" threatened to overwhelm their subject, now the center of a "Holy War." That Rosenstein was taking issue with all sides should have put her in a prime position to write a truly independent biography. She understood why Plath's use of anger and her exploration of women's lives and domestic routines should make her an icon for the feminist movement and a startling new figure in the history of Anglo-American literature. At the same time, the biographer expressed concern that Plath's own voice had been drowned out by programmatic arguments about what she stood for. Distinctions had to be made between Plath as a representative figure and Plath's singularity.

Writing on 23 November 1973 to Clare Court, a Court Green neighbor who had incurred Olwyn's wrath by writing a letter to the *TLS* praising Plath, A. Alvarez noted: "Miss Rosenstein seems better than most . . . She seems very thorough and also independent—though how long that will last, heaven only knows. . . . But I must confess that it's depressing to think that the unspeakable Olywn Hughes has managed to bully and insult you, too, into silence. She has tried that tactic on so many people that I despair of the truth of that sordid and tragic affair ever emerging." Poor Clare Court, she had been charmed by Sylvia's stories of the swifts, who took the thatch from her home to build nests of their own.

Perhaps the recalcitrance of the Plath estate was, in the end, enough to prevent Rosenstein from ever publishing her biography. She may also have been aware of another contender, Elizabeth Hinchliffe, a graduate of Wellesley High School, a *Mademoiselle* guest editor, and the author of a Wellesley College honors thesis on Plath. Hinchliffe had also spent her freshman year at Smith, thus appearing as yet another double that Plath herself would have appreciated. Judging by a manuscript in the Frances McCullough Papers at the University of Maryland in College Park, and by her correspondence in the Alvarez papers at the British Library, Hinchliffe did considerable research and interviewing, gathering intimate and even gruesome details that would not have served her well in dealings with the Plath estate. The Plath archives are silent on what happened to the Hinchliffe biography. McCullough's collection at the University of Maryland includes a letter from Olywn deeming Hinchliff's work "highly offensive and ludicrous." Ted Hughes later wrote to poet and biographer Andrew Motion about biographers who had come to grief attempting to write about Sylvia, noting that Linda Wagner-Martin was "so insensitive that she's evidently escaped the usual effects of undertaking this particular job—i.e. mental breakdown, neurotic collapse, domestic catastrophe—which in the past have saved us from several travesties of this kind being completed."

By 1973, Edward Butscher, not a timid soul, was already well on his way to producing the first full-length Plath biography, discovering that "English authors . . . reluctantly refused to see me on the ground that they could not reveal the truth of Sylvia's last years and still maintain social and/or business ties with Ted and Olwyn Hughes." Elizabeth Compton, a Devon neighbor of Sylvia's, wrote to Butscher, "If you wrote what I knew of Sylvia you could not publish it because Ted & Olwyn would sue you. 'The truth about Sylvia can only be told when you are dying,' Ted told me some weeks back."

Olwyn met with Butscher three times and responded in writing to his queries. At one point, she offered to act as his agent in the UK if he submitted his book to her and she approved of it. In early 1975, Olwyn sent detailed corrections of Butscher's biography, objecting, especially, to his sympathetic account of Sylvia after Ted had left her. In Olwyn's version, Sylvia had been aggressively jealous and had driven Ted out of his own home, thus making it certain he would turn to Assia, whose own behavior is excused because she was so much in love with Ted. Olwyn, seeking to mitigate Ted's treatment of Sylvia, campaigned relentlessly for a positive portrayal of Assia's actions—even securing Assia's friend, Edward Lucie-Smith, to write a character study that would soften her image in Butscher's book.

On 7 April 1975, Butscher replied, thanking Olwyn for saving him from some embarrassing errors, but also admitting he found her "massive missive" annoying. He answered Olwyn's concerns point-by-point, identifying sources and pointing out that many of her objections were to Sylvia's point of view, which the biographer was trying to honor. He did not intend to rewrite the book. When Olwyn demanded more changes and mentioned her intention to contact Butscher's publisher, he replied on 5 May 1975 that he deemed her response a threat. He encouraged her to carry through with it, saying Continuum Books would be delighted to advertise his biography as "THE BOOK THE HUGHES TRIED TO SUPPRESS!" He also wanted her to know that he had engaged a lawyer who had vetted his book and assured him he would win any legal action brought against him (Olywn had already suggested that certain passages might be libelous). Although he had initially believed in her sincerity, he now realized that too many of her "recent suggestions smack of a whitewash." He agreed to change some other wording at her suggestion, but that was as far as he could go. If he was denied permission to quote from Plath's work, the biographer promised to mount a letter-writing campaign to literary journals and newspapers decrying Olwyn's "pre-censorship" and "heavy-handed tactics," which would also be a subject of the preface to his biography. He did not consider these proposed actions threats— just aids to fulfilling his duty to "literature and objective scholarship."

Olwyn's reply on 12 May was forbearing, suggesting that Butscher's "rage" was the result of her hastily composed letter, which she had dispatched too soon because of the press of other business. But well into mid-July 1975, when the book was in the proofs stage and corrections would be costly to the author and publisher, Olwyn was still requesting changes and cuts—even after she had endorsed Harper's grant of permission to quote from Plath's work. Butscher agreed to a few more alterations, telling Olwyn it was too late to do anything more. Three years later, she engaged in correspondence with Peter Owen, Butscher's publisher for a collection of essays, *Sylvia Plath: The Woman and the Work,* complaining about the "horrible Butscher" as a "revengeful little sod."

Reviewing *Letters Home* in the *Los Angeles Times Book Review* (23 November 1975), poet and novelist Erica Jong complained that Plath's work had been muddled by "relatives of hers . . . anxious . . . to suppress the truth." To Jong, Ted, Olwyn, and Aurelia were no better than other commentators who had "axes to grind." In *The National Observer* (10 January 1976), Anne Tyler, a highly regarded novelist, was equally excoriating, calling the Sylvia of *Letters Home* a "wax image," and the collection not much better than a family scrapbook. In the *Southwest Review* (Summer 1976), scholar Jo Brans questioned the "reliability of the letters because of their editing." So many ellipses suggested tendentiousness. Aurelia's italicized commentary was dismissed as reductive rationalization.

Edward Butscher's *Sylvia Plath: Method and Madness,* appearing at almost the same time as the publication of *Letters Home,* provided an explanation for readers who puzzled over how the dutiful daughter in Aurelia's book could possibly have written the searing verse of Sylvia's final year. The biographer argued that Plath had to shed her female modesty and middle-class values to become the "bitch goddess" entirely consumed by her art. Like several critics, Sylvia's friend, Phil McCurdy, thought Butscher had pushed his thesis too far. "You reify too many traits," he wrote the biographer. In a subsequent letter to Butscher, McCurdy expressed his gratitude to Sylvia, who had made him a better man. "If it was just part of an unhealthy, manipulative—even unconscious—rationale on her part, I'm sure glad I was one of the objects!"

Although Butscher was accused of misogyny and superficial psychologizing, he proved an astute critic, establishing "almost all the formulas that later biographers would adopt and reinforce," Susan R. Van Dyne contends in *The Cambridge Companion to Sylvia Plath.* Hampered in some cases by his inability to name names (both Assia and Dick Norton were given pseudonyms), Butscher nevertheless nailed down the testimony of many important witnesses, while carefully assessing their reliability. A year later, in *Sylvia Plath: The Woman and the Work,* Butscher included important memoirs by Clarissa Roche and Elizabeth Sigmund (married to David Compton when she knew Sylvia at Court Green). Sigmund singled out Olwyn as "the most difficult person in Ted's family," one who "feared and resented Sylvia's talent and beauty, as well as her relationship with Ted."

In 1977, Ted Hughes published a collection of Plath's short stories, *Johnny Panic and the Bible of Dreams* (1977), followed in 1981 by *The Collected Poems,* with helpful notes and introductions, and then in 1982 a redacted edition of Sylvia's journals, edited by Frances McCullough. Hughes wanted McCullough to cut out references to his "uncouthness" because they upset his wife Carol. Passages critical of Aurelia had to be removed, as did various references to his friends. An exasperated McCullough wrote Hughes on 21 September 1981:

> The effect of a number of the cuts is to take away her sexuality. This seems to me really mistaken . . . It's absurd to think

that Aurelia might be embarrassed by Sylvia's having sexual feelings in college—it's one of Aurelia's big virtues in LET-TERS HOME that she talks frankly about sex to Sylvia and tries her best to seem liberated about it, whatever her true feelings. To take these passages out on the grounds that she might object just seems prudish, and it trivializes Sylvia. . . . There has already been so much question of censorship surrounding Plath that it would be much better simply to leave the unpleasant stuff in. I really think it would be counterproductive to censor it . . .

Undeterred, Hughes thought only of the humiliation of his wife and children. McCullough wrote to Olwyn nearly a decade later, after the publication of the journals, "There was a very real chance the book would be cancelled altogether because of the last set of cuts." The editor withdrew from the Plath field, complaining to Olwyn that she was tired of accusations that she was a "Hughes patsy trying to censor Plath into oblivion," only to be attacked by Olwyn as the "architect of a clever plot to inflame feminists."

As with *Letters Home,* the response of reviewers to Plath's journals was predictable. "What is really annoying are the long editorial shadows that fall over these papers," complained Marni Jackson in *Maclean's Magazine* (17 May 1982). "The decision to publish her journal should respect her contradictory selves; instead, the editing makes us feel that Plath's husband, mother and editor are peering over our shoulders as we read. . . ." Like many reviewers, Miriam Levine in the *American Book Review* rued Hughes's admission that he had destroyed one of Plath's journals and lost another. In "The Second Destruction of Sylvia Plath," Steven Gould Axelrod argued in *American Poetry Review* that like Plath's last poems, her last journal, which Hughes destroyed, was probably a masterpiece. Axelrod cited the comments of several other scholars and critics, who deemed the editing of Plath's work a "scandal." Taking aim at Hughes's introduction to the journals, in which Ted suggests, "All her writing appears like notes and jottings, directing attention towards that central problem—herself," Axelrod concludes that it was "quite possible that the writings that we have been prevented from seeing have directed attention toward other central problems— for example, the problem of Ted Hughes himself." Hughes's role in stewardship of Plath's posthumous career was, in short, nothing less than appalling.

Not only had Hughes rearranged the order of Plath's *Ariel* poems to suit his proprietary view of her genius, he invidiously divided *The Collected Poems* into two sections, one of them a sort of consignment ghetto called "Juvenilia." The "mature" poems date from 1956, the year she met Hughes. Thus Plath's development is occluded and incomplete in *The Collected Poems*. The volume's exclusivity has no place for poems like "Mad Girl's Love Song," for example, a favorite of many Plath enthusiasts.

Linda Wagner-Martin, intending to write a feminist biography that would do full justice to her subject's work, made an issue of the Plath estate's effort to bully biographers by withholding permission to quote from Plath's materials if the biographers' interpretations diverged from the estate's. Altogether Wagner-Martin cut something like fifteen thousand words from her book when it became clear she could not get permission to conduct close readings of Plath's writing. The exasperated biographer wrote to Elizabeth Compton, "No mention of Assia allowed, for example. Well, then the separation just looked like Sylvia *had* lost her mind." As A. Alvarez remarked, Olwyn and Ted had a "Soviet view of history," believing that "you could airbrush people out." Perhaps most upsetting to Ted Hughes was Wagner-Martin's skepticism about his claim that he and Plath could have reconciled. Ted and Olwyn then decided it was more important than ever to find a replacement for Lois Ames, so that the estate's version of Plath's life could begin to rectify the damage done to them by unauthorized biographies.

For Dido Merwin, who had come to loathe Plath and lionize Ted, any biographer who thought Sylvia committed suicide after realizing her ties to her husband were severed had it wrong. Ted was a "quintessential, ineradicable, irreplaceable part of Sylvia's myth," Dido instructed Wagner-Martin in a letter (18 September 1985). Sylvia never meant to end her life, Dido was certain. Rather, Sylvia's actions were meant to scare Ted into a reconciliation. In effect, Dido was building the case for what would become Anne Stevenson's authorized biography, which would also shift the focus to Sylvia's faults and her manipulative sensibility. Dido pithily summed up the anti-Plath position in April 1986: "It was above all her phenomenal sense of drama. Her gift for timing and organization. The ability to create the maximum embarrassment, shame, consternation and dismay and of course guilt, as a comeback to anything that displeased her, which brought to mind a character out of Strindberg." In the end, what is so troubling about Dido Merwin's memoir of Sylvia is that she is so *certain* of her point of view and so content in her animus, seeing no merit whatever in a feminist analysis of Plath's life and dismissing Wagner-Martin's narrative as a "whitewash." A good deal of Dido's letter was later incorporated into Stevenson's book as an appendix.

Dido claimed a kind of absolute authority because she was *there*, a tactic often employed against a biographer who was not. And yet, just one example of her misreading of Hughes demonstrates why eyewitness testimony can be unreliable. Dido fumed over Sylvia's arrogating the one decent room for writing in the cramped London flat she shared with Ted, consigning him to a card table in a hallway. But Ted later told Anne Stevenson, "One of the best [writing] places I ever had was the hallway of the flat in Chalcot Square—a windowless cubicle just big enough for a chair."

On 25 August 1985, Anne Stevenson wrote to Ted Hughes, informing him that Viking Penguin had offered her a contract to write a short biography of Sylvia Plath. The money was too good to refuse, she admitted. Disavowing "rampant" feminism and determined to be "tactful," she assured him that he could remove any offending passages. Hughes replied in the autumn of 1986 that he received her letter with the "usual dismay." To him, biographers were strangers whose concoctions derived from "a few hearsay legendary bits and pieces." But Hughes seemed more resigned than outraged. Even old friends were now "spilling the beans." He was probably thinking of Lucas Myers, who a week later sent Hughes a memoir. Myers had complied with Hughes's request to delete passages from Hughes's letters to Myers that might be taken the wrong way. Yet Hughes sold these very letters to Emory, and they were

later reproduced in an edition of his correspondence. With Olwyn's encouragement, Stevenson persevered while Hughes dealt
with Jane Anderson's lawsuit, alleging that Hughes had allowed
the libel of her in *The Bell Jar* to be perpetuated and amplified in
the film adaptation of the novel. The suit, finally settled in 1987 by
AVCO Embassy, producers of the film adaptation of *The Bell Jar*,
cost him nothing.

It does not seem possible to discern any consistency or logic in
Hughes's management of his papers and Plath's, perhaps because
his view of their marriage kept changing. To Myers, Hughes wrote
that he regretted, for example, that he had colluded in the publication of *Letters Home*, which burnished the myth of Sylvia as martyr
and absolved Aurelia. The problem, Hughes told Myers, was that
he had "coddled Sylvia"—the very point that Dido Merwin had
driven home in her memoir. He should just have carried on in his
own way instead of deferring to Plath, Hughes concluded.

By mid-1987, Anne Stevenson had abandoned the Viking Penguin project for a full-length biography to be published by Houghton Mifflin and supervised by the heavy-handed Olwyn. Stevenson
possessed a promising background for a Plath biographer. She was
an American who made England her home. She was a member of
Plath's generation. She was a poet. As she wrote to her editor, Peter
Davison, on 29 December 1986, she understood Plath's "uncanny
identification with archetypal myth-figures (Isis, the Black Goddess) and her striving to be both antitheses of herself: Successful
American Woman on Smith Girl lines and Great Imaginary Poet-
Earth Goddess. . . ."

But almost immediately, Stevenson ran into trouble, reporting
to Davison on 25 February 1987, that she had little direct access to
Ted and could not "get around" Olwyn's "fixed ideas" about him.
After a trip to the Lilly Library at Indiana University, Stevenson
wrote her editor that Olwyn could not see how her own biases in-
terfered with the biography Anne wanted to write. At the Lilly,
Anne discovered a letter Sylvia wrote over the 1960–61 Christmas
holiday during a visit to the Hughes home. Sylvia had adopted her
customary absolutist reaction to personal criticism: "Olwyn made
such a painful scene that I can never stay under the same roof with

her again. She has never hidden her resentment of me and her relation to Ted is really quite pathological." Although Anne had come
to discount many of Sylvia's extreme statements—especially her
attacks on Ted after their marriage broke up—on the subject of
Olwyn, Anne was "beginning to think Sylvia was right."

Olwyn was an indispensable resource for Stevenson, who gained
access to papers and interviewees unavailable to previous biographers. Davison, no fan of Sylvia's, believed that Stevenson had the
opportunity to dispel the myth of the martyred Sylvia, but he realized that Olwyn was getting in the way. When he asked her to let
Stevenson alone, an offended Olwyn shot back at Stevenson on 20
August 1987, denying that she was trying to "run the show." To
Davison, Olwyn expressed her anger at "Anne's ferocious (on occasions) resentment of my help." The biographer's insinuation that
Olwyn was trying to "sway the tenor of the book," and Davison's
belief that Anne could do the book on her own depressed Olwyn,
who did not see how Anne could get on without "constant hints,
help and overseeing." As usual, Olwyn objected to the portrayal of
Ted, claiming that material Stevenson wanted to include was "slan-
derous." Even worse, in a letter to Anne on 13 September, Olwyn
accused the biographer of identifying with her subject! Beware of
empathy, Olwyn admonished. She assured Anne she was nothing
like Sylvia, even if Anne—Olwyn averred—now and then threw a
Sylvia-like tantrum.

Davison stood by his author, telling Olwyn that he sympathized with "Anne's feeling that you sometimes give the sense of
looking over her shoulder. It is hard enough to decide what to
write on a page without imagining someone else is listening. . . ."
But Olwyn declared Stevenson was hardly better than the "appalling Wagner." Olwyn had, in short, "backed the wrong horse."
Davison jockeyed between Stevenson and Hughes, bolstering the
former and placating the latter. While Stevenson worried that the
book would ruin her reputation, Olwyn asserted she was saving
the biographer's good name and demanded 25 percent of the royalties for all her work, which had kept Anne up to the mark. Davison, with a book seven months overdue, finally lost patience and
flatly told Olwyn in a letter dated 13 January 1988 that he was near

the point of withdrawing the book from publication. Olwyn, he said, had taken it over, inserting passages in her own style that clashed with Anne's. Even worse, Olwyn demanded 40 percent of the royalties, a demand that Edward Lucie-Smith, one of Olwyn's friends, would not have been surprised to learn about. As much as he loved Olwyn, he had told Edward Butscher that she was a "cow" about business. Davison could not make it plainer to her: If Olwyn did not approve the manuscript the publisher would be sending her in three days, Stevenson's biography would be cancelled for "non-delivery."

In a letter dated 17 February and marked "not sent," a fed up Davison summed up Olwyn's attitude: "Something is wrong. Someone has blundered. You do not approve, you are not satisfied, and you will withdraw Ted's statement, or Ted's permission to quote his letters . . ." He had no reason to suppose any text he edited would "receive approval from *you*." Davison concluded that it simply was not possible for Olwyn to "let go." Olwyn wore "too many hats." Many years later Davison confided to Smith archivist Karen V. Kukil that in the normal course of things, his correspondence would have been shredded. In this case, however, he wanted a record of what had happened.

Why such a savvy editor permitted himself to become mired in such a mess deserves comment. Davison had been enticed by the access that not only Olwyn but also Ted (who had lunched with Davison and talked over the biography) promised. But access, it turned out, meant adherence to Olwyn's ever-expanding provisos. Ironically, she exhibited exactly the kind of monomaniacal behavior that she attributed to Sylvia. In his unsent letter, Davison said he had come to realize that Sylvia had poisoned Olwyn's life. But when both Olwyn and Anne both agreed to abide by Davison's adjudication of their work, he decided to proceed, noting that the book had "survived, barely, a series of major operations, during which the doctors seemed to have disagreed in their diagnoses and prescriptions." Warfare continued, with Anne charging, "Whatever Sylvia's faults, she cannot have been more self-blind or perverse in her treatment of people she tried to use than yourself," and Olwyn replying that Stevenson was thwarting her "in Sylvia fashion."

The result was very close to what Olwyn wanted. She had worn down both editor and biographer to the point where Olwyn begrudgingly called the book "ok." Making the best of it, Davison wrote both of them to say how pleased he was with the book that was now balanced between Anne's "softness" and Olwyn's "asperity." When the biography appeared, to mixed reviews, it contained Anne Stevenson's note stating that *Bitter Fame* was virtually a work of joint authorship—an admission Olwyn had resisted, but settled for in lieu of putting herself forward as the book's co-biographer.

On 22 April 1989, *The Independent* published a long letter from Hughes rebutting several charges made against him by Ronald Hayman, who linked Hughes's alleged neglect of Plath's grave with his appalling handling of her estate and her biographers. Hughes rightly noted he had never taken court action against a biographer, but he acknowledged that the estate had denied biographers permission to quote from Plath's work, in effect using copyright as a form of censorship. He seemed to think that just because the biographers had been able to publish, no harm had been done. As for her grave, he confessed his inability to maintain the site because of constant pilfering and defacement of her stone (three times the name Hughes had been gouged out so that only the name Sylvia Plath remained). To Hughes, such desecration confirmed his belief that his own right to commemorate Plath had been debased.

Although Paul Alexander attempted to enlist Ted Hughes's cooperation—at least in so far as an interview was concerned—the biographer decided to steer clear of the Plath estate after Hughes turned him down. Alexander had one memorable encounter with Olwyn, who reported it to Frances McCullough: "Alexander really seems to me pretty hopeless . . . Did I tell you his big inspiration? Who do you think, he asks, those letters she wanted stamps for on the last night went to? I point out they were probably just an excuse to find out if neighbour would let nurse in next morning. I think he announces, eyes agleam, they were to . . . Sassoon! I advised him maybe he should stick to writing fiction. . . ." Alexander wrote a "fair use" biography, published in 1991, relying on summary and brief quotations. He produced a very detailed book, making extensive use of Plath's archives and hundreds of interviews with those who knew her. On 19 August 1992, the Plath estate contacted Alexander's publisher, Penguin USA. Penguin's senior vice president and general counsel, Alan J. Kaufman, replied:

> I have had the work in question carefully and thoroughly legally vetted prior to publication. I am therefore taken by surprise by your letter alleging that there are numerous passages which grossly defame your client, Ted Hughes.
>
> As a responsible publisher we are interested to learn, with great specificity, exactly which passages in the work you allege to be defamatory to your client.

No legal action was taken. Ted wrote to Olwyn on 26 August, advising her not to get into a newspaper debate with Alexander, as no one remembers what is said in newspapers, which only want "hot copy." Olwyn should write her own book. Stevenson's was "catastrophic," he added with rhetorical flourish, "because everything that was said there was heard as if you got her to say it—and as if I got you to get her to say it." Only books get through to new readers, he argued. "Nothing else is accessible to them. Think of the advance too." Although it has been said that Olwyn is working on her memoirs, she has yet to publish any.

Ronald Hayman's *The Death and Life of Sylvia Plath* (1991) took a bolder line than Alexander had done. Hayman argued that Plath had crossed the line between life and art, and that her greatest work virtually demanded to be read alongside her biography. In other words, the conventional biographer's argument that the life helped to illuminate the work had been abrogated in favor of a fusion of the two, making the estate's withholding of material and its efforts to control the flow of information about Plath all the more reprehensible. How exactly were biographers to distinguish between the private and public Plath? Although Plath scholarship has moved away from conflating the poet and her work, Hayman's argument has been difficult to dismiss. Kathleen Connors and Sally Bayley note in *Eye Rhymes: Sylvia Plath's Art of the Visual* (2007) that the "boundaries between Plath literary critics, biographers, and devotees" who worship at the "altar of Plath," remain unclear.

In 1991, on 11 February, the anniversary of Sylvia Plath's suicide, Janet Malcolm met with Olwyn Hughes to discuss a projected book, which became *The Silent Woman* (1994). Like Judith Kroll, Malcolm describes Olwyn as "forbidding and imposing." Disdaining the plodding earnestness of biographers who pretend to be neutral or objective, Malcolm then dispatches Olwyn with gusto: "She is like the principal of a school or the warden of a prison: students or inmates come and go, while she remains." Indeed, in Malcolm's film noir, Olwyn becomes Mrs. Danvers welcoming Rebecca (the callow biographer) to Court Green, the Mandalay of Plath biography. One half expects Malcolm to include the Daphne DuMaurier line, "Last night I dreamed I went to Mandalay again."

But Malcolm is rewarded only with Olwyn's grudging agreement to take the importunate writer for a look at the exterior of the Fitzroy Road flat. Much of their conversation centers on how Olwyn had to "nanny" Anne Stevenson along to no avail, since Anne still got Sylvia "wrong." Malcolm notes that suicide always leaves the survivors in the wrong. Nothing can be done about it, because Plath remains "silent, powerful"—and in the right. Malcolm characterizes Olwyn's demand that Anne remove an account of Sylvia's attack on Olwyn as the only available method of replying to Plath—even though Sylvia's harsh words can themselves be interpreted as a bias the reader is perfectly capable of detecting. Olwyn, Malcolm implies, is unable to let the biographer and the reader do their work. In spite of Malcolm's criticism, Olwyn and her brother left Malcolm alone—perhaps because she had such obvious scorn for biographers who do not trouble to make the Hugheses into fully rounded human beings coping with an impossible situation, wishing both to protect their privacy and do justice to Plath's work. Ted Hughes realized that Malcolm was on the estate's side, and yet prior to publication he still tried to ferret out what she would write about Olwyn. Malcolm replied on 16 September 1992 that of course Olwyn figured in the narrative, but she was not the "central figure." The cagey biographer added, "I feel by telling you this I am saying more than I should (you may feel I am saying too little) . . ."

A brilliant stylist, Malcolm evokes the problematics of biography. How can biographers possibly know the truth? As Dido Merwin said, they were not *there*. Of course, by this logic, Malcolm, too, is suspect. But presumably she is more honorable because at least she concedes (indeed wallows in) the fallibility of biography. But memoirs written after the fact are no less fallible, which is why Malcolm focuses on Hughes's letters, showcasing him as a brilliant interpreter of Plath's work. Malcolm is right to emphasize that in his letters Ted expresses virtually no animus toward Plath. But it is hard to see why his later letters should be taken as the last word. In the end, Malcolm seems to have put herself in thrall to Ted Hughes, wishing, like Olwyn, to safeguard him from predators.

Ted Hughes, however, did not see matters this way. To him, Malcolm had adopted the guise of an objective truth-teller, painfully and regretfully revealing the "bad as well as the good because that's the truth." Her concoction of psychoanalytical commentary and "self-doubt" conveyed an impression of "helpless verisimilitude." Malcolm knew her audience and knew how it would eagerly devour a controversial book written with the patented Malcolm style. And Ted understood, as he warned Olwyn, that she was the "main target." By now, Ted was just part of the "trampled field."

In *Birthday Letters* (1998), poems addressed to Plath and written over a thirty-five year period, Ted Hughes finally provided his own apologia. The work is difficult to assess as biography, since it bears the same relation to reality as Plath's creative work. And yet a poem like "Fulbright Scholars" is hard to resist, because it is such an antidote to the sour memoirs of his friends. By mentioning Plath's "Veronica Lake" bang, he evokes not only Sylvia's glamour in postwar Cambridge, but also how she exuded so much more style than his contemporaries. She was so American and so romantic, a dream girl coming to him off the movie screen, his own Marilyn Monroe. *Birthday Letters* is not a record of what happened, but a crafted memory of what Sylvia Plath meant to Ted Hughes.

In hindsight, Hughes describes himself in "Visit" as auditioning for the lead role in Plath's drama. Hughes evokes the power of the "brand" her teeth marks left for nearly a month after she bit him. The blood rite of their first meeting is subsumed in "The Shot" in Plath the "god-seeker," an Isis looking for an Osiris to worship—although Hughes does not name his god. He remains first among the god-candidates after she jettisons the "ordinary jocks," but it is remarkable in these poems how he subjects his persona to her quest, replicating precisely the pattern of those biographies of her that he abhorred.

Birthday Letters also reveals how little Hughes knew of his wife's inner turmoil until, like her biographers, he could read her journals and accompany her on that last desperate pursuit of Richard Sassoon in Paris. And like Plath's biographers, Hughes can only re-create her suffering. He, too, was not *there*. He guesses and speculates, presuming that poetry, rather than biography, has license to re-create Plath's life. And he falls for the Plath myth just like so many others, in "18 Rugby Street" imagining her visiting the "shrines" of her sojourns with Sassoon. How, Hughes wonders, was Plath "conjuring" him?

Was it Plath's death that made Hughes write in such a supplicating way? In an astonishing scene of abasement, he refers not to his weapons but to her "artillery," as he imagines her climbing the stairs of his flat after her failed effort to secure Sassoon. Plath practically gives off sparks with the "pressure" of her "effervescence," suggesting an eruptive nature that fairly overwhelmed Hughes. Even if this is the hyperbole of hindsight, it reveals how all encompassing the Sylvia Plath myth had become for more than just her biographers. It is Plath, a goddess with "aboriginal" thick lips, who initiates Hughes into the mysteries. She flies about his London flat like a spirit he cannot contain, her face like the sea, subject to all sorts of weather and the play of sun and moon. A devotee of astrology—its vocabulary suffuses *Birthday Letters*—Hughes seems bound by the charts of her moods, merely "hanging around" until she can shape him. What is odd here is the absence of Sylvia's Ted Hughes—at least the one she thought of as a god. Why is the titan Plath described in her letters, poems, and journals absent from *Birthday Letters*?

Hughes occasionally provides striking vignettes of their

mythologized daily life, such as one involving Sylvia's distress when she does not find him at their meeting place and rides a taxi like a chariot, in search of him. He marvels in "Fate Playing" at her "molten" eyes and face when she greets him as though he had "come back from the dead," the answer to a priestess's prayer. Then he "knew what it was / To be a miracle." Here Hughes discloses why Sylvia Plath was so irresistible. He even turns her taxi driver into a "small god," treating her eruption of joy as an act of nature drenching the "cracked earth" in the "cloudburst" of her emotions. In "The Owl," the childlike abandon Plath took in nature awakened Hughes's own "ecstatic boyhood," bringing back to him an elemental rapture he had previously experienced only with his beloved older brother. In "A Pink Wool Knitted Dress," Hughes pictures his wedding as the marriage of the swineherd to the princess, the postwar threadbare "not quite . . . Frog-Prince" bound to Plath's transfigured and flaming personage. On their honeymoon, described in "Your Paris," he is like her dog, sniffing out the fear and corruption in the collaborationist city, while she basks in the aura of her expatriate predecessors: Miller, Fitzgerald, Hemingway, and Stein. While he is mired in history, she soars into the mythos of her own making.

During their Benidorm honeymoon in Spain, Hughes seems for the first time to emerge from Plath's spell, noting in "You Hated Spain" how the primitive cult of the bullfight frightened her. In contrast, he felt quite at home, perceiving clearly—perhaps for the first time—the part of her that was still a "bobby-sox American." Drawing calmed her and was also an assertion of her mastery that had a beneficial impact on Hughes, who felt "released"—an apparent allusion to the stress her fluctuating moods inflicted on him. When Plath fell ill (a case of food poisoning) he felt empowered, enjoying the role of mothering her as he had been mothered—although her fevered fear of death, her crying "wolf," aroused his distrust of her overwrought sensibility. How would he know when she was truly at the last extreme? That question haunts the persona Hughes creates for himself in *Birthday Letters,* as he tries to read Sylvia Plath, who has tied him to her quest for fame. Otherwise, he might have been, as he puts it in "Ouija," "fishing off a rock / In Western Australia."

In "The Blue Flannel Suit," Hughes describes Sylvia aboard a liner taking them off to America, once again invoking a life that seemed plotted for him. In "Child's Park," Plath is so potent that she has a "plutonium secret"—a phrase reminiscent of those 1950s articles that saluted Marilyn Monroe as the "atomic blonde." It seems from these poems that what really undid Hughes in America was his feeling that he was feeding off of Plath. His humiliation is palpable in "9 Willow Street," where he calls himself a "manikin in your eyeball." Unlike his wife, Hughes explains in "The Fifty-Ninth Bear," he had no need to make their "dud scenario into a fiction," aggrandizing their brief brush with the beast outside their tent in Yellowstone Park into a story of a husband hounded to his death by his importunate wife. There is in Hughes, as there was in Arthur Miller, a primordial dread of becoming entirely absorbed in his wife's imago. He treats their trip to the Grand Canyon as Plath's pilgrimage to the Delphic oracle, seeking a sign about the fate of her six-week old pregnancy. Is it any wonder that this couple came to grief, trying to live on the level of the gods? Before their embarkation for America, Sylvia had dreamed that country would make Hughes an even greater poet. But poems like "Grand Canyon" suggest the vastness of American geography only made him yearn for the narrow cobbled streets of home.

"Haunted" is hardly the word for what Hughes has to say in "Black Coat" about Plath's penetrating "paparazzo sniper" eye, as she lined him up against a seascape, pinioning him with her camera, and transforming him—in his imagination and hers—into her father, crawling out of the sea and sliding "into me." This poem amplifies the thrust of Plath's autobiographical essays, which transform Otto Plath into a powerful sea beast that in Hughes's retrospective poem sends a shiver through him, freezing him forever in her lens. Caught in Plath's double vision, Hughes realizes he has become a palimpsest of her memories and desires.

Hughes concedes in "Stubbing Wharfe" that Plath had a reach like the Atlantic, but that whereas he reveled in the idea of a home in the dark valleys of his boyhood, she saw there "blackness," the "face of nothingness." She triumphed because, as he announces in "Remission," she submitted to an "oceanic" pregnancy, becoming the very type of the fruitful woman of time immemorial, the Venus of Willendorf. When Hughes mentions Plath's Indian midwife, who appears to be a deity from the Ganges, the image of voluptuous female idols hanging off of Indian temples comes to mind. No wonder, then, that in "Isis" Hughes imagines childbirth as his wife's stripping of her "death-dress"—or was this only an interruption of her attraction to death as the father of herself? Hughes can be no more certain than her biographers, but he pictures her here as a vessel of life, an Isis carrying "what had never died, never known Death."

In "The Lodger," the move to Court Green becomes an announcement of Hughes's disintegrating life, which makes him feel "already posthumous." The change of venue is part of the "wrong road taken" theme that pervades this part of *Birthday Letters*. Images of him digging a garden are transformed into images of him digging his own grave. He treats his betrayal of himself very much like the story of the self and its double that so entranced Plath. Indeed, Hughes presents himself as being overtaken by another, an "alien joker." In "The Table," his double becomes her father, so that Hughes pictures himself not as Plath's salvation, but as her doom, an actor deprived of his script on an "empty stage." He had lost, in other words, his own conception of their marriage.

From here on Hughes seems to withdraw himself from Plath's imago, dreading in "Dream Life" her descent into the crypt of her imagination, and sensing the futility of his efforts to hypnotize her into courage and calm. She was, in his retrospective sense of destiny, preparing herself for the gas chamber. In "The Rabbit Catcher" he pictures himself once again trailing after Plath like a dog, trying to attune himself to her volatile moods. Prey to her hostility, he wonders if she is expressing her own "doomed self," or responding to something "Nocturnal and unknown to me"—the closest Hughes comes to reflecting on his own culpability. Yet he capitulates to the "new myth," as he calls it, which would take her back to her father—as surely as the beekeeping she performs in "The Bee God" as a bow to her "Daddy."

Assia Wevill makes her fated appearance in "Dreamers" as a Lamia-like demon that entrances Hughes, who recovers the dreamer in himself by falling in love with her. The poem seems too pat, part of a mythology, but not part a record of what actually happened. A hard-pressed Hughes writes as though he can only succumb to Assia, "filthy with erotic mystery," the antithesis of his well-scrubbed wife, who in "The Beach" sought the sea as a means of scouring away the dinginess of a grubby England still camouflaged in wartime grime.

The Hughes who said reconciliation with Plath remained a possibility emerges briefly in "The Inscription," which reflects his confusion over the signals she gave him—demanding that he remain with her, or insisting he "vanish off the earth." In "Night-Ride with Ariel," he attributes her unwillingness to recommit to him as having been influenced by the constellation of women in her life: her mother, Mrs. Prouty, Ruth Beuscher, and Mary Ellen Chase—all of whom he labels jammers of Plath's "wavelengths," confusing her with their advice. Hughes adds his own rueful insight in "A Picture of Otto": "I was a whole myth too late to replace you." After that, *Birthday Letters* trails off in an enigmatic ending, and Hughes never comes to terms with his role in the marriage's final phase. In *Howls and Whispers,* published the same year in a limited edition and overlooked except by a few scholars, Hughes addresses several more letters to Plath. This time he makes even less room for his own psychology and responsibility, producing unpolished work that is "excessively vituperative or self-pitying," to use the words of critic Lynda K. Buntzen, who notes the poet's "lack of control."

Responses to *Birthday Letters* were mixed, ranging from high praise for its poetry and candor, to dismissals of its rather flat prose-like lines and exculpatory thrust. Some thought Hughes placed the burden of failure on Plath's own Electra complex—although he does not explicitly indulge in Freudian explanations. In the main, Hughes seems to have done himself some good by finally delivering his own diagnosis of Plath's life and death. In *Ariel's Gift: Ted Hughes, Sylvia Plath and the Story of Birthday Letters* (2000), Erica Wagner seemed to start a new trend in Plath exegesis, arguing that Hughes "honors the work and the person of Sylvia Plath. There is no greater gift of love than that honor."

Diane Middlebrook's *Her Husband* (2003) presents a meticulous and compassionate exploration of what the two poets owed one another. Indeed, Middlebrook's book is the best answer to those who cudgel biographers with the assertion, "You weren't *there*." Benefiting from the perspective afforded by earlier biographies, and from a close reading of the Plath and Hughes texts, Middlebrook easily surpasses in insight the memoirists who claim the privileges of proximity. Eschewing much biographical speculation, Middlebrook seemed to earn even the grudging respect of Olwyn Hughes, who took issue with some of the biographer's facts but also praised her insights. But Middlebrook, reverent in her treatment of Ted Hughes's devotion to literature—especially to his reading of Robert Graves's *The White Goddess*—ultimately lets Hughes off the hook: "Hughes's marriage was the doing of the White Goddess, who had laid claim to Ted Hughes through the agency of Sylvia Plath: Hughes had no choice." This sense of predestination suffuses *Birthday Letters,* absolving Hughes by making him no more than a figure in an allegory. Plath herself was aware of Hughes's tendency to turn away from ratiocination in favor of horoscopes and predestination. In "Hill of Leopards," an alternative title for Plath's aborted novel, "Falcon Yard," Jess, modeled after Plath, challenges her lover, clearly a version of Hughes, over his reliance on horoscopes to suss out human character. "It's so deterministic," she observes.

Conspicuously absent from *Birthday Letters* is any reckoning of Plath's final days and hours. On 11 October 2010, the *New Statesman* published "Last Letter," Hughes's own coda, unearthed from his British Library archive. The poem, apparently never finished, is a departure in tone, which is perhaps why Hughes chose not to complete it for *Birthday Letters.* "Last Letter" is very much of the moment, focused on the contingency of events as he wonders about the timing of his last meeting with Plath—and why she called him, burned her letter to him, and acted as though he had somehow thwarted her design. She had apparently expected her letter not to be delivered on a Friday, but after the weekend was over. When Hughes arrived at her flat that Friday, two days before her death, she was upset. What did her note say? Did it announce her suicide, or was it just the cry for help that Hughes later mentioned to Aurelia? Judging by the murkiness of Hughes's verse, his visit to Plath produced no resolution. Like all her other exegetes, he can only speculate about what happened. He imagines her phoning his empty flat. At the time, he was, in fact, bedding another poet, Susan Alliston, in the same building where he first bedded Plath and later spent his wedding night. Alliston was apparently a relief from Sylvia and Assia the two "needles," as they are referred to in "Last Letter." He imagines Plath hearing the ringing in her receiver, a scene reminiscent of Marilyn Monroe attached to her phone, simultaneously reaching out to and saying good-bye to the world she had wooed and lost. Just a few hours later, a telephone call informs him of his wife's death.

Ted Hughes, who died on 28 October 1998, remained evasive to the end, providing no corrective to the myth he had done so much to foster, even as he decried its development—and never for a moment analyzed his role as renegade priest. Elaine Feinstein's biography of Hughes, published in 2003, was not much help to Olwyn. On 25 May, Olwyn wrote to filmmaker Pawel Pawlikowski, charging that *Ted Hughes: The Life of a Poet* was "wildly inaccurate" and "gossipy."

Ted's daughter, Sylvia Plath's sole surviving child (Nicholas committed suicide on 16 March 2009, after struggling with periodic depression), has adopted her father's attitude, accusing the BBC producers of the film *Sylvia* (2003) of voyeuristic motivations, creating a "Sylvia suicide doll" for the "peanut eaters." In 2004, in a preface to the restored edition of *Ariel,* which rectified the changes Ted Hughes made in the first published version of Plath's masterpiece, Frieda relayed her father's explanation that he had omitted some poems because they would hurt living persons, and others because they were weaker than those he added to Plath's original arrangement. Frieda also attacked Aurelia, claiming that as "small child" (she was little more than two years old) she observed her grandmother encouraging Sylvia to order Ted out of Court Green. The Hughes Papers at Emory University include other examples of Frieda's animosity toward Aurelia. And exhibiting considerable animosity toward the "strangers" who have possessed and reshaped her mother, Frieda describes a caring father who helped her keep the memory of her mother alive. That bond with him makes her disdainful of others who have enshrined her mother in their own pantheon. She is aghast that her "more temperate [compared to her mother] and optimistic" father has been vilified. Hughes never liked seeing Assia's name in print next to his, and Frieda's fealty to him results in turning Assia into "the other woman" in the preface.

When English Heritage proposed putting a blue commemorative plaque on the Fitzroy Road building, Frieda insisted that it be placed on the wall of 3 Chalcot Square, where her parents had lived for nearly two years and where they wrote some of their best work. The ensuing attacks from those who believed the plaque should be at the Fitzroy Road residence exacerbated Frieda's anger about the way her mother has been "dissected, analyzed, reinterpreted, reinvented, fictionalized, and in some cases completely fabricated." Still, like her father, Frieda has come forward with an *Ariel*—only this time it is exactly what those analyzers and reinventors have desired for nearly five decades: a Sylvia Plath composed by the poet herself, silent no more.

APPENDIX A

Sylvia Plath and Carl Jung

The Smith archive includes several pages of notes Plath took while reading Carl Jung's *The Development of Personality*. Unfortunately, no dates are affixed to the passages that Plath copied out, and she does not annotate her responses to them. Plath scholar Judith Kroll suggests this material dates from late 1962, because it deals with "many topics relevant to her concerns near the end of her life." Uninterested in dealing with Plath in biographical terms—or at least unwilling to do so—Kroll, like Diane Middlebrook and Jacqueline Rose, is more concerned with exploring how both Plath and Hughes made use of Jung in their work. As Margaret Dickie Uroff notes, Plath wrote her mother about reading Jung for her senior thesis on Dostoevsky, and Plath herself notes in a 4 October 1959 journal entry that reading Jung confirms her use of certain images in her "Mummy" story—especially that of the child dreaming of a "loving, beautiful mother as a witch or animal," and another image of the "eating mother . . . all mouth." Although critics like Kroll and Rose shy away from the biographical approach, Plath herself had no problem with it, concluding that she was the "victim" of what she wrote and not an "analyst. My 'fiction' is only a naked recreation of what I felt, as a child and later, must be true."

Less fastidious than her academic commentators, Plath realized that her "fiction" could be read both ways: as stories and as accounts of her own life. The problems for the biographer, however, are chronology and causation. It would be illuminating to know if

Kroll is right about the passages coming so late in Plath's development as an individual and as a writer. Then Jung is a kind of "proof" for Plath, and also, perhaps, a catalyst for her final burst of creativity. If the passages come earlier, a case could be made for them as influences, writing that shaped her psyche and her style. Critic Tim Kendall argues that Jung served as Plath's vindication while she also becomes "her own case history." It is the same dual role—both victim and analyst of her victimhood—she plays in "Daddy," Kendall concludes.

This discussion of Plath and Jung appears in an appendix precisely because her handwritten quotations from Jung cannot be dated and thus cannot be confidently inserted into a narrative of her life. Even so, what Plath copied explains certain mysteries that appear in her journals and letters. To begin with, what exactly did Aurelia do to Sylvia that made her both grateful and hostile? Both the Smith and Emory archives contain letters from a mystified Aurelia, who emphasized how tactful and tolerant she tried to be with Sylvia.

Carl Jung ratified much of what Sylvia (and her fictional alterego, Esther) felt, observing that parents "set themselves the fanatical task of 'doing the best for the children' and 'living only for them.'" As a result, parents never develop themselves, so focused are they on thrusting their "best" down their children's' throats. "This so-called 'best' turns out to be the very things the parents have most badly neglected in themselves. Thus children are goaded on to achieve their parents' most dismal failures and are loaded with ambitions that are never fulfilled." Precisely so. Aurelia writes in the introduction to *Letters Home* that after the first year of her marriage, she realized she would have no peace with Otto unless she did exactly as he said. Her own proud independence, her literary interests, would have to be subordinated to his work. In a letter to Ted Hughes that is in the Emory archive, an agonized Aurelia tells Ted (years after Sylvia's death) how she longed to share her joy in literature, instead of constantly playing the nurturing mother—not only to Sylvia, but also to Ted when the couple visited—and she did everything in her power to make them comfortable, never demanding any time for herself. One of Aurelia's notes in the Smith archive welcomes Ted and Sylvia home with the announcement that the refrigerator is not only full, it is stocked with ready-made meals. She did not want a dependent life for Sylvia, and yet Sylvia found it hard not to replicate her mother's marriage to a powerful man. She "inherited" the desire to abase herself—which haunted her even as she arose from her bed with Ted to become her own person and poet.

Aurelia's insistence that she did not project herself onto Sylvia is countered by Jung: "The infectious nature of the parents' complexes can be seen from the effect their mannerisms have on their children. Even when they make completely successful efforts to control themselves, so that no adult could detect the least trace of a complex, the children will get wind of it somehow." Jung told the story of a mother with three loving daughters who were disturbed about their dreams, which all had to do with her turning into a ravening animal. Years later, the women went insane, dropping onto all fours and imitating the sounds of wolves and pigs. All this and more Plath noted in four pages of verbatim passages.

Plath copied out other passages in Jung that attacked the "sanctity of motherhood," noting that mothers had produced their share of lunatics, idiots, and criminals. As much as Plath embraced motherhood, she also found she had a profound need not to sentimentalize it. She pointed out in letters to Paul and Clarissa Roche that taking care of children was an exhausting enterprise. No wonder she became enraged when her husband told her family life was becoming too much for him. Her death, in a way, finally forced fatherhood on him, making it his inescapable fate.

A final page of passages on marriage may indicate why Kroll believed Plath was reading Jung in the latter part of 1962. Jung describes marriage as a return to childhood and to the mother's womb in an effort to recapture the community of feeling that adults so rarely achieve. As parents, husband and wife become part of the "life urge." But this initial harmony inevitably turns to anguish and pain for anyone who puts a premium on individuality and independence. Sometimes the Jung quoted in Plath's copied-out passages sounds very like her own verse, as here, where he describes the trajectory of marriage: "First it was passion, then it became a duty & finally an intolerable burden, a vampire that battens on the life of its creator." In Ted Hughes, in other words, Sylvia had created a monster.

APPENDIX B

Sylvia Plath's Library

Plath underlined, starred, and annotated the following passages in books now part of her collection at Smith College. These selections reflect her wide reading in literature, philosophy, and theology that led her to believe in the primacy of the poet. In literature, especially in the work of D. H. Lawrence, she could read the prophecy of her own life and the means by which she would accomplish her own death.

[W]hile all of us, at bottom, pursue only our private interest, we wear these fair disguises in order to put others off their guard, and expose them the more to our wiles and machinations. [In the right-hand margin, Plath wrote, "good."]
  —David Hume, *An Inquiry Concerning Human Understanding*

[T]he hateful white light of understanding which floats like scum on the eyes of all white, oh, so white, English and American women, with their understanding voices and their deep, sad words, and their profound good spirits. Pfui! [Plath wrote, "ouch!"]
  —D. H. Lawrence, *Studies in Classic American Literature*

The artist must be inhuman, extra-human, he must stand in a queer aloof relationship to our humanity . . . Literature is not a calling, it is a curse, believe me! . . . It begins by your feeling yourself set apart, in a curious sort of opposition to the nice, regular people . . . the poet as the most highly developed of human beings, the poet as saint.

—Thomas Mann, *Tonio Kröger*

Everything seemed to have gone smash for the young man. He could not paint. . . . Everything seemed so different, so unreal. There seemed no reason why people should go along the street, and houses pile up in the daylight. There seemed no reason why these things should occupy the space, instead of leaving it empty. His friends talked to him: he heard the sounds, and he answered. But why there should be the noise of speech he could not understand. [Next to this passage, Plath wrote, "cf. July 1953"]

—D. H. Lawrence, *Sons and Lovers*

O strange happiness, that seeketh the alliance of Death to win its crown. . . . It must needs be a forcible evil, that has power to make a man (nay, a wise man) to be his own executioner. . . . A wise man is indeed to endure death with patience, but that must come *ab externo* from another man's hand and not from his own. [In the left-hand margin, Plath wrote, "Why?"] But these men teaching that he may do it himself, just needs confess that the evils are intolerable which force a man to such an extreme impropriety. [Plath wrote, "yes."]

—St. Augustine, *The City of God*

[T]hose who pursue philosophy right study to die; and to them of all men death is least formidable.

—Plato

Marriage was a ghastly disillusion to him [Herman Melville], because he looked for perfect marriage. [Plath wrote in the margin, "All our grievances come from not being able to be alone." And on the next page she put an exclamation mark next to the following passage.] Melville came home to face out the long rest of his life. He married and had an ecstasy of a courtship and fifty years of disillusion.

—D. H. Lawrence, *Studies in Classic American Literature*

It was her deep distrust of her husband—this was what darkened the world.

—Henry James, *Portrait of a Lady*

APPENDIX C

David Wevill

On 10 July 2010, I wrote the following to David Wevill:

> I wonder if I could try your patience and ask if you would reply to a few questions via email. I know it was a long time ago, but I would very much like a sentence or two about how Sylvia Plath appeared to you. What was it like to be in her physical presence? Even a vague impression would be helpful. A related question: Do you remember noticing any change in her from the first time you met her to the last? For example: Did she look thinner? I'd be very grateful for even a sentence or two, which I would not use without getting your explicit permission.

On 19 July 2010, David Wevill replied:

> I did not notice a change in Sylvia's appearance while I knew her: she was slender (lean), looked fit, bore herself well. Personally she was witty, affable, had a quick smile, her conversation was bright and covered a wide range, she seemed interested in people and their lives, she could gossip but not cruelly. She and Ted seemed to complement each other, not contradict. I sensed no tensions there. Later I came to think some effort went into this—not so much an act, as a willed self-control? We four got on well, it seemed the start of a

friendship, with much in common. As for the Assia biography, I came to know Eilat and Yehuda and liked them. They
had done their homework and talked with many people. The
story they had to tell was hard, tragic, and I think there were
problems of tone and judgement as to what to include and
leave out, and parts I found too sensational. Inaccuracies,
some. I never threatened to kill anyone; I did not walk the
streets at night with a knife; or plead with Assia to stay (rather,
the other way around). . . . As for Sylvia, I wish I could help
you. For nearly half a century I've tried to keep from getting
involved in what became almost an investigative industry.

On 22 December 2011, I wrote to David Wevill again, saying I
wished to reprint his 10 July 2010 reply to me, and that I wanted to
do so without any comment of mine attached to his statement. He
agreed that I could do so.

APPENDIX D

Elizabeth Compton Sigmund

On 14 January 2012, I journeyed to Cornwall to see Elizabeth Sigmund for a two-day talk about Sylvia Plath. Elizabeth was married to the writer David Compton when she became a good friend of Sylvia's during the Court Green period. Elizabeth also had a good opportunity to observe Ted and the Hughes-Plath marriage. She has become one of the major players in a conflict that unfortunately is likely to go on as long as the Punic Wars, arraying Olwyn, Ted— and even Ted's second wife, Carol, and Sylvia's daughter, Frieda— against Elizabeth, Al Alvarez, and Clarissa Roche, joined later by biographers Linda Wagner-Martin and Ronald Hayman. The latter side, appalled at Olwyn's handling of the Plath estate, and critical of Assia's role in seducing Ted away from his Devon home and family, identifies with Sylvia's grievances and deplores the vitriol in Anne Stevenson's biography. Elizabeth showed me a letter from Olwyn to Clarissa Roche, written on 24 March 1986, which sums up the war in two brief sentences: "You liked her. I think she was pretty straight poison." I went to Elizabeth seeking some understanding of why Ted left Sylvia. Virtually nothing in reports of his behavior while living with Plath—and certainly nothing in letters of his that have so far surfaced—signals anything like the depth of unhappiness that he expressed to his sister Olwyn shortly after he left Sylvia.

Later, Olwyn sought to extenuate her brother's actions by pointing out that Sylvia had ordered Ted out of the house. In other words, it was not his doing, not his choice. But a letter he wrote to Olwyn, sent shortly after his leaving Court Green, shows he wanted out of the marriage. It was rather typical of him to let Sylvia actually declare the start of hostilities—just as it was nearly always the case that he let women, including Sylvia, seem the aggressor. Ted, like the female spirit who appears to him in his radio play, "Difficulties of a Bridegroom," and in the persona he fashions for himself in *Birthday Letters,* was a curiously passive victim of an irresistible destiny. Ted was a sexual predator, Al Alvarez told me, but the prey had to become visible and come to him—"to show," I added in conversation with Alvarez.

Elizabeth Compton Sigmund's testimony is crucial, in part because initially she was quite fond of Ted Hughes. She did not regard him as a dour, if romantic, Heathcliff. She only got involved in the acrimony concerning how the marriage ended when Olwyn became upset that Elizabeth was not following the party line with regard to Ted's behavior—a party line Olwyn had established. Then Olwyn began writing that in fact Elizabeth had only seen Sylvia and Ted on perhaps a dozen occasions and was nothing like a good friend of the couple (this despite Sylvia's dedicating *The Bell Jar* to Elizabeth and David Compton).

In Elizabeth's papers, two letters from Aurelia tell what Olwyn does not want told. On 11 April 1963, Aurelia wrote to Elizabeth, "I know what good friends you and your husband had been to my girl when she was so shocked by the change that came into her marriage." After learning that Ted had installed Elizabeth to take care of Court Green in his absence, Aurelia wrote again on 5 May: "I want to say that there is no one in all England I would rather have in Court Green, doing what you are doing, than you. From the first moment I saw you, I rejoiced that Sylvia had such a fine and lovely a friend. Indeed I wish to see you when I come in June . . . I am glad to think of you at Court Green." And more than a decade later, after the Plath wars had heated up, Aurelia wrote to Elizabeth on 18 May 1976, "When I met you . . . I thought you were one of the most beautiful, radiant women I ever saw. My heart went out to you in affection from the very start."

In May 1963, Ted sent a letter to Elizabeth instructing her to be wary about what she told Aurelia, because Sylvia's mother had been "casting a spy-ring" around him as part of a plot to wrest the children away from him. Wary about what? I wanted to know. Elizabeth could not think of what Ted had in mind. In June, he asked her to hide albums and other memorabilia that Aurelia was sure to snatch up. Uncomfortable about these instructions, Elizabeth did go through the contents of a desk, but she saw nothing she wanted to hide away. In July, Ted made clear that he held Aurelia partially responsible for the breakup of his marriage, writing to David Compton, "My effort to get away from her was a large part of my leaving Court Green last summer & starting the fire I wasn't able to put out." When Elizabeth made it clear she could not follow orders, Olwyn exacted her punishment, making sure that Sylvia's children never saw Elizabeth again.

In the course of two days, I recorded Elizabeth's reminiscences and looked through her extraordinary files, which include articles about Ted, Sylvia, and Olwyn, as well as letters sent to Elizabeth from Aurelia, Olwyn, and others, and correspondence involving Olwyn, Clarissa Roche, and Linda Wagner-Martin, and a few of Sylvia's own letters. What I include below are the exact words of Elizabeth's testimony, edited only to clarify chronology and eliminate repetition. I am grateful to her for verifying the accuracy of this account.

Elizabeth first became aware of the couple when they were on the BBC program "Two of a Kind," describing their rather cramped lodgings that gave them little room to write. So she wrote to them describing her lovely house in North Devon that included an orchard: "My husband is a writer too, and we'd love you to come stay and have a holiday. I can look after the children because I'm well used to that, and you three can go off and write." She went on to tell me: "And my husband who was very cynical said, 'You silly woman. You won't have an answer from them.' And of course for a year I didn't. Then I got a letter from Ted saying, 'We too are living in a thatched home and farmhouse a few miles from you. Come and have a meal with us.'" To Elizabeth, it seemed a rock solid marriage that would never, ever be broken.

> They seemed to be so much a unit. And it grew because when they came up to visit us, and they went to look at a stream near us, you could see there was such closeness. But Sylvia was talking to me and Ted was talking with David about rights and money as all writers do. David was writing science fiction and whodunits and stuff like that. Sylvia said to me, "What other things do you do?" And I said, "Well I do some canvassing for the Liberal Democrats," and she jumped up and rushed to Ted and shook him and said, "I've found a committed woman!" Our local MP, Mark Bonham Carter, got to know Sylvia and was very fond of her. We talked quite a bit about the military industrial complex. She was extremely politically aware.

To my questions, "Did Ted talk politics? Was he interested at all?" Elizabeth replied:

> Now I'm glad you asked that question because nobody ever asked me this. I was going up to a meeting in the House of Commons about chemical weapons [Elizabeth was active in the movement to abolish them], and Ted happened to be at the station too. He said, "Oh, can I come along?" He'd never been to the House of Commons. We walked around, and he looked at the great marble busts, and he said, "I want to knock them down, crush their heads." Ted had this feeling against people in power and the class system. But then of course when it came to being Poet Laureate, he had to go cringe before the Queen, and he wrote in a letter to me that because he was having an affair with a thrice married woman [Assia] his parents were saying he would never be made a knight. He was laughing at them for that.
> It was a sad mixture of feelings I had about Ted. Because when I went to London [in early March 1963] after Sylvia's

death, the nanny [taking care of Sylvia's children] told me Assia had moved in [to the Fitzroy Road flat]. I said, "Where is she?" The nanny said, "She's having one of those operations." I said, "Do you mean an abortion?" She said, "Yes." When they came back into the flat, Assia went straight up past the kitchen to the stairs to Sylvia's bedroom, and Ted came into the kitchen and stood back against the wall, and he did look like a whipped dog. He really did look dreadful. And he said to me, "It doesn't fall to many men to murder a genius." And I said, "Well, you didn't murder her." And he said, "I might just as well have done." So my first impression was here was a man absolutely destroyed by what had happened. He said, "I hear the wolves howling." [They were near the Regent's Park Zoo.] It seems appropriate. I got this impression that he was guilt ridden.

Later Ted's Aunt Hilda, who was taking care of the children, told Elizabeth that Assia had arrived at the Fitzroy Road flat after Sylvia's death and, according to Elizabeth, announced:

"I'm moving in." "No, you're not," Hilda replied. "I'm sorry, but I am, and I shall win," and she did. Aunt Hilda then went to Court Green. Talk about Northern Yorkshire women [I had told Elizabeth about Al Alvarez's comment that Olwyn and Ted were Northern peasants who cared too much about money], when I saw her, she said, "Has your husband earned any more money this time?" I got to know all of them. Ted's parents. [This was the period when Ted asked Elizabeth and David to live in Court Green and look after it, the period when Assia visited and sensed Elizabeth's loyalty to Sylvia.] This was the very first time I met Olwyn. She was very pleasant to me in her own sort of fierce way.

Before I knew about you I tried last year to contact Wagner-Martin [who had corresponded with Elizabeth and interviewed her over the phone] because I felt very strongly that someone must write a book that tells the story of Olwyn because nobody's really done it—only hints and bits. Ted's position was very odd because he knew I was faithful to Sylvia's memory. He liked me. [Some years later] on the train to Exeter . . . [not far from Court Green, Elizabeth, returning to her seat, encountered Ted and his second wife, Carol Hughes.] She rose up, looked up at me and said, "Don't worry, we'll move." I said, "You don't have to move." She said, "Come on, Ted." And he got up with the bags and he just trailed after her.

But Elizabeth remembered happier days when Ted would sing and entertain friends. "You've made Ted human," Daniel Craig told Elizabeth when he came to talk to her during his preparation to play Hughes in the film *Sylvia*. Elizabeth added: "There were those bits when [Ted] came to our house and drank coffee and sang, when he was quite a normal, ordinary person. I remember one Christmas Eve he came and took his children and three of my children on to Dartmoor. We stopped at the top of the moor. A streak of sunlight was coming through the clouds, and he said, 'Look, children, that's the eye of God.'"

SOURCES

Abbreviations:

AP:	Aurelia Plath
BL:	Ted and Olwyn Hughes Papers, British Library
CP:	Sylvia Plath, *The Collected Poems*
EB:	Edward Butscher, *Sylvia Plath: Method and Madness*
EBP:	Edward Butscher Papers, Smith College Library, Special Collections
ECS:	Elizabeth Compton Sigmund Papers
Emory:	Ted Hughes Papers, Emory University
JP:	*Johnny Panic and the Bible of Dreams*
LH:	*Letters Home*
Lilly:	Sylvia Plath Papers, Lilly Library, Indiana University
LWM:	Linda Wagner-Martin, *Sylvia Plath: A Literary Life*
Maryland:	Frances McCullough Papers, Special Collections, University of Maryland, College Park
OH:	Olwyn Hughes
PA:	Paul Alexander, *Rough Magic: A Biography of Sylvia Plath*
Smith:	Sylvia Plath Papers, Smith College Library, Special Collections
SP:	Sylvia Plath
SPCH:	Linda W. Wagner, *Sylvia Plath: The Critical Heritage*

SPWW:	Edward Butscher, *Sylvia Plath: The Woman and the Work*
TH:	Ted Hughes
THL:	*Letters of Ted Hughes*

Wherever possible, I have built this biography on primary sources I have read in the archives at Smith College, Indiana University, Emory University, the University of Maryland, and the British Library. I am grateful to Peter K. Steinberg, author of a perceptive introduction to Sylvia Plath, for providing additional primary sources. *Letters Home,* Karen V. Kukil's scrupulous edition of Sylvia Plath's journals, and Christopher Reid's *Letters of Ted Hughes* form part of the bedrock of my narrative.

Although I diverge at various points from previous Plath biographies, I don't see how my book could have been written without them. As Plath's first biographer, Edward Butscher interviewed for the first time many of the key figures in his subject's life. To be sure, Butscher made errors, and his "bitch goddess" thesis has been deplored, but he nevertheless deserves an honored place in Plath biography as a pathfinder, and my debt to him shows in the notes below. Paul Alexander accomplished a good deal in discovering much new material about Plath's family and her childhood. His command of the details of Plath biography is such that I consulted his book continually as I composed my own. Linda Wagner-Martin's literary biography was the first effort to integrate a full discussion of her subject's literary sensibility and her life from a feminist perspective. I have often consulted Ronald Hayman's elegant and succinct biography when deciding how to handle some of the thornier issues in Plath's life.

Anne Stevenson is the only biographer to have had the sanction of the Plath estate and, as such, her work has certain built-in advantages in terms of access to material and the ability to quote. But it also has the disadvantages of the authorized biographer beholden to the literary executor. Paul Alexander wisely decided not to deal with the estate, so as to remain independent. I had several conversations with him while he was researching Plath's life and concluded then that should I ever attempt a Plath biography, I would not seek cooperation from the estate. The result, as in Alexander's case, is that I have quoted very sparingly in order to produce a fair use biography.

In my acknowledgments, I thank everyone I interviewed for this biography. My bibliography lists those books I found helpful in constructing my narrative. Below I have listed only those sources for individual chapters that are not identified in the text.

Acknowledgments: For my extended critique of Janet Malcolm's *The Silent Woman,* see *Biography: A User's Guide.*

Introduction: The word "Isis" appears on the typescript of "Edge," SP's last completed poem.

I first adumbrated the idea of SP as the Marilyn Monroe of modern literature in "Visions of Sylvia Plath," the *New York Sun,* 17/2/04. Jacqueline Rose has something quite different in mind when she calls Plath the "Marilyn Monroe of the literati." That may be true, but implicity in Rose's words is the idea of a myth superimposed upon Plath. My point is that Plath herself made the connection to Monroe, who appeared to the poet in a dream-like vision of the creative, aspiring self, seeking a new look, and an ever-greater vision of self-fulfillment. I am indebted to Peter K. Steinberg, who discovered the rejected line in "A Winter's Tale" in the *New Yorker* papers in the New York Public Library.

Plath's parody of *Dragnet:* SP to Gordon Lameyer, 27/6/54, Maryland.

In *No Man's Land,* Sandra Gilbert and Susan Gubar mention the *Varsity* photo layout as an example of "female impersonation" akin to promotional strategies used by Edith Sitwell, Marianne Moore, Edna St. Vincent Millay, and Elinor Wylie. But the term impersonation does an injustice, it seems to me, to SP's motivations. She was not merely impersonating what others wanted. She was far more implicated in her culture than such a term implies. Gilbert and Gubar reveal their misapprehension of Plath when they move away from the episode at Cambridge and begin a new paragraph with the words, "More seriously, in the same year Plath produced a poem . . ." SP calling herself Betty Grable may have been a joke, but it was also a part of her deeply ingrained need to display herself—and not just part of what Gilbert and Gubar call her "dutifully sexualized self."

Stella Dallas as portrayed on the radio is a strong-willed and resourceful mother—much more positively portrayed than the lower class character of Prouty's novel.

Chapter 1: For the details of SP's childhood and early schooling I draw on her stories and essays published in JP and on EBP, as well as on Elizabeth Hinchliffe's unpublished manuscript, "The Descent of Ariel: The Death of Sylvia Plath," available at BL and Maryland. Wilbury Crockett's impressions of Sylvia are taken from his 26/7/74 letter to AP in the Frances McCullough Papers at Maryland. In essays, poems, and fiction, SP drew on details of her life to create a persona, a mythology of the self, and the critic has a right to question how much of her retrospective writing is true. For example, she draws on her mother's family experience during World War I, when German Americans were also under suspicion, to heighten her portrait of Otto the German. But what is true? Certain facts can, of course, be established. But in a figure as protean as SP, fact and fabulation are not easily disentangled.

SP's early writings, including her letters from camp, are at Lilly. Her school reports are at Smith.

Susan R. Van Dyne cites AP's 1/12/78 letter to Judith Kroll.

Sylvia often saw the world in terms of the movies. Her Philipps Junior High School report (14/5/46) on Longfellow's poem *Evangeline* observes that the work would make an "effective movie scene, especially in technicolor," with a mob of men "blazing with anger" protesting the decree that they must forfeit their lands to the crown. In their mad rush to the doorway, they shout, "Down with tyrants."

Chapter 2: SP's letters to Hans, to Marcia Brown, to Ann Davidow, Enid Epstein, Phil McCurdy, and Sally Rogers are at Smith.

Jane Anderson's deposition, and the deposition of her therapist, are in *Jane Anderson v. AVCO Embassy Pictures*, which is in the Smith archive, as are SP's letters to Anderson.

Letters to SP from Eddie Cohen, Dick Norton, Elizabeth Drew, Gordon Lameyer, and Richard Sassoon are at Lilly.

In SPWW, Gordon Lameyer says of his first impression, "I felt she came on too strong with her enthusiasms, as if a little too sophomoric and immature." SP, however, seems to have detected no such resistance to her ebullience.

For the meaning of skalshalala meat I am indebted to Susan Plath Winston, Warren Plath's daughter. She adds in an email to Karen V. Kukil, "We used that term in our household, too, growing up, but I believe it originated with my dad and Sylvia."

SP's letter to Olive Higgins Prouty: LH.

The originals of SP's letters to her mother are at Lilly and make fascinating reading, especially when set beside the edited versions in LH.

I am indebted to Nanci A. Young, College Archivist at Smith, for information about the college's posture exams and photographs.

"Initiation": JP.

AP's letter to Dick Norton is at Lilly.

Chapter 3: Robert Gorham Davis's letter to AP is at Lilly, and SP's letters to Gordon Lameyer are at Maryland. For Davis's and George Gibian's impressions of Plath, see George Gibian's letter in EBP.

SP's letters to Warren and Olive Higgins Prouty's letters to AP are in LH and at Lilly.

See SPWW, for Laurie Levy's recollections of SP's *Mademoiselle* month.

SP's listing of her extracurricular activities at Smith is reprinted in a 1/5/53 letter sent to her from *Mademoiselle*, now at Lilly, as are other correspondence and materials relating to Plath's guest editorship.

"In the Mountains," "Tongues of Stone," and "The Wishing Box": JP.

"much of a commitment": *Jane Anderson,* Smith.

"Anyone who did not know": 2/9/82, Emory.

Wilbury Crockett's impressions of Sylvia: WC to AP, 26/7/74, Maryland.

I'm grateful to Karen V. Kukil for making available to me a photocopy of SP's senior thesis, "The Magic Mirror: A Study of the Double in Two of Dostoevsky's Novels."

SP's description of Alfred Kazin jibes exactly with the man I knew. His letter of recommendation is at Smith.

I am indebted to Helen Lane for her memoir, Constance Blackwell, Kathleen Knight, Judy Denison, Marilyn Martin, Ellen Ouelette, Barbara Russell Kornfield, Anne Mohegan Smith, CB Follett, Barbara Schulz Larson, Darryl Hafter, and Ravelle Silberman Brickman for speaking to me about SP's years at Smith and for answering my email inquiries.

SP's mention of her "very attractive, but nervous mother" is in an undated letter (c. December 1954) at Smith.

Constance Blackwell says that Sassoon's friends called him "Dick," but since SP refers to him in her journal as Richard, I have adopted her practice.

Chapter 4: SP's letters to Elinor Friedman Klein and Marcia Brown are at Smith. SP's letters to Mallory Wober are at Kings College, Cambridge, and Wober's letter to Edward Butscher is in EBP. An excerpt from Elinor Friedman Klein's memoir of Plath appears in SPCH. Wendy Campbell's memoir is included in Newman.

See SPWW for Jane Baltzell Kopp's memoir and Dorothea Krook's reminiscences, including Krook's description of SP's girlish clothing. For more on Kopp, see SP to AP, 5/3/56 in LH.

Edward Butscher could find no one in the amateur theater group who had a distinct impression of Plath, but then she belonged to the club for only one term and appeared in just a few minor roles.

SP to AP: 24/3/56, LH.

Selling matches on the Place Pigalle: SP to Elinor Friedman Klein, 10/2/56.

TH's description of the "large fine room": THL.

OH had a characteristically benign gloss on the first encounter between Sylvia and Ted. On 11 March 1987, she wrote to scholar Marjorie Perloff to say that Ted's own recollection of the meeting was that he "accidentally dislodged an earring and the headband in the embrace—when Sylvia was rather drunk. One has to read this description in the context of her then Baudelairean, Grande Amoureuse image of herself—heavily under the influence of Sassoon": ECS.

"biggest seducer in Cambridge": TH's friends have complained about this comment, made by Hamish Stewart, who, Daniel Huws claims, hardly knew TH. Lucas Myers and others insist TH had very few girlfriends. Huws can only remember two and is certain Sylvia was far more experienced than TH. Huws may well be right, but as he acknowledges, that is not what Sylvia wanted. Perceiving TH as a seducer was in keeping with the kind of danger and risk taking she seemed determined to pursue.

For Marilyn Monroe's quest for a "white knight," see my biography of Marilyn Monroe.

See PA for a discussion of Olive Higgins Prouty's letter to SP about TH.

TH's 7 July letter to his brother, Gerald, is at Emory and is not included in THL.

SP's response to the bullfight: PA, EB, AS.

Sassoon's letter to SP: Lilly.

"The Widow Mangada": JP.

OH's letters to Diane Middlebrook: Emory.

Fragments of "Falcon Yard": Emory.

Chapter 5: "She was very amusing": 8/7/57 BL.

"tall, thin": TH to OH, 8/7/57 BL.

The Roches' response to SP's journals is included in the TH archive at Emory.

Grace Schulman's remarks stem from my brief conversation with her in the corridors of the Baruch College English department, where she gave me a copy of her book, *First Loves and Other Adventures,* which includes her essay on SP and TH at Yaddo.

"laughter and even tears": BL.

Daniel Aaron's impressions of SP's teaching are quoted in Davison, *The Fading Smile*.

slapping Sylvia out of her rages: Frances McCullough to David McCullough, 7/7/74, Maryland.

"Hardcastle Crags": The place is identified in TH's notes to CP.

a "tense and withdrawn SP": Davison, *The Fading Smile*.

"clumsy irony": Davison, *Half Remembered*.

"very deferential": Davison, *The Fading Smile*.

"willowy, long-waisted": Quoted in Davison, *The Fading Smile*.

"The Fifty-Ninth Bear": JP.

Chapter 6: SP's calendar and letters to Marcia Brown and Lynne Lawner are at Smith.

"craggy Yorkshire handsomeness": quoted in Leeming.

OH's hectoring letters: Several example of OH's riding herd on Stevenson are in Stevenson's papers at Smith and in Frances McCullough's papers at Maryland.

"virtuoso qualities": SPCH includes important reviews of *The Colossus*.

"the white of human extinction": See Marjorie Perloff, "Angst and Animism in the Poetry of Sylvia Plath," Wagner, *Critical Essays on Sylvia Plath*.

"Mothers": JP.

"dutiful" and "hardworking": SP to James, Smith, 14/11/61.

"to great effect": See the notes section of CP.

Chapter 7: Letters to SP from Dr. Beuscher and A. Alvarez are at Smith, as are SP's letters to Clarissa Roche and OH. TH's last week of visits to SP, recounted in diary notes he wrote up about a week after her death, are in BL. Winifred Davies's letter to Aurelia, and Aurelia's description of a letter Ted's mother sent to her, are at Maryland.

Assia as a Jezebel: Trevor Thomas recalls SP called Assia such. SP's reaction may seem melodramatic, but as Yehuda Koren and

Eilat Negev report, Assia had a reputation as a femme fatale. Edward Lucie-Smith, a friend to Assia, later called her "devious," although he did not explicitly relate this trait to her seduction of TH. On the contrary, both Lucie-Smith (two of his letters are included in EBP) and OH, as she later told Butscher, thought Sylvia's jealousy had driven TH into Assia's arms. Assia later told OH that she had asked a man to call Court Green on her behalf. Was it Lucie-Smith? He worked in the same office as Assia. He told Butscher he was writing on OH's request and that Butscher was not to quote him. OH gave her account of how her brother's affair with Assia began in letters to Anne Stevenson that are now in the Smith archive.

pouring out of the phone like mud: "Words heard, by accident, over the phone," dated 9/9/62, CP.

"The blood jet is poetry": "Kindness," CP.

"*little* man": To Gerry Becker, one of the last people to see SP alive, she confided that she and Ted made love "like giants." See Jillian Becker's memoir, *Giving Up*.

"He says": SP's letter to Mrs. Prouty, 29/9/62: Lilly. The letter to AP, dated 26/9/62, was published in AP's edition of *Letters Home*, but TH insisted that AP excise the portion of the letter quoted here. Previous biographers have treated SP's versions of what TH said to her warily, but much of what she writes about his manner, behavior, and even the wording of his comments is replicated in Assia Wevill's accounts of his treatment of her. See Yehuda Koren and Eilat Negev.

an excursion to Ireland: Accounts of the Irish episode vary widely—and rightly so, since SP's views of TH were in flux, and Richard Murphy's version, included in Stevenson, reads like a soap opera. SP's letters to Murphy are in ECS.

"A story": This and subsequent quotations are taken from journal entries Plath wrote when she was eighteen. Nothing changed in her later years concerning her views of eternity, suicide, and writing. SP often mistakenly confused it's and its.

"scare you off": the exchanges between OH and Alvarez are at the BL.

"It has always seemed to me": Peter Porter, "Ted Hughes and

Sylvia Plath: A Bystander's Recollections," *Australian Book Review,* August 2001: http://www.australianbookreview.com.au/past-issues /online-archive/153.

"She is the phoenix": BL.

On destiny's doorstep: the details about SP's discovery of the Fitzroy Road flat are from her letter to Olive Higgins Prouty 20/11/62, Smith.

Emily Hahn: I experienced Hahn's generosity and high spirits when I interviewed her for my biography of Rebecca West. She took an immediate interest in my work and helped to arrange interviews with others. Lessing was also helpful to me, but, like SP, I encountered a temperament much cooler than Hahn's.

By 2 January: The details in this paragraph are drawn from SP's essay, "Snow Blitz," in JP.

"If she felt any qualms": Alexander, *Ariel Ascending,* prints the fullest version of TH's introduction to SP's journals.

SP's last wracking weekend: My account corrects earlier biographies. Becker has expressed dissatisfaction with previous biographers' accounts, saying they "suppressed" her information "or distorted it, not only with inaccuracies but also by tailoring it to make a point."

Dr. Horder: see http://www.camdennewjournal.com/feature-literature-could-i-have-done-more-sylvia-plath-poets-doctor-john -horder-his-role-her-final-d.

our mothers: I vividly recall speaking with Becker about her mother, who was also a writer, while researching my biography of Rebecca West. Jillian had very hard feelings about a demanding parent that would have helped form the bond with SP.

"all one's energy": Alvarez, *The Savage God.*

thrust her head as far as she could: Jillian Becker learned this detail from a police officer attached to the London coroner's office.

In "The Descent of Ariel: The Death of Sylvia Plath," a manuscript deposited in both the British Library and the University of Maryland, Elizabeth Hinchliffe concludes that Plath did not put her head in the oven until perhaps 7:30 or 8:00 a.m. Plath had asked Trevor Thomas the night before her death what time he would leave for work; 8:30, as usual, was his reply. Plath, Hinchliffe surmises, expected Thomas to smell the gas before he departed for work and come to the rescue. Sylvia did not anticipate that her pacing back and forth would keep Thomas up much of the night, or that he would take a sleeping pill, which then combined with the gas seeping into his apartment. Thus knocked out, Thomas could not save her. The reconstruction of Plath's last hours hinges, however, on knowing exactly when Plath turned on the gas. Dr. Horder believed that Sylvia had gassed herself at about 4:00 a.m., and he told Stevenson that even if Plath had been found alive, her mind would have been destroyed.

Chapter 8: AP's correspondence with Frances McCullough is at Maryland.

"she had free and controlled access": quoted in Clark.

"that hate": SP's marks, annotations, and underlining in her books are at Smith, as are the two letters from Dido Merwin to Linda Wagner-Martin, and correspondence to and from AP. My account of Edward Butscher's research is drawn from EBP, which includes the letters from Olwyn Hughes. The letters to Anne Stevenson from OH and Peter Davison are also at Smith, as are Stevenson's letters to Davison and OH.

"Please don't": BL.

"reincarnated Cleopatra": to OH, BL.

"very nice": BL.

it "became increasingly difficult": Holder.

"Notes Toward a Biography": reprinted in Newman.

"I am so sick": Smith.

"Plath or her publisher": email from Frances McCullough to Beth Alvarez, 8/2/12, forwarded to me.

"Ted told me": Maryland.

"Miss Rosenstein seems": ECS.

Poor Clare Court: interview with Elizabeth Compton Sigmund.

"so insensitive that": quoted in Malcolm.

"English authors": SPWW.

"If you wrote": Elizabeth Compton to EB, 24/1/74.

Butscher's request for an interview: "In Search of Sylvia," SPWW.

"For me": Smith.

"Olwyn, of course": Emory.

the "mob": THL does not include the entire correspondence between AP, TH, and Frances McCullough, but it is available at Emory and at Maryland, College Park.

Reviews of *Letters Home:* SPCH.

"You reify": 4/2/75, EBP.

"If it was just": 11/2/75, EBP.

"There was a very real chance": 30/4/91, Maryland.

"the effect of": Emory.

"no mention of Assia": ECS.

"a Soviet view of history": interview with A. Alvarez.

"rampant" feminism: Emory.

"spilling the beans": TH to Victor Kovner, the attorney defending him in the Jane Anderson lawsuit, Emory.

"central figure": Emory.

"I have had the work in question": Emory.

"hot copy": BL.

"bad as well as the good": 26/8/92, BL.

Eschewing much biographical speculation: Emory.

"It's so deterministic": Emory.

"excessively vituperative": Bayley.

"Sylvia suicide doll": Frieda's comments are quoted in Jamie Wilson, "Frieda Hughes Attacks BBC for Film on Plath," *Guardian,* 3/2/03.

In "Nicholas Hughes, Sylvia Plath's Son, Commits Suicide," *Huffington Post,* 23/3/09, Frieda is quoted as saying her brother had been depressed.

"wildly inaccurate": ECS.

BIBLIOGRAPHY

Alexander, Paul. *Rough Magic: A Biography of Sylvia Plath.* Viking-Penguin, 1991. Kindle edition, new introduction, 2003.

——, ed. *Ariel Ascending: Writings about Sylvia Plath.* Harper & Row, 1985.

Alliston, Susan. *Poems and Journals, 1960–1969.* Richard Hollis, 2010.

Alvarez, A. *The Savage God: A Study of Suicide.* Random House, 1972.

——. *When Did It All Go Right?* William Morrow, 2000.

Axelrod, Steven Gould. *Sylvia Plath: The Wound and the Cure of Words.* Johns Hopkins University Press, 1990.

Badia, Janet. *Sylvia Plath and the Mythology of Women Readers.* University of Massachusetts Press, 2011.

Bayley, Sally, and Tracy Brain, eds. *Representing Sylvia Plath.* Cambridge University Press, 2011.

Becker, Jillian. *Giving Up: The Last Days of Sylvia Plath.* St. Martin's Press, 2003.

Brain, Tracy. *The Other Sylvia Plath.* Longman, 2001.

Butscher, Edward. *Sylvia Plath: Method and Madness.* Seabury, 1976. Kindle edition, 2003.

——, ed. *Sylvia Plath: The Woman and the Work.* Dodd, Mead, 1977.

Clark, Heather. *The Grief of Influence: Sylvia Plath and Ted Hughes.* Oxford University Press, 2011.

Connors, Kathleen, and Sally Bayley. *Eye Rhymes: Sylvia Plath's Art of the Visual.* Oxford University Press, 2007.

Davison, Peter. *The Fading Smile: Poets in Boston from Robert Lowell to Sylvia Plath.* W. W. Norton, 1994.

———. *Half-Remembered: A Personal History.* Story Line Press, 1991.

"Education: Woman & Man at Yale." *Time,* 20 March 1972.

Farber, Leslie. *Lying, Despair, Jealousy, Envy, Sex, Suicide, Drugs, and the Good Life.* Basic Books, 1976.

Feinstein, Elaine. *Ted Hughes: The Life of a Poet.* W. W. Norton, 2001.

Ferretter, Luke. *Sylvia Plath's Fiction: A Critical Study.* Edinburgh University Press, 2010.

Gilbert, Sandra M., and Susan Gubar. *No Man's Land: The Place of the Woman Writer in the Twentieth Century.* Volumes 1 and 2. Yale University Press, 1988–89.

Gill, Jo, ed. *The Cambridge Companion to Sylvia Plath.* Cambridge University Press, 1976.

Hall, Caroline King Barnard. *Sylvia Plath Revised.* Twayne, 1998.

Hayman, Ronald. *The Death and Life of Sylvia Plath.* Birch Lane, 1991.

Heinz, Drue. "The Art of Poetry." *Paris Review.* Spring 1995.

Helle, Anita, ed. *The Unraveling Archive: Essays on Sylvia Plath.* University of Michigan Press, 2007.

Holder, Doug. "Lois Ames: Confidante to Sylvia Plath and Anne Sexton." Interview 2005. http://dougholder.blogspot.com/2009/11/lois-ames-confidante-to-sylvia-plath.html.

Hughes, Ted. *Birthday Letters.* Farrar, Straus & Giroux, 1998.

———. *Howls and Whispers.* Gehenna, 1998.

———. *Letters of Ted Hughes.* Ed. Christopher Reid. Faber & Faber, 2009.

Huws, Daniel. *Memories of Ted Hughes, 1952–1963.* Five Leaves, 2010.

Kazin, Alfred. *New York Jew.* Syracuse University Press, 1996.

Kendall, Tim. *Sylvia Plath: A Critical Study.* Faber & Faber, 2001.

Kirk, Connie Ann. *Sylvia Plath: A Biography.* Prometheus Books, 2009.

Koren, Yehuda Koren, and Eilat Negev. *Lover of Unreason: Assia Wevill, Sylvia Plath's Rival and Ted Hughes's Doomed Love.* Carroll & Graf, 2006.

Kroll, Judith. *Chapters in a Mythology: The Poetry of Sylvia Plath*. Sutton, 2007.

Kukil, Karen V., ed. *The Unabridged Journals of Sylvia Plath*. Anchor Books, 2000. Kindle Edition, 2007.

Lane, Gary. *Sylvia Plath: New Views on the Poetry*. Johns Hopkins University Press, 1979.

Larschan, Richard. "Art and Artifice in Sylvia Plath's Self-Portrayals," in *Life Writing: Autobiography, Biography, and Travel Writing in Contemporary Literature*. Ed. Koray Melikoglu. Ibidem Press, 2007.

Lawrence, D. H. *The Man Who Died* (1929). Kindle edition, 2011.

Leeming, David. *Stephen Spender: A Life in Modernism*. Henry Holt, 1999.

Lever, Janet, and Pepper Schwartz. *Women at Yale: Liberating a College Campus*. Allen Lane, 1971.

Malcolm, Janet. *The Silent Woman: Sylvia Plath and Ted Hughes*. Knopf, 1994.

Middlebrook, Diane. *Anne Sexton: A Biography*. Random House, 1991.

———. *Her Husband: Hughes and Plath—A Marriage*. Viking, 2003.

Myers, Lucas. *Crow Steered/Bergs Appeared*. Proctor's Hall, 2001.

———. *An Essential Self: Ted Hughes and Sylvia Plath*. Five Leaves, 2011.

Newman, Charles, ed. *The Art of Sylvia Plath*. Indiana University Press, 1970.

Peel, Robin. *Writing Back: Sylvia Plath and Cold War Politics*. Fairleigh Dickinson University Press, 2002.

Plath, Aurelia, ed. *Letters Home: Correspondence, 1950–1963*. Harper & Row, 1975.

Plath, Sylvia. *Ariel: The Restored Edition*. HarperCollins, 2004.

———. *The Bell Jar*. Harper & Row, 1971. Kindle Edition, 2008.

———. *The Collected Poems*. Harper & Row, 1981.

———. *Johnny Panic and the Bible of Dreams: Short Stories, Prose and Diary Excerpts*. HarperPerennial, 2000.

Reid, Christopher, ed. *Letters of Ted Hughes*. Farrar, Straus & Giroux, 2008. Kindle Edition, Faber & Faber, 2011.

Rollyson, Carl. *Biography: A User's Guide*. Ivan R. Dee, 2008.

———. *Marilyn Monroe: A Life of the Actress*. UMI Research Press, 1986. Reprinted in paperback by DaCapo, 1993.

————. *Rebecca West: A Modern Sybil.* iUniverse, 2008. Kindle edition, 2009.

Rose, Jacqueline. *The Haunting of Sylvia Plath.* Harvard University Press, 1992.

Schulman, Grace. *First Loves and Other Adventures.* University of Michigan Press, 2010.

Schweizer, Bernard. *Rebecca West: Heroism, Rebellion, and the Female Epic.* Greenwood, 2001.

Steinberg, Peter K. *Sylvia Plath.* Chelsea House, 2004. Kindle edition, 2004.

Steiner, Nancy Hunter. *A Closer Look at Ariel: A Memory of Sylvia Plath.* Harpers Magazine Press, 1973.

Stevenson, Anne. *Bitter Fame: A Life of Sylvia Plath.* Houghton Mifflin, 1989.

Thomas, Trevor. "Last Encounters." Privately printed, nd.

Uroff, Margaret Dickie. *Sylvia Plath and Ted Hughes.* University of Illinois Press, 1980.

Van Dyne, Susan R. *Revising Life: Sylvia Plath's Ariel Poems.* University of North Carolina Press, 1994.

Wagner, Erica. *Ariel's Gift: Ted Hughes, Sylvia Plath and the Story of Birthday Letters.* W. W. Norton, 2000.

Wagner, Linda W., ed. *Critical Essays on Sylvia Plath.* G. K. Hall, 1984.

————, ed. *Sylvia Plath: The Critical Heritage.* Routledge, 1988.

Wagner-Martin, Linda. *Sylvia Plath: A Biography.* St. Martin's Press, 1987.

————. *Sylvia Plath: A Literary Life.* Palgrave Macmillan, 2003.

Wootten, William. "That Alchemical Power: The Literary Relationship of A. Alvarez and Sylvia Plath." *Cambridge Quarterly,* September 2010.

INDEX

Aaron, Daniel, 154, 160–61, 292

Abels, Cyrilly, 63

"Above the Oxbow," 166

Akutowicz, Edwin, 83

Aldermaston marchers, 174

Alexander, Paul, 4, 15, 48, 178, 257, 286–87

"All the Dead Dears," 134–35

Alliston, Susan, 213–14, 223, 267

Allyson, June, 72

Alvarez, Al, 225, 294
   Hughes, T., and, 241–42
   on Hughes, O., 240
   letters, 196–97
   meeting of, 175–76
   on Plath, S., 232
   relationship with, 211–13, 218–20
   reviews of, 179
   visit of, 192

Amateur Dramatic Club, 95, 97

ambition, 42, 76, 99

America, 10, 145–46

"America! America!", 85

"America the Beautiful," 10

American Book Review, 251

American Poetry Review, 251

Americanism, 114

Ames, Lois, 236, 239, 246

Anderson, Jane, 69, 74, 117–18, 254, 289

"Angst and Animism in the Poetry of Sylvia Plath," 292

appendicitis, 180–83

Apuleius, 1

Arendt, Hannah, 205

"Ariel," 211, 215

Ariel (Plath, S.), 218, 236, 237, 252, 267, 268

Ariel's Gift: Ted Hughes, Sylvia Plath and the Story of Birthday Letters (Wagner), 265

Arnold, Matthew, 14–15

"Arraignment," 242

"The Arrival of the Bee Box," 204

The Art of Loving (Fromm), 200

Arvin, Newton, 151

astrology, 140, 171, 261

The Atlantic Monthly, 87, 88, 125,
    127, 168, 215

atomic bomb, 24, 174

Auden, W. H., 57, 58, 175, 176

Augustine, St., 274

Axelrod, Steven Gould,
    27, 251–52

babysitting jobs, 36–37, 38,
    45–46

Badia, Janet, 242, 244

"Balloons," 224, 226

Barbizon Hotel, 62

Bartholomew Fair, 98

"Battle-Scene from the Comic
    Operatic Fantasy *The Seafarer*,"
    152

Bayley, Sally, 258–59

BBC, 124, 176, 177, 182, 192

"The Beach," 265

Beales, Joan, 16

"The Bear," 165

Becker, Gerry, 293

Becker, Jillian, 224, 228–29, 293,
    294

"The Bee God," 264

beekeeping, 204

behavior, 66, 85, 183

The Bell Jar (movie), 254

The Bell Jar (Plath, S.), 6, 28, 49, 61
    copyrights of, 239
    Davison on, 159
    dedication of, 280
    first draft of, 187
    influences on, 64

interpretation of, 188
    McCullough on, 245
    publication of, 208, 217, 238–39,
        241
    reviews of, 224

Belmont Hotel, 43–45

Benny, Jack, 17, 19–20

Beuscher, Ruth, 67, 69, 160–64,
    199–200

biking, 133

biographers, xiii, 4, 246–48, 252,
    259–60, 286–87
    Hughes, T., and, 257

birth, 8

Birthday Letters (Hughes, T.), 188,
    260–64
    censorship of, 266
    personas in, 280
    response to, 265

"A Birthday Present," 201, 202–3

Bitter Fame (Stevenson), 257

"Bitter Strawberries," 24, 63

"Black Coat," 263

Black Lamb and Gray Falcon (West),
    64

"Blackberrying," 187

The Blackboard Jungle, 136–37

Blackwell, Betsy Talbot, 61

Blackwell, Constance, 76, 77, 78,
    290

Blake, William, 103

"The Blue Flannel Suit," 263

Boddy, Michael, 111–12

The Bookseller, 180

Boston, 148, 151, 155, 158–59

Boston Herald, 8, 15

Boston University, 164

Bourjaily, Vance, 63
Bowen, Elizabeth, 61, 62
Bowles, Sally, 112
Bradford, 8
Brans, Jo, 249
Brown, Marcia, 34, 35, 89, 120
   letters, 45, 110, 129–30, 141,
      170, 226
   visit, 50, 123
Buck, David, 98
Buckley, Maureen, 38–39
Buckley, William F., Jr., 39
Bulganin, Nicolai, 115
bullfighting, 121–22, 262
Bumblebees and Their Ways
    (Plath, O.), 8
Bundy, Leo, 159
Buntzen, Lynda K., 265
"Burning the Letters," 196
Bus Stop, 209
Butscher, Edward, 11, 15–16, 56,
    113, 250, 286
   Hughes, O., meeting with,
    248–49

Cambridge, 94–96
   Christmas at, 98–99
   exams, 127
   letters at, 98–99
   mentors at, 101
   return to, 124
   schedule at, 97
The Cambridge Companion to Sylvia
    Plath (Van Dyne), 250
Cambridge University, 2–3
Campbell, Wendy, 116, 174–75

camping, 167
Campus Cat, 60
Cape Cod, 141–42, 158
career, marriage and, 35, 100
Carter, Mark Bonham, 282
Cary, Joyce, 134
Catcher in the Rye (Salinger), 61, 64,
    115
censorship, 252
   of *Birthday Letters,* 266
   copyright and, 257
   of journals, Hughes, T.,
    250–52
   sexuality and, 250–52
Chaikin, Celia, 240
"Character Notebook," 135
Chase, Mary Ellen, 89, 116,
    131
chilblains, 190
"Child," 224
childbirth. *See* pregnancy
childhood, 8–25
   camp, 16–17
   end of, 148–49
   first kiss, 23
   hurricane of September 21st,
    1938, 12–13
   interests, 15–16, 19
   jobs, 23
   ocean and, 9, 12, 14–15, 16, 156,
    164
   Plath, O., death of, 13–14, 81
children, 156, 164, 242. *See also*
    Hughes, Frieda Rebecca;
    Hughes, Nicolas
   colds of, 220
   confession about, 209

children (*continued*)
  longing for, 158, 164–65
  Plath, A., as caretaker of,
    233–34
"Child's Park," 263
Christian Science, 45–46
The Christian Science Monitor, 8, 24,
  100–101, 123
Ciardi, John, 89, 90
"Circus in Three Rings," 90, 104,
  109
The City of God (St. Augustine), 274
Cohen, Eddie, xiv, 26, 33, 135
  advice of, 54, 70
  letters, 27–31, 33, 38, 39, 51
  Plath's, S., rejection of, 34
  on recovery, 79–80
  relationship with, 31–32, 35, 48
Cohen, Marvin, 148, 241, 243
Cold War, 88, 189
Collected Plays (Yeats), 214
The Collected Poems (Plath, S.),
  104, 143, 144, 182, 250
  errors in, 243–44
  Hughes, T., division of, 252
  "Juvenilia," 252
Colman, Ronald, 20
The Colossus (Plath, S.), 157, 179,
  182, 292
Compton, David, 279
Connors, Kathleen, 258–59
Continuum Books, 248
"Contusion," 224
cooking, 37, 81, 130, 141
Coover, Robert, 64
copyright, censorship and, 257
Court, Clare, 247

Court Green, 184–86, 192, 194–95,
  234–35, 264
Coward, Noël, 62
Craig, Anna C., 18
Craig, Daniel, 284
creativity, 65, 166
  of Hughes, T., 126
  marriage and, 35
  teaching and, 146
Crockett, Wilbury, 20, 288
  on suicide of Plath, S., 18–19
  visit of, 69–70
Crow Steered/Bergs Appeared (Myers),
  114, 172
Curie, Marie, 6, 55
"Cut," 209–11, 212

"Daddy," 11, 21, 178, 203, 205–6,
  244
  rejection of, 211
  review of, 237
Dalrymple, Florence, 147
Darkness Visible (Styron), 203
Davidow, Ann, 29, 32, 189
  dropping out of, 34
  letters, 36, 167
  visit, 175
Davies, Winifred, 198–99
Davis, Robert Gorham, 67, 289
Davison, Peter, 168, 254, 256,
  292
  relationship with, 91–92
  visit, 159–60, 175
death, 7, 67, 103, 231. *See also*
  suicide
  childbirth and, 264

consciousness and, 230
  of Hughes, T., 267
  philosophy and, 274
  of Plath, O., 13–14, 81
  writing and, 201–2
The Death and Life of Sylvia Plath
  (Hayman), 4, 258
Denison, Judy, 55, 73
"Departure of the Ghost (After Paul
  Klee)," 152
depression, 53, 64–65, 156, 159
  despair, 27–28, 34
  dynamics of, 203
  emergence from, 69–70
  medication, 227, 230
"The Descent of Ariel: The Death
  of Sylvia Plath," 288, 294
"The Detective," 203
The Development of Personality
  (Jung), 269
"Dialogue of the Damned," 51
"Dialogue Over a Ouija Board,"
  143–45
Dickinson, Emily, 15, 237
discipline, 30–31, 131
"The Disquieting Muses," 153
divorce, 197, 200, 201, 207, 209–11,
  213, 234
"Doom of Exiles," 75
"Doomsday," 58
Dostoevsky, Fyodor, 85, 86
The Double (Dostoevsky), 85
"Doubletake," 217
"Dream Life," 264
"Dream Woman Muse," 145
"Dreamers," 264–65
dreams, 44, 46–47

Drew, Elizabeth, 58, 67–68, 150
Dyson, A. E., 179

"Edge," 71, 203, 226, 230, 287
"Eichman in Jerusalem," 205–6
"18 Rugby Street," 261
"Electra on Azalea Path," 165–66
electroconvulsive treatments, 66,
  69, 74, 160
Eliot, T. S., 5, 74, 137, 138, 175
Elizabethan Club, 76
Ellison, Ralph, 17
Elwin, Malcolm, 216
"An End," 26–27
England, 86, 128–29, 171, 180–81,
  225. *See also* Fulbright
"Epitaph for Fire and Flower," 128
Epstein, Elinor, 237
Epstein, Enid, 47, 71
Evangeline, 288
Ewell, Tom, 4
*Eye Rhymes: Sylvia Plath's Art of the
  Visual* (Bayley & Connors),
  258–59

The Fading Smile (Davison), 160, 292
Fainlight, Ruth, 215
"Falcon Yard," 132–33, 135, 141,
  148, 167, 266
fan letters, 37–38
Farber, Leslie, 227
fascism, 206
"Fate Playing," 262
Faulkner, William, 165
"The Fearful," 215

Feinstein, Elaine, 103, 122, 176, 267
feminism, 242–43, 246–47, 251
fiction, 42, 269–70
"The Fifty-Ninth Bear," 41, 167–68,
    263
First Loves and Other Adventures
    (Schulman), 291
Fisher, Alfred, 148–49, 151
Fisher, John, 138–39
Follett, CB ("Lyn"), 72
"For a Fatherless Son," 200–201
"The Forsaken Merman," 14–15
Frances McCullough Papers, 83,
    247, 288
"Frieda Hughes Attacks BBC for
    Film on Plath," 296
Fromm, Erich, 200
Fulbright, 2–3, 86
    application for, 84
    marriage and, 119, 127–28
    renewal of, 108–9
"Fulbright Scholars," 260
Fuller, Roy, 179
Fulton, George, 11

Gaitskill, Hugh, 128
Gardner, Ava, 6
Gellhorn, Martha, 231
Gendron, Valerie, 47
genealogy, 22
Generation of Vipers (Wylie, P.), 41
Gibian, George, 67, 88, 149, 150
Giving Up (Becker), 228, 293
God, 14, 284
Godden, Rumer, 62
The Golden Ass (Apuleius), 1

The Golden Notebook (Lessing), 217
Gone with the Wind, 108
Goodall, Pat, 223
Goodman, Ann, 190
Goodman, Leo, 175, 190
"The Goring," 122
"Grand Canyon," 263
grave marker, 7, 257
Graves, Robert, 6, 266
Greenwood, Esther, 187–88
Guggenheim Fellowship, 166, 171,
    176
Gyllenhaal, Maggie, 183

Hafter, Daryl, 29, 84–85
Hahn, Emily, 217, 294
Half-Remembered (Davison), 91
Hall, Caroline King Barnard, 108
Hall, Donald, 83, 236
Harcourt, 169
"Hardcastle Crags," 156–57
Hardwick, Elizabeth, 164, 241
Hardy, Thomas, 23–24
Harper's, 58, 129, 131–32, 137
Harris, Phil, 20
Harvard, 62, 64, 65, 152–53
"Haunted," 263
Haupt, Gary, 109, 113
Haven House, 29, 38–39
The Hawk in the Rain (Hughes, T.),
    131–32, 137
Hayman, Ronald, 4, 104, 257,
    258, 286
Hecht, Anthony, 151
Heinemann, 173
Henley, William Ernest, 38

Her Husband (Middlebrook), 6, 266

Herself Surprised (Cary), 134

"Hill of Leopards," 266

Hinchcliffe, Elizabeth, 11, 247, 288, 294

history, 30–31

histrionics, 52

Hitler, Adolf, 9, 11, 12, 49

Holm, Alex, 78

Holocaust, 9, 12, 21, 205, 206, 209

homesickness, 93, 98, 220

honeymoon, 120, 121, 262

Horder, John, 214, 218, 220, 227–31, 233

The Horse's Mouth (Cary), 134

hospitalization, 227–28

Houghton Mifflin, 254

The House of Aries (Hughes, T.), 178

Howls and Whispers (Hughes, T.), 265

The Hudson Review, 166

Hughes, Carol, 241, 284

Hughes, Edith, 177, 235

Hughes, Frieda Rebecca, 173–74, 181, 221, 267, 296

Hughes, Nicholas, 189, 192, 296

Hughes, Olwyn, 21, 127, 135
  Alexander and, 257–58
  Butscher meeting with, 248–49
  Cohen, M., on, 243
  as custodian of Plath's, S., work, 243–44
  hatred of Plath, S., 178–79
  Hughes, T., letters to, 138–39
  Kroll and, 243
  letters, 178, 267
  Malcolm and, 259–60

  meeting of, 129
  on Plath, S., 279
  Stevenson, Anne, and, 254–57
  visit, 170
  on Wevill, A., suicide, 240

Hughes, Ted, 110–11, 137, 173, 178
  abuse of, 155
  Alvarez and, 241–42
  on America, 145–46
  arguments with, 130–31, 155, 161
  Ariel rearrangement, 252
  Auden and, 176
  BBC readings of, 124, 176, 182, 192
  biographers and, 257
  censorship of journals, 250–52
  The Collected Poems division of, 252
  competition with Plath, S., 212
  creativity of, 126
  day job of, 109
  death of, 267
  divorce, 197, 200, 201, 207, 209–11, 213, 234
  education of, 102
  faith in, 132
  fame of, 177
  farewell love letter to, 229
  fatherhood of, 181–82
  feminist reaction to, 242–43
  fishing of, 191
  Guggenheim Fellowship of, 166, 171, 176
  guilt of, 283
  Harper's prize win of, 131–32, 137
  Harvard reading of, 152–53

Hughes, Ted (*continued*)
 hatred of, 233
 Hayman's charges against, 257
 Horder on, 233
 hygiene of, 152
 infidelity of, 155, 194–95, 241
 jealousy of, 163
 letters, 125, 126–27, 164, 286
 Letters Home and, 119, 245–46
 letters to Hughes, O., 138–39,
  232–33
 letters to parents, 121–22, 167
 love letters of, 2, 113
 love poems of, 113
 lovemaking with, 111–12, 113
 on marriage, 185, 198
 marriage to, 1–2, 5–6, 18, 119,
  125, 141–42, 155, 157–58,
  162–63, 172, 191, 192, 225,
  279–80
 marriage to Orchard, 241
 meeting of, 101–3, 291
 Merwin, D., on, 252–53
 Morgan and, 242–43
 parents, 124
 physical appearance of, 101–2
 Plath, W., meeting of, 123
 on Plath, S., 232
 as Poet Laureate, 282
 poetry critique of, 127
 politics and, 282–83
 popular prose of Plath, S., and, 3
 pregnancy involvement of,
  174
 privacy and, 2, 6
 Prouty and, 148
 Prouty on, 116–17

"Pursuit," 103–4, 107, 109
 reaction to suicide of Wevill, A.,
  239–40
 reconciliation, plans for, 223,
  225, 227, 233, 252–53
 relationship with, 114–18, 125
 sadism of, 117
 Sassoon, R., on marriage to,
  122–23
 as school teacher, 128, 131
 stories of, 126
 success of, 133
 on suicide, 232–33
 at UMASS, 149, 155
 violence and, 104
 wardrobe of, 153
Hughes, William, 177
The Hughes Papers, 267
Hume, David, 273
Humphrey, Dorothy L., 16
Hunter, Nancy, 55, 75, 78, 81,
 135
hurricane, 12–13
Huws, Daniel, 169, 291
hygiene, 19

identity, 28
 fan letters and, 37–38
 loss of, 222
 at Smith College, 29
"In the Mountains," 56
The Independent, 257
Indiana University, 176
"Initiation," 48–49
*An Inquiry Concerning Human
 Understanding* (Hume), 273

"The Inscription," 265
"Invictus," 38
The Invisible Man, 17
Irwin, 81–82
Isis, 1, 6, 106–8, 135–36
"Isis," 264

Jackson, Marni, 251
Jackson, Shirley, 61
"The Jailor," 208, 209
James, Henry, 52, 85, 275
*Jane Anderson v. AVCO Embassy
    Pictures*, 289
Jezebel, 197
jobs
    babysitting, 36–37, 38, 45–46
    at Belmont Hotel, 43–45
    childhood, 23
    at Massachusetts General
        Hospital, 159–60
    routine of, 45
    waiting tables, 37, 43–45
Joe's Pizza, 50, 52
John Birch Society, 189
Johnny Panic and the Bible of Dreams
    (Plath, S.), 3, 250
"Johnny Panic and the Bible of
    Dreams" (Plath, S.), 160, 166
Jong, Erica, 249
journalism, 29, 42
journals, Hughes, T., censorship of,
    250–52
Joyce, James, 56
Judas, 106
Jung, Carl, 269
    on marriage, 271–72

on motherhood, 271
Plath, A., and, 270–71
"Juvenilia," 252

Kaufman, Alan J., 258
Kazin, Alfred, 74, 86–87, 89
Kendall, Tim, 270
Kennedy, John F., 189
Kent, Clark (Superman), 10
Kerouac, Jack, 37
Kesey, Ken, 160
Khrushchev, Nikita, 189
"Kindness," 224
King's Chapel, 94
kissing, 23
Klein, Elinor, 84, 108–9, 159
Klotz, Myron, 51–52, 55–56
Knight, Kathleen, 73
knowledge, 46
Kopp, Jane Baltzell, 96–97
Korean War, 23
Kornfield, Barbara Russell, 146–47
Kroll, Judith, 9, 22, 206, 243, 269–70
Krook, Dorothea, 105, 107, 109,
    127–28, 135
Kukil, Karen V., 256, 286, 289, 290
Kunitz, Stanley, 160, 165

Ladies Home Journal, 88, 153, 186,
    189, 209
"Lady Lazarus," 201, 211
Lameyer, Gordon, xiv, 56, 67, 77, 135
    letters, 68, 70, 90–91
    relationship with, 78, 89
    reunion with, 113

Lane, Helen, 73, 82

Lane, Lois (Superman), 10–11

Larschan, Richard, 12, 119

"Last Letter," 266–67

Lawner, Lynne, 173, 174

Lawrence, D. H., 105, 107, 136, 175, 273, 274–75

Lawrence House, 54–55, 72

Lawson, Helen, 15–16

Leavis, F. R., 94–95

"Lesbos," 208

Lessing, Doris, 136, 217, 243

Let's Make Love, 206

letters, xiv

  Akutowicz, 83

  Alvarez, 196–97

  Anderson, 74

  Brown, 45, 110, 129–30, 141, 170, 226

  at Cambridge, 98–99

  Christmas cards, 189

  Cohen, E., 27–31, 33, 38, 39, 51

  copyright of, 245

  Davidow, 36, 167

  Drew, 67–68

  fan, 37–38

  farewell love letter to Hughes, T., 229

  Hughes, O., 178, 267

  Hughes, T., 125, 126–27, 164, 286

  Hughes, T., love, 2, 229

  Hughes, T., to Hughes, O., 138–39, 232–33

  Klein, 108–9

  Lameyer, 68, 70, 90–91

  McCurdy, 75

  Neupert, 20–21, 23, 34

  Norton, D., 40–41, 50

  Plath, A., 10, 16, 28, 29, 37–38, 83–87, 110, 137, 204–5, 209, 225–26

  Plath, W., 51–52, 59, 93, 114, 120

  Prouty, 32–33, 97, 116–17, 134

  Rogers, 71–72

  Sassoon, R., 91, 98, 111

  Smith College, 28–29

  suicide in, 32

  summer camp, 17–18

  Wevill, A., 234

  Wober, 98, 99

Letters Home (Plath, S.), 30, 70, 132, 136

  Hughes and, 119, 245–46

  introduction to, 270

  publication of, 245, 254

  reviews of, 249–50, 251

Letters of Ted Hughes (Reid), 286

Levenson, Christopher, 135

Lever, Janet, 76–77

Levine, Miriam, 251

Levy, Laurie, 62, 64

library, 273–75

Lilly Library, 254

Lind, Louise, 18

The Listener, 207

literary criticism, 94–95, 140, 244

Little, Marybeth, 60–61

"The Lodger," 264

The London Magazine, 137, 167

Longfellow, Henry Wadsworth, 288

looks. *See* physical appearance

Lord Byron's Wife (Elwin), 216

Los Angeles Book Review, 249

"The Lovesong of J. Alfred
    Prufrock," 74
Lowell, Robert, 164, 165, 183, 237
Loy, Myrna, 67
Lucas, Victoria, 217
Lucie-Smith, Edward, 248, 256, 293
Lupercal (Hughes, T.), 173

Maclean's Magazine, 251
"Mad Girl's Love Song," 77, 109, 252
Mademoiselle, 115
    assessment of Plath, S., 63
    deadlines at, 62, 63
    guest editorship at, 60–62
    prizes, 26, 42–43
    routine at, 80
Madrid, 121–22
"The Magic Mirror: A Study of the
    Double in Two of Dostoevsky's
    Novels," 290
Malcolm, Janet, 2, 259–60, 287
"The Man He Killed," 23–24
"The Man Who Died," 105–6, 136
Mann, Thomas, 22, 273–74
marriage
    career and, 35, 100
    creativity and, 35
    divorce, 197, 200, 201, 207,
        209–11, 213, 234
    Fulbright and, 119, 127–28
    honeymoon, 120, 121, 262
    Hughes, T., on, 185, 198
    to Hughes, T., 1–2, 5–6, 18, 119,
        125, 141–42, 155, 157–58,
        162–63, 172, 191, 192, 225,
        279–80

Jung on, 271–72
    Melville and, 274–75
    of Monroe, 141–42
    to Orchard, Hughes, 241
    reconciliation plans, 223, 225,
        227, 233, 252–53
    Sassoon, R., on Hughes, 122–23
    secret wedding, 119–22
    separation, 199
    writing and, 163
Martin, Marilyn, 72, 74, 78
masochism, 82, 103
Massachusetts General Hospital,
    159–60
materialism, 46, 128, 140
Maxwell, William, 74
McCarthyism, 88
McCullough, Frances, 83, 155, 234,
    245–46, 250–51
    Hughes, O., and, 257–58
McCurdy, Phil, 19, 73, 75, 79, 250
McLean hospital, 115
medication, 227, 230
"Medusa," 207–8, 244
Melville, Herman, 274–75
men, 162
menstrual cycle, 159, 165
mental health, 64–65
Merwin, Dido, 171–72, 175, 183,
    191, 252–53
Merwin, W. S., 150–51, 171, 183, 191
Middlebrook, Diane, 6, 19, 266, 269
Milbanke, Anna Isabella, 216
Millay, Edna St. Vincent, 3, 202
Miller, Arthur, 4, 5, 108, 139,
    168–69, 263
Miller, Karl, 211

miscarriage, 180

money, 143, 166, 234–35, 282

Monroe, Marilyn, 1, 26, 108, 169,
    206, 263
    autobiographical performances
        of, 209
    behavior of, 139
    marriage of, 5, 141–42
    Plath's, S., dream of, 4–5
    psychiatric treatment of, 164
    as role model to Plath, S., 4–6

Monster (Morgan), 242–43

mood swings, 32, 38, 224, 238

Moore, Marianne, 89, 90, 207

Moorehead, Alan, 176–77

Morgan, Robin, 242–43

"Morning Song," 174

"Mothers," 186

Motion, Andrew, 247

Ms., 246

The Munich Mannequins," 224

Murphy, Richard, 197, 198

"Mussel Hunter at Rock Harbor,"
    156, 158

"My Heart Belongs to Daddy," 206

Myers, Lucas, 102, 110, 114, 119–20,
    129, 172, 253–54

"Mystic," 224

The Nation, 120

National Health Service (England),
    171, 180–81, 225

The National Observer, 249

National Review, 39

nature, 115

Neibuhr, Reinhold, 35

Neupert, Hans-Joachim, 20–21,
    23, 34

New Statesman, 186, 191, 211, 216,
    266

New York City, 57, 155

New York Jew (Kazin), 87

The New Yorker, 61, 87, 101, 127
    first-reading contract of, 180
    poems accepted into, 156–58,
        166, 187
    rejections from, 5, 58, 115, 154,
        215

"Night-Ride with Ariel," 265

"9 Willow Street," 263

Nixon, Richard, 174

No Man's Land, 287

"Nocturne," 156

Northampton, 145

Norton, Dick, xiv, 167–68
    breakup with, 57
    career of, 41
    emotional problems of, 48
    journal entry on, 35–36
    letters, 40–41, 50
    relationship with, 35–36, 38, 40,
        42, 47, 48, 52–53
    tuberculosis of, 49, 57
    writing of, 52, 56–57

Norton, Perry, 19, 35, 48, 51

"Notes Toward a Biography," 236

Now, Voyager (Prouty), 197

The Observer, 176, 241–42

ocean, childhood and, 9, 12, 14–15,
    16, 156, 164

"Ocean 1212-W," 85

O'Connor, Frank, 62, 64

Odets, Clifford, 177

O'Hara, Scarlett, 17–18

On Native Grounds (Kazin), 86

On the Beach (Shute), 34

One Flew Over the Cuckoo's Nest
    (Kesey), 160

O'Neill, Eugene, 48

O'Neill-Roe, Susan, 209–10

Orchard, Carol. *See* Hughes, Carol

Orr, Peter, 6, 212, 217

Ouelette, Ellen, 55, 153

"Ouija," 262–63

Ouija board, 129, 157

Owen, Peter, 249

"The Owl," 262

pacifism, 20, 24–25, 63, 129

The Painted Caravan: A Penetration
    into the Secrets of Tarot Cards
    (Rakoczi), 232

panic, 139

"Paralytic," 224

Paris, 99

Paris Review, 114

Partisan Review, 166

"Paula Brown's Snowsuit," 87

Pawlikowski, Pawel, 267

Penguin USA, 258

perfectionism, 86, 146

Perloff, Marjorie, 182, 291, 292

personality, 96–97

Peyre, Henri, 77

Philippian, 8

physical appearance, 19, 73–75, 96,
    277–78

"A Picture of Otto," 265

"A Pink Wool Knitted Dress," 262

Plath, Aurelia (mother), 2, 8, 9, 13,
    15, 245
  as caretaker of children, 233–34
  as confidant, 22
  hatred of, 161–62
  Hughes, F., attack of, 267
  Jung and, 270–71
  letter to Sigmund, 280
  letters, 10, 16, 28, 29, 37–38,
    83–87, 110, 137, 204–5, 209,
    225–26
  morals of, 17–18
  self-sacrifice of, 59
  suicide and, 162
  ulcers of, 161–62
  visit of, 118–19, 183–84

Plath, Otto (father), 8, 263
  death of, 13–14, 81
  "Electra on Azalea Path,"
    165–66
  gravestone of, 165–66
  Nazism and, 12
  Ouija board communication
    with, 157
  politics of, 20
  as professor, 11–12

Plath, Warren (brother), 11, 12,
    289
  Hughes, T., meeting of, 123
  letters, 51–52, 59, 93, 114, 120
  visit, 185
  wife of, 208

Plato, 274

Poe, Edgar Allen, 96–97

"Poem," 15

poetry, 128, 158. *See also* writing
  beginning of, 13, 14
  confessional, 165
  early interest in, 10–11
  Hughes critique of, 127
  hurricane of September 21st, 1938
    and, 13
  Plath, S., on, 3
  pleasure of, 204
  villanelle, 58
Poetry, 120, 127
Point Shirley, 14
"Point Shirley," 164
politics
  in England, 128–29
  of Plath, O., 20
  Sigmund on Hughes, T., and,
    282–83
Pope, Alexander, 212
"Poppies in July," 196
Porter, Cole, 206
Porter, Peter, 212, 293–94
The Portrait of a Lady (James),
    85, 275
positive thinking, 64
posture, 29–30
pregnancy, 73, 142–43, 263
  due date, 171
  effect of, 169
  Hughes, T., involvement with,
    174
  labor/delivery, 173–74, 189–90
  miscarriage, 180
  natural childbirth, 171–72
  second, 180
  third, 184
The Prince and the Showgirl, 142

prizes, 3, 15
  Hughes, T., *Harper's* prize, 131–32,
    137
  Mademoiselle, 26, 42–43
  Seventeen, 48–49
prose, 3, 158
Prouty, Olive Higgins, 2, 18, 142, 197
  gifts from, 185
  Hughes, T., and, 116–17, 148
  letters, 32–33, 97, 116–17, 134
  as mentor, 49
  nervous breakdown of, 68
  scholarship from, 32
  visit to, 80
The Public Burning (Coover), 64
Punic Wars, 279–80
"Pursuit," 103–4, 107, 109, 125

Quinn, Kay, 82

"The Rabbit Catcher," 264
radio, writing for, 46
Rainbow Press, 243
Rakoczi, Basil Ivan, 232
Random House, 239
rape, 33, 40, 82–83, 110
readings, 89
rebirth, 107, 183
reconciliation, plans for, 223, 225,
    227, 233, 252–53
"Reconsidering Sylvia Plath," 246
recorded voice, 124
recovery, 67–69, 79–80, 105, 130
"Redcoats," 210
Redgrove, Peter, 240

Reid, Christopher, 286

rejections, 21, 24, 26, 84, 161
  from *The Atlantic Monthly,* 215
  of "Daddy," 211
  of "Lady Lazarus," 211
  from *The New Yorker,* 5, 58, 115,
    154, 215
  from Yale Younger Poets, 148–49,
    167

relationships, 31. *See also* marriage
  with Alvarez, 211–13, 218–20
  with Cohen, E., 31–32, 35, 48
  with Davison, 91–92
  with Hughes, T., 114–18, 125
  with Irwin, 81–82
  with Lameyer, 78, 89
  with Norton, D., 35–36, 38, 40,
    42, 47, 48, 52–53
  romance, 40
  with Sassoon, R., 76–79, 89, 108,
    122–23
  with Wober, 95

religion, materialism and, 46

Rich, Adrienne, 149, 152–53

River Cam, 94

RMS *Queen Elizabeth,* 138

Roche, Clarissa, 179, 215
  memoirs, 250
  visit, 194, 201, 209, 220–21, 228

Roche, Paul, 209

Roethke, Theodore, 165, 179, 183

Rogers, Sally, 71–72

Rose, Jacqueline, 144, 269

Rosenstein, Harriet, 246

*Rough Magic: A Biography of Sylvia
  Plath* (Alexander), 4

Rowe, Susan O'Neill, 215

Salinger, J. D., 61, 64, 115, 127

Sanctuary (Faulkner), 165

Sassoon, Richard, 135, 212,
    290
  on Hughes, T., marriage,
    122–23
  letters, 91, 98, 111
  loss of, 100, 104–5
  rape and, 110
  relationship with, 76–79, 89, 108,
    122–23
  sexuality of, 77, 78
  Swiss girlfriend of, 100

Sassoon, Siegfried, 24, 76

The Saturday Evening Post, 88

Saturday's Child (Morgan), 243

The Savage God: A Story of Suicide
  (Alvarez), 192, 212–13, 219,
    241, 294

Saxton grant, 186–87

scars, 80

schedule
  at Cambridge, 97
  writing, 130, 207, 226

scholarship, 23, 26, 32, 72

schooling, 9–10, 13, 18–20

Schulman, Grace, 150, 291

Schwartz, Merrill, 147

Schwartz, Pepper, 76–77

science, 50–51

"The Second Destruction of Sylvia
  Plath," 251–52

self-doubt, 65

self-wounds, 65–66, 80

The Seven Year Itch, 4

Seventeen, 8, 26, 27, 48–49

The Sewanee Review, 166

Sexton, Anne, 1, 165, 201
sexuality, 91, 288, 293
  abuse, 82
  censorship and, 250–52
  dating, 31
  first kiss, 23
  guilt and, 79
  Martin on, 78
  rape, 33, 40, 82–83, 110
  of Sassoon, R., 77, 78
The Shadow, 2
The Shadow, 9
"The Shadow" (Plath), 166
Shakespeare, William, 16, 18
Shaw, George Bernard, 202
Shaw, Irwin, 61
"Sheep in Fog," 223–24
"The Shot," 261
Shute, Nevil, 34
sickness, 30
Sigmund, Elizabeth Compton, 170,
    192, 196, 235, 248, 250, 252
  on Hughes, T., and politics, 282–83
  Plath, A., letter to, 280
  testimony of, 280–84
Silberman, Ravelle, 72–73, 148
The Silent Woman (Malcolm), 259,
    287
Sillitoe, Alan, 239
Simon, Jody, 84
Skouras, Plato, 39
sleep, 53, 54, 146
sleeping pills, 201, 228
Smith, Anne Mohegan, 147
Smith Alumnae Quarterly, 115
Smith College, xiii, 8, 22, 154
  alumni, 73

  course load at, 39
  Haven House room at, 29
  hiatus from, 67–68
  identity at, 29
  letters at, 28–29
  mood swings at, 32
  physical exams at, 29–30
  return to, 71–72
  scholarship to, 23, 26, 72
  teaching position at, 134, 146–48,
    154
  worry about studies at, 30
Smith Review, 42, 56, 58, 60
smoking, 201, 207
"Snow Blitz," 222
Somerset Maugham award, 173
Sons and Lovers (Lawrence), 274
Sontag, Susan, 3–4, 32
sororities, 48–49
Southwest Review, 249
Spender, Stephen, 175
Springfield Daily News, 61
St. Botolph's Review, 101
Stafford, Jean, 168
Starbuck, George, 165, 167
Steinberg, Peter K., 5, 83, 286, 287
Steiner, Nancy Hunter, 55, 83
Stella Dallas (Prouty), 18, 32, 142,
    197
Stevenson, Adlai, 90
Stevenson, Anne, 103–4, 178,
    219–20, 253, 286
  Hughes, O., and, 254–57
  on Wevill, 236
Stewart, Hamish, 291
"Stings," 204
Strange Interlude (O'Neill), 48

"Stubbing Wharfe," 263–64
Studies in Classic American Literature
    (Lawrence), 273, 274–75
style, 3, 71, 96, 214–15
Styron, William, 203, 227
Suez crisis, 128
suicide, 7, 65, 130
    Akutowicz on, 83
    attempt, first, 13, 66–67, 70–75,
        83, 91, 105, 164, 201
    attraction of, 71
    Crockett on, 18–19
    discovery of, 231
    egoism and, 49
    father and, 74
    by gas, 230–31, 239–40, 295
    Hughes, T., on, 232–33
    isolation and, 227
    in letters, 32
    Plath, A., and, 162
    popularization of, 241–42
    preparation for, 231
    Sexton on, 1
    Thomas and, 294–95
    time of, 294–95
    of Wevill, 239–40
    of Woolf, 133
suitors, 80, 92
summer camp, 16–18
"And Summer Will Not Come
    Again," 26–28
sunbathing, 106
"Sunday at the Mintons,"
    26, 42–43, 47, 56
Superman, 9, 10–11, 22
"Sweetie Pie and the Gutterman,"
    166

Swenson, May, 149
Sylvia, 130, 179, 267, 284
Sylvia Plath: Method and Madness
    (Butscher), 249–50
*Sylvia Plath: The Woman and the
    Work* (Owen), 249

"The Table," 264
Tate, Allen, 110
teaching, 150
    creativity and, 146
    at Smith College, 134, 146–48,
        154
    Socratic method, 147
Teasdale, Sara, 26–27, 49
Ted Hughes: The Life of a Poet
    (Feinstein), 267
temperament, 21, 28, 197–98
The Tempest (Shakespeare), 16
"That Widow Mangada," 122,
    123
therapy. *See* recovery
The Thinking Body (Todd), 30
Thomas, Dylan, 62, 117
Thomas, Trevor, 216–18, 221–22,
    224, 230, 294–95
"Three Women: A Poem for
    Three Voices," 191, 192,
    195–96
Time, 237
Todd, Mabel Elsworth, 30
"Tongues of Stone," 69, 70,
    105–6
Tonio Kröger (Mann), 273–74
"Totem," 224
Trafalgar Square, 174

Tri-Quarterly, 236–37
Truslow, Jane, 175
"Tulips," 182–83
"Two of a Kind," 180, 281–82

UMASS. *See* University of
    Massachusetts
University of Chicago, 31
University of Maryland, 247
University of Massachusetts
    (UMASS), 149, 155
Uroff, Margaret, 104, 269

Van Dyne, Susan R., 250, 288
"Verbal Calisthenics," 58
"Veronica Lake," 260
Viking Penguin, 253, 254
villanelle, 58
violence, Hughes, T., and, 104
"Visions of Sylvia Plath," 287
"Visit," 260–61

Wagner, Erica, 265
Wagner-Martin, Linda, 247, 252,
    286
Wain, John, 179
war, 9, 12, 21, 23–24. *See also specific
    types*
wedding. *See* marriage
Weeks, Edward, 90
Weissbort, Daniel, 185, 238
Wellesley High School, 18
Wells, H. G., 103
Welty, Eudora, 127, 168

Wesker, Arnold, 177·
West, Rebecca, 64, 103, 120, 294
Wevill, Assia, 184, 191, 194, 212,
    214, 268
    abortion of, 283
    in biographies of Plath, S., 252
    in "Dreamers," 264–65
    effect of Plath, S., fame on, 236,
        238
    Hughes, O., on, 240
    letters, 234
    Plath's, S., innate understanding
        of, 215
    reputation as femme fatal, 293
    Stevenson, A., on, 236
    suicide of, 239–40
    Wevill, D., on, 278
Wevill, David, 184, 191, 194, 212,
    277–78
White, E. B., 61
The White Goddess (Graves), 266
Wilde, Oscar, 144
Wilkes, Ashley, 31
"William Wilson," 96–97
Williams, William Carlos, 24
Wilson, Don, 20
Winston, Susan Plath, 289
"A Winter's Tale," 5, 287
"The Wishing Box," 71, 126
Wober, Mallory, 95, 98, 99, 135
The Woman and the Work (Butscher),
    113
*Women at Yale: Liberating a College
    Campus* (Lever & Schwartz, P.),
    76–77
Woodrow Wilson fellowship
    application, 87

Woolf, Virginia, 28, 49, 133, 141,
    175
Wooten, William, 220
Wordsworth, William, 46
World War I, 22, 124, 288
World War II, 24, 205
writer's block, 130, 133, 151–52
    hatred of Plath, A., and, 162
    of Hughes, T., 141
writing, 71. *See also* poetry
    death and, 201–2
    love of, 88
    marriage and, 163
    schedule, 130, 207, 226

Wunderlich, Ray, 57
Wuthering Heights, 123–24
Wylie, Elinor, 3
Wylie, Philip, 41

Yaddo, 166, 169
Yale, 39, 76–77
Yale Younger Poets, 88, 130,
    148–49, 167
Yeats, W. B., 214
"You Hated Spain," 122, 262
Young, Nanci A., 289
"Your Paris," 262